THE BHAGAVAD-GITA

THE BHAGAVAD-GITA

with Samskrit Text, free Translation into English, a Word-for Word translation, and an Introduction on Samskrit Grammar.

BY

ANNIE BESANT

AND

BHAGAVAN DAS

GYAN

Published by

GYAN

Gyan Publishing House
5, Ansari Road
Daryaganj, New Delhi-110002
Phone: 011-47034999, 9811692060
E-mail: books@gyanbooks.com

Distribution Network
gyanbooks.com
India, USA, Canada, UK, Australia

ISBN: 978-93-6208-306-7 (HB)
First Published, 1905

2nd Impression 2024

Printed at: Gyan Press, Delhi.

THE BHAGAVAD-GITA
Author: ANNIE BESANT AND BHAGAVAN DAS

THE BHAGAVAD-GÎTÂ

THE BHAGAVAD-GÎTÂ

With Samskṛit Text, free translation into English, a word-for-word translation, and an Introduction on Samskṛit Grammar.

BY

ANNIE BESANT

AND

BHAGAVÂN DÂS.

THEOSOPHICAL PUBLISHING SOCIETY

LONDON AND BENARES

1905.

CONTENTS.

PAGE.

INTRODUCTORY NOTE ON SAMSKRIT GRAMMAR......... i—xviii

Gita Mahatmyam.—The greatness of the *Gita* as described in the *Varaha-Purana* xxi

Gita-Karadi-Nyasah.—The Tantra way of 'practising' the *Gita.* xxvii

Gita-Dhyanam.—'The Thought-Form of the *Gita* for purposes of meditation xxxi

CHAP: I. *Arjuna Vishada-Yoga.*—Arjuna inspects the rival forces—He describes the evil consequent on the battles of kinsfolk ... ... 1—22

CHAP: II. *Sankhya-Yoga.*—Arjuna refuses to fight —Shrî Kṛishṇa counsels Arjuna not to grieve over the mere destruction of transient bodies, because the inner Self can never be slain—or even because the bodies must die in any case— and so to perform the duty of the Kṣhattriya with untroubled mind —thereby gaining fame in this and happiness in the other world, incidentally—though duty should be performed for its own sake and not for any ulterior reward, as it is performed by sages of steady mind—Arjuna asks for a more particular description of such—Shrî Kṛishṇa complies, laying stress on the attainment of wisdom and the absence of desire. ... ... 23—56

PAGE.

CHAP: III. *Karma-Yoga.*—Arjuna asks how these are compatible with such terrible action as that of slaughter—Shri Kṛishṇa's preliminary reconciliation of the two: "perform the action that is duty, but without attachment"—a cursory allusion to the system of the world-wheel, which gives rise to the various Dharmas, duties—Arjuna enquires why men fail in duty—Shri Kṛishṇa replies, cursorily as yet. ... ... 57—76

CHAP: IV. *Jnana-Vibhaga-Yoga*—Shri Kṛishṇa again lays stress on the necessity of Wisdom, right-thought, right-reason, and in this connection describes the many forms of Yoga—He adverts to His own previous incarnations, in reply to a question of Arjuna's (and so incidentally strengthens the allusion, made before, to world-cycles, without an understanding of which true enlightenment is not possible). ... ... 77—95

CHAP: V. *Karma-Sannyasa-Yoga.*—Arjuna repeats his question as to the inconsistency between 'renunciation' and 'action'—Shri Kṛishṇa answers (indirectly, by describing the happy condition of those who renounce the fruits of action but continue to perform it as duty, knowing that all proceeds from the Supreme Self. ... ... 96—109

CHAP: VI. *Adhyatma-Yoga.*—Shri Kṛishṇa continues his description of the Yogi—Arjuna asks how the condition may be attained—Shri Kṛishṇa

PAGE.

answers: "by dispassion and perseverent practice." —Arjuna asks: "what are the consequences of failure in Yoga?"—Shrî Kṛiṣhṇa replies: "a better birth, greater opportunity and devotion to the Supreme Self, and final attainment of Mokṣha." 110—130

CHAP: VII. *Jnana-Yoga.*—Shrî Kṛiṣhṇa describes the natures of wisdom and unwisdom—the Glories of the Self (the knowledge of which constitutes the wisdom whereby the possessor thereof performs his duty unflinchingly). ... ... 131—143

CHAP: VIII. *Akshara-Brahma-Yoga.*—(The subject matter of the previous chapter is continued.) Arjuna asks what is the nature of Brahman, of Adhyâtma, Adhibhûta, and Adhidaiva—Shrî Kṛiṣhṇa describes these and also incidentally mentions how Brahman may be reached by the living as well as the departing Jîva. ... 144—157

CHAP: IX. *Raja-Vidya-Raja-Guhya-Yoga.*—Shrî Kṛiṣhṇa continues his statement of "the Royal Secret, the final wisdom," the possession of which confers Immortality, *viz.* the recognition of and devotion to the Supreme Self—also describes the results of devotion to minor personal Gods (Îshvaras of systems &c.) ... ... 158—173

CHAP: X. *Vibhuti-Yoga.*—The Glories of the Supreme Self ... ... 174—191

CHAP: XI. *Vishvarupa-darshana-Yoga.*—Shrî Kṛiṣhṇa compresses into one illuminating vision all the

PAGE.

results of lengthened explanations, and makes Arjuna see directly that he and all his fellow-beings are part of the life of Îshvara—that they are what they are by His gift (in the personal aspect of the Supreme Self, manifesting as an Individual Îshvara)—that it is their duty to endeavour, feebly as they may, to repay this great debt by obeying His will, and that His will, in the present instance is the destruction of Kṣhattriyas. ... 192—224

CHAP: XII. *Bhakti-Yoga.*—Arjuna, perceiving the difference between the Unmanifested Eternal and the manifested Îshvara, incidentally asks which is the better method, fixing the mind on the one or on the other—Shrî Kṛiṣhṇa answers: "the former is the more difficult, and by that method too, Jîvas have to pass to the stage and state of (a personal) Îshvara." (He thereby stimulates deeper enquiry, to which He leaves the discovery that the two systems are really not distinct, that the *one* system is to fix the mind on the Eternal, and, in *subordination* to that supreme fact, to work by the will of the Îshvara to whom we belong. .... 225—233

CHAP: XIII. *Kshetra-Kshetrajna-vibhaga-Yoga.*—Shrî Kṛiṣhṇa expounds the difference between Puruṣha and Prakṛiti as part of the supreme science, the wisdom which raises the Jîva above doubt and makes him steady in action (as Arjuna should be. ... ... 234—248

PAGE.

CHAP: XIV. *Guna-traya-vibhaga-Yoga.*—The subject of the preceding chapter is continued and the three guṇas of Prakṛiti are dealt with. ... 249—260

CHAP: XV. *Purushottama-Yoga.*—Shrî Kṛishṇa carries on the subject of the 13th discourse, and deals specially with the Purushа, in the aspect of the Abstract Self as well as the aspect of a manifested Îshvara ... ... 261—270

CHAP: XVI. *Daivasura-Sampad-vibhaga-Yoga.*—Shrî Kṛishṇa goes on to describe, as another essential part of the highest science, and having, further, an immediate bearing on the issue before Arjuna, the dual nature of all the creatures of Îshvara, divine and demoniac, good and evil—He tells how the former class, to which Arjuna belongs, necessarily perform their duty, in accordance with the Shâstras (and battle against the latter to prevent them from harming the innocent). ... 271—281

CHAP: XVII. *Shraddha-traya-vibhaga-Yoga.*—Arjuna asks Shrî Kṛishṇa to describe what is the essence of all true action and what is not, also what characterises all untrue action, according as the predominant motive-nature is Sâttvika, Râjasa, or tâmasa. ... ... 282—294

CHAP: XVIII. *Sannyasa-Yoga.*—Shrî Kṛishṇa sums up, finally, the whole teaching regarding the combination of renunciation of fruit of action with performance, which is the only means of secur-

PAGE.

ing ultimate happiness—Arjuna's doubts are solved; he is convinced and satisfied, and expresses his readiness to do his duty of battling with the unrighteous. ... ... 295—328

APPENDIX. ... ... 329—333

INDEX. ... ... 335—348

INTRODUCTION.

THIS edition of the *Bhagavad-Gîtâ* has been prepared for the use of those who, while studying this Hindu scripture mainly for the sake of its priceless teachings, wish, being little acquainted with Samskṛit, to utilise the text, thus gaining a fuller insight into the meaning than can be gained through a translation, and incidentally acquiring a better knowledge of that language also. A brief note on the grammar of Samskṛit, putting before the reader a few of the most salient features thereof, is therefore added here, as likely to be of use. It will help by giving a bird's eye view of the subject and thus some idea of how one part is connected with another. The details must of course be looked up in any large grammar, if needed.

I. Alphabet:—A complete alphabet would comprise hundreds, perhaps thousands, of single sounds. Out of these each human race or sub-race uses a comparatively small number, selected in accordance with the constitution of its vocal organs and of other aspects of its physical and superphysical being. There is a correspondence between all the parts of an organism; and the means and instruments of manifestation possessed by a race or nation, as by an individual, are, generally speaking, in correspondence with the 'ruling passion,' the 'main idea,' which that race or nation embodies and has to express. These 'ideas,' 'passions,' 'emotions,' 'glories,' 'aspects,' 'modifications,' of the Universal Self, Spirit, or Consciousness, are infinite; the world-process which endeavours to express them is infinite. One main idea (others being subordinate) is expressed by one individual, or one race, in any one time and space, 'beauty', 'strength,' 'comfort', 'peace,' 'war', 'science,' 'law', 'duty' 'right,' 'piety,' 'devotion,' &c. &c. The various members of a race, which is the embodiment and exponent of any one such main idea, have to use means of communication with each other to intensify that exposition, to make their lives fuller and deeper. This means, during the present cycle of evolution, is sound-language. In other cycles it may be sight-language, or touch-language, or smell-language, &c. &c. This sound-language is made up of single sounds, which, as said before, are in accordance with the 'body,' the physical constitution, of the race, which, again, is in accordance with its 'spirit,' its ruling idea. A race embodying sweetness and gentleness would unconsciously select the soft and sweet sounds for its language; another manifesting martial strength and spirit, the harsher and more definite ones.

The Samskṛit language, embodying *Dharma*, law and order, the instrument of a civilisation whose characteristics are systematisation, rounded comprehensiveness and completeness, an ordered arrangement of life from beginning to end, and in all departments, is therefore itself systematic. It uses fourteen vowels and thirty-five consonants, a total of seven sevens. Some put the nasal and the aspirate sounds— · *anusvâra* and : *visarga*—amongst the vowels, and so count them as sixteen and the consonants thirty-three. They are arranged systematically, according to the regions of the vocal apparatus whence they proceed, as gutturals, linguœ-radicals, palatals, cerebrals, dentals, labials, and certain combinations of these—beginning from the throat and proceeding outwards. As to why we have here two septenaries of vowels and five septenaries of consonants is a question which could possibly be answered by one who had sufficient knowledge of world-evolution to be able to say why the present human race has two hands and two feet and five senses of knowledge and five organs of action, and five fingers on each hand and five toes on each foot, &c. The question can only tantalise us. But we can vaguely see that if these sounds of the Samskṛit alphabet were multiplied systematically and permuted and combined, we should obtain a scheme which would cover all the languages of the earth, and bring into line all the very various-seeming sounds which constitute the several alphabets of these. *F. i.*, taking the linguœ-radicals, क, ख, ग, घ ङ, we find that ख, is the aspirate of क, that the guttural of this ख, *viz*, ख़, ḳh, has been appropriated by the Persian race and language and has disappeared from Samskṛit; that ग, is only a deepening of क; and that घ is the aspirate of ग; that the guttural of क़ *i. e.*, q̣, and of ग़, *i. e.*, g̣h, again, have disappeared from Samskṛit and been appropriated by the Arabic race and language; that ङ़, is the nasal of ग, as now pronounced, and that the nasals of the other letters, क, ख, घ, &c., &c., are not present in Samskṛit, but may possibly be present in some of the so-called savage languages, as 'snorts' and 'grunts' of various kinds.

This process of elimination, of the disappearance of sounds and letters, may be witnessed as being in progress even to-day. In Samskṛit the vowels ऋ, ॠ, ऌ, ॡ, have practically disappeared from use; their outer written form is preserved, but for all practical purposes of pronunciation they have merged into र and ल.

The distinction between श and ष is on the wane; the probability, judging by the rules of pronunciation given by Pâṇiṇi, is that ष in another form of the Persian ḳh mentioned above, as the discarded ़ क is that of the Arabic q̣ and the similarly abandoned ़ प of the Persian pḥ or f.

The nasal letters again ङ, ञ, ण, न, have a tendency to run, all of them, into the single न, in the mouths of those who are not particularly careful. So in English, sounds which originally existed when such words as 'daughter' (Persian *duḳhtar*, Samskṛit *duhitâ*), and 'night' (Samskṛit *nakta*) &c. were brought over, have now disappeared except perhaps in some village dialects, though the spelling continues as before. The reason of this may be suggested thus. According to the variety of the aspects of consciousness embodied in a people will be the variety of sounds, or letters employed by them; as the one variety diminishes or expands so will the other: if the word *laugh* were pronounced as *lawgh* as it probably was in the beginning, and as it is still by 'uneducated' people, it would imply a greater and a somewhat coarser heartiness; pronounced as *lâf* it indicates a toning down of the uncontrolled animal spirit, into a much more mild and refined condition of feeling. In America, and in some English circles, it is becoming further shortened into *laff*.

The Samskṛit Alphabet:

	SIMPLE.		COMPOUND.	
	Short	*Long*	*Short*	*Long.*
Vowels:	अ	आ	ए=(अ or आ + इ or ई)	ऐ=(अ or आ + ए)
	इ	ई	ओ=(अ or आ + उ or ऊ)	औ=(अ or आ + ओ).

उ ऊ
ऋ ॠ
ऌ ॡ

Cosonants क ख ग घ ङ.
च छ ज झ ञ.
ट ठ ड ढ ण.
त थ द ध न.
प फ ब भ म.
य र ल व,
श ष स ह.

Classified in various ways with reference to स्थान and प्रयत्न, the 'place' in the vocal apparatus and the special kind of 'effort' required to pronounce it.

There are only a few verses now current, as to the psychophysics of sound and language, in Pâṇini's *Shikshâ*, and these are not very intelligible in the absence of full explanations. They may be summarised thus: The Self cognising facts by means of the *Buddhi* (Reason) inspires the *Manas* (intelligence) with the desire to speak; the *Manas* strikes the *kâyâgni*—the fire of the body; and it in turn sets in motion the *mâruta*, the wind or breath that moving in the chest generates the *Mandra* sound; that, again, rising to the palate (or the crown of the head) and rebounding thence passes to the mouth and produces articulate sounds, classified according to tone, time, place, effort, &c., &c.

II. *Sandhi or Coalescence of sounds or letters*—In connection with these letter sounds, arises the first difficulty of Samskṛit Grammar, *Sandhi*, the coalescence of sounds. When one word is followed by another, in quick succession of pronunciation, the natural tendency is for the tail of the first and the head of the second to get mixed up: This mixture sometimes takes a shape which, while no doubt always retaining traces of the components, is not always analysable into these components by the beginner. The coalescence takes place in all languages, and offers one of the chief difficulties to the foreigner; but in other languages, for the most part, no attempt is made to express in writing the spoken sound. Thus the Frenchman says "le'pti," but he always writes "le petit." In Samskṛit writing the spoken sound is imitated. The detailed rules on this subject, which two sounds mixing make up which third sound, are many. The generalised rule may be stated to be that if the student will pronounce the two letters *correctly* and quickly in succession, the resultant sound, compelled by his own vocal apparatus, will also be in accordance with the grammatical rule on the subject. Briefly, the grammatical rule is only a description of the physiological fact. This appears not only in the case of actual coalescence, but in the influence of one sound on another separated from it by one or more intervening ones. Thus, according to the ordinary rule the word राम declined into its instrumental form, should be रामेन, but after pronouncing the cerebral *r* in its exact Samskṛit shade, the vocal apparatus of the Indian finds it difficult to adjust itself rapidly to pronounce the dental-nasal *n* न properly, even when another labial nasal *m* intervenes; it turns more readily to the allied and nearer cerebral-nasal ṇ, ण, and the result is रामेण.

Examples:

(a.) Conjunction of similar vowels: whether both short or both long, or one short and one long, the resultant is the long vowel.

कृतेन अर्थः = कृतेनार्थः (iii. 18.), आत्मना आत्मानं = आत्मनात्मानं (vi. 5.), च अपरे = चापरे (iv. 27.); and so with इ, उ, ऋः, उस्का-

मति ईश्वरः=उत्क्रामतीश्वरः (xv. 8.), तु उद्देशतः=तूद्देशतः (x. 4.) etc.

(b) *Conjunction of dissimilar vowels*: अ or आ followed by इ or ई gives ए, एका इह=एकेह (ii. 41.); by उ or ऊ gives ओ, श्रद्धया उपेतः=श्रद्धयोपेतः (vi. 37.); by ए or ऐ gives ऐ, न एवं=नैवं (ii. 38.); by ऋ gives अर्, देव ऋषिः=देवर्षिः (ii. 13.); by ओ or औ gives औ; इ followed by any dissimilar vowel gives य्, गच्छन्ति अनामयं= गच्छन्त्यनामयं (ii. 57.); so उ gives व् and ऋ, र्.

(c) *Visarga*: changes in five ways; it disappears, समवेताः युयुत्सवः=समवेता युयुत्सवः (i. 1.); it is dropped before a vowel and no further change occurs, कामः एषः=काम एषः (iii. 37.); it changes into ष, श and स, दुः कृतां=दुष्कृतां (iv. 8.), पांडवाः च= पांडवाश्च (i. 1.), यज्ञः तपः तथा=यज्ञस्तपस्तथा (xvii. 7.); it changes into ओ, यः मां=यो मां (vi. 30.), अजः अपि=अजोऽपि (iv. 6.) these cases being generally marked with ऽ. as सः अर्जुन=सोऽर्जुन (iv 9.)]; it is changed into र्, योनिः महद्ब्रह्म=योनिर्महद्ब्रह्म (xiv. 3.) The details of the rules causing these changes must be sought in a grammar.

(d) *Consonants*: The final consonant of one word is modified by the first consonant of the succeeding one. These changes are very numerous and intricate, and will only gradually become familiar; the following cases show the general principle above mentioned that the writing follows the sound; यत् ज्ञात्वा=यज्ज्ञात्वा (vii. 2.), यत् यत् विभूतिमत्=यद्यद्विभूतिमत् (x. 41.), यत् च=यच्च (x. 39.)

III. *Compounds.* When all cases of simple sandhi have been eliminated, the student is faced with another difficulty; words are compounded together, and only the last word of the compound is complete; the remaining word or words have their endings clipped off, and these have to be supplied before the compound becomes intelligible. Such compounds are called समास. They are of six chief kinds.

द्वन्द्व compounds; रागः च द्वेषः च = रागद्वेषौ (iii. 34.); पणवाः च आनकाः च गोमुखाः च = पणवानकगोमुखाः (i. 13.)

तत्पुरुष compounds; देवानाम् ईश = देवेश (xi. 45.); विस्मयेन आविष्टः = विस्मयाविष्टः (xi. 14.)

कर्मधारय *Compounds*; परमः आत्मा = परमात्मा (xv-17)

द्विगु *Compounds*; त्रयाणां गुणानां समाहारः = त्रैगुण्यम् (ii. 45.)

बहुव्रीहि *Compounds* विजितानि इंद्रियाणि यस्य सः = विजितेंद्रियः (vi. 8.); ब्रह्मणा संस्पर्शः यस्य तत् = ब्रह्मसंस्पर्शम् (vi. 28.)

अव्ययीभाव *Compounds*; आत्मनः विषये = अध्यात्मम्।

To solve these compounds it will be noticed that a knowledge of case-endings is necessary; it is the case-ending which is struck out in a compound, and the meaning of the compound depends on this eliminated case-ending. Hence the next step of the learner is to familiarise himself with the case-endings, of which every noun has twenty-one—7 cases in 3 numbers, singular, dual and plural.

IV. *Words.—(a) Declension of nouns.* Words are mainly of two kinds, names of things and names of actions, corresponding respectively to the cognition and action aspects of consciousness. Mediating between the two, binding them together, as desire binds cognition and action, is the third kind of word, the preposition; it forms a separate word in the modern languages, for various evolutionary reasons; but in the Samskṛit, it is hidden in and is a part of the noun itself, in the shape of the declensional termination, even as desire is hidden in the person, the actor, and is not something separate from him. Other parts of speech are off-shoots from these three principal ones. Nouns including pronouns are (i) simple, subdivided by gender into 3 classes, or (ii) derivative, i. e. to say, derived from verb-roots. Of course one theory, and probably the right one, is that all names or nouns are ultimately connected with and founded on some characteristic *action* of the object; but without going into the detail of the theory, it is enough for practical purposes to recognise that as the Samskṛit language now stands, some of its nouns may be regarded as, on their face, simple and some as derivative. To denote the kind of relation that exists between one noun and another, and also to give some indication of the kind of action passing between them, is the purpose of prepositional, or declensional, terminations. As *pre-positions*, distinguishing and *separating* marks of the *kinds* of the nouns concerned, showing the position or situation or case in which they are, whether nominative, or accusative, or instrumental, &c., with reference to each other, these declensional terminations are called *vibhaktis*; as indicating that some action passes between them, they are called *kârakas.*

Examples of declensions :

1st.	सन्यासः	[v. 1.]	उभौ	[v. 1]	पंडिताः	[v. 4]
2nd.	रथं	[i. 21]	अश्विनौ	[xi. 6]	लोकान्	[xi. 32]
3rd.	पुत्रेण	[i 3]	नराभ्याम		वैरैः	[xi. 53]
4th.	विनाशाय	[iv. 1]	,,		पापेभ्यः	
5th.	हस्तात	[ii. 30]	,,		पापेभ्यः	[xviii. 66]
6th.	लोकस्य	[v. 14]	तयोः	[iii. 34]	पुत्राणाम्	[i, 3]
7th.	मध्ये	[i. 21]	उभयोः	[i. 21]	गुणेषु	[iii. 28]

Âtmâ, crude form Âtman, is a typical form, and occurs very frequently in the *Gîtá* in the singular number.

1st. आत्मा [v. 21]
2nd. आत्मानम् [vi. 5]
3rd. आत्मना [vi. 5]
4th. आत्मने
5th. आत्मनः
6th. आत्मनः [vi. 6]
7th. आत्मनि [vi. 21]

Neuter nouns in their case-endings, except in those of the first and second cases, generally follow the masculine.

Thus कर्म crude form कर्मन्, has :

1st. कर्म (xviii. 8) कर्मणी कर्माणि (ix. 9)
2nd. „ (iii. 8) „ „ (vi. 30)

The feminine in इ may be taken as an example of the feminine declensions :

1st. मतिः (xviii. 78)
2nd. बुद्धिं (iii. 2)
3rd. बुद्ध्या (ii. 39)
4th. मत्यै or मतये
5th. बुद्धेः (iii. 43) or बुद्ध्याः
6th. „
7th. बुद्धौ (ii, 49)

(*b*) *Adjectives and adverbs &c.* Adjectives, words indicative of the 'qualities' of nouns, are declined in the same way as the latter, and when not compounded with these are always in "apposition" with them.

Adverbs are mostly 'Indeclinable' in Samskṛit. These indeclinables include also some words, however, which are not *adverbs ;* thus conjunctions and interjections are included here. Examples च, अति, अतीव, अथ. अभितः, अवश्यम्, अहोबत, अहो, इति, इव, इह, उत, एव, एवम्, कच्चित्, कथम, किन्तु, कृते, चेत्, तदा, तु, न, &c., &c., are of frequent occurrence.

(c) *Gender.* The marks of gender are very perplexed in Samskṛit : They belong to the noun only, as in most languages ; and not the verb, as in Hindi, Arabic or French. As a general rule, governing frequent cases, when the male base ends in a short अ, the corresponding female base ends in the long आ ; and the neuter in अं.

अपरः Singular of अपरान् (xvi–14)

अपरा (iii. 6) ; अपरं (iv– 4).

(d) *Verbs.* After nouns, verbs. The list of roots given by Paṇini numbers 2343; and each is capable of undergoing hundreds of inflectional or conjugational terminations, on account of moods and tenses, and causative, desiderative and repetitive forms of it, and all these again can be conjugated in the active or the passive form, and so on. But by the same processes of selection and elimination that have governed the number of the letters, the verb-roots in actual use in current Samskṛit are not many more than 500 and of these a very limited number of forms is used.

The tenses and moods are taken together and all called *vibhaktis* or *lakâras ;* and there are ten of such, *viz.*, six tenses and four moods. The tenses are, 1 present ; 3 past ; and 2 future; and the moods are Imperative, Potential, Benedictive and

Conditional. In common and unclassical Samskṛit, one form of the past, *viz*., the first preterite, is largely used, the other two being very infrequent; so the first future is seldom met with even in classical Samskṛit. Of the moods, the benedictive mood is very rarely used.

If the whole list of the 2343 roots were carefully examined, very many more roots would be found to be common between the several Âryan languages than are now noted. But, as said before in connection with the alphabet, the genius of each later language has selected out of the roots what were most suited to it, and the older race, the root-race, has correspondingly dropped them in its later career. It is as if there had been a partition of patrimony between heirs so that what one took the others could not retain.

These verbs are divided into ten classes; the external reason is that the verbs of each class resemble each other more than those of the other classes, in the general appearance of their conjugational forms. But this again requires a deeper why; and that is not traceable. If it could be said that there were ten main kinds of human action, we should have approximated to the answer wanted.

There are two main forms of conjugation, the परस्मै-पद "for another"; and the आत्मने-पद "for self". The former, generally speaking, belongs to the active voice, wherein one person does something to another; and the latter to the passive voice, wherein something is done 'to one self'. But while in the passive voice form of any verb *only* the आत्मनेपद form is used, in the active voice the परस्मैपद form is used only generally, and sometimes the आत्मनेपद form is used, and in some cases both.

The following forms occur frequently in the *Gîtâ.*

		परस्मैपद	SINGULAR.		PLURAL.
Present Tense.	3rd p.	परिशुष्यति	(i. 29)	सीदन्ति	(ii. 6)
	2nd p.	अर्हसि	(ii. 25)	"	
	1st p.	शक्नोमि	(i. 30)	विद्मः	(ii. 6)
First Preterite.	3rd p.	अब्रवीत्	(i. 2)		
	2nd p.	अन्वशोचः	(ii. 11)		
	1st p.	आसं	(ii. 12)		
Second Preterite.	3rd p.	उवाच	(i. 3)		
Third Preterite.	2nd p.	अगमः (in conjunction with मा drops अ, and acquires imperative meaning)	(ii. 3)		
First Future.	3rd p.	भविता	(ii. 20)		
	2nd p.	गन्तासि	(ii. 52)		
Second Future.	3d. p.	स्थास्यति	(ii. 53)	कथयिष्यन्ति	(i. 34)
	2nd p.	करिष्यसि	(ii. 33)	अवाप्स्यथ	(iii. 11)
	1st p.	प्रतियोत्स्यामि	(ii. 4)	भविष्यामः	(ii. 12)
Imperative Mood.	3rd p.	अस्तु	(ii. 47)	भावयन्तु	(iii 11)
	2nd p.	पश्य	(i. 3)	भावयत	(iii. 11)
Potential Mood.	3rd p.	स्यात्	(i. 36)	हन्युः	(i. 46)
	1st p.	आप्नुयाम्		जयेम	(ii. 6)

(The dual number is omitted, as not occurring in the *Gîtâ*)

आत्मनपद

Present Tense.	3rd p.	जायते	(i. 29)	सज्जन्ते	(iii. 29)
	2nd p.	भाषसे	(ii. 11)		
	1st p.	कांक्षे	(i. 32)		

First Preterite.	3rd p.	अकुर्वत:	(i. 1)
Second Future.	3rd p. —	मंस्यंते	(ii. 35)
	2nd p.	मोक्ष्यसे	(ii. 37)
	1st p.	योत्स्ये	(ii. 9)
Imperative Mood.	2nd p.	तितिक्षस्व	(ii. 14)
Potential Mood.	3rd p.	प्रभाषेत	(ii. 54)
	1st p.	भुञ्जीय	(ii. 5)

In the technical works on grammar, rules are given for the correct use of all the ten moods and tenses; thus the first preterite should be used when the event is older than the current day; the 2nd when it occurred outside the speaker's personal knowledge; and the 3rd in any case; and so the 1st future should be used when the event is expected very shortly. But these rules, as said before, are observed only in classical composition. There is also some reason to think that they do not represent accurately the real original distinctions. It is possible that the three pasts corresponded to the English 'imperfect' and 'pluperfect' &c.

The addition of prefixes entirely changes the meaning of the verb-root, as stated in the classical sbloka on the subject.

उपसर्गेण धात्वर्थो बलादन्यत्र नीयते ।
प्रहाराहारसंहारविहारपरिहारवत् ॥

" The prefex violently drags away elsewhere the meaning of the verb-root; thus, with the common root हृ, to take away, प्रहार means a blow, आहार food, संहार destruction विहार, play, and परिहार clearing away ". A careful analysis shows that the idea of taking away is present in some shape or other throughout all these.

Each verb-root is capable of being modified into a causative form, a desiderative form and a frequentative form; and each of these forms is capable of independent conjugation in all moods and tenses.

Causative; The causative verb is formed by the addition of इ, which becomes when the termination is added, य घातयति (ii. 21) he causes to kill, from हन् to kill; नियोजयसि (iii. 1) thou causest (me) to engage, from युज् to join; कार्यते (iii. 5) he is caused to do, from कृ to do; विचालयेत् (iii. 29) he may cause to be unsettled, from चल् to move; अवसादयेत् let (him) cause to sink down, from अवसद् to be cast down.

Desiderative; The desiderative verb expresses the wish of the agent; स is added, and the first letter is reduplicated युयुत्सवः (i. i) wishing to fight, from युध् to fight; जिजीविषामः (ii. 6) (we) wish to live, from जीव् to live; चिकीर्षुः (iii. 25) desiring to do, from कृ to do; आरुरुक्षोः (of the) wishing to ascend, from आरुह् to mount.

(*e*) *Derivative words.* Derivative words of various kinds, *e, g.* some indicating moods not covered by the regular conjugations, are formed by means of affixes.

(इच्छ) आप्तुं = (wish) to obtain (xii. 9).

(अशक्तोसि) कर्तुं = (art powerless) to do (xii. 11).

त्यक्त्वा = having abandoned (V. 10).

भूत्वा = having been (ii. 20).

Various participles, past, present and future, and some shades of tenses, which in Samskṛit behave like adjectives and so like nouns, are also thus derived. They are declined exactly like the nouns with which they may be in apposition:

पश्यन् = seeing (v. 8). शृण्वन् hearing (v. 8). आसीनः being seated (xiv. 23). हन्यमानः = being slain (ii. 20).

श्रोतव्यः = to be heard (ii. 52). कर्तव्यं = to be done (iii 22). कार्यं = to be done (xviii. 5).

प्रोक्तवान् = have (or hast, or has) said (iv. 1).

आविष्टः = seized or possessed with (i. 28). भक्तः = devoted (ix. 31). सक्तः attached (v. 12).

योत्स्यमानः = going to fight (i. 23).

Many nouns are formed by inflectional modifications of other nouns :

पार्थः, the son of पृथा. (ii. 3.)

कौंतेयः, the son of कुंती. (ii. 14.)

So सौभद्रः from सुभद्रा; द्रौपदेयः from द्रौपदी which itself is formed from द्रुपद &c. (i. 6.).

अक्लेद्यः, अदाह्यः, अशोष्यः &c. meaning 'not capable of क्लेदः, or दाहः, or शोषः &c., (ii. 24).

सत्वं = सत् + त्वं = good-ness :

अलोलुप्त्वं = un-avaricious-ness ; अतिमानिता = very-proud ness ; (xiv. 2).

ज्ञानी = ज्ञान-possessing ; (vii. 18).

ज्ञानवान् = do. ; (vii. 82).

कुतः (from किं) = 'from which (place), (ii. 2) ; ततः from तत्, = then, thence,' (vi. 45).

धर्म्यः = 'in accordance with धर्मः' (ii. 31) ;

अष्टधा = in अष्ट or eight ways (vii. 4). &c., &c., &c.,

V. *Sentences.* The two main forms of the sentence are: (1) that in the active voice, and (2) that in the passive.

(1) Active: न मां कर्माणि लिंपंति (iv. 14) = Actions do not stain me.

(2) Passive: लिप्यते न स पापेन (v. 10) = He is not stained by sin.

In construing a shloka the first thing to do is to separate out the words, so as to give to each its complete and independent existence; the coalesced tails and heads [सन्धि] are first dissolved into their component parts; then the compound words are separated, and any lacking case-endings supplied; then the words are arranged in their prose order. In Samskṛit order matters comparatively little, but still there is more inversion permissible in poetry than in prose. Let us take i. 2, 3.

दृष्ट्वा तु पांडवानीकं व्यूढं दुर्योधनस्तदा ।
आचार्यमुपसंगम्य राजा वचनमब्रवीत् ॥

Separated into independent words:

दृष्ट्वा तु (पांडवानीकं =) पांडवानाम् अनीकं व्यूढं दुर्योधनः तदा ।
आचार्यम् उपसंगम्य राजा वचनम् अब्रवीत् ॥

The prose-order:

तदा राजा दुर्योधनः पांडवानां अनीकं तु व्यूढं दृष्ट्वा आचार्यं उपसंगम्य वचनम् अब्रवीत् ॥

पश्यैतां पांडुपुत्राणामाचार्य महतीं चमूम् ।
व्यूढां द्रुपदपुत्रेण तव शिष्येण धीमता ॥

Separated into independent words:

पश्य एतां (पांडुपुत्राणाम् =) पांडोः पुत्राणाम् आचार्य महतीं चमूम् ।

व्यूढां (द्रुपदपुत्रेण =) द्रुपदस्य पुत्रेण तव शिष्येण धीमता ॥

The English prose-order of this would run.

हे आचार्य पश्य एतां महतीं चमूम् पांडोः पुत्राणाम् व्यूढां तव धीमता शिष्येण द्रुपदस्य पुत्रेण ॥

But in Samskṛit prose-order :

हे आचार्य तव धीमता शिष्येण द्रुपदस्य पुत्रेण व्यूढां एतां पांडोः पुत्राणाम् महतीं चमूम् पश्य ॥

—:0:—

THE BHAGAVAD-GÎTÂ

॥ अथ श्रीमद्भगवद्गीता ॥

अथ गीतामाहात्म्यम् ।

श्रीगणेशाय नमः ॥ श्रीराधारमणाय नमः ॥ धरोवाच ॥
भगवन्परमेशान भक्तिरव्यभिचारिणी ॥ प्रारब्धं भुज्यमानस्य
कथं भवति हे प्रभो ॥ १ ॥ विष्णुरुवाच ॥ प्रारब्धं भुज्यमा-
नो हि गीताभ्यासरतः सदा ॥ स मुक्तः स सुखी लोके कर्म-
णा नोपलिप्यते ॥ २ ॥ महापापादिपापानि गीताध्यानं करो-
ति चेत् ॥ क्वचित्स्पर्शं न कुर्वंति नलिनीदलमंबुवत् ॥ ३ ॥
गीतायाः पुस्तकं यत्र यत्र पाठः प्रवर्तते ॥ तत्र सर्वाणि ती-
र्थानि प्रयागादीनि तत्र वै ॥ ४ ॥ सर्वे देवाश्च ऋषयो यो-
गिनः पन्नगाश्च ये ॥ गोपाला गोपिका वापि नारदोद्धवपार्ष-
दैः ॥ ५ ॥ सहायो जायते शीघ्रं यत्र गीता प्रवर्तते ॥ यत्र
गीताविचारश्च पठनं पाठनं श्रुतम् ॥ तत्राहं निश्चितं पृथ्वि निवसा-
मि सदैव हि ॥ ६ ॥ गीताश्रयेऽहं तिष्ठामि गीता मे चोत्तमं
गृहम् ॥ गीताज्ञानमुपाश्रित्य त्रीन्लोकान्पालयाम्यहम् ॥ ७ ॥
गीता मे परमा विद्या ब्रह्मरूपा न संशयः ॥ अर्धमात्राक्षरा नि-
त्या स्वानिर्वाच्यपदात्मिका ॥ ८ ॥ चिदानंदेन कृष्णेन प्रोक्ता
स्वमुखतोऽर्जुनम् ॥ वेदत्रयी परानंदा तत्त्वार्थज्ञानसंयुता ॥ ९ ॥

योऽष्टादशजपो नित्यं नरो निश्चलमानसः ॥ ज्ञानसिद्धिं स ल-
भते ततो याति परं पदम् ॥ १० ॥ पाठे समग्रे ऽसंपूर्णे ततो-
ऽर्धं पाठमाचरेत् ॥ तदा गोदानजं पुण्यं लभते नात्र संशयः
॥ ११ ॥ त्रिभागं पठमानस्तु गंगास्नानफलं लभेत् ॥ षडंशं
जपमानस्तु सोमयागफलं लभेत् ॥ १२ ॥ एकाध्यायं तु यो
नित्यं पठते भक्तिसंयुतः ॥ रुद्रलोकमवाप्नोति गणो भूत्वा
वसेच्चिरम् ॥ १३ ॥ अध्यायं श्लोकपादं वा नित्यं यः पठते
नरः ॥ स याति नरतां यावन्मन्वंतरं वसुंधरे ॥ १४ ॥ गी-
तायाः श्लोकदशकं सप्त पंच चतुष्टयम् ॥ द्वौ त्रीनेकं तदर्धं
वा श्लोकानां यः पठेन्नरः ॥ १५ ॥ चंद्रलोकमवाप्नोति वर्षा-
णामयुतं ध्रुवम् ॥ गीतापाठसमायुक्तो मृतो मानुषतां व्रजेत्
॥ १६ ॥ गीताभ्यासं पुनः कृत्वा लभते मुक्तिमुत्तमाम् ॥ गी-
तेत्युच्चारसंयुक्तो म्रियमाणो गतिं लभेत् ॥ १७ ॥ गीतार्थश्र-
वणासक्तो महापापयुतोऽपि वा ॥ वैकुण्ठं समवाप्नोति विष्णुना
सह मोदते ॥ १८ ॥ गीतार्थं ध्यायते नित्यं कृत्वा कर्माणि
भूरिशः ॥ जीवन्मुक्तः स विज्ञेयो देहांते परमं पदम् ॥ १९ ॥
गीतामाश्रित्य बहवो भूभुजो जनकादयः ॥ निर्धूतकल्मषा लोके
गीता याताः परं पदम् ॥ २० ॥ गीतायाः पठनं कृत्वा मा-
हात्म्यं नैव यः पठेत् ॥ वृथा पाठो भवेत्तस्य श्रम एव ह्युदाहृ-

तः ॥ २१ ॥ एतन्माहात्म्यसंयुक्तं गीताभ्यासं करोति यः ॥ स तत्फलमवाप्नोति दुर्लभां गतिमाप्नुयात् ॥ २२ ॥ सूत उवाच ॥ माहात्म्यमेतद्गीताया मया प्रोक्तं सनातनम् ॥ गीतांते च पठेद्यस्तु यदुक्तं तत्फलं लभेत् ॥ २३ ॥ इति श्रीवाराहपुराणे श्रीगीतामाहात्म्यं संपूर्णम् ॥

———:o:———

THE BHAGAVAD-GÎTÂ.

THE GREATNESS OF THE GÎTÂ.

Hail to Shrî Gaṇeṣha! Hail to the Lover of Râdhâ!

Dharâ (the Earth) said: O Blessed One, O Supreme Ruler, how may unfaltering devotion arise in him who is constrained by prârabdha karma, O Lord?

(1). Viṣhṇu said: He who, constrained by prârabdha karma, is ever assiduously practising the Gîtâ, he is liberated, he is happy in this world, he is not stained by karma.

(2). If he study the Gîtâ, then can no sin stain him, as water stains not the lotus-leaf.

(3). Where is the book of the Gîtâ, where its reading is performed, there are all holy places, there indeed Prayâga and the rest.

(4). All Devas, Ṛiṣhis, Yogîs and Pannagas, also Gopâlas and Gopîs also, with Nârada, Uddhava, and their train.

(5). Help comes swiftly where the Gîtâ is recited. Where the discussion of the Gîtâ, the recitation, the teaching, of it is heard, there I, O Earth, doubtless ever abide.

(6). I dwell in the retreat of the Gîtâ ; the Gîtâ is My best abode. Having mastered the wisdom of the Gîtâ, I protect the three worlds.

(7). The Gîtâ is My supreme science, it is verily the form of Brahman. It is the half-syllable eternal (the dot on the ॐ), everlasting, the ineffable essence of the Self,

(8). Spoken by Kṛiṣhṇa, the Omniscient, the Blessed, to Arjuna with His own mouth, the three Vedas, the final bliss, the exposition of the knowledge of the Tattvas.

(9). The man who constantly repeats the eighteen discourses with unwavering mind, he will obtain perfect wisdom and reach the supreme goal.

(10). If the complete recitation be impossible, then may one half be read. Then he doubtless obtains merit, equal to the gift of a cow.

(11). By the reading of a third part, he may obtain

the fruit of bathing in Gangâ. By the repetition of a sixth part, he may obtain the fruit of the Soma-sacrifice.

(12). He who daily reads a single discourse with devotion, he, having become a Gaṇa, obtains Rudraloka and therein long abides.

(13). The man who daily reads a quarter-shloka, he, O Earth, remains a man during a manvantara.

(14). The man who should read ten, seven, five, four, two, three, one, or half a shloka of the Gîtâ,

(15). He securely obtains Chandraloka for ten thousand years. Ever engaged in the reading of the Gîtâ, passing through death, he would return to humanity.

(16). Having again practised the Gîtâ, he obtains the supreme liberation. Engaged in the utterance, "Gîtâ," the dying reaches the path.

(17). Attached to the hearing of the Gîtâ, even the great sinner attains to Vaikuntha, and rejoices with Vishṇu.

(18). He who meditates on the meaning of the Gîtâ, having performed actions abundantly, he should be known as a Jîvanmukta, and at the ending of the body reaches the supreme goal.

(19). Having taken refuge in the Gîtâ, many Kings,

Janaka and the rest, praised in the world, being cleansed from sins, have gone to the supreme goal.

(20). Having accomplished the reading of the Gîtâ, he who should not also read this description of its greatness, his reading is in vain, and his labour is lost.

(21). He who performs the practice of the Gîtâ, associated with this discourse on its Greatness, he obtains the fruit, he may reach the path difficult of obtainment.

(22). Sûta said: He who should read this eternal Greatness of the Gîtâ, proclaimed by me, at the end of the Gîtâ, should obtain that fruit which has been described.

(23). Thus in the blessed Vârâhapurâṇa the greatness of the Gîtâ is set forth.

Note. The statements made above, as to the value of reading portions, or the whole, of the *Gîtâ*, may seem at first sight to be somewhat fantastic. They should not be construed as meaning the mere reading, the lip-repetition, of verses, but rather as the mastering and assimilation of the spirit of the *Gîtâ*, and the life-repetition thereof. The man who has thus wrought the *Gîtâ* into his life is a Jîvanmukta, and the assimilation of one shloka, of several, of a quarter of the *Gîtâ*, and so on, mark various stages in human evolution, each of which has its own appropriate fruit.

अथ गीताकरादिन्यासः ।

ॐ अस्य श्रीभगवद्गीतामालामंत्रस्य भगवान्वेदव्यास ऋषिः ॥ अनुष्टुप् छंदः ॥ श्रीकृष्णः परमात्मा देवता ॥ अशोच्यानन्वशोचस्त्वं प्रज्ञावादांश्च भाषस इति बीजम् ॥ सर्वधर्मान्परित्यज्य मामेकं शरणं व्रजेति शक्तिः ॥ अहं त्वा सर्वपापेभ्यो मोक्षयिष्यामि मा शुच इति कीलकम् ॥ नैनं छिंदंति शस्त्राणि नैनं दहति पावक इत्यंगुष्ठाभ्यां नमः ॥ न चैनं क्लेदयंत्यापो न शोषयति मारुत इति तर्जनीभ्यां नमः ॥ अच्छेद्योऽयमदाह्योऽयमक्लेद्योऽशोष्य एव चेति मध्यमाभ्यां नमः ॥ नित्यः सर्वगतः स्थाणुरचलोऽयं सनातन इत्यनामिकाभ्यां नमः ॥ पश्य मे पार्थ रूपाणि शतशोऽथ सहस्रश इति कनिष्ठिकाभ्यां नमः ॥ नानाविधानि दिव्यानि नानावर्णाकृतीनि चेति करतलकरपृष्ठाभ्यां नमः ॥ इति करन्यासः ॥ अथ हृदयादिन्यासः ॥ नैनं छिंदंति शस्त्राणि नैनं दहति पावक इति हृदयाय नमः ॥ न चैनं क्लेदयंत्यापो न शोषयति मारुत इति शिरसे स्वाहा ॥ अच्छेद्योऽयमदाह्योऽयमक्लेद्योऽशोष्य एव चेति शिखायै वषट् ॥ नित्यः सर्वगतः स्थाणुरचलोऽयं सनातन इति कवचाय हुम् ॥ पश्य मे पार्थ रूपाणि शतशोऽथ सहस्रश इति नेत्रत्रयाय वौषट् ॥ नानाविधानि

दिव्यानि नानावर्णाकृतीनि चेति अस्त्राय फट् ॥ श्रीकृष्णप्रीत्यर्थे पाठे विनियोगः ॥

—:o:—

The Arrangement Of The Hands etc. For The Gîtâ.

ॐ The Blessed Veda-Vyâsa is the Ṛiṣhi of this *Bhagavad-Gîtâ* mantra. The metre is the anuṣhṭup. Shrî Kṛiṣhṇa, the Supreme Self, is its Devatâ. "Thou grievest for those that should not be grieved for, yet speakest words of wisdom:" such is the Bîja. "Abandoning all duties, come unto me alone for shelter:" such is the Shakti. "I will liberate thee from all sins; sorrow not:" such is the Kilakam. "Weapons cleave him not, nor fire burneth him;" thus: "To the two thumbs, all hail!" "Nor waters wet him, nor wind drieth him away;" thus: "To the two index fingers, all hail!" "Uncleavable he, incombustible he, neither to be wetted nor dried away;" thus: "To the two middle fingers, all hail!" "Perpetual, all-pervasive, stable, immovable, ancient;" thus: "To the two nameless (fourth) fingers, all hail!" "Behold, O Pârtha, my Forms, a hundred-fold, a thousand-fold;" thus: "To the two little fingers, all hail!" "Various in kind, divine, various in colours;" thus: "To the two palms and backs of the hands, all hail!" Such is the disposition of the hands. Now as to the disposition of the heart and the other organs. "Weapons cleave him not, nor fire burneth him;" thus: "To the heart, all hail!" "Nor waters wet him, nor wind drieth him away;" thus: "To the head, svâhâ!" Uncleavable he, incombustible he, neither to be wetted nor dried away;" thus: "To the shikhâ, vaṣhaṭ!" "Perpetual, all-pervasive, stable, immovable;" thus: "To the encasement, huṅ!" "Behold, O Pârtha, my Forms, a hundred-fold, a thousand-fold;" thus: "To the fire-weapon, phaṭ!" For the propitiation of Shrî Kṛishṇa the reading is enjoined.

Note. A mantra, in the Hindu religion, has a Rishi, who gave it; A metre, which governs the inflection of the voice. A Devatâ—a supernatural being, higher or lower—as its informing power. The Bîja, seed, is a significant word, or series of words, which gives it a special power; sometimes this word is a sound which harmonises with the key-note of the individual using it, and varies with the individual; sometimes this word expresses the essence of the mantra, and the result of the mantra is the flower springing from this seed; this essence of the *Gîtâ* is in the words quoted. The Shakti is the energy of the *form* of the mantra, i. e. the vibration-forms set up by its sounds; these in the *Gîtâ* carry the man to the Lord. The Kîlakam, the pillar, is that which supports and makes strong the mantra; this is the ceasing of sorrow, by the freeing from imperfections.

Then follow certain special directions, intended to set up relations between the centres in the man's body and the corresponding centres in the body of the Lord—the universe. The thumbs, the earth-symbol, are connected with the physical plane, and are utilised in control of its subtle forces. The index fingers, the water-symbol, are connected with the astral plane, and are similarly used with astral forces. The middle fingers, the fire-symbol, the apex of the pyramid of the hand, are similarly used with mental forces. The fourth fingers, the air-symbol, are similarly used with buddhic forces. The little fingers, the most powerful in the subtle worlds, are the âkâsha-symbol, and are similarly used with âtmic forces. The other organs of the body are the other poles of the magnet of the body: thumbs and heart; index fingers and head; middle fingers and the point of juncture of the occipital and parietal sutures; the fourth fingers and the sûkshma sharira; the little fingers and the creative organ. These are the positive and negative poles of the magnet we call the body; either may be positive, either negative, according to the object aimed at, but they work together.

From other stand-points, these dispositions may be regarded as having on the one hand, an inhibitory, or, on the other, a stimulative effect on the physical or subtler function of the organs concerned, according to the purpose in view in the subsequent meditation or practice.

To the western world these correspondences may seem fantastic and superstitious; to the eastern world, in which the faint tradition of the Great Science lingers, they sound as echoes of a mightier age, when Gods and Men walked familiarly together in the Hidden Ways.

———:0:———

अथ गीताध्यानम् ।

ॐ पार्थाय प्रतिबोधितां भगवता नारायणेन स्वयं व्यासेन ग्रथितां पुराणमुनिना मध्येमहाभारतम् ॥ अद्वैतामृतवर्षिणीं भगवतीमष्टादशाध्यायिनीमंब त्वामनुसंदधामि भगवद्गीते भवद्वेषिणीम् ॥ १ ॥ नमोऽस्तु ते व्यास विशालबुद्धे फुल्लारविंदायतपत्रनेत्र ॥ येन त्वया भारततैलपूर्णः प्रज्वालितो ज्ञानमयः प्रदीपः ॥ २ ॥ प्रपन्नपारिजाताय तोत्रवेत्रैकपाणये ॥ ज्ञानमुद्राय कृष्णाय गीतामृतदुहे नमः ॥ ३ ॥ सर्वोपनिषदो गावो दोग्धा गोपालनंदनः ॥ पार्थो वत्सः सुधीर्भोक्ता दुग्धं गीतामृतं महत् ॥ ४ ॥ वसुदेवसुतं देवं कंसचाणूरमर्दनम् ॥ देवकीपरमानंदं कृष्णं वंदे जगद्गुरुम् ॥ ५ ॥ भीष्मद्रोणतटा जयद्रथजला गांधारनीलोत्पला शल्यग्राहवती कृपेण वहनी कर्णेन वेलाकुला ॥ अश्वत्थामविकर्णघोरमकरा दुर्योधनावर्तिनी सोत्तीर्णा खलु पाण्डवै रणनदी कैवर्तकः केशवः ॥ ६ ॥ पाराशर्यवचः सरोजममलं गीतार्थगंधोत्कटं नानाख्यानककेसरं हरिकथासंबोधनाबोधितम् ॥ लोके सज्जनषट्पदैरहरहः पेपीयमानं मुदा भूयाद्भारतपङ्कजं कलिमलप्रध्वंसि नः श्रेयसे ॥ ७ ॥ मूकं करोति वाचालं पंगुं लंघयते गिरिं ॥ यत्कृपा तमहं वंदे परमानंदमा-

धवम् ॥ ८ ॥ यं ब्रह्मावरुणेंद्ररुद्रमरुतः, स्तुन्वंति दिव्यैः स्तवैर्वेदैः सांगपदक्रमोपनिषदैर्गायंति यं सामगाः ॥ ध्यानावस्थिततद्गतेन मनसा पश्यंति यं योगिनो यस्यांतं न विदुः सुरासुरगणा देवाय तस्मै नमः ॥ ९ ॥ इति ध्यानम् ॥

—:o:—

THE MEDITATION ON GÎTÂ.

ॐ Taught by the Blessed Nârâyaṇa Himself to Arjuna; compiled by Vyâsa, the ancient Muni, in the midst of the *Mahâbhârata*; I meditate on thee, O Mother, O Bhagavad-Gîtâ, the blessed, the pourer-forth of the nectar of Advaita, destroyer of rebirth. Hail to thee, O Vyâsa, large-minded one, with eyes like the petals of the opened lotus; by whom the lamp of knowledge, filled with the oil of the *Mahâbhârata*, has been lighted. To the Pârijâta-kalpataru of the suppliant, to the holder of the whip, to Kṛiṣhṇa as Teacher, milker of the Gîtâ-nectar, all hail! All the Upaniṣhats are the cows; the Milker is the joy of the cowherds; Pârtha is the calf; the man of high intelligence is the enjoyer; the milk is the great nectar of the Gîtâ. I worship Vâsudeva, the charioteer, the God, the destroyer of Kamsa and Châṇûra, the supreme joy of Devakî, Kṛiṣhṇa, Guru of the world. With Keshava as helmsman, verily was crossed by the Pâṇḍavas that battle-river, whose banks were Bhîṣhma and Droṇa, whose water was Jayadratha, whose blue lotus was Gândhâra, whose crocodile was Shalya, whose current was Kripa, whose billows were Karṇa, whose terrible alligators were Asvatthâmâ and Vikarṇa, whose whirlpool was Duryodhana. May this Lotus of the *Mahâbhârata* be for our good, born on the lake of the words of Pârâsharya, sweet with the fragrance of the meaning of the Gîtâ, pollened with many stories, unfolding to the sun of the history of Hari, sucked by the bees of good men in the world day by day, cleanser of the stains of Kali. I salute Him, Mâdhava, the supreme Bliss, whose grace makes the dumb man eloquent, and the cripple a climber of mountains. Whom Brahmâ, Varuṇa, Indra, Rudra, and the Maruts praise with divine songs; whom the Sâma-chanters sing with the Vedas and with Aṅgas, in the pada and krama methods with the Upaniṣhats; whom Yogîs see by the mind fixed in meditation, to Him going; whose end Suras and Asuras know not; to that God, all hail!

———:o:———

ॐ

॥ अथ श्रीमद्भगवद्गीता प्रारभ्यते ॥

HERE THE BLESSED LORD'S SONG IS BEGUN.

धृतराष्ट्र उवाच ।

धर्मक्षेत्रे कुरुक्षेत्रे समवेता युयुत्सवः ।
मामकाः पाडवाश्चैव किमकुर्वत संजय ॥ १ ॥

Dhṛitarâṣhṭra said:

On the holy plain, on the field of Kuru, gathered together, eager for battle, what did they, O Sañjaya, my people and the Pâṇḍavas?

धृतराष्ट्रः Dhṛitarâṣhṭra; उवाच said; धर्मक्षेत्रे = धर्मस्य क्षेत्रे of dharma, in (on) the field; कुरुक्षेत्रे = कुरोः क्षेत्रे of Kuru, in (on) the field; समवेताः gathered together; युयुत्सवः wishing to fight; मामकाः mine; पांडवाः = पांडोः पुत्राः of Pâṇḍu, the sons; च and; एव also; किम् what; अकुर्वत did they; संजय O Sañjaya.

संजय उवाच ।

दृष्ट्वा तु पांडवानीकं व्यूढं दुर्योधनस्तदा ।
आचार्यमुपसंगम्य राजा वचनमब्रवीत् ॥ २ ॥

Sañjaya said :

Having seen arrayed the army of the Pâṇḍavas, the Râjâ Duryodhana approached his teacher,[1] and spake these words : (2)

संजयः Sañjaya ; उवाच said ; दृष्ट्वा having seen ; तु indeed ; पांडवानीकं = पांडवानां अनीकं of the Pâṇḍavas, the army ; व्यूढं arrayed ; दुर्योधनः Duryodhana ; तदा then ; आचार्यम् the teacher ; उपसंगम्य having approached ; राजा the King (Duryodhana) ; वचनम् speech ; अब्रवीत् said :

पश्यैतां पाडुपुत्राणामाचार्य महतीं चमूम् ।
व्यूढां द्रुपदपुत्रेण तव शिष्येण धीमता ॥ ३ ॥

Behold this mighty host of the sons of Pâṇḍu, O teacher, arrayed by the son of Drupada, thy wise disciple. (3)

पश्य behold ; एतां this ; पांडुपुत्राणाम् = पांडोः पुत्राणाम् of Pâṇḍu, the sons ; आचार्य O teacher ; महतीं great ; चमूम् army ; व्यूढां arrayed ; द्रुपदपुत्रेण = द्रुपदस्य पुत्रेण of Drupada, by the son ; तव thy ; शिष्येण (by) disciple ; धीमता (by) wise.

अत्र शूरा महेष्वासा भीमार्जुनसमा युधि ।
युयुधानो विराटश्च द्रुपदश्च महारथः ॥ ४ ॥

Heroes are these, mighty bowmen, to Bhîma and Arjuna equal in battle; Yuyudhâna, Virâṭa, and Drupada of the great car :[2] (4)

---

1 Droṇa, the son of Bhâradvâja.

2 Technically, one able to fight alone ten thousand bowmen.

अत्र here; शूराः heroes; महेष्वासाः = महान्तः इष्वासाः येषां ते, great, bows, whose (are), they (इष्वासः = यः इषुं अस्यति that which, the arrow, throws); भीमार्जुनसमाः = भीमस्य अर्जुनस्य समाः of Bhîma, of Arjuna, equal; युधि in battle; युयुधानः Yuyudhâna; विराटः Virața; च and; द्रुपदः Drupada; च and; महारथः = महान् रथो यस्य सः great, chariot, whose, he.

धृष्टकेतुश्चेकितानः काशिराजश्च वीर्यवान् ।
पुरुजित्कुंतिभोजश्च शैब्यश्च नरपुंगवः ॥ ५ ॥

Dhrishțaketu, Chekitâna, and the valiant Râjâ of Kâshî; Purujit and Kuntibhoja, and Shaibya, bull [1] among men; (5)

धृष्टकेतुः Dhrishtaketu; चेकितानः Chekitâna; काशिराजः = काश्याः राजा of Kâshî, the King; च and; वीर्यवान् valiant; पुरुजित् Purujit; कुंतिभोजः Kuntibhoja; च and; शैब्यः Shaibya; च and; नरपुंगवः = नरेषु पुंगवः among men, bull.

युधामन्युश्च विक्रांत उत्तमौजाश्च वीर्यवान् ।
सौभद्रो द्रौपदेयाश्च सर्व एव महारथाः ॥ ६ ॥

Yudhâmanyu the strong, and Uttamaujâ the brave; Saubhadra and the Draupadeyas, [2] all of great cars. (9)

युधामन्युः Yudhâmanyu; च and; विक्रांतः the strong; उत्तमौजाः Uttamaujâ; च and; वीर्यवान् valiant; सौभद्रः Saubhadra; द्रौपदेयाः

---

1 The bull, as the emblem of manly strength and vigour, is often used as an epithet of honour.

2 Abhimanyu, the son of Subhadrâ and Arjuna, and the sons of Draupadî.

Draupadeyas ; च and ; सर्व all ; एव even ; महारथाः great car-warriors.

अस्माकं तु विशिष्टा ये तान्निबोध द्विजोत्तम ।
नायका मम सैन्यस्य संज्ञार्थं तान्ब्रवीमि ते ॥७॥

Know further all those who are our chiefs, O best of the twice-born, the leaders of my army; these I name to thee for thy information : (7)

अस्माकं ours ; तु indeed ; विशिष्टाः the best ; ये who ; तान् those ; निबोध know (thou) ; द्विजोत्तम द्विजेषु उत्तम among the twice-born, O best ; नायकाः the leaders ; मम my ; सैन्यस्य of army ; संज्ञार्थं=सज्ञायाः अर्थे, of recognition, for the sake : तान् these ; ब्रवीमि (I) speak ; ते of (to) thee.

भवान्भीष्मश्च कर्णश्च कृपश्च समितिंजयः ।
अश्वत्थामा विकर्णश्च सौमदत्तिस्तथैव च ॥ ८ ॥

Thou, lord and Bhîṣhma, and Karṇa, and Kṛipa, conquering in battle ; Ashvatthâmâ, Vikarṇa, and Saumadatti[1] also ; (8)

भवान् your honour ; भीष्मः Bhîṣhma ; च and ; कर्णः Karṇa ; च and ; कृपः Kṛipa ; च and ; समितिंजयः=समितिं जयति assemblage, conquers ; अश्वत्थामा Ashvatthâmâ ; विकर्णः Vikarṇa ; च and ; सौमदत्तिः Saumadatti ; तथा thus ; एव even ; च and.

अन्ये च बहवः शूरा मदर्थे त्यक्तजीविताः ।
नानाशस्त्रप्रहरणाः सर्वे युद्धविशारदाः ॥ ९ ॥

---

1 The son of Somadatta.

And many others, heroes, for my sake renouncing their lives, with divers weapons and missiles, and all well-skilled in war. (9)

अन्ये others; च and; बहवः many; शूराः heroes; मदर्थे = मम अर्थे my, for sake; त्यक्तजीविताः = त्यक्तं जीवितं यैः ते renounced, life, by whom, they; नानाशस्त्रप्रहरणाः = नाना शस्त्राणि प्रहरणानि येषां ते various, weapons, means of striking, whose, they; सर्वे all; युद्धविशारदाः = युद्धे विशारदाः in battle, skilled.

अपर्याप्तं तदस्माकं बलं भीष्माभिरक्षितम् ।
पर्याप्तं त्विदमेतेषां बलं भीमाभिरक्षितम् ॥१०॥

Yet insufficient seems this army of ours, though marshalled by Bhîṣhma, while that army of theirs seems sufficient, though marshalled by Bhîma;[1] (10)

अपर्याप्तं insufficient; तद् that; अस्माकं our; बलं force; भीष्माभिरक्षितम् = भीष्मेण अभिरक्षितम् by Bhîṣhma, commanded (or protected); पर्याप्तं sufficient; तु indeed; इदम् this; एतेषां of theirs; भीमाभिरक्षितम् = भीमेन अभिरक्षितम् by Bhîma, commanded.

अयनेषु च सर्वेषु यथाभागमवस्थिताः ।
भीष्ममेवाभिरक्षंतु भवंतः सर्व एव हि ॥ ११ ॥

Therefore in the rank and file let all, standing firmly in their respective divisions, guard Bhîṣhma, even all ye Generals." (11)

---

1 The commentators differ in their interpretation of this verse; Ânandagiri takes it to mean just the reverse of Shridhara Svâmî "aparyâptam" being taken by the one as "insufficient," by the other as "unlimited."

अयनेषु in the lines of troops; च and; सर्वेषु (in) all; यथाभागम् according to division; अवस्थिताः standing; भीष्मम् Bhîṣhma; एव even; अभिरक्षन्तु guard; भवंतः your honours; सर्वे all; एव even; हि indeed (particle to complete metre).

तस्य संजनयन्हर्षं कुरुवृद्धः पितामहः ।
सिंहनादं विनद्योच्चैः शंखं दध्मौ प्रतापवान् ॥१२॥

To enhearten him, the Ancient of the Kurus, the Grandsire, the glorious, blew his conch, sounding on high a lion's roar. (12)

तस्य of (in) him; संजनयन् generating; हर्षं joy; कुरुवृद्धः = कुरुषु वृद्धः among the Kurus, the ancient; पितामहः the grandfather; सिंहनादं = सिंहस्य नादं of a lion, the roar; विनद्य sounding; उच्चैः on high (or loudly); शंखं a conch; दध्मौ blew; प्रतापवान् the glorious.

ततः शंखाश्च भेर्यश्च पणवानकगोमुखाः ।
सहसैवाभ्यहन्यंत स शब्दस्तुमुलोऽभवत् ॥१३॥

Then conches and kettledrums, tabors and drums and cowhorns suddenly blared forth, and the sound was tumultuous. (13)

ततः then; शंखाः conches; च and; भेर्यः kettledrums; च and; पणवानकगोमुखाः = पणवाः च आनकाः च गोमुखाः च tabors, and, drums, and, cowhorns, and; सहसा suddenly; एव also; अभ्यहन्यंत were struck; सः that; शब्दः sound; तुमुलः tumultuous; अभवत् was.

ततः श्वेतैर्हयैर्युक्ते महति स्यंदने स्थितौ ।
माधवः पांडवश्चैव दिव्यौ शंखौ प्रदध्मतुः ॥१४॥

Then, stationed in their great war-chariot, yoked to white horses, Mâdhava[1] and the son of Pâṇḍu[2] blew their divine conches, (14)

ततः then; श्वेतैः (with) white; हयैः with horses; युक्ते (in) yoked; महति (in) great; स्यंदने in war-chariot; स्थितौ (two) standing; माधवः Mâdhava; पांडवः the son of Pâṇḍu; च and; एव also; दिव्यौ (two) divine; शंखौ (two) conches; प्रदध्मतुः (two) blew.

पाचजन्यं हृषीकेशो देवदत्तं धनंजयः।
पौंड्रं दध्मौ महाशंखं भीमकर्मा वृकोदरः ॥१५॥

Pâñchajanya by Hṛishîkesha, and Devadatta by Dhanañjaya.[3] Vṛikodara,[4] of terrible deeds, blew his mighty conch, Paundra; (15)

पांचजन्यं Pânchajanya; हृषीकेशः = हृषीकाणाम् ईशः of the senses, the lord; देवदत्तं Devadatta; धनंजयः = धनं जयति इति wealth, wins, thus; पौंड्रं Paundra; दध्मौ blew; महाशंखं great conch; भीमकर्मा = भीमं कर्म यस्य सः fearful, deed, whose, he; वृकोदरः = वृकस्य इव उदरं यस्य सः a wolf's, like, stomach, whose, he.

अनंतविजयं राजा कुंतीपुत्रो युधिष्ठिरः।
नकुलः सहदेवश्च सुघोषमणिपुष्पकौ ॥ १६ ॥

---

1 Shrî Kṛishṇa. 2 Arjuna.

3 Pâñchajanya, Shrî Kṛishṇa's conch, was made from the bones of the giant Pañchajana, slain by Him; the title Hṛishikesha is given to Shrî Kṛishṇa, and Dhanañjaya to Arjuna, whose conch is the "God-given."

4 Bhîma; the meaning of the name of his conch is doubtful.

The Râjâ Yudhiṣhṭhira, the son of Kuntî, blew Anantavijaya; Nakula and Sahadeva, Sughoṣha and Maṇipuṣhpaka.[1] (16)

अनंतविजयं Anantavijaya ; राजा the King ; कुंतीपुत्रो = कुंत्याः पुत्रः of Kuntî, the son ; युधिष्ठिरः Yudhiṣhṭhira ; नकुलः Nakula ; सहदेवः Sahadeva ; च and ; सुघोषमणिपुष्पकौ = सुघोषं च मणिपुष्पकं च Sughosha, and Maṇipuṣhpaka, and.

काश्यश्च परमेष्वासः शिखंडी च महारथः ।
धृष्टद्युम्नो विराटश्च सात्यकिश्चापराजितः ॥ १७ ॥

And Kâshya,[2] of the great bow, and Shikhaṇḍî, the mighty car-warrior, Dhṛiṣhṭadyumna and Virâṭa and Sâtyaki, the unconquered. (17)

काश्यः Kâshya ; च and ; परमेष्वासः = परमः इष्वासः यस्य सः excellent, bow, whose, he ; शिखंडी Shikhaṇḍî ; च and ; महारथः great car-warrior ; धृष्टद्युम्नः Dhṛiṣhtadyumna ; विराटः Virâṭa ; च and ; सात्यकिः Sâtyaki ; च and ; अपराजितः unconquered.

द्रुपदो द्रौपदेयाश्च सर्वशः पृथिवीपते ।
सौभद्रश्च महाबाहुः शंखान्दध्मुः पृथक्पृथक् ॥ १८ ॥

Drupada and the Draupadeyas, O Lord of earth, and Saubhadra, the mighty-armed, on all sides their several conches blew. (18)

---

1 The conches of the remaining three brothers were named respectively, "endless victory," "honey-tone" and "jewel-blossom."

2 The King of Kâshî, the modern Benares.

द्रुपदः Drupada ; द्रौपदेयाः Draupadeyas ; च and ; सर्वशः from all sides ; पृथिवीपते = पृथिव्याः पते of earth, O Lord ; सौभद्रः Saubhadra ; च and ; महाबाहुः = महान्तौ बाहू यस्य सः (two) great, (two) arms, whose, he ; शंखान् conches ; दध्मुः blew ; पृथक् severally ; पृथक् severally.

स घोषो धार्तराष्ट्राणां हृदयानि व्यदारयत् ।
नभश्च पृथिवीं चैव तुमुलो व्यनुनादयन् ॥ १९ ॥

That tumultuous uproar rent the hearts of the sons of Dhṛitarâṣhṭra, filling the earth and sky with sound. (19)

सः that ; घोषः uproar ; धार्तराष्ट्राणां = धृतराष्ट्रस्य पुत्राणां of Dhṛitarâṣhṭra, of the sons ; हृदयानि the hearts ; व्यदारयत् rent ; नभः sky ; च and ; पृथिवीम् earth ; च and ; एव also ; तुमुलः tumultuous ; व्यनुनादयन् filling with sound.

अथ व्यवस्थितान्दृष्ट्वा धार्तराष्ट्रान्कपिध्वजः ।
प्रवृत्ते शस्त्रसंपाते धनुरुद्यम्य पांडवः ॥ २० ॥

Then, beholding the sons of Dhṛitarâṣhṭra standing arrayed, and the flight of missiles about to begin, he whose crest is an ape, the son of Pâṇḍu, took up his bow, (20)

अथ now ; व्यवस्थितान् standing (in order) ; दृष्ट्वा having seen ; धार्तराष्ट्रान् the sons of Dhṛitarâṣhṭra ; कपिध्वजः = कपिः ध्वजे यस्य सः an ape, in flag, whose, he ; प्रवृत्ते in (the state of) having begun ; शस्त्रसंपाते = शस्त्राणाम् संपाते of weapons, in the falling ; धनुः bow ; उद्यम्य having taken up ; पांडवः the son of Pâṇḍu.

हृषीकेशं तदा वाक्यमिदमाह महीपते ।

अर्जुन उवाच ।

सेनयोरुभयोर्मध्ये रथं स्थापय मेऽच्युत ॥ २१ ॥

And spake this word to Hṛiṣhîkesha, O Lord of earth:

Arjuna said:

" In the midst, between the two armies, stay my chariot, O Achyuta, (21)

हृषीकेशं to Hṛiṣhikesha; तदा then; वाक्यम् sentence; इदम् this; आह said; महीपते = मह्याः पते of earth, O Lord; अर्जुन Arjuna; उवाच said; सेनयोः of the (two) armies; उभयोः (of) both; मध्ये in the middle; रथं car; स्थापय stop; मे my; अच्युत O Immutable.

यावदेतान्निरीक्षेऽहं योद्धुकामानवस्थितान् ।

कैर्मया सह योद्धव्यमस्मिन्रणसमुद्यमे ॥ २२ ॥

That I may behold these standing, longing for battle, with whom I must strive in this out-breaking war; (22)

यावत् while; एतान् these; निरीक्षे see; अहं I; योद्धुकामान् = योद्धुं कामो येषां ते to fight, desire, whose, they; अवस्थितान् standing; कैः with whom; मया by me; सह together; योद्धव्यम् must be fought; अस्मिन् in this; रणसमुद्यमे = रणस्य समुद्यमे of war, in the uprising.

योत्स्यमानानवेक्षेऽहं य एतेऽत्र समागताः ।
धार्तराष्ट्रस्य दुर्बुद्धेर्युद्धे प्रियचिकीर्षवः ॥ २३ ॥

And gaze on those here gathered together, ready to fight, desirous of pleasing in battle the evil-minded son of Dhṛitarâṣhṭra. (23)

योत्स्यमानान् these going to fight; अवेक्षे see; अहं I; ये who; एते these; अत्र here; समागताः gathered together; धार्तराष्ट्रस्य of the son of Dhṛitarâṣhṭra; दुर्बुद्धेः (of the) evil-minded; युद्धे in fight; प्रियचिकीर्षवः=प्रियस्य चिकीर्षवः of the pleasure, desirous to do.

संजय उवाच ।

एवमुक्तो हृषीकेशो गुडाकेशेन भारत ।
सेनयोरुभयोर्मध्ये स्थापयित्वा रथोत्तमम् ॥ २४ ॥

Sañjaya said:

Thus addressed by Guḍâkesha,[1] Hṛiṣhîkesha, O Bhârata, having stayed that best of chariots in the midst, between the two armies, (24)

एवम् thus; उक्तः addressed; हृषीकेशः Hṛiṣhîkesha; गुडाकेशेन=गुडाकायाः ईशेन of sleep, by the lord; भारत O Bhârata; सेनयोः of the (two) armies; उभयोः (of) both; मध्ये in the middle; स्थापयित्वा having stayed; रथोत्तमम्=रथानां उत्तमम् of chariots, the best.

---

1 Arjuna.

भीष्मद्रोणप्रमुखतः सर्वेषां च महीक्षिताम् ।
उवाच पार्थ पश्यैतान्समवेतान्कुरूनिति ॥ २५॥

Over against Bhîshma, Drona and all the rulers of the world, said: "O Pârtha, behold these Kurus gathered together." (25)

भीष्मद्रोणप्रमुखतः = भीष्मस्य च द्रोणस्य च प्रमुखतः of Bhîshma, and of Drona, and, in presence; सर्वेषां of all; च and; महीक्षिताम् = मही क्षियति इति महीक्षित् तेषां the earth, sees, such, (is) the protector of the earth, of them; उवाच said; पार्थ O Pârtha; पश्य behold; एतान् these; समवेतान् gathered; कुरून् Kurus; इति thus.

तत्रापश्यत्स्थितान्पार्थः पितृनथ पितामहान् ।
आचार्यान्मातुलान्भ्रातृन्पुत्रान्पौत्रान्सखींस्तथा ॥ २६॥

Then saw Pârtha standing there uncles and grandfathers, teachers, mother's brothers, cousins, sons and grandsons, comrades, (26)

तत्र there; अपश्यत् saw; स्थितान् standing; पार्थः Pârtha; पितृन् fathers; अथ also; पितामहान् grandfathers; आचार्यान् teachers; मातुलान् maternal uncles; भ्रातृन् brothers; पुत्रान् sons; पौत्रान् grandsons, सखीन् friends; तथा too.

श्वशुरान्सुहृदश्चैव सेनयोरुभयोरपि ।
तान्समीक्ष्य स कौंतेयः सर्वान्बंधूनवस्थितान् ॥ २७॥

Fathers-in-law and friends also in both armies.

Seeing all these kinsmen, thus standing arrayed, Kaunteya,[1] (27)

श्वशुरान् fathers-in-law ; सुहृदः good-hearts; च and ; एव also ; सेनयोः in (two) armies; उभयोः (in) both ; अपि also; तान् these ; समीक्ष्य having seen ; सः he ; कौंतेयः Kaunteya; सर्वान् all ; बंधून relatives; अवस्थितान् standing.

कृपया परयाऽऽविष्टो विषीदान्निदमब्रवीत् ।
अर्जुन उवाच ।
दृष्ट्वेमं स्वजनं कृष्ण युयुत्सुं समुपास्थितम् ॥२८॥

Deeply moved to pity, this uttered in sadness :

Arjuna said:

Seeing these, my kinsmen, O Kṛishṇa, arrayed eager to fight,

कृपया by pity ; परया (by) extreme ; आविष्टः entered (filled); विषीदन् sorrowing ; इदम् this ; अब्रवीत् said ; अर्जुनः Arjuna ; उवाच said; दृष्ट्वा having seen ; इमं this; स्वजनम्=स्वस्य जनम् of one's own, people ; कृष्ण O Krishṇa ; युयुत्सुं wishing to fight ; समुपस्थितम् standing together.

सीदंति मम गात्राणि मुखं च परिशुष्याति ।
वेपथुश्च शरीरे मे रोमहर्षश्च जायते ॥ २९ ॥

My limbs fail and my mouth is parched, my body quivers, and my hair stands on end, (29)

1 The son of Kuntī, Arjuna.

सीदंति fail; मम my; गात्राणि limbs; मुखं mouth; च and; परिशुष्यति dries up: वेपथुः shivering; च and: शरीरे in body; मे my; रोमहर्षः=रोम्णाम् हर्षः of the hairs, excitement; च and; जायते arises.

गांडीवं स्रंसते हस्तात्त्वक्चैव परिदह्यते।
न च शक्नोम्यवस्थातुं भ्रमतीव च मे मनः॥३०॥

Gâṇḍiva slips from my hand, and my skin burns all over; I am not able to stand, and my mind is whirling, (30)

गांडीवं Gâṇḍiva; स्रंसते slips; हस्तात् from hand; त्वक् skin; च and; एव also; परिदह्यते burns all over: न not; च and; शक्नोमि (I) am able; अवस्थातुं to stand; भ्रमति wanders; इव like; च and; मे my; मनः mind.

निमित्तानि च पश्यामि विपरीतानि केशव।
न च श्रेयोऽनुपश्यामि हत्वा स्वजनमाहवे॥३१॥

And I see adverse omens, O Keshava.[1] Nor do I foresee any advantage from slaying kinsmen in battle. (31)

निमित्तानि causes (omens); च and; पश्यामि (I) see; विपरीतानि opposed; केशव [1] O Keshava; न not; च and; श्रेयः the better (the good); अनुपश्यामि (I) foresee; हत्वा having killed; स्वजनम् kinsfolk; आहवे in battle.

1 An epithet explained by some as meaning: "he who has fine or luxuriant hair, केश;" by others as meaning: he who sleeps, शेते, in the waters, के."

न कांक्षे विजयं कृष्ण न च राज्यं सुखानि च ।
किं नो राज्येन गोविंद किं भोगैर्जीवितेन वा ॥३२॥

For I desire not victory, O Krishṇa, nor kingdom, nor pleasures; what is kingdom to us, O Govinda, what enjoyment, or even life? (32)

न not; कांक्षे (I) desire; विजयं victory; कृष्ण O Krishṇa; न not; च and; राज्यं kingdom; सुखानि pleasures; च and; किं what; नः to us; राज्येन by (or with) kingdom; गोविंद O Govinda; किं what; भोगैः by (or with) pleasures; जीवितेन by (or with) life; वा or.

येषामर्थे कांक्षितं नो राज्यं भोगाः सुखानि च ।
त इमेऽवस्थिता युद्धे प्राणांस्त्यक्त्वा धनानि च ॥३३॥

Those for whose sake we desire kingdom, enjoyments and pleasures, they stand here in battle, abandoning life and riches—

येषाम् of whose; अर्थे sake; कांक्षितं (is) desired; नः of us; राज्यं kingdom; भोगाः enjoyments; सुखानि pleasures; च and; ते those; इमे these; अवस्थिताः are standing; युद्धे in battle; प्राणान् life-breaths; त्यक्त्वा having abandoned; धनानि riches; च and.

आचार्याः पितरः पुत्रास्तथैव च पितामहाः ।
मातुलाः श्वशुराः पौत्राः श्यालाः संबंधिनस्तथा ॥३४॥

Teachers, fathers, sons, as well as grandfathers,

mother's brothers, fathers-in-law, grandsons, brothers-in-law, and other relatives. (34)

आचार्याः teachers; पितरः fathers; पुत्राः sons; तथा thus; एव also; च and; पितामहाः grandfathers; मातुलाः maternal uncles; श्वशुराः fathers-in-law; पौत्राः grandsons; श्यालाः brothers-in-law; संबंधिनः relatives; तथा too.

एतान्न हंतुमिच्छामि घ्नतोऽपि मधुसूदन ।
अपि त्रैलोक्यराज्यस्य हेतोः किं नु महीकृते ॥३५॥

These I do not wish to kill, though myself slain, O Madhusûdana, even for the sake of the kingship of the three worlds; how then for earth? (35)

एतान् these; न not; हंतुम् to kill; इच्छामि (I) wish; घ्नतः slaying; अपि although; (i. e. although they be slaying me) मधुसूदन O Madhusûdana; अपि even; त्रैलोक्यराज्यस्य = त्रैलोक्यस्य राज्यस्य of three worlds, of kingdom; हेतोः of cause (for the sake of); किं how; नु then; महीकृते = मह्याः कृते of earth, for the sake.

निहत्य धार्तराष्ट्रान्नः का प्रीतिः स्याज्जनार्दन ।
पापमेवाश्रयेदस्मान्हत्वैतानाततायिनः ॥ ३६ ॥

Slaying these sons of Dhṛitarâṣhṭra, what pleasure can be ours, O Janârdana?[2] killing these desperadoes sin will but take hold of us. (36)

---

1 The slayer of Madhu, a demon.

2 "Destroyer of the people." Shri Kṛiṣhṇa as the warrior conquering all forms of evil.

निहत्य having slain; धार्तराष्ट्रान् sons of Dhritarâshtra; नः to us; का what; प्रीतिः pleasure; स्यात् may be; जनार्दन O Janârdana; पापम् sin; एव also; आश्रयेत् would attach; अस्मान् to us; हत्वा having killed; एतान् these; आततायिनः desperadoes.

तस्मान्नार्हा वयं हंतुं धार्तराष्ट्रान्स्वबांधवान् ।
स्वजनं हि कथं हत्वा सुखिनः स्याम माधव ॥३७॥

Therefore we should not kill the sons of Dhritarâshtra, our relatives; for how, killing our kinsmen, may we be happy, O Mâdhava? (37)

तस्मात् therefore; न (are) not; अर्हाः deserving, (ought); वयम् we; हंतुं to kill; धार्तराष्ट्रान् the sons of Dhritarâshtra; स्वबांधवान् own relatives; स्वजनं kinsfolk; हि indeed; कथं how; हत्वा having killed; सुखिनः happy; स्याम may (we) be; माधव O Mâdhava.

यद्यप्येते न पश्यंति लोभोपहतचेतसः ।
कुलक्षयकृतं दोषं मित्रद्रोहे च पातकम् ॥३८॥

Although these, with intelligence overpowered by greed, see no guilt in the destruction of a family, no crime in hostility to friends, (38)

यदि if; अपि even; एते these; न not; पश्यंति see; लोभोपहतचेतसः = लोभेन उपहतं चेतः येषां ते by greed, carried away, mind, whose, they; कुलक्षयकृत = कुलस्य क्षयेन कृतं of a family, by the destruction, made; दोषं fault (evil); मित्रद्रोहे = मित्राणाम् द्रोहे of friends, in hostility; च and; पातकम् crime.

2

कथं न ज्ञेयमस्माभिः पापादस्मान्निवर्तितुम् ।
कुलक्षयकृतं दोषं प्रपश्यद्भिर्जनार्दन ॥ ३९ ॥

Why should not we learn to turn away from such a sin, O Janârdana, who see the evils in the destruction of a family ? (39)

कथं how ; न not ; ज्ञेयम् to be known ; अस्माभिः by us ; पापात् from sin ; अस्मात् (from) this ; निवर्तितुम् to turn away ; कुलक्षयकृतं =(as shl. 28) caused by the destruction of a family ; दोषं evil ; प्रपश्यद्भिः by the seeing (by us who see) ; जनार्दन O Janârdana.

कुलक्षये प्रणश्यन्ति कुलधर्माः सनातनाः ।
धर्मे नष्टे कुलं कृत्स्नमधर्मोऽभिभवत्युत ॥ ४० ॥

In the destruction of a family the immemorial family traditions[1] perish ; in the perishing of traditions lawlessness overcomes the whole family ; (40)

कुलक्षये = कुलस्य क्षये of a family, in the destruction ; प्रणश्यन्ति perish ; कुलधर्माः = कुलस्य धर्माः of the family, the duties ; सनातनाः immemorial ; धर्मे in the (state of) duty ; नष्टे being destroyed ; कुलं the family ; कृत्स्नम् the whole ; अधर्मः lawlessness ; अभिभवति overcomes ; उत indeed.

---

1 Dharma ; this is a wide word primarily meaning the essential nature of a thing ; hence, the laws of its being, its duty ; and it includes religious rites—appropriate to those laws—customs, also righteousness.

अधर्माभिभवात्कृष्ण प्रदुष्यंति कुलस्त्रियः ।
स्त्रीषु दुष्टासु वार्ष्णेय जायते वर्णसंकरः ॥ ४१ ॥

Owing to predominance of lawlessness, O Kṛiṣhṇa, the women of the family become corrupt; women corrupted, O Vârṣhṇeya, there ariseth caste-confusion; (41)

अधर्माभिभवात् = अधर्मस्य अभिभवात् of lawlessness, from prevalence ; कृष्ण O Kriṣhṇa ; प्रदुष्यंति become wicked ; कुलस्त्रियः = कुलस्य स्त्रियः of the family, women ; स्त्रीषु in (the state of) women ; दुष्टासु (being) wicked ; वार्ष्णेय O Varṣhṇeya; जायते arises ; वर्णसंकरः = वर्णस्य संकरः of caste, confusion.

संकरो नरकायैव कुलघ्नानां कुलस्य च ।
पतंति पितरो ह्येषां लुप्तपिंडोदकक्रियाः ॥ ४२ ॥

This confusion draggeth to hell the slayers of the family and the family ; for their ancestors fall, deprived of rice-balls and libations. (42)

संकरः confusion; नरकाय (is) for hell; एव also; कुलघ्नानाम् of the slayers of the family, कुलस्य of the family; च and; पतंति fall; पितरः the ancestors; हि verily; एषां of these ; लुप्तपिंडोदकक्रियाः = लुप्ता पिंडस्य च उदकस्य च क्रिया येषां ते lost, of rice-balls, and of water, and, the rite, of whom, they.

दोषैरेतैः कुलघ्नानां वर्णसंकरकारकैः ।
उत्साद्यंते जातिधर्माः कुलधर्माश्च शाश्वताः ॥ ४३ ॥

By these caste-confusing misdeeds of the slayers of the family, the everlasting caste customs and family customs are abolished. (43)

दोषैः by sins; एतैः (by) these; कुलघ्नानां of the family-slayers; वर्णसंकरकारकैः = वर्णस्य संकरस्य कारकैः of caste, of the confusion, by the doers; उत्साद्यन्ते are destroyed; जातिधर्माः = जातेः धर्माः of the caste, customs; कुलधर्माः = कुलस्य धर्माः of the family, customs; च and; शाश्वताः everlasting.

उत्सन्नकुलधर्माणां मनुष्याणां जनार्दन ।
नरके नियतं वासो भवतीत्यनुशुश्रुम ॥ ४४ ॥

The abode of the men whose family customs are extinguished, O Janârdana, is everlastingly in hell. Thus have we heard. (44)

उत्सन्नकुलधर्माणां = उत्सन्नः कुलस्य धर्मः येषां ते destroyed, of the family, customs, of whom, they; मनुष्याणां of men; जनार्दन O Janârdana; नरके in hell; नियतं fixed; वासः dwelling: भवति is; इति thus; अनुशुश्रुम we have heard.

अहो बत महत्पापं कर्तुं व्यवसिता वयम् ।
यद्राज्यसुखलोभेन हंतुं स्वजनमुद्यताः ॥ ४५ ॥

Alas! in committing a great sin are we engaged, we who are endeavouring to kill our kindred from greed of the pleasures of kingship. (45)

अहो alas; बत alas; महत् great; पापं sin; कर्तुं to do; व्यवसिताः prepared; वयम् we; राज्यस्य सुखस्य लोभेन of kingdom.

of pleasure, by greed; हंतुं to kill; स्वजनम् (our) own relatives; उद्यताः uprisen.

यदि मामप्रतीकारमशस्त्रं शस्त्रपाणयः ।
धार्तराष्ट्रा रणे हन्युस्तन्मे क्षेमतरं भवेत् ॥ ४६ ॥

If the sons of Dhṛitarâṣhṭra, weapon-in-hand, should slay me, unresisting, unarmed, in the battle, that would for me be the better. (46)

यदि if; मां me; अप्रतीकारं without retaliation (unresisting); अशस्त्रं weaponless; शस्त्रपाणयः=शस्त्राणि पाणिषु येषां ते weapons, in hands, whose, they; धार्तराष्ट्राः the sons of Dhṛitarâṣhṭra; रणे in the battle; हन्युः may slay; तत् that; मे of me; क्षेमतरं better; भवेत् would be.

संजय उवाच ।

एवमुक्त्वाऽर्जुनः संख्ये रथोपस्थ उपाविशत् ।
विसृज्य सशरं चापं शोकसंविग्नमानसः ॥ ४७ ॥

Sañjaya said:

Having thus spoken on the battle-field, Arjuna sank down on the seat of the chariot, casting away his bow and arrow, his mind overborne by grief. (47)

संजयः Sañjaya; उवाच said; एवम् thus; उक्त्वा having said, अर्जुनः Arjuna; संख्ये in the battle; रथोपस्थे=रथस्य उपस्थे of the chariot, in the seat; उपाविशत् sank down; विसृज्य having cast away; सशरं=शरेण सह with the arrow, together;

चापं bow; शोकसंविग्नमानसः=शोकेन संविग्नं मानसं यस्य सः by sorrow, agitated, mind, whose, he;

इति श्रीमद्भगवद्गीतासूपनिषत्सु ब्रह्मविद्यायां योगशास्त्रे श्रीकृष्णार्जुन—
संवादेऽर्जुनविषादयोगो नाम प्रथमोऽध्यायः।

Thus in the Upanishats of the glorious Bhagavad-Gîtâ, the science of the ETERNAL, the scripture of Yoga, the dialogue between Shri Krishna and Arjuna, the first discourse, entitled:

THE YOGA OF THE DESPONDENCY OF ARJUNA.

इति thus; श्रीमद्भगवद्गीतासु in the blessed Bhagavad-Gîtâs; उपनिषत्सु in the Upanishats; ब्रह्मविद्यायां=ब्रह्मणः विद्यायां of the ETERNAL, in the science; योगशास्त्रे=योगस्य शास्त्रे of Yoga, in the scripture; श्रीकृष्णार्जुनसंवादे=श्रीकृष्णस्य च अर्जुनस्य च संवादे, of Shrî Krishna, and, of Arjuna, and, in the dialogue; अर्जुनविषादयोगः=अर्जुनस्य विषादस्य योगः of Arjuna, of despondency, the Yoga; नाम name; प्रथमः first; अध्यायः discourse.

SECOND DISCOURSE.

संजय उवाच ।

तं तथा कृपयाविष्टमश्रुपूर्णाकुलेक्षणम् ।

विषीदंतमिदं वाक्यमुवाच मधुसूदनः ॥ १ ॥

Sanjaya said:

To him thus with pity overcome, with smarting brimming eyes, despondent, Madhusûdana spake these words: (1)

तं to him; तथा thus; कृपया with pity; आविष्टम् penetrated; अश्रुपूर्णाकुलेक्षणम्=अश्रुभिः पूर्णे च आकुले च ईक्षणे यस्य तं: with tears, filled, and, restless (smarting), and, (two) eyes, whose, him; विषीदंतं (to the) despondent; इदं this; वाक्यम् speech; उवाच spake; मधुसूदनः Madhusûdana.

श्रीभगवानुवाच ।

कुतस्त्वा कश्मलमिदं विषमे समुपस्थितम् ।

अनार्यजुष्टमस्वर्ग्यमकीर्तिकरमर्जुन ॥ २ ॥

The Blessed Lord said:

Whence hath this dejection befallen thee in this perilous strait, ignoble, heaven-closing, infamous, O Arjuna? (2)

कुतः whence; त्वा thee; कश्मलम् dejection; इदं this; विषमे in difficulty; समुपस्थितम happened; अनार्यजुष्टम=अना-

यैः जुष्टम् by non-Âryans, rejoiced in (practised); अस्वर्ग्यम् unheavenly (not leading to Svarga) ; अकीर्तिकरम् un-fame-making अर्जुन O Arjuna.

क्लैब्यं मास्म गमः पार्थ नैतत्त्वय्युपपद्यते ।
क्षुद्रं हृदयदौर्बल्यं त्यक्त्वोत्तिष्ठ परंतप ॥ ३ ॥

Yield not to impotence, O Pârtha! it doth not befit thee. Shake off this paltry faint-heartedness! Stand up, Parantapa! (3)

क्लैब्यं to weakness; मा not; स्म (pleonastic particle,; गमः go; पार्थ O Pârtha: न not; एतत् this; त्वयि in thee: उपपद्यते is fitting; क्षुद्रं mean: हृदयदौर्बल्यं = हृदयस्य दौर्बल्यं of the heart, weakness; त्यक्त्वा having abandoned; उत्तिष्ठ stand up; परंतप = परान् तपति others (foes) consumes (he who).

अर्जुन उवाच ।

कथं भीष्ममहं संख्ये द्रोणं च मधुसूदन ।
इषुभिः प्रतियोत्स्यामि पूजार्हावरिसूदन ॥ ४ ॥

Arjuna said:

How, O Madhusûdana, shall I attack Bhîṣhma and Droṇa with arrows in battle? they who are worthy of reverence, O slayer of foes. (4)

कथं how; भीष्मम Bhîṣhma; अहं I; संख्ये in battle; द्रोणं Droṇa; च and; मधुसूदन O Madhusûdana; इषुभिः with arrows; प्रतियोत्स्यामि shall I attack; पूजार्हौ = पूजाया: अर्हौ

of worship, the deserving (two) : अरिसूदन=अरीणाम् सूदन of enemies, O slayer.

गुरूनहत्वा हि महानुभावान्
श्रेयो भोक्तुं भैक्ष्यमपीह लोके ।
हत्वार्थकामांस्तु गुरूनिहैव
भुंजीय भोगान्रुधिरप्रदिग्धान् ॥ ५ ॥

Better in this world to eat even the beggars' crust, than to slay these most noble Gurus. Slaying these Gurus, our well-wishers,[1] I should taste of blood-besprinkled feasts. (5)

गुरून् the Gurus ; अहत्वा not having slain ; हि indeed ; महानुभावान्=महान् अनुभावो येषां तान् great, splendour, whose, them ; श्रेयः better ; भोक्तुं to eat ; भैक्ष्यम alms ; अपि even ; इह here ; लोके in world ; हत्वा having slain ; अर्थकामान्=अर्थं कामयंति इति तान् wealth (or good), (they) desire, thus, them ; तु indeed ; गुरून् Gurus ; इह here ; एव also ; भुंजीय I should eat ; भोगान् foods ; रुधिरप्रदिग्धान=रुधिरेण प्रदिग्धान् with blood, stained.

---

[1] अर्थकामान्=अर्थं (धनं) कामयन्ते=अर्थकामाः तान् they who covet wealth; or अर्थं (मन अर्थं=हितं) कामयन्ते they who desire (my) artha *i.e.* good or welfare; another reading is अर्थकामात्=(अर्थस्य कामः तस्मात्) from greed of wealth.

More often translated, "greedy of wealth," but the word is used elsewhere for well-wisher, and this term is more in accordance with the tone of Arjuna's remarks.

न चैतद्विद्मः कतरन्नो गरीयो
यद्वा जयेम यदि वा नो जयेयुः ।
यानेव हत्वा न जिजीविषाम:
तेऽवस्थिताः प्रमुखे धार्तराष्ट्राः ॥ ६ ॥

Nor know I which for us be the better, that we conquer them or they conquer us—these, whom having slain we should not care to live, even these arrayed against us, the sons of Dhṛitarâṣhṭra. (6)

न not; च and; एतत् this; विद्मः (we) know; कतरत् which; नः for us; गरीयः more important; यत् that; वा or; जयेम (we) should conquer; यदि if; वा or; नः us; जयेयुः (they) should conquer; यान् whom; एव even; हत्वा having slain; न not; जिजीविषामः (we) wish to live; ते those; अवस्थिताः (are) standing; प्रमुखे in face; धार्तराष्ट्राः sons of Dhṛitarâṣhṭra.

कार्पण्यदोषोपहतस्वभावः
पृच्छामि त्वां धर्मसंमूढचेताः ।
यच्छ्रेयः स्यान्निश्चितं ब्रूहि तन्मे
शिष्यस्तेऽहं शाधि मां त्वां प्रपन्नम् ॥ ७ ॥

My heart is weighed down with the vice of faintness; my mind is confused as to duty. I ask thee which may be the better—that tell me decisively. I am thy disciple, suppliant to Thee ; teach me. (7)

कार्पण्यदोषोपहतस्वभावः = कार्पण्यस्य दोषेण उपहतः स्वभावः यस्य सः of commiseration, by the fault, attacked, nature, whose, he ; पृच्छामि (I) ask ; त्वां thee ; धर्मसंमूढचेताः = धर्मे संमूढं चेतः यस्य सः in (as to) duty, confused, whose, he ; यत् which ; श्रेयः better ; स्यात् may be ; निश्चितं decisively ; ब्रूहि speak ; तत् that ; मे of (to) me ; शिष्यः disciple ; ते of thee ; अहं I ; शाधि teach ; माम् me ; त्वां to thee ; प्रपन्नम् suppliant.

नहि प्रपश्यामि ममापनुद्याद्

यच्छोकमुच्छोषणमिंद्रियाणाम् ।

अवाप्य भूमावसपत्नमृद्धं

राज्यं सुराणामपि चाधिपत्यम् ॥ ८ ॥

For I see not that it would drive away this anguish that withers up my senses, if I should attain unrivalled monarchy on earth, or even the sovereignty of the Shining Ones. (8)

नहि not; प्रपश्यामि (I) see ; मम my ; अपनुद्यात् may drive away ; यत् that ; शोकम् grief ; उच्छोषणम् drier-up ; इंद्रियाणाम् of my senses ; अवाप्य having obtained ; भूमौ in the earth ; असपत्नम् unrivalled ; राज्यं kingdom ; सुराणाम् of the Suras ; अपि even ; च and ; आधिपत्यम् lordship.

संजय उवाच ।

एवमुक्त्वा हृषीकेशं गुडाकेशः परंतप ।

न योत्स्य इति गोविंदमुक्त्वा तूष्णीं बभूव ह ॥९॥

Sanjaya said:

Guḍâkesha, conqueror of his foes, having thus addressed Hṛishîkesha, and said to Govinda, "I will not fight!" became silent. (9)

एवं thus; उक्त्वा having spoken; हृषीकेशं to Hṛishikesha; गुडाकेश: Guḍâkesha; परंतप: destroyer of foes; न not; योत्स्ये (I) will fight; इति thus; गोविंदम् to Govinda; उक्त्वा having said; तूष्णीं silent; बभूव became; ह (particle).

तमुवाच हृषीकेशः प्रहसन्निव भारत ।
सेनयोरुभयोर्मध्ये विषीदंतमिदं वचः ॥ १० ॥

Then Hṛishîkesha, smiling, as it were O Bhârata, spake these words, in the midst of the two armies, to him, despondent. (10)

तम् to him; उवाच said; हृषीकेश: Hṛishikesha; प्रहसन् smiling; इव as it were; भारत O Bhârata; सेनयो: of the (two) armies; उभयो: (of) both; मध्ये in the middle; विषीदंतम despondent; इदं this; वच: word.

श्रीभगवानुवाच ।

अशोच्यानन्वशोचस्त्वं प्रज्ञावादांश्च भाषसे ।
गतासूनगतासूंश्च नानुशोचंति पंडिताः ॥११॥

The Blessed Lord said:

Thou grievest for those that should not be grieved for, yet speakest words of wisdom.[1] The wise grieve neither for the living nor for the dead. (11)

अशोच्यान् unbewailable; अन्वशोचः hast bewailed; त्वं thou; प्रज्ञावादान्=प्रज्ञायाः वादान् of wisdom, words; च and; भाषसे speakest; गतासून्=गताः असवः येषां तान् gone, life-breaths, whose, those; अगतासून् not, gone, life-breaths, whose, those; च and; न not; अनुशोचंति grieve; पंडिताः the wise.

न त्वेवाहं जातु नासं न त्वं नेमे जनाधिपाः ।
न चैव न भविष्यामः सर्वे वयमतः परम् ॥ १२ ॥

Nor at any time verily was I not, nor thou, nor these princes of men, nor verily shall we ever cease to be, hereafter. (12)

न not; तु indeed; एव also; अहं I; जातु at any time; न not; आसम् was; न not; त्वम् thou; न not; इमे these; जनाधिपाः=जनानां अधिपाः of the people, lords; न not; च and; एव also; न not; भविष्यामः shall be; सर्वे all; वयम् we; अतः from this (time); परम् after.

देहिनोऽस्मिन्यथा देहे कौमारं यौवनं जरा ।
तथा देहांतरप्राप्तिर्धीरस्तत्र न मुह्यति ॥ १३ ॥

As the dweller in the body experienceth, in the body, childhood, youth and old age, so passeth he on to

1 Words that sound wise but miss the deeper sense of wisdom.

another body; the steadfast one grieveth not thereat. (13)

देहिनः of the embodied; अस्मिन् in this; यथा as; देहे in body; कौमारं childhood; यौवनं youth; जरा old age; तथा so; देहान्तरप्राप्तिः=देहान्तरस्य प्राप्तिः of another body, the obtaining; धीरः the firm; तत्र there; न not; मुह्यति grieves.

मात्रास्पर्शास्तु कौंतेय शीतोष्णसुखदुःखदाः ।
आगमापायिनोऽनित्यास्तांस्तितिक्षस्व भारत ॥१४॥

The contacts of matter, O son of Kuntî, giving cold and heat, pleasure and pain, they come and go, impermanent; endure them bravely, O Bhârata. (14)

मात्रास्पर्शाः=मात्रायाः स्पर्शाः of the matter, the touches; तु indeed; कौंतेय O Kaunteya; शीतोष्णसुखदुःखदाः=शीतं च उष्णं च सुखं च दुःखं च ददति इति cold, and, heat, and, pleasure, and, pain, and, give; thus आगमापायिनः=आगमः च अपायः च येषां ते, coming, and, going, and, whose, they; अनित्याः transitory; तान् these; तितिक्षस्व bear (thou); भारत O Bhârata.

यं हि न व्यथयंत्येते पुरुषं पुरुषर्षभ ।
समदुःखसुखं धीरं सोऽमृतत्वाय कल्पते ॥१५॥

The man whom these torment not, O chief of men, balanced in pain and pleasure, steadfast, he is fitted for immortality. (15)

यं whom; हि indeed; न not; व्यथयन्ति torment; एते these; पुरुषं man; पुरुषर्षभ=पुरुषाणां ऋषभ of men, O best;

समदुःखसुखं = समं दुःखं च सुखं च यस्य सः equal, pain and pleasure, and whose (to whom), him ; धीरं firm : सः he ; अमृतत्वाय for immortality ; कल्पते becomes fit.

नासतो विद्यते भावो नाभावो विद्यते सतः ।
उभयोरपि दृष्टोऽन्तस्त्वनयोस्तत्त्वदर्शिभिः ॥१६॥

The unreal hath no being ; the real never ceaseth to be ; the truth about both hath been perceived by the seers of the Essence of things. (16)

न not ; असतः of the non-existent ; विद्यते is ; भावः being ; न not ; अभावः non-being ; विद्यते is ; सतः of the existent ; उभयोः of the two ; अपि also ; दृष्टः (has been) seen ; अंतः the end (the final truth) ; तु indeed ; अनयोः of these ; तत्त्वदर्शिभिः by the truth-seeing.

अविनाशि तु तद्विद्धि येन सर्वमिदं ततम् ।
विनाशमव्ययस्यास्य न कश्चित्कर्तुमर्हति ॥१७॥

Know THAT to be indestructible by whom all this is pervaded. Nor can any work the destruction of that imperishable One. (I)

अविनाशि indestructible ; तु indeed ; तद् That ; विद्धि know (thou) ; येन by whom ; सर्वं all ; इदं this ; ततं (has been) spread ; विनाशम् the destruction ; अव्ययस्य of the imperishable ; अस्य of this ; न not ; कश्चित् anyone ; कर्तुम् to do ; अर्हति is able.

अंतवंत इमे देहा नित्यस्योक्ताः शरीरिणः ।

अनाशिनोऽप्रमेयस्य तस्माद्युध्यस्व भारत ॥१८॥

These bodies of the embodied One, who is eternal, indestructible and boundless, are known as finite. Therefore fight, O Bhârata. (18)

अंतवंत: having end; इमे these; देहाः bodies; नित्यस्य of the everlasting; उक्ताः (are) said; शरीरिणः of the embodied; अनाशिनः of the indestructible; अप्रमेयस्य of the immeasurable; तस्मात् therefore; युध्यस्व fight (thou); भारत O Bhârata.

य एनं वेत्ति हंतारं यश्चैनं मन्यते हतम् ।
उभौ तौ न विजानीतो नायं हंति न हन्यते ॥१९॥

He who regardeth this as a slayer, and he who thinketh he is slain, both of them are ignorant. He slayeth not, nor is he slain. (19)

यः he who; एनं this; वेत्ति knows; हंतारं slayer; यः he who; च and; एनं this; मन्यते thinks; हतम् slain; उभौ the two; तौ those; न not; विजानीतः (two) know; न not; अयं this; हंति kills; न not; हन्यते is killed.

न जायते म्रियते वा कदाचि-
न्नायं भूत्वा भविता वा न भूयः ।
अजो नित्यः शाश्वतोऽयं पुराणो
न हन्यते हन्यमाने शरीरे ॥२०॥

He is not born, nor doth he die: nor having been, ceaseth he any more to be; unborn, perpetual, eternal and ancient, he is not slain when the body is slaughtered. (20)

न not; जायते is born; म्रियते dies; वा or; कदाचित् at any time; न not; अयं this; भूत्वा having been; भविता will be; वा or; न not; भूयः (any) more; अजः unborn; नित्यः perpetual; शाश्वतः eternal; अयं this; पुराणः ancient; न not; हन्यते is killed; हन्यमाने (in) being killed; शरीरे in body.

वेदाऽविनाशिनं नित्यं य एनमजमव्ययम् ।
कथं स पुरुषः पार्थ कं घातयति हंति कम् ॥२१॥

Who knoweth him indestructible, perpetual, unborn, undiminishing, how can that man slay, O Pârtha, or cause to be slain? (21)

वेद knows; अविनाशिनं indestructible; नित्यं perpetual; यः who; एनं this; अजं unborn; अव्ययम् undiminishing; कथं how; सः he (that); पुरुषः man; पार्थ O Pârtha; कं whom; घातयति causes to be slain; हंति kills; कम् whom.

वासांसि जीर्णानि यथा विहाय
नवानि गृह्णाति नरोऽपराणि ।
तथा शरीराणि विहाय जीर्णा-
न्यन्यानि संयाति नवानि देही ॥ २२ ॥

As a man, casting off worn-out garments, taketh new

ones, so the dweller in the body, casting off worn-out bodies, entereth into others that are new. (22)

वासांसि garments; जीर्णानि worn-out; यथा as; विहाय having cast away; नवानि new; गृह्णाति takes; नरः a man; अपराणि others; तथा so; शरीराणि bodies; विहाय having cast away; जीर्णानि worn-out; अन्यानि to others; संयाति goes; नवानि (to) new; देही the embodied (one).

नैनं छिंदंति शस्त्राणि नैनं दहति पावकः ।
न चैनं क्लेदयंत्यापो न शोषयति मारुतः ॥२३॥

Weapons cleave him not, nor fire burneth him, nor waters wet him, nor wind drieth him away. (23)

न not; एनं this; छिंदंति cleave; शस्त्राणि weapons; न not; एनं this; दहति burns; पावकः fire; न not; च and; एनं this; क्लेदयंति wet; आपः waters; न not; शोषयति dries; मारुतः wind.

अच्छेद्योऽयमदाह्योऽयमक्लेद्योऽशोष्य एव च ।
नित्यः सर्वगतः स्थाणुरचलोऽयं सनातनः ॥२४॥

Uncleavable he, incombustible he, and indeed neither to be wetted nor dried away; perpetual, all-pervasive, stable, immovable, ancient, (24)

अच्छेद्यः uncleavable; अयं this; अदाह्यः incombustible; अयं this; अक्लेद्यः unwettable; अशोष्यः undryable; एव also; च and; नित्यः perpetual; सर्वगतः = सर्वस्मिन् गतः into all, gone; स्थाणुः stable; अचलः immovable; अयं this; सनातनः ancient.

अव्यक्तोऽयमचिंत्योऽयमविकार्योऽयमुच्यते ।
तस्मादेवं विदित्वैनं नानुशोचितुमर्हसि ॥ २५ ॥

Unmanifest, unthinkable, immutable, he is called; therefore knowing him as such, thou shouldst not grieve.

(25)

अव्यक्तः unmanifest ; अयं this ; अचिंत्यः inconceivable ; अयं this ; अविकार्यः immutable ; अयं this ; उच्यते is called ; तस्मात् therefore ; एवं thus ; विदित्वा having known ; एनं this ; न not ; अनुशोचितुम् to grieve ;अर्हसि (thou) oughtest.

अथ चैनं नित्यजातं नित्यं वा मन्यसे मृतम् ।
तथापि त्वं महाबाहो नैनं शोचितुमर्हसि ॥ २६ ॥

Or if thou thinkest of him as being constantly born and constantly dying, even then, O mighty-armed, thou shouldst not grieve. (26)

अथ now ; च and ; एनं this ; नित्यजातं = नित्यं जातं constantly, born; नित्यं perpetually; वा or; मन्यसे (thou) thinkest; मृतम् dead ; तथा so ; अपि also ; त्वं thou ; महाबाहो = महान्तौ बाहू यस्य (त्वं) great (two) arms, whose, (O thou) ; न not; एनं this; शोचितुम् to grieve ; अर्हसि (thou) oughtest.

जातस्य हि ध्रुवो मृत्युर्ध्रुवं जन्म मृतस्य च ।
तस्मादपरिहार्येऽर्थे न त्वं शोचितुमर्हसि ॥ २७ ॥

For certain is death for the born, and certain is birth for the dead; therefore over the inevitable thou shouldst not grieve. (27)

जातस्य of the born; हि indeed; ध्रुवः certain; मृत्युः death; ध्रुवं certain; जन्म birth; मृतस्य of the dead; च and; तस्मात् therefore; अपरिहार्ये (in) inevitable; अर्थे in matter; न not; त्वं thou; शोचितुम् to grieve; अर्हसि (thou) oughtest.

अव्यक्तादीनि भतानि व्यक्तमध्यानि भारत ।
अव्यक्तनिधनान्येव तत्र का परिदेवना ॥ २८ ॥

Beings are unmanifest in their origin, manifest in their midmost state, O Bhârata, unmanifest likewise are they in dissolution. What room then for lamentation? (28)

अव्यक्तादीनि = अव्यक्तं आदिः येषां ते unmanifest, beginning, whose, they; भूतानि beings; व्यक्तमध्यानि = व्यक्तं मध्यं येषां तानि manifest, middle, whose, they; भारत O Bhârata; अव्यक्तनिधनानि = अव्यक्तं निधनं येषां तानि unmanifest, destruction, whose, they; एव also: तत्र there; का what; परिदेवना lamentation.

आश्चर्यवत्पश्यति कश्चिदेन-
माश्चर्यवद्वदति तथैव चान्यः ।
आश्चर्यवच्चैनमन्यः शृणोति
श्रुत्वाऽप्येनं वेद न चैव कश्चित् ॥ २९ ॥

As marvellous one regardeth him; as marvellous another speaketh thereof; as marvellous another heareth thereof; yet having heard, none indeed understandeth. (29)

आश्चर्यवत् as wonderful; पश्यति sees; कश्चित् some one; एनं this; आश्चर्यवत् as wonderful; वदति speaks; तथा so; एव also; च and; अन्यः another; आश्चर्यवत् as wonderful; च and; एनं this; अन्यः another; शृणोति hears; श्रुत्वा having heard; अपि even; एनं this; वेद knows; न not; च and; एव also; कश्चित् anyone.

देही नित्यमवध्योऽयं देहे सर्वस्य भारत ।
तस्मात्सर्वाणि भूतानि न त्वं शोचितुमर्हसि ॥३०॥

This dweller in the body of everyone is ever invulnerable, O Bhârata; therefore thou shouldst not grieve for any creature. (30)

देही the embodied; नित्यं always; अवध्यः invulnerable; अयं this; देहे in the body; सर्वस्य of all; भारत O Bhârata; तस्मात् therefore; सर्वाणि (for) all; भूतानि creatures; न not; त्वं thou; शोचितुम् to grieve; अर्हसि (thou) shouldst.

स्वधर्ममपि चावेक्ष्य न विकंपितुमर्हसि ।
धर्म्याद्धि युद्धाच्छ्रेयोऽन्यत्क्षत्रियस्य न विद्यते ॥३१॥

Further, looking to thine own duty, thou shouldst not tremble; for there is nothing more welcome to a Kṣhattriya than righteous war. (31)

स्वधर्मम् = स्वस्य धर्मं of own, duty; अपि also; च and; अवेक्ष्य having seen; न not; विकंपितुम् to tremble; अर्हसि (thou) oughtest; धर्म्यात् (than) righteous; हि indeed; युद्धात् than war; श्रेयः better; अन्यत् other; क्षत्रियस्य of the Kshattriya; न not; विद्यते is.

यदृच्छया चोपपन्नं स्वर्गद्वारमपावृतम् ।
सुखिनः क्षत्रियाः पार्थ लभन्ते युद्धमीदृशम् ॥ ३२ ॥

Happy the Kshattriyas, O Pârtha, who obtain such a fight, offered unsought as an open door to heaven. (32)

यदृच्छया by chance; च and; उपपन्नं happened; स्वर्गद्वारम् = स्वर्गस्य द्वारं of heaven, door; अपावृतं opened; सुखिनः happy; क्षत्रियाः kshattriyas; पार्थ O Pârtha; लभन्ते obtain; युद्धम् battle; ईदृशम् like this.

अथ चेत्त्वमिमं धर्म्यं संग्रामं न करिष्यसि ।
ततः स्वधर्मं कीर्तिं च हित्वा पापमवाप्स्यसि ॥ ३३ ॥

But if thou wilt not carry on this righteous warfare, then, casting away thine own duty and thine honour, thou wilt incur sin. (33)

अथ now; चेत् if; त्वम् thou; इमम् this; धर्म्यं righteous; संग्रामं battle; न not; करिष्यसि (thou) wilt do; ततः then; स्वधर्मं own duty; कीर्तिम् fame; च and; हित्वा having thrown away; पापं sin; अवाप्स्यसि (thou) wilt obtain.

अकीर्तिं चापि भूतानि कथयिष्यंति तेऽव्ययाम्।
संभावितस्य चाकीर्तिर्मरणादतिरिच्यते ॥ ३४ ॥

Men will recount thy perpetual dishonor, and, to one highly esteemed, dishonor exceedeth death. (34)

अकीर्तिं dishonor; च and; अपि also; भूतानि creatures; कथयिष्यंति will relate; ते thy; अव्ययाम् undiminishing; संभावितस्य of the honored; च and; अकीर्तिः dishonor; मरणात् than death; अतिरिच्यते exceeds.

भयाद्रणादुपरतं मंस्यंते त्वां महारथाः।
येषां च त्व बहुमतो भूत्वा यास्यासि लाघवम्॥३५॥

The great car-warriors will think thee fled from the battle from fear, and thou that wast highly thought of by them, wilt be lightly held. (35)

भयात् from fear; रणात् from the battle; उपरतं withdrawn; मंस्यंते will think; त्वां thee; महारथाः the great car-warriors; येषां of whom; च and; त्वं thou; बहु much; मतः thought (of); भूत्वा having been; यास्यंसि wilt go; लाघवम् to lightness.

अवाच्यवादांश्च बहून्वदिष्यंति तवाहिताः।
निंदंतस्तव सामर्थ्यं ततो दुःखतरं नु किम् ॥३६॥

Many unseemly words will be spoken by thine enemies, slandering thy strength; what more painful than that? (36)

अवाच्यवादान् = अवाच्यान् वादान् improper to be spoken, words; च and; बहून् many; वदिष्यंति will say; तव thy; अहिता: non-friends; निंदंत: slandering; तव thy; सामर्थ्यं power; तत: than that; दु:खतरं more painful; नु indeed; किम् what.

हतो वा प्राप्स्यसि स्वर्गं जित्वा वा भोक्ष्यसे महीम् ।
तस्मादुत्तिष्ठ कौंतेय युद्धाय कृतनिश्चयः ॥ ३७ ॥

Slain, thou wilt obtain heaven; victorious, thou wilt enjoy the earth; therefore stand up, O son of Kuntî, resolute to fight. (37)

हत: slain; वा or; प्राप्स्यसि (thou) wilt obtain; स्वर्गं heaven; जित्वा having conquered; वा or; भोक्ष्यसे (thou) wilt enjoy; महीम the earth; तस्मात् therefore; उत्तिष्ठ stand up; कौंतेय O Kaunteya; युद्धाय for battle; कृतनिश्चय: = कृत: निश्चय: येन स: made, decision, by whom, he.

सुखदुःखे समे कृत्वा लाभालाभौ जयाजयौ ।
ततो युद्धाय युज्यस्व नैवं पापमवाप्स्यासि ॥ ३८ ॥

Taking as equal pleasure and pain, gain and loss, victory and defeat, gird thee for the battle; thus thou shalt not incur sin. (38)

सुखदु:खे = सुखं च दु:खं च pleasure, and, pain, and; समे equal; कृत्वा having made; लाभालाभौ = लाभ: च अलाभ: च gain, and, loss, and; जयाजयौ = जय: च अजय: च, victory, and, defeat, and; तत: then; युद्धाय for the battle; युज्यस्व join (thou); न not; एवं thus; पापं sin; अवाप्स्यासि (thou) shalt obtain.

एषा तेऽभिहिता सांख्ये बुद्धियोंगे त्विमां शृणु ।
बुद्ध्या युक्तो यया पार्थ कर्मबंधं प्रहास्यसि ॥३९॥

This teaching set forth to thee is in accordance with the Sâṅkhya; hear it now according to the Yoga, imbued with which teaching, O Pârtha, thou shalt cast away the bonds of action. (39)

एषा this; ते of (to) thee; अभिहिता (is) declared; सांख्ये in Sâṅkhya; बुद्धिः knowledge; योगे in the Yoga; तु indeed; इमां this; शृणु hear; बुद्ध्या with knowledge; युक्तः joined; यया with which; पार्थ O Pârtha; कर्मबंधं = कर्मणः बंधं of karma, the bond; प्रहास्यसि (thou) shalt cast away.

नेहाभिक्रमनाशोऽस्ति प्रत्यवायो न विद्यते ।
स्वल्पमप्यस्य धर्मस्य त्रायते महतो भयात् ॥४०॥

In this there is no loss of effort, nor is there transgression. Even a little of this knowledge [1] protects from great fear. (40)

न not; इह here; अभिक्रमनाशः = अभिक्रमस्य नाशः of effort, destruction; अस्ति is; प्रत्यवाय: transgression; न not; विद्यते is; स्वल्पम् very little; अपि even; अस्य of this; धर्मस्य duty; त्रायते protects; महतः (from) great; भयात् from fear.

व्यवसायात्मिका बुद्धिरेकेह कुरुनंदन ।
बहुशाखा ह्यनंताश्च बुद्धयोऽव्यवसायिनाम् ॥४१॥

1 Dharma.

The determinate reason is but one-pointed, O joy of the Kurus; many-branched and endless are the thoughts of the irresolute. (41)

व्यवसायात्मिका = व्यवसायः आत्मा यस्याः सा determination, soul, whose, she; बुद्धिः thought; एका one; इह here; कुरुनंदन = कुरूणां नंदन of the Kurus, O rejoicer; बहुशाखाः = बह्व्यः शाखाः यासां ताः many, branches, whose, those; हि indeed; अनंताः endless; च and; बुद्धयः thoughts; अव्यवसायिनाम् of the irresolute.

यामिमां पुष्पितां वाचं प्रवदंत्यविपश्चितः ।
वेदवादरताः पार्थ नान्यदस्तीति वादिनः ॥ ४२ ॥

Flowery speech is uttered by the foolish, rejoicing in the letter of the Vedas, O Pârtha, saying: "There is naught but this." (42)

याम् which; इमां this; पुष्पितां flowery; वाचं speech; प्रवदंति utter; अविपश्चितः the un-wise; वेदवादरताः = वेदस्य वादे रताः of the Veda, in the word, rejoicing; पार्थ Pârtha; न not; अन्यत् other; अस्ति is; इति thus; वादिनः saying.

कामात्मानः स्वर्गपरा जन्मकर्मफलप्रदाम् ।
क्रियाविशेषबहुलां भोगैश्वर्यगतिं प्रति ॥ ४३ ॥

With desire for self, [1] with heaven for goal, they offer birth as the fruit of action, and prescribe many and

[1] Those whose very self is desire, Kâma, and who therefore act with a view to win heaven and also rebirth to wealth and rank.

various ceremonies for the attainment of pleasure and lordship. (43)

कामात्मानः = कामः आत्मा येषां ते desire, soul, whose, they; स्वर्गपराः = स्वर्गः परः येषां ते heaven, highest, whose, they; जन्मकर्मफलप्रदाम् = जन्म एव कर्मणः फलं (इव) प्रददाति तां (re) birth, alone, of action, fruit, (as,) gives, that (which); क्रियाविशेषबहुलां = क्रियाणां विशेषाः बहुलाः यस्यां तां of actions, varieties, many, in which, that; भोगैश्वर्यगतिं = भोगस्य च ऐश्वर्यस्य च गतिं of enjoyment, and, of sovereignty, and, the gaining; प्रति towards (for the sake of).

भोगैश्वर्यप्रसक्तानां तयाऽपहृतचेतसाम् ।
व्यवसायात्मिका बुद्धिः समाधौ न विधीयते॥४४॥

For them who cling to pleasure and lordship, whose minds are captivated by such teaching, is not designed this determinate Reason, on contemplation steadily bent.[1] (44)

भोगैश्वर्यप्रसक्तानां = भोगे च ऐश्वर्ये च प्रसक्तानां in enjoyment, and, in lordship, and, of the attached; तया by that; अपहृतचेतसाम् =

1 The following is offered as an alternative translation of shlokas 42, 43, 44.

"The flowery speech that the unwise utter, O Pârtha, clinging to the word of the Veda, saying there is nothing else, ensouled by selfish desire and longing after heaven—(the flowery speech) that offereth only rebirth as the (ultimate) fruit of action, and is full of (recommendations to) various rites for the sake of (gaining) enjoyments and sovereignty,—the thought of those who are misled by that (speech) and cling to pleasures and lordship, not being inspired with resolution, is not engaged in concentration."

अपहृतं चेतः येषां तेषां dragged away, mind, whose, of them; व्यवसायात्मिका determinate (see 41); बुद्धिः thought; समाधौ in Samâdhi; न not; विधीयते is fixed.

त्रैगुण्यविषया वेदा निस्त्रैगुण्यो भवार्जुन ।
निर्द्वन्द्वो नित्यसत्त्वस्थो निर्योगक्षेम आत्मवान् ॥ ४५ ॥

The Vedas deal with the three attributes;[1] be thou above these three attributes, O Arjuna; beyond the pairs of opposites, ever steadfast in purity,[2] careless of possessions, full of the SELF. (45)

त्रैगुण्यविषयाः = त्रैगुण्यं विषयः येषां ते the three attributes, subject-matter, whose, they; वेदाः (the) Vedas; निस्त्रैगुण्यः without the three attributes; भव be; अर्जुन O Arjuna; निर्द्वन्द्वः without the pairs (of opposites); नित्यसत्त्वस्थः = नित्यं सत्त्वे तिष्ठति इति constantly, in sattva, (who) dwells, thus; निर्योगक्षेमः = न अस्ति योगः च क्षेमः च यस्य सः not, is, earning, and, maintaining, and, whose, he; आत्मवान् full of the Self.

यावानर्थ उदपाने सर्वतः संप्लुतोदके ।
तावान्सर्वेषु वेदेषु ब्राह्मणस्य विजानतः ॥ ४६ ॥

All the Vedas are as useful to an enlightened Brâhmaṇa, as is a tank in a place covered all over with water. (46)

---

1 Guṇas = attributes, or forms of energy. They are Sattva, rhythm or purity; Rajas, activity or passion; Tamas, inertia or darkness.

2 Sattva.

यावान् as much; अर्थः use; उदपाने in a small pool; सर्वतः everywhere; संप्लुतोदके = संप्लुते उदके (in the state of a place being) flooded, (in, *i. e.*, with) water; तावान् so much; सर्वेषु (in) all; वेदेषु in the Vedas; ब्राह्मणस्य of the Brâhmaṇa; विजानतः (of) learned.

कर्मण्येवाधिकारस्ते मा फलेषु कदाचन ।
मा कर्मफलहेतुर्भूर्मा ते संगोऽस्त्वकर्मणि ॥४७॥

Thy business is with the action only, never with its fruits; so let not the fruit of action be thy motive, nor be thou to inaction attached. (47)

कर्मणि in the action; एव only; अधिकारः right; ते thee; मा not; फलेषु in the fruits; कदाचन at any time; मा not; कर्मफलहेतुः = कर्मणः फलं हेतुः यस्य सः of action, fruit, motive, whose, he; भूः be; मा not; ते thy; संगः attachment; अस्तु let (there) be; अकर्मणि in inaction.

योगस्थः कुरु कर्माणि संगं त्यक्त्वा धनंजय ।
सिद्ध्यसिद्ध्योः समो भूत्वा समत्वं योग उच्यते ॥४८॥

Perform action, O Dhanañjaya, dwelling in union with the divine, renouncing attachments, and balanced evenly in success and failure: equilibrium is called yoga. (48)

योगस्थः yoga-seated; कुरु, perform; कर्माणि actions; संगं attachment; त्यक्त्वा having abandoned; धनंजय O Dhanañjaya; सिद्ध्यसिद्ध्योः = सिद्धौ च असिद्धौ च in success, and, in non-success, and; समः the same; भूत्वा having become; समत्वं equality; योगः yoga; उच्यते is called.

दूरेण ह्यवरं कर्म बुद्धियोगाद्धनंजय ।
बुद्धौ शरणमन्विच्छ कृपणाः फलहेतवः ४९ ॥

Far lower than the Yoga of Discrimination is action, O Dhanañjaya. Take thou refuge in the Pure Reason; pitiable are they who work for fruit. (49)

दूरेण by far; हि indeed; अवरं inferior; कर्म action; बुद्धियोगाद् = बुद्धेः योगात् of discrimination, than the yoga; धनंजय O Dhanañjaya; बुद्धौ in (the) Pure Reason; शरणं refuge; अन्विच्छ, seek; कृपणाः pitiable; फलहेतवः = फलं हेतुः येषां ते fruit, motive, whose, they.

बुद्धियुक्तो जहातीह उभे सुकृतदुष्कृते ।
तस्माद्योगाय युज्यस्व योगः कर्मसु कौशलम् ॥५०॥

United to the Pure Reason, one abandoneth here both good and evil deeds, therefore cleave thou to yoga; yoga is skill in action. (50)

बुद्धियुक्तः = बुद्ध्या युक्तः with knowledge, endowed; जहाति (he) throws away; इह here; उभे both; सुकृतदुष्कृते = सुकृतं च दुष्कृतं च good deed, and, evil deed, and; तस्मात् therefore; योगाय for (to) yoga; युज्यस्व be united, (prepare); योगः yoga; कर्मसु in actions; कौशलम् skill.

कर्मजं बुद्धियुक्ता हि फलं त्यक्त्वा मनीषिणः ।
जन्मबंधविनिर्मुक्ताः पदं गच्छंत्यनामयम् ॥ ५१ ॥

The Sages, united to the Pure Reason, renounce the fruit which action yieldeth, and, liberated from the bonds of birth, they go to the blissful seat. (51)

कर्मजं action-born; बुद्धियुक्ताः united to Buddhi (see 50); हि indeed; फलं the fruit; त्यक्त्वा having abandoned; मनीषिणः the wise; जन्मबंधविनिर्मुक्ताः = जन्मनः बंधात् विनिर्मुक्ताः of birth, from the bondage, freed; पदं the abode; गच्छंति go; अनामयं painless.

यदा ते मोहकलिलं बुद्धिर्व्यतितरिष्यति ।
तदा गंतासि निर्वेदं श्रोतव्यस्य श्रुतस्य च ॥५२॥

When thy mind shall escape from this tangle of delusion, then thou shalt rise to indifference as to what has been heard and shall be heard. (52)

यदा when; ते thy; मोहकलिलं = मोहस्य कलिलं of delusion, the confusion; बुद्धिः mind; व्यतितरिष्यति will cross; तदा then; गंतासि (thou) shalt go; निर्वेदं to indifference; श्रोतव्यस्य of (what) should be heard; श्रुतस्य of (what) has been heard; च and.

श्रुतिविप्रतिपन्ना ते यदा स्थास्यति निश्चला ।
समाधावचला बुद्धिस्तदा योगमवाप्स्यसि ॥ ५३ ॥

When thy mind, bewildered by the Shruti, shall stand immovable, fixed in contemplation, then shalt thou attain unto yoga. (53)

श्रुतिविप्रतिपन्ना = श्रुतिभिः विप्रतिपन्ना by scripture-texts, distracted; ते thy; यदा when; स्थास्यति shall stand; निश्चला immovable; समाधौ in Samâdhi; अचला unmoved; बुद्धिः Pure Reason; तदा then; योगं to yoga; अवाप्स्यसि (thou) shalt attain.

अर्जुन उवाच ।

स्थितप्रज्ञस्य का भाषा समाधिस्थस्य केशव ।
स्थितधीः किं प्रभाषेत किमासीत व्रजेत किम् ॥५४॥

Arjuna said:

What is the mark of him who is stable of mind, steadfast in contemplation, O Keshava? how doth the stable-minded talk, how doth he sit, how walk? (54)

स्थितप्रज्ञस्य = स्थिता प्रज्ञा यस्य तस्य steady, intelligence, whose, his; का what; भाषा definition; समाधिस्थस्य = of the Samâdhi-seated; केशव O Keshava; स्थितधीः = स्थिता धीः यस्य सः fixed, mind, whose, he; किं what; प्रभाषेत may (he) speak; किं what (how); आसीत may (he) sit; व्रजेत may (he) walk; किं what (how).

श्री भगवानुवाच ।

प्रजहाति यदा कामान्सर्वान्पार्थ मनोगतान् ।
आत्मन्येवात्मना तुष्टः स्थितप्रज्ञस्तदोच्यते ॥५५॥

The Blessed Lord said:

When a man abandoneth, O Pârtha, all the desires of the heart, and is satisfied in the SELF by the SELF, then is he called stable in mind. (55)

प्रजहाति (he) throws away; यदा when; कामान् desires; सर्वान् all; पार्थ O Pârtha; मनोगतान् = मनः गतान् to the mind, gone; आत्मनि in the Self; एव only: आत्मना by the Self; तुष्टः satisfied; स्थितप्रज्ञः steadfast in mind (see 54); तदा then; उच्यते (he) is called.

दुःखेष्वनुद्विग्नमनाः सुखेषु विगतस्पृहः।
वीतरागभयक्रोधः स्थितधीर्मुनिरुच्यते ॥ ५६ ॥

He whose mind is free from anxiety amid pains, indifferent amid pleasures, loosed from passion, fear and anger, he is called a sage of stable mind. (56)

दुःखेषु in pains; अनुद्विग्नमनाः = न उद्विग्नं मनः यस्य सः not agitated, mind, whose, he; सुखेषु in pleasures; विगतस्पृहः = विगता स्पृहा यस्य सः gone, desire, whose, he; वीतरागभयक्रोधः = वीतः रागः च भयं च क्रोधः च यस्य सः gone, desire, and, fear, and, anger, and whose, he; स्थितधीः steady-minded (see 54); मुनिः sage; उच्यते (he) is called.

यः सर्वत्रानभिस्नेहस्तत्तत्प्राप्य शुभाशुभम्।
नाभिनंदति न द्वेष्टि तस्य प्रज्ञा प्रतिष्ठिता ॥५७॥

He who on every side is without attachments, whatever hap of fair and foul, who neither likes nor dislikes, of such a one the understanding is well-poised. (57)

यः he who; सर्वत्र everywhere; अनभिस्नेहः un-attached; तत् that; तत् that (whatever); प्राप्य having obtained; शुभाशुभम् = शुभं च अशुभं च pleasant, and, unpleasant, and; न not; अभि-

नंदति rejoices; न not; द्वेष्टि hates; तस्य of him; प्रज्ञा the intelligence; प्रतिष्ठिता is established.

यदा संहरते चायं कूर्मोऽङ्गानीव सर्वशः ।
इंद्रियाणींद्रियार्थेभ्यस्तस्य प्रज्ञा प्रतिष्ठिता ॥५८॥

When, again, as a tortoise draws in on all sides its limbs, he withdraws his senses from the objects of sense, then is his understanding well-poised. (58)

यदा when; संहरते draws in; च and; अयं this one; कूर्मः tortoise; अङ्गानि limbs; इव like; सर्वशः everywhere; इन्द्रियाणि the senses; इंद्रियार्थेभ्यः = इंद्रियाणाम् अर्थेभ्यः of the senses, from the objects; तस्य of him; प्रज्ञा the intelligence; प्रतिष्ठिता is established.

विषया विनिवर्तंते निराहारस्य देहिनः ।
रसवर्जं रसोऽप्यस्य परं दृष्ट्वा निवर्तते ॥ ५९ ॥

The objects of sense, but not the relish for them,[1] turn away from an abstemious dweller in the body; and even relish turneth away from him after the Supreme is seen. (59)

विषयाः the objects of sense; विनिवर्तंते turn away; निराहारस्य (of the) foodless; देहिनः of the embodied; रसवर्जं = रसं वर्जयित्वा relish, excepting; रसः relish; अपि even; अस्य of him; परं the Supreme; दृष्ट्वा having seen; निवर्तते turns away.

---

1 The objects turn away when rejected, but still desire for them remains; even desire is lost when the Supreme is seen.

यततो ह्यपि कौंतेय पुरुषस्य विपश्चितः ।
इंद्रियाणि प्रमाथीनि हरंति प्रसभं मनः ॥ ६० ॥

O son of Kuntî, the excited senses of even a wise man, though he be striving, impetuously carry away his mind. (60)

यततः of the endeavouring; हि indeed; अपि even; कौंतेय O Kaunteya; पुरुषस्य of man; विपश्चितः (of the) wise; इंद्रियाणि the senses; प्रमाथीनि (the) uptearing; हरंति carry away; प्रसभं impetuously; मनः the mind.

तानि सर्वाणि संयम्य युक्त आसीत मत्परः ।
वशे हि यस्येंद्रियाणि तस्य प्रज्ञा प्रतिष्ठिता ॥ ६१ ॥

Having restrained them all, he should sit harmonised, I his supreme goal; for whose senses are mastered, of him the understanding is well-poised. (61)

तानि them; सर्वाणि all; संयम्य having restrained; युक्तः joined; आसीत should sit; मत्परः = अहं परः यस्य सः I, supreme goal, whose, he; वशे in control; हि indeed; यस्य of whom; इंद्रियाणि senses; तस्य of him; प्रज्ञा the intelligence; प्रतिष्ठिता (is) established.

ध्यायतो विषयान्पुंसः संगस्तेषूपजायते ।
संगात्संजायते कामः कामात्क्रोधोऽभिजायते ॥ ६२ ॥

Man, musing on the objects of sense, conceiveth an

attachment to these; from attachment ariseth desire; from desire anger cometh forth; (62)

ध्यायतः (of the) meditating; विषयान् (on) objects (of the senses); पुंसः of the man; संगः attachment; तेषु in them; उपजायते is born; संगात् from attachment; संजायते arises; कामः desire; कामात् from desire; क्रोधः anger; अभिजायते is produced.

क्रोधाद्भवति संमोहः संमोहात्स्मृतिविभ्रमः ।
स्मृतिभ्रंशाद् बुद्धिनाशो बुद्धिनाशात्प्रणश्यति ॥ ६३ ॥

From anger proceedeth delusion; from delusion confused memory; from confused memory the destruction of Reason; from destruction of Reason he perishes. (63)

क्रोधात् from anger; भवति becomes; संमोहः delusion; संमोहात् from delusion; स्मृतिविभ्रमः = स्मृतेः विभ्रमः of memory, confusion; स्मृतिभ्रंशात् = स्मृतेः भ्रंशात् of memory, from confusion; बुद्धिनाशः = बुद्धेः नाशः of Reason, destruction; बुद्धिनाशात् from destruction of Reason; प्रणश्यति (he) perishes.

रागद्वेषवियुक्तैस्तु विषयानिंद्रियैश्चरन् ।
आत्मवश्यैर्विधेयात्मा प्रसादमधिगच्छति ॥ ६४ ॥

But the disciplined self, moving among sense-objects with senses free from attraction and repulsion mastered by the SELF, goeth to Peace. (64)

रागद्वेषवियुक्तैः = रागेण च द्वेषेण च वियुक्तैः with (from) attraction, and, (from) repulsion, and, (from) disjoined; तु indeed; विषयान् objects (of sense); इंद्रियैः with senses; चरन् moving

(after); आत्मवश्यैः = आत्मनः वश्यैः of the Self. (by) the controlled; विधेयात्मा = विधेयः आत्मा यस्य सः subdued, self, whose, he; प्रसादं to peace; अधिगच्छति attains.

प्रसादे सर्वदुःखानां हानिरस्योपजायते ।
प्रसन्नचेतसो ह्याशु बुद्धिः पर्यवतिष्ठते ॥ ६५ ॥

In that Peace the extinction of all pains ariseth for him; for of him whose heart is peaceful the Reason soon attaineth equilibrium. (65)

प्रसादे in (the state of) peace; सर्वदुःखानां = सर्वेषां दुःखानां (of) all, of pains; हानिः destruction; अस्य of him; उपजायते arises; प्रसन्नचेतसः = प्रसन्नं चेतः यस्य तस्य peaceful, mind, whose, his; हि indeed; आशु quickly; बुद्धिः the Reason; पर्यवतिष्ठते settles down.

नास्ति बुद्धिरयुक्तस्य न चायुक्तस्य भावना ।
न चाभावयतः शांतिरशांतस्य कुतः सुखम् ॥ ६६ ॥

There is no pure Reason for the non-harmonised, nor for the non-harmonised is there concentration; for him without concentration there is no peace, and for the unpeaceful how can there be happiness? (66)

न not; अस्ति is; बुद्धिः Reason; अयुक्तस्य of the uncontrolled; न not; च and; अयुक्तस्य of the uncontrolled; भावना meditation; न not; च and; अभावयतः of the non-meditating; शांतिः peace; अशांतस्य of the unpeaceful; कुतः whence; सुखं happiness.

इंद्रियाणां हि चरतां यन्मनोऽनुविधीयते ।
तदस्य हरति प्रज्ञां वायुर्नावमिवांभसि ॥ ६७ ॥

Such of the roving senses as the mind yieldeth to, that hurries away the understanding, just as the gale hurries away a ship upon the waters. (67)

इंद्रियाणां of the senses; हि indeed; चरताम् moving; यत् which; मनः the mind; अनुविधीयते is conformed to; तत् that; अस्य of him; हरति carries away; प्रज्ञां the intelligence; वायुः the wind; नावं the ship; इव like; अंभसि in the water.

तस्माद्यस्य महाबाहो निगृहीतानि सर्वशः ।
इंद्रियाणींद्रियार्थेभ्यस्तस्य प्रज्ञा प्रतिष्ठिता ॥ ६८ ॥

Therefore, O mighty-armed, whose senses are all completely restrained from the objects of sense, of him the understanding is well-poised. (68)

तस्मात् therefore; यस्य of whom; महाबाहो O mighty-armed (see 26); निगृहीतानि restrained; सर्वशः everywhere; इंद्रियाणि the senses; इंद्रियार्थेभ्यः (see 58) from the objects of the senses; तस्य of him; प्रज्ञा the intelligence; प्रतिष्ठिता (is) established.

या निशा सर्वभूतानां तस्यां जागर्ति संयमी ।
यस्या जाग्रति भूतानि सा निशा पश्यतो मुनेः ॥ ६९ ॥

That which is the night of all beings, for the disciplined man is the time of waking; when other beings are waking, then is night for the Muni who seeth.[1] (69)

या which; निशा night; सर्वभूतानां = सर्वेषां भूतानां (of) all, of beings; तस्यां in that; जागर्ति wakes; संयमी the disciplined (one); यस्यां in which; जाग्रति wake; भूतानि creatures; सा that; निशा night; पश्यतः (of the) seeing; मुनेः of the muni.[1]

आपूर्यमाणमचलप्रतिष्ठं

समुद्रमापः प्रविशंति यद्वत् ।

तद्वत्कामा यं प्रविशंति सर्वे

स शांतिमाप्नोति न कामकामी ॥ ७० ॥

He attaineth Peace, into whom all desires flow as rivers flow into the ocean, which is filled with water but remaineth unmoved—not he who desireth desires. (70)

आपूर्यमाणम् (ever) being filled; अचलप्रतिष्ठं = अचला प्रतिष्ठा यस्य तं unmoving, status, whose, him; समुद्रम् (in) to the ocean; आपः waters; प्रविशंति enter; यद्वत् as; तद्वत् so; कामाः (objects of) desires; यं (in) to whom; प्रविशंति enter; सर्वे all; सः he; शांतिम् peace; आप्नोति obtains; न not; कामकामी = कामानां कामी of (objects of) desires, the desirer.

विहाय कामान्यः सर्वान्पुमांश्चरति निःस्पृहः ।

---

1 The Sage is awake to things over which the ordinary man sleeps, and the eyes of the Sage are open to truths shut out from the common vision, while *vice versâ* that which is real for the masses is illusion for the Sage.

निर्ममो निरहंकारः स शांतिमधिगच्छति ॥७१॥

Who so forsaketh all desires and goeth onwards free from yearnings, selfless and without egoism—he goeth to Peace. (71)

विहाय having thrown away ; कामान् desires ; यः he who ; सर्वान् all ; पुमान् man ; चरति goes ; निःस्पृहः without-desire ; निर्ममः without-mine (ness) ; निरहंकारः without-egoism ; सः he ; शांतिं to peace ; अधिगच्छति attains.

एषा ब्राह्मी स्थितिः पार्थ नैनां प्राप्य विमुह्यति ।
स्थित्वाऽस्यामंतकालेऽपि ब्रह्म निर्वाणमृच्छति ॥७२॥

This is the Eternal state, O son of Prithâ. Having attained thereto none is bewildered. Who, even at the death-hour, is established therein, he goeth to the Nirvâṇa of the Eternal. (72)

एषा this ; ब्राह्मी of Brahman ; स्थितिः status ; पार्थ O Pârtha ; न not ; एनां this ; प्राप्य having obtained ; विमुह्यति is confused ; स्थित्वा having sat (been established) ; अस्यां in this ; अन्तकाले =अन्तस्य काले of the end, in the time ; अपि even ; ब्रह्मनिर्वाणम् =ब्रह्मणः निर्वाणम् of Brahman, to Nirvâṇa ; ऋच्छति attains.

इति श्रीमद्भगवद्गीता० सांख्ययोगो नाम द्वितीयोऽध्यायः ॥

Thus in the glorious BHAGAVAD-GÎTÂ the second discourse entitled:

YOGA BY THE SÂNKHYA.

THIRD DISCOURSE.

अर्जुन उवाच ।

ज्यायसी चेत्कर्मणस्ते मता बुद्धिर्जनार्दन ।
तत्किं कर्मणि घोरे मां नियोजयसि केशव ॥ १ ॥

Arjuna said:

If it be thought by thee that knowledge is superior to action, O Janârdana, why dost thou, O Keshava, enjoin on me this terrible action? (1)

ज्यायसी superior; चेत् if; कर्मणः than action; ते of (by) thee; मता thought; बुद्धिः knowledge; जनार्दन O Janârdana; तत् then; किम् why; कर्मणि in action; घोरे (in) terrible; मां me; नियोजयसि (thou) engagest; केशव O Keshava.

व्यामिश्रेणेव वाक्येन बुद्धिं मोहयसीव मे ।
तदेकं वद निश्चित्य येन श्रेयोऽहमाप्नुयाम् ॥ २ ॥

With these perplexing words Thou only confusest my understanding; therefore tell me with certainty the one way by which I may reach bliss? (2)

व्यामिश्रेण (with) intermixed; इव as it were; वाक्येन with speech; बुद्धिं understanding; मोहयसि (thou) confusest; इव as it were; मे my; तत् so; एकं one; वद speak; निश्चित्य having decided; येन by which; श्रेयः better (the good); अहं I; आप्नुयाम् may obtain.

श्रीभगवानुवाच ।

लोकेऽस्मिन्द्विविधा निष्ठा पुरा प्रोक्ता मयाऽनघ ।
ज्ञानयोगेन सांख्यानां कर्मयोगेन योगिनाम् ॥ ३ ॥

The Blessed Lord said :

In this world there is a twofold path, as I before said, O sinless one: that of yoga by knowledge, of the Sâṅkhyas ; and that of yoga by action, of the Yogîs. (3)

लोके in world ; अस्मिन् (in) this ; द्विविधा twofold ; निष्ठा belief ; पुरा formerly ; प्रोक्ता said ; मया by me ; अनघ O sinless one ; ज्ञानयोगेन = ज्ञानस्य योगेन of knowledge, by yoga ; सांख्यानाम् of the Sâṅkhyas ; कर्मयोगेन = कर्मणः योगेन of action, by yoga ; योगिनाम् of the yogîs.

न कर्मणामनारंभान्नैष्कर्म्यं पुरुषोऽश्नुते ।
न च संन्यसनादेव सिद्धिं समधिगच्छति ॥ ४ ॥

Man winneth not freedom from action by abstaining from activity, nor by mere renunciation doth he rise to perfection. (4)

न not ; कर्मणाम् of actions ; अनारंभात् from (by) non-commencement ; नैष्कर्म्यं inactivity ; पुरुषः man ; अश्नुते obtains ; न not ; च and ; संन्यसनात् from (by) renunciation ; एव only ; सिद्धिं perfection ; समधिगच्छति attains.

नहि कश्चित्क्षणमपि जातु तिष्ठत्यकर्मकृत् ।

कार्यते ह्यवशः कर्म सर्वः प्रकृतिजैर्गुणैः ॥ ५ ॥

Nor can anyone, even for an instant, remain really actionless; for helplessly is everyone driven to action by the qualities born of nature. (5)

नहि not; कश्चित् anyone; क्षणम् a moment; अपि even; जातु in reality; तिष्ठति stands; अकर्मकृत् un-action-performing; कार्यते is made to do; हि indeed; अवशः helpless; कर्म action; सर्वः all; प्रकृतिजैः (by) the nature-born; गुणैः qualities.

कर्मेन्द्रियाणि संयम्य य आस्ते मनसा स्मरन् ।
इन्द्रियार्थान्विमूढात्मा मिथ्याचारः स उच्यते ॥ ६ ॥

Who sitteth, controlling the organs of action, but dwelling in his mind on the objects of the senses, that bewildered man is called a hypocrite. (6)

कर्मेन्द्रियाणि = कर्मणां इंद्रियाणि of actions, the organs; संयम्य having controlled; यः who; आस्ते sits; मनसा by the mind; स्मरन् remembering; इंद्रियार्थान् the objects of the senses (see ii. 58.); विमूढात्मा = विमूढः आत्मा यस्य सः confused, mind, whose, he; मिथ्याचारः = मिथ्या आचारः यस्य सः false, conduct, whose, he; सः he; उच्यते is called.

यस्त्विन्द्रियाणि मनसा नियम्यारभतेऽर्जुन ।
कर्मेन्द्रियैः कर्मयोगमसक्तः स विशिष्यते ॥ ७ ॥

But who, controlling the senses by the mind, O

Arjuna, with the organs of action, without attachment, performeth yoga by action [1], he is worthy. (7)

यः who; तु indeed; इन्द्रियाणि the senses; मनसा by the mind; नियम्य having controlled; आरभते commences; अर्जुन O Arjuna; कर्मेन्द्रियैः by the organs of action; कर्मयोगम् karma-yoga; असक्तः unattached; सः he; विशिष्यते excels.

नियतं कुरु कर्म त्वं कर्म ज्यायो ह्यकर्मणः ।
शरीरयात्राऽपि च ते न प्रसिद्ध्येदकर्मणः ॥ ८ ॥

Perform thou right action, for action is superior to inaction, and, inactive, even the maintenance of thy body would not be possible. (8)

नियतं prescribed; कुरु do; कर्म action; त्वं thou; कर्म action; ज्यायः better; हि indeed; अकर्मणः than inaction; शरीरयात्रा = शरीरस्य यात्रा of the body, pilgrimage; अपि even; च and; ते thy; न not; प्रसिद्ध्येत् may succeed; अकर्मणः from (by) inaction.

यज्ञार्थात्कर्मणोऽन्यत्र लोकोऽयं कर्मबंधनः ।
तदर्थं कर्म कौंतेय मुक्तसंगः समाचर ॥ ९ ॥

The world is bound by action, unless performed for the sake of sacrifice; for that sake, free from attachment, O son of Kuntî, perform thou action. (9)

यज्ञार्थात् = यज्ञस्य अर्थात् of sacrifice, (from) for the sake of;

---

1 Karma-Yoga is the consecration of physical energy on the Divine Altar, *i. e.*, the using of one's organs of action simply in service, in obedience to Law and Duty.

कर्मणः from (than) action; अन्यत्र otherwise; लोकः the world; अयं this; कर्मबंधनः=कर्म बंधनं यस्य सः action, bond, whose, it; तदर्थं=तस्य अर्थं of that, for the sake; कर्म action; कौंतेय O Kaunteya; मुक्तसंगः=मुक्तः संगो येन सः abandoned, attachment, by whom, he; समाचर perform.

सहयज्ञाः प्रजाः सृष्ट्वा पुरोवाच प्रजापतिः ।
अनेन प्रसविष्यध्वमेष वोऽस्त्विष्टकामधुक् ॥ १० ॥

Having in ancient times emanated mankind together with sacrifice, the Lord of emanation said: "By this shall ye propagate; be this to you the giver of desires[1]; (10)

सहयज्ञाः=यज्ञेन सह with sacrifice, together; प्रजाः the peoples; सृष्ट्वा having emanated; पुरा formerly; उवाच said; प्रजापतिः Prajâpati; अनेन by this; प्रसविष्यध्वम् shall propagate (ye); एष this; वः of you; अस्तु let be; इष्टकामधुक्= इष्टान् कामान् दोग्धि desired. objecte, milks.

देवान्भावयतानेन ते देवा भावयंतु वः ।
परस्परं भावयंतः श्रेयः परमवाप्स्यथ ॥ ११ ॥

"With this nourish ye the shining ones and may the shining ones nourish you; thus nourishing one another, ye shall reap the supremest good. (11)

देवान् the Gods; भावयत nourish (ye); अनेन by this; ते those; देवाः Gods; भावयंतु may nourish; वः you; परस्परं

1 The cow of Indra, from which each could milk what he wished for; hence the giver of desired objects.

each other; भावयंतः nourishing; श्रेयः good; परं the highest; अवाप्स्यथ (ye) shall obtain.

इष्टान्भोगान्हि वो देवा दास्यंते यज्ञभाविताः ।
तैर्दत्तानप्रदायैभ्यो यो भुंक्ते स्तेन एव सः ॥१२॥

"For, nourished by sacrifice, the Shining Ones shall bestow on you the enjoyments you desire." A thief verily is he who enjoyeth what is given by Them without returning Them aught. (12)

इष्टान् desired; भोगान् enjoyments; हि indeed; वः to you; देवाः the Gods; दास्यंते will give; यज्ञभाविताः=यज्ञेन भाविताः by sacrifice, nourished; तैः by them; दत्तान् given; अप्रदाय not having given (returned); एभ्यः to these; यः who; भुंक्ते enjoys; स्तेनः thief; एव only; सः he.

यज्ञशिष्टाशिनः संतो मुच्यंते सर्वकिल्बिषैः ।
भुंजते ते त्वघं पापा ये पचंत्यात्मकारणात् ॥ १३ ॥

The righteous, who eat the remains of the sacrifice, are freed from all sins; but the impious, who dress food for their own sakes, they verily eat sin. (13)

यज्ञशिष्टाशिनः=यज्ञस्य शिष्टं अश्नंतिते of the sacrifice, remains, (who) eat, they; संतः the good; मुच्यंते are freed; सर्वकिल्बिषैः =सर्वैः किल्बिषैः by (from) all, by (from) sins; भुंजते enjoy; ते those; तु indeed; अघं evil; पापाः sinners; ये who; पचंति cook; आत्मकारणात्=आत्मनः कारणात् of the self, from (for the) cause (sake).

अन्नाद्भवंति भूतानि पर्जन्यादन्नसंभवः ।
यज्ञाद्भवति पर्जन्यो यज्ञः कर्मसमुद्भवः ॥ १४ ॥

From food creatures become; from rain is the production of food; rain proceedeth from sacrifice; sacrifice ariseth out of action; (14)

अन्नात् from food; भवंति become; भूतानि creatures; पर्जन्यात् from rain; अन्नसंभवः = अन्नस्य संभवः of food, the production; यज्ञात् from sacrifice; भवति becomes; पर्जन्यः rain; यज्ञः sacrifice; कर्मसमुद्भवः = कर्मणः समुद्भवः यस्यः तत् from action, the arising, whose, that.

कर्म ब्रह्मोद्भवं विद्धि ब्रह्माऽक्षरसमुद्भवम् ।
तस्मात्सर्वगतं ब्रह्म नित्यं यज्ञे प्रतिष्ठितम् ॥१५॥

Know thou that from Brahma action groweth, and Brahman from the Imperishable cometh. Therefore the Eternal, the all-permeating, is ever present in sacrifice. (15)

कर्म action; ब्रह्मोद्भवं = ब्रह्मणः उद्भवः यस्य तत् from Brahma (the Vedas), arising, whose, that; विद्धि know; ब्रह्म Brahma; अक्षरसमुद्भवम् = अक्षरात् समुद्भवः यस्य तत्, from the Imperishable, arising, whose, that; तस्मात् therefore; सर्वगतं everywhere-going; ब्रह्म Brahman; नित्यं constantly; यज्ञे in sacrifice; प्रतिष्ठितम् (is) established.

एवं प्रवर्तितं चक्रं नानुवर्तयतीह यः ।

अघायुरिंद्रियारामो मोघं पार्थ स जीवति ॥ १६ ॥

He who on earth doth not follow the wheel thus revolving, sinful of life and rejoicing in the senses, he, O son of Prithâ, liveth in vain. (16)

एवं thus; प्रवर्तितं set turning; चक्रं wheel; न not; अनुवर्तयति follows; इह here; यः who; अघायुः = अघं आयुः यस्य सः evil, life, whose, he; इंद्रियारामः = इंद्रियेषु आरामः यस्य सः in the senses, rejoicing, whose, he; मोघं uselessly; पार्थ O Pârtha; सः he; जीवति lives.

यस्त्वात्मरतिरेव स्यादात्मतृप्तश्च मानवः ।

आत्मन्येव च संतुष्टस्तस्य कार्यं न विद्यते ॥ १७ ॥

But the man who rejoiceth in the SELF, with the SELF is satisfied, and is content in the SELF, for him verily there is nothing to do. (17)

यः who; तु indeed; आत्मरतिः = आत्मनि रतिः यस्य सः in the Self, pleasure, whose, he; एव only; स्यात् may be; आत्मतृप्तः = आत्मना तृप्तः by the Self, satisfied; च and; मानवः the man; आत्मनि in the Self; एव only; च and; संतुष्टः contented; तस्य of him; कार्यं (work) to be done; न not; विद्यते is.

नैव तस्य कृतेनार्थो नाकृतेनेह कश्चन ।

न चास्य सर्वभूतेषु कश्चिदर्थव्यपाश्रयः ॥ १८ ॥

For him there is no interest in things done in this

world, nor any in things not done, nor doth any object of his depend on any being. (18)

न not; एव even; तस्य of him; कृतेन with action; अर्थः concern; न not; अकृतेन with inaction; इह here; कश्चन any; न not; च and; अस्य of this one; सर्वभूतेषु = सर्वेषु भूतेषु (in) all, in creatures; कश्चित् any; अर्थस्य of (an) interest; व्यपाश्रयः dependence.

तस्मादसक्तः सततं कार्यं कर्म समाचर ।
असक्तो ह्याचरन्कर्म परमाप्नोति पूरुषः ॥ १९ ॥

Therefore, without attachment, constantly perform action which is duty, for by performing action without attachment, man verily reacheth the Supreme. (19)

तस्मात् therefore; असक्तः unattached; सततं always; कार्यं (necessary) to be done; कर्म action; समाचर perform; असक्तः unattached; हि indeed; आचरन् performing; कर्म action; परं the Supreme; आप्नोति obtains; पूरुषः man.

कर्मणैव हि संसिद्धिमास्थिता जनकादयः ।
लोकसंग्रहमेवापि संपश्यन्कर्तुमर्हसि ॥ २० ॥

Janaka and others indeed attained to perfection by action; then having an eye to the welfare of the world also, thou shouldst perform action. (20)

कर्मणा by action; एव only; हि indeed; संसिद्धिम् to perfection; आस्थिताः attained; जनकादयः = जनकः आदिः येषां ते Janaka, the beginning, whose, they; लोकसंग्रहम् = लोकस्य संग्रहम् of the world, welfare; एव even; अपि also; संपश्यन् looking to; कर्तुम् to do; अर्हसि thou shouldst.

यद्यदाचरति श्रेष्ठस्तत्तदेवेतरो जनः ।
स यत्प्रमाणं कुरुते लोकस्तदनुवर्तते ॥ २१ ॥

Whatsoever a great man doeth, that other men also do; the standard he setteth up, by that the people go. (21)

यत् what; यत् what; आचरति does; श्रेष्ठः the best; तत् that; तत् that; एव only; इतरः the other; जनः people; सः he यत् what; प्रमाणं measure (authority); कुरुते makes; लोकः the world (people); तत् that; अनुवर्तते follows.

न मे पार्थाऽस्ति कर्तव्यं त्रिषु लोकेषु किंचन ।
नानवाप्तमवाप्तव्यं वर्त एव च कर्मणि ॥ २२ ॥

There is nothing in the three worlds, O Pârtha, that should be done by Me, nor anything unattained that might be attained; yet I mingle in action. (22)

न not; मे of me; पार्थ O Pârtha; अस्ति is; कर्तव्यं to be done; त्रिषु (in the) three; लोकेषु worlds; किंचन anything; न not; अनवाप्तम् unobtained; अवाप्तव्यं to be obtained; वर्ते exist (I); एव also; च and; कर्मणि in action.

यदि ह्यहं न वर्तेयं जातु कर्मण्यतंद्रितः ।
मम वर्त्मानुवर्तंते मनुष्याः पार्थ सर्वशः ॥ २३ ॥

For if I mingled not ever in action, unwearied, men all around would follow My path, O son of Pṛitha. (23)

यदि if; हि indeed; अहं I; न not; वर्तेयं should exist; जातु (always); कर्मणि in action; अतंद्रितः unwearied; मम my; वर्त्म path; अनुवर्तन्ते follow; मनुष्याः men; पार्थ O Pârtha; सर्वशः everywhere.

उत्सीदेयुरिमे लोका न कुर्यां कर्म चेदहम् ।
संकरस्य च कर्ता स्यामुपहन्यामिमाः प्रजाः ॥२४॥

These worlds would fall into ruin, if I did not perform action; I should be the author of confusion of castes, and should destroy these creatures. (24)

उत्सीदेयुः would be destroyed; इमे these; लोकाः worlds; न not; कुर्यां if (I) perform; कर्म action; चेत् if; अहं I; संकरस्य of confusion; च and; कर्ता author; स्याम् (I) would be; उपहन्याम् (I) would slay; इमाः these; प्रजाः peoples.

सक्ताः कर्मण्यविद्वांसो यथा कुर्वंति भारत ।
कुर्याद्विद्वांस्तथाऽसक्तश्चिकीर्षुर्लोकसंग्रहम् ॥२५॥

As the ignorant act from attachment to action, O Bhârata, so should the wise act without attachment, desiring the welfare of the world. (25)

सक्ताः attached; कर्मणि in (to) action; अविद्वांसः the unwise; यथा as; कुर्वंति act; भारत O Bhârata; कुर्यात् should act; विद्वान् the wise man; तथा so; असक्तः unattached; चिकीर्षुः desiring to make; लोकसंग्रहम् (see 20) the welfare of the world.

न बुद्धिभेदं जनयेदज्ञानां कर्मसंगिनाम् ।
जोषयेत्सर्वकर्माणि विद्वान्युक्तः समाचरन् ॥२६॥

Let no wise man unsettle the mind of ignorant people attached to action; but acting in harmony with Me let him render all action attractive. (26)

न not; बुद्धिभेदं = बुद्धेः भेदं of the reason, the breaking-up; जनयेत् should produce; अज्ञानां of the unknowing; कर्मसंगिनाम् = कर्मणि संगो येषां तेषां in action, attachment, whose, of them; जोषयेत् should cause (others) to like; सर्वकर्माणि = सर्वाणि कर्माणि all, actions; विद्वान् the wise man; युक्तः united, (balanced); समाचरन् performing.

प्रकृतेः क्रियमाणानि गुणैः कर्माणि सर्वशः ।
अहंकारविमूढात्मा कर्ताऽहमिति मन्यते ॥२७॥

All actions are wrought by the qualities of nature only. The self, deluded by egoism, thinketh: "I am the doer." (27)

प्रकृतेः of nature; क्रियमाणानि being performed; गुणैः by the qualities; कर्माणि actions; सर्वशः everywhere; अहंकारविमूढात्मा = अहंकारेण विमूढः आत्मा यस्य सः by egoism, deluded, self, whose, he; कर्ता the doer; अहं I; इति thus; मन्यते thinks.

तत्त्ववित्तु महाबाहो गुणकर्मविभागयोः ।
गुणा गुणेषु वर्तंत इति मत्वा न सज्जते ॥२८॥

But he, O mighty-armed, who knoweth the essence of the divisions of the qualities and functions, holding that "the qualities move amid the qualities,"[1] is not attached. (28)

तत्त्ववित् the essence-knower ; तु indeed ; महाबाहो O mighty-armed (ii. 26) ; गुणकर्मविभागयोः = गुणानाम् च कर्मणाम् च विभागयोः of the qualities, and, of the actions, and, of the (two) divisions[2] ; गुणाः the qualities; गुणेषु in the qualities ; वर्त्तंते exist ; इति thus ; मत्वा having thought ; न not ; सज्जते is attached.

प्रकृतेर्गुणसंमूढाः सज्जंते गुणकर्मसु ।
तानकृत्स्नविदो मंदान्कृत्स्नविन्न विचालयेत् ॥ २९ ॥

Those deluded by the qualities of nature are attached to the functions of the qualities. The man of perfect knowledge should not unsettle the foolish whose knowledge is imperfect. (29)

प्रकृतेः of nature ; गुणसंमूढाः = गुणैः संमूढाः by the qualities, deluded ; सज्जंते are attached ; गुणकर्मसु = गुणानां कर्मसु of the qualities, in the actions ; तान् those ; अकृत्स्नविदः not-all-

---

[1] The qualities as sense-organs move amid the qualities as sense-objects. A suggested reading is : " The functions dwell in the propensities."

[2] गुणकर्मविभागयोः (*a*) Shankara says ; "of guṇa-vibhâga and karma-vibhâga "=of the *class* of guṇas and the *class* of karmas ; or (*b*) vibhâga=apportionment, arrangement , the arrangements of guṇas and of karmas. or the *relations* of them.

knowing; मन्दान् the slow; कृत्स्नवित् the all-knowing; न not; विचालयेत् should unsettle.

मयि सर्वाणि कर्माणि संन्यस्याऽध्यात्मचेतसा ।
निराशीर्निर्ममो भूत्वा युद्धयस्व विगतज्वरः ॥३०॥

Surrendering all actions to Me, with thy thoughts resting on the supreme SELF, from hope and egoism freed, and of mental fever cured, engage in battle. (30)

मयि in me; सर्वाणि all; कर्माणि actions; संन्यस्य having abandoned; अध्यात्मचेतसा = अध्यात्मनि चेतसा in the Self, with mind; निराशीः unhoping; निर्ममः without 'mine'; भूत्वा having become; युद्ध्यस्व fight (thou); विगतज्वरः = विगतः ज्वरो यस्य सः gone, fever, whose, he.

ये मे मतमिदं नित्यमनुतिष्ठंति मानवाः ।
श्रद्धावंतोऽनसूयंतो मुच्यंते तेऽपि कर्मभिः ॥३१॥

Who abide ever in this teaching of Mine, full of faith and free from cavilling, they too are released from actions. (31)

ये (they) who; मे my; मतम् opinion; इदं this; नित्यं constantly; अनुतिष्ठंति follow; मानवाः men; श्रद्धावंतः faith-filled; अनसूयंतः not cavilling; मुच्यंते are freed; ते they; अपि also; कर्मभिः by (from) actions.

ये त्वेतदभ्यसूयंतो नानुतिष्ठंति मे मतम् ।
सर्वज्ञानविमूढांस्तान्विद्धि नष्टानचेतसः ॥३२॥

Who carp at My teaching and act not thereon, senseless, deluded in all knowledge, know thou these mindless ones as fated to be destroyed. (32)

ये who ; तु indeed; एतत् this ; अभ्यसूयंत: carping at ; न not ; अनुतिष्ठंति follow ; मे my ; मतम् opinion ; सर्वज्ञानविमूढान् = सर्वस्मिन् ज्ञाने विमूढान् (in) all, in knowledge, deluded ; तान् these ; विद्धि know (thou); नष्टान् destroyed ; अचेतसः mind-less.

सदृशं चेष्टते स्वस्याः प्रकृतेर्ज्ञानवानपि ।
प्रकृतिं याति भूतानि निग्रहः किं करिष्यति ॥३३॥

Even the man of knowledge behaves in conformity with his own nature ; beings follow nature ; what shall restraint avail ? (33)

सदृशं conformably ; चेष्टते behaves ; स्वस्याः (of) his own ; प्रकृतेः of nature ; ज्ञानवान् the wise man ; अपि even ; प्रकृतिं to nature : यांति go ; भूतानि creatures ; निग्रहः restraint ; किं what ; करिष्यति will do.

इंद्रियस्येंद्रियस्यार्थे रागद्वेषौ व्यवस्थितौ ।
तयोर्न वशमागच्छेत्तौ ह्यस्य परिपंथिनौ ॥३४॥

Affection and aversion for the objects of sense abide in the senses; let none come under the dominion of these two ; they are obstructors of the path. (34)

इंद्रियस्य of the sense ; इंद्रियस्य of the sense ; अर्थे in the object ; रागद्वेषौ = रागः च द्वेषः च attraction, and, repulsion, and ; व्यवस्थितौ seated ; तयोः of these (two) ; न not ; वशम् (under the) control; आगच्छेत् let (him) come; तौ these (two); हि indeed; परिपंथिनौ (two) obstructors of the way.

श्रेयान्स्वधर्मो विगुणः परधर्मात्स्वनुष्ठितात् ।
स्वधर्मे निधनं श्रेयः परधर्मो भयावहः ॥३५॥

Better one's own duty, though destitute of merit, than the duty of another well-discharged. Better death in the discharge of one's own duty; the duty of another is full of danger. (35)

श्रेयान् better; स्वधर्मः own-duty; विगुणः without (good) quality; परधर्मात् = परस्य धर्मात् of another, than the duty; स्वनुष्ठितात् (than) well done; स्वधर्मे in own duty; निधनं death श्रेयः better; परधर्मः another's duty; भयावहः fear-bringing.

अर्जुन उवाच ।

अथ केन प्रयुक्तोऽयं पापं चरति पूरुषः ।
अनिच्छन्नपि वार्ष्णेय बलादिव नियोजितः ॥३६॥

Arjuna said:

But dragged on by what does a man commit sin, reluctantly indeed, O Vârṣhṇeya, as it were by force constrained? (36)

अथ now; केन by what; प्रयुक्तः impelled; अयम् this; पापं sin; चरति does; पूरुषः man: अनिच्छन् undesiring; अपि even; वार्ष्णेय O Vârṣhṇeya; बलात् by force; इव as it were; नियोजितः compelled.

श्रीभगवानुवाच ।

काम एष क्रोध एष रजोगुणसमुद्भवः ।
महाशनो महापाप्मा विद्ध्येनमिह वैरिणम् ॥३७॥

The Blessed Lord said:

It is desire, it is wrath, begotten by the quality of mobility; all-consuming, all-polluting, know thou this as our foe here on earth. (37)

कामः desire; एषः this; क्रोधः wrath; एषः this; रजोगुणसमुद्भवः = रजसः गुणात् समुद्भवः यस्य सः of mobility, from the quality, birth, whose, it; महाशनः = महत् अशनं यस्य सः great, devouring, whose, it; महापाप्मा very hurtful; विद्धि know (thou); एनं this; इह here; वैरिणम् the foe.

धूमेनाऽऽव्रियते वह्निर्यथाऽऽदर्शो मलेन च ।
यथोल्बेनावृतो गर्भस्तथा तेनेदमावृतम् ॥३८॥

As a flame is enveloped by smoke, as a mirror by dust, as an embryo is wrapped by the amnion, so This[1] is enveloped by it. (38)

धूमेन by smoke; आव्रियते is enwrapped; वह्निः fire; यथा as आदर्शः a mirror; मलेन by dust; च and; यथा as; उल्बेन by the amnion; आवृतः enwrapped; गर्भः embryo; तथा so; तेन by it; इदं this; आवृतम् enwrapped.

---

[1] The universe: "This" as opposed to "THAT," the ETERNAL. Some say "This" stands for "knowledge."

आवृतं ज्ञानमेतेन ज्ञानिनो नित्यवैरिणा ।
कामरूपेण कौंतेय दुष्पूरेणानलेन च ॥३९॥

Enveloped is wisdom by this constant enemy of the wise in the form of desire, which is insatiable as a flame. (39)

आवृतं enveloped; ज्ञानं wisdom; एतेन (by) this; ज्ञानिनः of he wise man; नित्यवैरिणा by the constant enemy; कामरूपेण = कामः रूपं यस्य सः desire, body, whose, he; कौंतेय O Kaunteya; दुष्पूरेण (by) the unfillable; अनलेन by flame; च and.

इंद्रियाणि मनो बुद्धिरस्याधिष्ठानमुच्यते ।
एतैर्विमोहयत्येष ज्ञानमावृत्य देहिनम् ॥४०॥

The senses, the mind and the Reason are said to be its seat; by these, enveloping wisdom, it bewilders the dweller in the body. (40)

इंद्रियाणि the senses; मनः the mind; बुद्धिः the reason; अस्य of this; अधिष्ठानम् the seat; उच्यते is called; एतैः by these; विमोहयति bewilders; एषः this; ज्ञानम् wisdom; आवृत्य having enveloped; देहिनम् the embodied one.

तस्मात्त्वमिंद्रियाण्यादौ नियम्य भरतर्षभ ।
पाप्मानं प्रजहि ह्येनं ज्ञानविज्ञाननाशनम् ॥४१॥

Therefore, O best of the Bharatas, mastering first

the senses, do thou slay this thing of sin, destructive of wisdom and knowledge. (41)

तस्मात् therefore; त्वम् thou; इंद्रियाणि the senses; आदौ in the beginning; नियम्य having controlled; भरतर्षभ = भरतानां ऋषभ of the Bharatas, O best; पाप्मानं sin; प्रजहि slay; हि indeed; एनं this; ज्ञानविज्ञाननाशनम् = ज्ञानस्य च विज्ञानस्य च नाशनम्, of knowledge, and, of special knowledge, destroyer.

इंद्रियाणि पराण्याहुरिंद्रियेभ्यः परं मनः ।
मनसस्तु परा बुद्धिर्यो बुद्धेः परतस्तु सः ॥४२॥

It is said that the senses are great; greater than the senses is the mind; greater than the mind is the Reason; but what is greater than the Reason, is HE.[1] (42)

इंद्रियाणि the senses; पराणि superior; आहुः (they) say; इंद्रियेभ्यः than the senses; परं superior; मनः mind; मनसः than the mind; तु indeed; परा superior; बुद्धिः the Reason; यः who; बुद्धेः than the Reason; परतः greater; तु indeed; सः he.

एवं बुद्धेः परं बुद्ध्वा संस्तभ्यात्मानमात्मना ।
जहि शत्रुं महाबाहो कामरूपं दुरासदम् ॥४३॥

Thus understanding Him as greater than the Reason, restraining the self by the SELF, slay thou, O mighty-armed, the enemy in the form of desire, difficult to overcome. (43)

एवं thus; बुद्धेः than the Reason; परं the greater; बुद्ध्वा having

1 The Supreme.

known; संस्तभ्य having steadied; आत्मानम् the self; आत्मना by the Self; जहि slay (thou); शत्रुं the enemy; महाबाहो (ii. 26); O mighty-armed; कामरूपं (39) (of) the form of desire; दुरासदम् difficult to approach.

इति श्रीमद्भगवद्गीतासूप० कर्मयोगो नाम तृतीयोऽध्यायः ।

Thus in the glorious BHAGAVAD-GÎTÂ...the third discourse, entitled:

THE YOGA OF ACTION.

FOURTH DISCOURSE.

श्रीभगवानुवाच ।

इमं विवस्वते योगं प्रोक्तवानहमव्ययम् ।
विवस्वान्मनवे प्राह मनुरिक्ष्वाकवेऽब्रवीत् ॥१॥

The Blessed Lord said:

This imperishable yoga I declared to Vivasvân; Vivasvân taught it to Manu; Manu to Ikṣhvâku told it. (1)

इमं this; विवस्वते to Vivasvân; योगं yoga; प्रोक्तवान् spoke; अहं I; अव्ययम् imperishable; विवस्वान् Vivasvân; मनवे to Manu; प्राह said; मनुः Manu; इक्ष्वाकवे to Ikṣhvâku; अब्रवीत् spake.

एवं परंपराप्राप्तमिमं राजर्षयो विदुः ।
स कालेनेह महता योगो नष्टः परंतप ॥२॥

This, handed on down the line, the King-Sages knew. This yoga by great efflux of time decayed in the world, O Parantapa. (2)

एवं thus; परंपराप्राप्तम् = परंपरया प्राप्तम् by succession, obtained; इमं this; राजर्षयः the king-sages; विदुः know; सः this; कालेन by time; इह here; महता (by) great; योगः yoga; नष्टः destroyed; परंतप O Parantapa.

स एवाऽयं मया तेऽद्य योगः प्रोक्तः पुरातनः ।
भक्तोऽसि मे सखा चेति रहस्यं ह्येतदुत्तमम् ॥ ३ ॥

This same ancient yoga hath been to-day declared to thee by Me, for thou art My devotee and My friend; it is the supreme Secret. (3)

सः this; एव even; अयम् this; मया by me; ते to thee; अद्य to-day; योगः yoga; प्रोक्तः declared; पुरातनः ancient; भक्तः devotee; असि (thou) art; मे my; सखा friend; च and; इति thus; रहस्यं secret; हि indeed; एतत् this; उत्तमम् best.

अर्जुन उवाच ।

अपरं भवतो जन्म परं जन्म विवस्वतः ।
कथमेतद्विजानीयां त्वमादौ प्रोक्तवानिति ॥४॥

Arjuna said:

Later was thy birth, earlier the birth of Vivasvân; how then am I to understand that Thou declaredst it in the beginning? (4)

अपरं later; भवतः of thee; जन्म the birth; परं earlier; जन्म the birth; विवस्वतः of Vivasvân; कथं how; एतत् this; विजानीयाम् may (I) understand; त्वं thou; आदौ in the beginning; प्रोक्तवान् declaredst; इति thus.

श्रीभगवानुवाच ।

बहूनि मे व्यतीतानि जन्मानि तव चार्जुन ।
तान्यहं वेद सर्वाणि न त्वं वेत्थ परंतप ॥५॥

The Blessed Lord said:

Many births have been left behind by Me and by

thee, O Arjuna. I know them all, but thou knowest not thine, O Parantapa. (5)

बहूनि many; मे my; व्यतीतानि past; जन्मानि births; तव thy; च and; अर्जुन O Arjuna; तानि these; अहं I; वेद know; सर्वाणि all; न not; त्वं thou; वेत्थ knowest; परंतप O Parantapa.

अजोऽपि सन्नव्ययात्मा भूतानामीश्वरोऽपि सन् ।
प्रकृतिं स्वामधिष्ठाय संभवाम्यात्ममायया ॥६॥

Though unborn, the imperishable SELF, and also the Lord of all beings, brooding over nature, which is Mine own, yet I am born through My own Power.[1] (6)

अजः unborn; अपि also; सन् being; अव्ययात्मा = अव्ययः आत्मा यस्य सः undecaying, self, whose, he; भूतानाम् of beings; ईश्वरः the Lord; अपि also; सन् being; प्रकृतिं nature; स्वाम् my own; अधिष्ठाय resting on; संभवामि (I) become; आत्ममायया = आत्मनः मायया of the Self, by the mâyâ.[1]

यदा यदा हि धर्मस्य ग्लानिर्भवति भारत ।
अभ्युत्थानमधर्मस्य तदात्मानं सृजाम्यहम् ॥७॥

Whenever there is decay of righteousness, O Bhârata, and there is exaltation of unrighteousness, then I Myself come forth; (7)

---

[1] Mâyâ, the power of thought that produces form, which is transient and therefore unreal compared with the eternal Reality: hence Mâyâ comes to be taken as the power of producing illusion.

यदा when; यदा when; हि indeed; धर्मस्य of duty; ग्लानिः decay; भवति is; भारत O Bhârata; अभ्युत्थानम् rising up; अधर्मस्य of sin; तदा then; आत्मानम् myself; सृजामि send forth; अहं I.

परित्राणाय साधूनां विनाशाय च दुष्कृताम् ।
धर्मसंस्थापनार्थाय संभवामि युगे युगे ॥ ८ ॥

For the protection of the good, for the destruction of evil-doers, for the sake of firmly establishing righteousness, I am born from age to age. (8)

परित्राणाय for the protection; साधूनां of the good; विनाशाय for the destruction; च and; दुष्कृताम् of evil-doers; धर्मसंस्थापनार्थाय = धर्मस्य संस्थापनस्य अर्थाय of duty, of the establishing, for the sake: संभवामि (I) am born; युगे in age: युगे in age.

जन्म कर्म च मे दिव्यमेवं यो वेत्ति तत्त्वतः ।
त्यक्त्वा देहं पुनर्जन्म नैति मामेति सोऽर्जुन ॥ ९ ॥

He who thus knoweth My divine birth and action, in its essence, having abandoned the body, cometh not to birth again, but cometh unto Me, O Arjuna. (9)

जन्म birth; कर्म action; च and; मे my; दिव्यं divine; एवं thus: यः who; वेत्ति knows; तत्त्वतः from (in) reality; त्यक्त्वा having abandoned; देहं the body; पुनः again; जन्म to birth; न not; एति comes; माम् to me; एति comes; सः he; अर्जुन O Arjuna.

वीतरागभयक्रोधा मन्मया मामुपाश्रिताः ।
बहवो ज्ञानतपसा पूता मद्भावमागताः ॥ १० ॥

Freed from passion, fear and anger, filled with Me, taking refuge in Me, purified in the fire of wisdom, many have entered into My being. (10)

वीतरागभयक्रोधाः = वीतः रागः च भयं च क्रोधः च येषां ते gone, desire, and, fear, and, anger, and, whose, they; मन्मया full of me; माम् to me; उपाश्रिताः resorting; बहवः many; ज्ञानतपसा = ज्ञानस्य तपसा of wisdom, by the austerity; पूताः purified; मद्भावम् = मम भावम् (to) my being; आगताः (have) come.

ये यथा मां प्रपद्यंते तांस्तथैव भजाम्यहम् ।
मम वर्त्मानुवर्तंते मनुष्याः पार्थ सर्वशः ॥ ११ ॥

However men approach Me, even so do I welcome them, for the path men take from every side is Mine, O Pârtha. (11)

ये who; यथा as; माम् to me; प्रपद्यंते approach; तान् them; तथा so; एव even; भजामि welcome; अहं I; मम my; वर्त्म path; अनुवर्तंते follow; मनुष्याः men; पार्थ O Pârtha; सर्वशः everywhere.

कांक्षंतः कर्मणां सिद्धिं यजंत इह देवताः ।
क्षिप्रं हि मानुषे लोके सिद्धिर्भवति कर्मजा ॥ १२ ॥

They who long after success in action on earth sacrifice to the Shining Ones; for in brief space verily, in this world of men, success is born of action. (12)

कांक्षंतः desiring; कर्मणां of actions; सिद्धिं success; यजंते (they) sacrifice to; इह here; देवताः the Shining Ones; क्षिप्रं quickly; हि indeed; मानुषे in the human; लोके (in the) world; सिद्धिः success; भवति is; कर्मजा karma-born.

चातुर्वर्ण्यं मया सृष्टं गुणकर्मविभागशः।
तस्य कर्तारमपि मां विद्ध्यकर्तारमव्ययम् ॥ १३ ॥

The four castes were emanated by Me, by the different distribution of qualities and actions; know Me to be the author of them, though the actionless and inexhaustible. (13)

चातुर्वर्ण्यं the four castes; मया by me; सृष्टं emanated; गुणकर्मविभागशः = गुणानाम् च कर्मणाम् च विभागशः of qualities and of actions, and, by division; तस्य of it; कर्तारम् the author; अपि also; माम् me; विद्धि know; अकर्तारम् unacting; अव्ययम् inexhaustible.

न मां कर्माणि लिंपंति न मे कर्मफले स्पृहा।
इति मां योऽभिजानाति कर्मभिर्न स बध्यते॥ १४॥

Nor do actions affect Me, nor is the fruit of action desired by Me. He who thus knoweth Me is not bound by actions. (14)

न not; माम् me; कर्माणि actions; लिंपंति stain; न not; मे of me; कर्मफले = कर्मणः फले of action, in the fruit; स्पृहा desire;

इति thus; माम् me; यः who; अभिजानाति knows; कर्मभिः by actions; न not; सः he; बध्यते is bound.

एवं ज्ञात्वा कृतं कर्म पूर्वैरपि मुमुक्षुभिः ।
कुरु कर्मैव तस्मात्त्वं पूर्वैः पूर्वतरं कृतम् ॥१५॥

Having thus known, our forefathers, ever seeking liberation, performed action; therefore do thou also perform action, as did our forefathers in the olden time. (15)

एवं thus; ज्ञात्वा having known; कृतं (was) done; कर्म action; पूर्वैः by ancients; अपि also; मुमुक्षुभिः (by) desirous of mokṣha; कुरु do; कर्म action; एव even; तस्मात् therefore; त्वं thou; पूर्वैः by ancients; पूर्वतरं (in the) past; कृतम् done.

किं कर्म किमकर्मेति कवयोऽप्यत्र मोहिताः ।
तत्ते कर्म प्रवक्ष्यामि यज्ज्ञात्वा मोक्ष्यसेऽशुभात्॥१६॥

"What is action, what inaction?" Even the wise are herein perplexed. Therefore I will declare to thee the action by knowing which thou shalt be loosed from evil. (16)

किं what; कर्म action; किं what; अकर्म inaction; इति thus; कवयः poets; अपि also; अत्र here; मोहिताः (are) confused; तत् that (therefore); ते of (to) thee; कर्म action; प्रवक्ष्यामि will (I) declare; यत् which; ज्ञात्वा having known; मोक्ष्यसे (thou) shalt be freed; अशुभात् from sin.

कर्मणो ह्यपि बोद्धव्यं बोद्धव्यं च विकर्मणः ।
अकर्मणश्च बोद्धव्यं गहना कर्मणो गतिः ॥१७॥

It is needful to discriminate action, to discriminate unlawful action, and to discriminate inaction; mysterious is the path of action. (17)

कर्मण: of action; हि indeed; अपि also; बोद्धव्यं should be known; बोद्धव्यं should be known; च and; विकर्मण: of wrong action; अकर्मण: of inaction; च and; बोद्धव्यं should be known; गहना deep; कर्मण: of action; गति: the path.

कर्मण्यकर्म यः पश्येदकर्मणि च कर्म यः ।
स बुद्धिमान्मनुष्येषु स युक्तः कृत्स्नकर्मकृत् ॥१८॥

He who seeth inaction in action, and action in inaction, he is wise among men, he is harmonious, even while performing all action. (18)

कर्मणि in action; अकर्म inaction; य: who; पश्येत् may see; अकर्मणि in inaction; च and; कर्म action; य: who; सः he; बुद्धिमान् wise; मनुष्येषु in men; स: he; युक्त: balanced; कृत्स्नकर्मकृत् = कृत्स्नं कर्म करोति य: स: all, action, does, who, he.

यस्य सर्वे समारंभाः कामसंकल्पवर्जिताः ।
ज्ञानाग्निदग्धकर्माणं तमाहुः पंडितं बुधाः ॥१९॥

Whose works are all free from the moulding of desire, whose actions are burned up by the fire of wisdom, him the wise have called a Sage. (19)

यस्य of whom; सर्वे all; समारंभा: beginnings; कामसंकल्पवर्जिता: = कामै: च संकल्पै: च वर्जिता: by desire, and, by imaginations, and, untouched; ज्ञानाग्निदग्धकर्माणं = ज्ञानस्य अग्निना दग्धानि कर्माणि यस्य तं of knowledge, by the fire, consumed, actions, whose, him; तम् him; आहु: call; पंडितं learned; बुधा: wise.

त्यक्त्वा कर्मफलासंगं नित्यतृप्तो निराश्रय:।
कर्मण्यभिप्रवृत्तोऽपि नैव किंचित्करोति स:॥२०॥

Having abandoned attachment to the fruit of action, always content, nowhere seeking refuge, he is not doing anything, although doing actions. (20)

त्यक्त्वा having abandoned; कर्मफलासंगं = कर्मण: फले आसंगं of action, in (to) the fruit, attachment, नित्यतृप्त: always-contented; निराश्रय: without dependence; कर्मणि in action; अभिप्रवृत्त: engaged; अपि also; न not; एव even; किंचित् anything; करोति does; स: he.

निराशीर्यतचित्तात्मा त्यक्तसर्वपरिग्रह:।
शारीरं केवलं कर्म कुर्वन्नाप्नोति किल्बिषम्॥२१॥

Hoping for naught, his mind and self controlled, having abandoned all greed, performing action by the body alone he doth not commit sin. (21)

निराशी: not hoping, (wishing); यताचित्तात्मा = यतं चित्तं च आत्मा च यस्य स: = controlled, mind, and, self, and, whose, he; त्यक्तसर्वपरिग्रह: = त्यक्त: सर्व: परिग्रहो येन स: abandoned, all, taking, by whom, he; शारीरं bodily; केवलं only; कर्म action; कुर्वन् doing; न not; आप्नोति obtains; किल्बिषम् sin.

यदृच्छालाभसंतुष्टो द्वंद्वातीतो विमत्सरः।
समः सिद्धावसिद्धौ च कृत्वापि न निबध्यते॥२२॥

Content with whatsoever he obtaineth without effort, free from the pairs of opposites, without envy, balanced in success and failure, though acting he is not bound. (22)

यदृच्छालाभसंतुष्टः = यदृच्छया लाभेन संतुष्टः by chance, with gain, contented; द्वंद्वातीतः = द्वंद्वं अतीतः the pairs, gone beyond; विमत्सरः un-envious; समः equal; सिद्धौ in success; अ-सिद्धौ in non-success; च and; कृत्वा having done; अपि even; न not निबध्यते is bound.

गतसंगस्य मुक्तस्य ज्ञानावस्थितचेतसः।
यज्ञायाचरतः कर्म समग्रं प्रविलीयते ॥ २३ ॥

Of one with attachment dead, harmonious, with his thoughts established in wisdom, his works sacrifices, all action melts away. (23)

गतसंगस्य = गतः संगः यस्य तस्य gone, attachment, whose, of him; मुक्तस्य of the liberated; ज्ञानावस्थितचेतसः = ज्ञाने अवस्थितं चेतः यस्य तस्य in wisdom, established, mind, whose, his; यज्ञाय for sacrifice; आचरतः (of) acting; कर्म action; समग्रं entirely; प्रविलीयते is dissolved.

ब्रह्मार्पणं ब्रह्म हविर्ब्रह्माग्नौ ब्रह्मणा हुतम् ।
ब्रह्मैव तेन गंतव्यं ब्रह्मकर्मसमाधिना ॥ २४ ॥

The ETERNAL the oblation, the ETERNAL the clarified butter, are offered in the ETERNAL the fire by the ETERNAL; unto the ETERNAL verily shall he go who in his action meditateth wholly upon the ETERNAL. (24)

ब्रह्म Brahman; अर्पणं (the act) of offering; ब्रह्म Brahman; हविः the offering (the thing offered); ब्रह्माग्नौ = ब्रह्मण: अग्नौ of Brahman, in the fire; ब्रह्मणा by Brahman; हुतम् (is) offered: ब्रह्म Brahman; एव only; तेन by him; गंतव्यं (is) to be attained, ब्रह्मकर्मसमाधिना = ब्रह्म एव कर्म तस्मिन् समाधिः यस्य तेन Brahman, only, action, in that, meditation, whose, by him;

दैवमेवापरे यज्ञं योगिनः पर्युपासते ।
ब्रह्माग्नावपरे यज्ञं यज्ञेनैवोपजुह्वति ॥ २५ ॥

Some Yogîs offer up sacrifice to the Shining Ones; others sacrifice only by pouring sacrifice into the fire of the ETERNAL; (25)

दैवम् divine; एव only; अपरे some; यज्ञं sacrifice; योगिनः yogis; पर्युपासते practise; ब्रह्माग्नौ = ब्रह्मण: अग्नौ of Brahman, in the fire; अपरे others; यज्ञं sacrifice; यज्ञेन by sacrifice; एव even; उपजुह्वति offer up.

श्रोत्रादीनींद्रियाण्यन्ये संयमाग्निषु जुह्वति ।
शब्दादीन्विषयानन्य इंद्रियाग्निषु जुह्वति ॥ २६ ॥

Some pour as sacrifice hearing and the other senses into the fires of restraint; some pour sound and the other objects of sense into the fires of the senses as sacrifice; (26)

श्रोत्रादीनि = श्रोत्रं आदिः येषाम् तानि hearing, the beginning, whose, them; इंद्रियाणि the senses; अन्ये others; संयमाग्निषु = संयमस्य अग्निषु of restraint (concentration), in the fires; जुह्वति sacrifice; शब्दादीन् = शब्दः आदिः येषाम् तान् sound, the beginning, whose, them; विषयान् sense-objects; अन्ये others इंद्रियाग्निषु = इंद्रियाणाम् अग्निषु of the senses, in the fires; जुह्वति sacrifice;

सर्वाणींद्रियकर्माणि प्राणकर्माणि चापरे ।
आत्मसंयमयोगाग्नौ जुह्वति ज्ञानदीपिते ॥ २७ ॥

Others again into the wisdom-kindled fire of union attained by self-control, pour as sacrifice all the functions of the senses and the functions of life; (27)

सर्वाणि all; इंद्रियकर्माणि = इंद्रियाणाम् कर्माणि of the senses, actions; प्राणकर्माणि = प्राणस्य कर्माणि of the breath, actions; च and; अपरे others; आत्मसंयमयोगाग्नौ = आत्मनः संयम एव योगः तस्य अग्नौ of the self, the restraint, even, yoga, of that, in the fire; जुह्वति sacrifice; ज्ञानदीपिते = ज्ञानेन दीपिते by wisdom, lighted.

द्रव्ययज्ञास्तपोयज्ञा योगयज्ञास्तथाऽपरे ।
स्वाध्यायज्ञानयज्ञाश्च यतयः संशितव्रताः ॥२८॥

Yet others the sacrifice of wealth, the sacrifice of austerity, the sacrifice of yoga, the sacrifice of silent reading and wisdom, men concentrated and of effectual vows; (28)

द्रव्ययज्ञाः = द्रव्येण यज्ञः येषां ते by substances, sacrifice, whose, they; तपोयज्ञाः = तपः यज्ञः येषां ते austerity, sacrifice, whose, they; योगयज्ञाः = योगः यज्ञः येषां ते yoga, sacrifice, whose, they; तथा so; अपरे others; स्वाध्यायज्ञानयज्ञाः = स्वाध्यायः च ज्ञानं च यज्ञः येषां ते, study, and, knowledge, and, sacrifice, whose, they; च and; यतयः the restrained (anchorites); संशितव्रताः = संशितं व्रतं येषाम् ते sharp (difficult), vows, whose, they.

अपाने जुह्वति प्राणं प्राणेऽपानं तथाऽपरे ।

प्राणापानगती रुद्ध्वा प्राणायामपरायणाः ॥ २९ ॥

Yet others pour as sacrifice the outgoing breath in the incoming, and the incoming in the outgoing, restraining the flow of the outgoing and incoming breaths, solely absorbed in the control of breathing; (29)

अपाने in incoming breath; जुह्वति sacrifice; प्राणं outgoing breath; प्राणे in outgoing breath; अपानं incoming breath; तथा thus; अपरे others; प्राणापानगती = प्राणस्य च अपानस्य च गती, of prâṇa, and, of apâna, (the two) courses; रुद्ध्वा having restrained; प्राणायामपरायणाः = प्राणायामः परायणं येषां ते prâṇâyâma, final refuge, whose, they.

अपरे नियताहाराः प्राणान्प्राणेषु जुह्वति ।

सर्वेऽप्येते यज्ञविदो यज्ञक्षपितकल्मषाः ॥ ३० ॥

Others, regular in food, pour as sacrifice their life-breaths in life-breaths. All these are knowers of sacrifice, and by sacrifice have destroyed their sins. (30)

अपरे others; नियताहाराः = नियतः आहारः येषाम् ते restrained, food, whose, they; प्राणान् life-breaths; प्राणेषु in life-breaths; जुह्वति sacrifice; सर्वे all; अपि also; एते these; यज्ञविदः sacrifice-knowers; यज्ञक्षपितकल्मषाः = यज्ञेन क्षपितः कल्मषः येषाम् ते by sacrifice, thrown away, sins, whose, they.

यज्ञशिष्टामृतभुजो यांति ब्रह्म सनातनम् ।
नायं लोकोऽस्त्ययज्ञस्य कुतोऽन्यः कुरुसत्तम ॥३१॥

The eaters of the life-giving remains of sacrifice go to the changeless ETERNAL. This world is not for the non-sacrificer, much less the other, O best of the Kurus. (31)

यज्ञशिष्टामृतभुजः = यज्ञस्य शिष्टं अमृतं भुंजंति ये ते of the sacrifice, remains, immortal (ambrosia) eat, who, they; यांति go; ब्रह्म to Brahman; सनातनम् eternal; न not; अयम् this; लोकः world; अस्ति is; अ-यज्ञस्य of the non-sacrificer; कुतः whence; अन्यः other; कुरुसत्तम = कुरूणाम सत्तम of the Kurus, O best.

एवं बहुविधा यज्ञा वितता ब्रह्मणो मुखे ।
कर्मजान्विद्धि तान्सर्वानेवं ज्ञात्वा विमोक्ष्यसे ॥३२॥

Many and various sacrifices are thus spread out before the ETERNAL.[1] Know thou that all these are born of action, and thus knowing thou shalt be free. (32)

[1] "In the Vedas" is another interpretation.

एवं thus; बहुविधाः manifold; यज्ञाः sacrifices; वितताः spread; ब्रह्मणः of Brahman (or Veda); मुखे in the face; कर्मजान् action-born; विद्धि know (thou); तान् them; सर्वान् all; एवं thus; ज्ञात्वा having known; विमोक्ष्यसे thou shalt be freed.

श्रेयान्द्रव्यमयाद्यज्ञाज्ज्ञानयज्ञः परंतप ।
सर्वं कर्माखिलं पार्थ ज्ञाने परिसमाप्यते ॥ ३३ ॥

Better than the sacrifice of any objects is the sacrifice of wisdom, O Parantapa. All actions in their entirety, O Pârtha, culminate in wisdom. (33)

श्रेयान् better; द्रव्यमयात् (than) made up of objects; यज्ञात् than sacrifice; ज्ञानयज्ञः = ज्ञानस्य यज्ञः of wisdom, the sacrifice; परंतप O Parantapa; सर्वं all; कर्म action; अखिलं without remainder; पार्थ O Pârtha; ज्ञाने in wisdom; परिसमाप्यते is finished.

तद्विद्धि प्रणिपातेन परिप्रश्नेन सेवया ।
उपदेक्ष्यंति ते ज्ञानं ज्ञानिनस्तत्त्वदर्शिनः ॥ ३४ ॥

Learn thou this by discipleship, by investigation, and by service. The wise, the seers of the Essence of things, will instruct thee in wisdom. (34)

तत् that; विद्धि know; प्रणिपातेन by obeisance; परिप्रश्नेन by questioning; सेवया by service; उपदेक्ष्यंति shall teach; ते of (to) thee; ज्ञानं wisdom; ज्ञानिनः the wise; तत्त्वदर्शिनः the truth-seeing.

यज्ज्ञात्वा न पुनर्मोहमेवं यास्यसि पाडव ।
येन भूतान्यशेषेण द्रक्ष्यस्यात्मन्यथो मयि ॥ ३५ ॥

And having known this, thou shalt not again fall into this confusion, O Pâṇḍava; for by this thou wilt see all beings without exception in the SELF, and thus in Me. (35)

यत् that; ज्ञात्वा having known; न not; पुनः again; मोहम् delusion; एवं thus; यास्यसि (thou) shalt go; पांडव O Pâṇḍava; येन by this; भूतानि creatures; अ-शेषेण (by) without-remainder; द्रक्ष्यसि (thou) shalt see; आत्मनि in the self; अथो that is; मयि in me.

अपि चेदसि पापेभ्यः सर्वेभ्यः पापकृत्तमः ।
सर्वं ज्ञानप्लवेनैव वृजिनं संतरिष्यसि ॥ ३६ ॥

Even if thou art the most sinful of all sinners, yet shalt thou cross over all sin by the raft of wisdom. (36)

अपि even; चेत् if; असि (thou) art; पापेभ्यः than sinners; सर्वेभ्यः (than) all; पापकृत्तमः most-sin-doing; सर्वं all; ज्ञानप्लवेन = ज्ञानस्य प्लवेन of wisdom, by the raft; एव only; वृजिनं sin; संतरिष्यसि (thou) shalt cross over.

यथैधांसि समिद्धोऽग्निर्भस्मसात्कुरुतेऽर्जुन ।
ज्ञानाग्निः सर्वकर्माणि भस्मसात्कुरुते तथा ॥३७॥

As the burning fire reduces fuel to ashes, O Arjuna, so doth the fire of wisdom reduce all actions to ashes. (37)

यथा as; एधांसि fuels; समिद्धः kindled; अग्निः fire; भस्मसात्

(to) ashes; कुरुते makes; अर्जुन O Arjuna; ज्ञानाग्निः = ज्ञानस्य अग्निः of wisdom, fire; सर्वकर्माणि = सर्वाणि कर्माणि all actions; भस्मसात् (to) ashes; कुरुते makes; तथा so.

नहि ज्ञानेन सदृशं पवित्रमिह विद्यते।
तत्स्वयं योगसंसिद्धः कालेनात्मनि विंदति ॥ ३८॥

Verily there is no purifier in this world like wisdom; he that is perfected in yoga finds it in the SELF in due season. (38)

नहि not; ज्ञानेन by (to) wisdom; सदृशं similar; पवित्रम् purifier; इह here; विद्यते is: तत् that; स्वयं itself; योगसंसिद्धः = योगे संसिद्धः in yoga, perfected; कालेन by (in) time; आत्मनि in the self; विंदति finds.

श्रद्धावाँल्लभते ज्ञानं तत्परः संयतेन्द्रियः।
ज्ञानं लब्ध्वा परां शांतिमचिरेणाधिगच्छति ॥ ३९॥

The man who is full of faith obtaineth wisdom, and he also who hath mastery over his senses; and having obtained wisdom he goeth swiftly to the Supreme Peace. (39)

श्रद्धावान् the faithful; लभते obtains; ज्ञानं wisdom; तत्परः intent; संयतेन्द्रियः = संयतानि इंद्रियाणि यस्य सः controlled, senses, whose he; ज्ञानं wisdom; लब्ध्वा having obtained; परां (to) the highest; शांतिम् to peace; अ-चिरेण without-delay; अधिगच्छति goes

अज्ञश्चाश्रद्दधानश्च संशयात्मा विनश्यति ।
नायं लोकोऽस्ति न परो न सुखं संशयात्मनः ॥४०॥

But the ignorant, faithless, doubting self goeth to destruction; nor this world, nor that beyond, nor happiness, is there for the doubting self. (40)

अ-ज्ञः un-knowing; च and; अ-श्रद्दधानः non-believing; च and; संशयात्मा = संशयः आत्मा यस्य सः: doubt, self, whose, he; विनश्यति is destroyed; न not; अयं this; लोकः world; अस्ति is; न not; परः beyond; न not; सुखं happiness; संशयात्मनः of (for) the doubting-self.

योगसंन्यस्तकर्माणं ज्ञानसंछिन्नसंशयम् ।
आत्मवंतं न कर्माणि निबध्नंति धनंजय ॥ ४१॥

He who hath renounced action by yoga, who hath cloven asunder doubt by wisdom, who is ruled by the SELF[1], actions do not bind him, O Dhanañjaya. (41)

योगसंन्यस्तकर्माणं = योगेन संन्यस्तं कर्म येनतं by Yoga, renounced, action, by whom, him; ज्ञानसंछिन्नसंशयम् = ज्ञानेन संछिन्नः संशयः यस्य सः by knowledge, cut away, doubt, whose, him, आत्मवंतं possessing the Self; न not; कर्माणि actions; निबध्नंति bind; धनंजय O Dhanañjaya.

तस्मादज्ञानसंभूतं हृत्स्थं ज्ञानासिनाऽऽत्मनः ।
छित्त्वैनं संशयं योगमातिष्ठोत्तिष्ठ भारत ॥४२।

---

1 Madhusûdana explains *âtmavantam* as "always watchful."

Therefore, with the sword of the wisdom of the SELF cleaving asunder this ignorance-born doubt, dwelling in thy heart, be established in yoga. Stand up, O Bhârata. (42)

तस्मात् therefore; अज्ञानसंभूतं = अज्ञानात् संभूतम from ignorance, born; हृत्स्थं heart-seated; ज्ञानासिना = ज्ञानस्य असिना of wisdom, by the sword; आत्मनः of the Self; छित्त्वा having cloven; एनं this; संशयं doubt; योगम् yoga; आतिष्ठ practice; उत्तिष्ठ stand up; भारत O Bhârata.

इति श्रीमद्भगवद्गीतासूप० ज्ञानविभागयोगो नाम चतुर्थोऽध्यायः ।

Thus in the glorious BHAGAVAD-GÎTÂ ...the fourth discourse, entitled:

THE YOGA OF WISDOM.

FIFTH DISCOURSE.

अर्जुन उवाच ।

संन्यासं कर्मणां कृष्ण पुनर्योगं च शंससि ।
यच्छ्रेय एतयोरेकं तन्मे ब्रूहि सुनिश्चितम् ॥ १ ॥

Arjuna said:

Renunciation of actions, thou praisest, O Kṛishṇa, and then also yoga. Of the two which one is the better? That tell me conclusively. (1)

संन्यासम् renunciation ; कर्मणां of actions ; कृष्ण O Kṛishṇa ; पुनः again ; योगं yoga ; च and ; शंससि praisest (thou) ; यत् which ; श्रेयः better ; एतयोः of these two ; एकं one ; तत् that ; मे of (to) me ; ब्रूहि speak ; सुनिश्चितम् well-determined.

श्रीभगवानुवाच ।

संन्यासः कर्मयोगश्च निःश्रेयसकरावुभौ ।
तयोस्तु कर्मसंन्यासात्कर्मयोगो विशिष्यते ॥ २ ॥

The Blessed Lord said :

Renunciation and yoga by action both lead to the highest bliss; of the two, yoga by action is verily better than renunciation of action. (2)

संन्यासः renunciation ; कर्मयोगः action-yoga ; च and ; निःश्रेयसकरौ (two) highest-happiness-makers ; उभौ both ; तयोः of these two ; तु indeed ; कर्मसंन्यासात् = कर्मणः संन्यासात्

of action, than renunciation ; कर्मयोगः action-yoga ; विशिष्यते excels.

ज्ञेयः स नित्यसंन्यासी यो न द्वेष्टि न काङ्क्षति ।
निर्द्वंद्वो हि महाबाहो सुखं बंधात्प्रमुच्यते ॥ ३ ॥

He should be known as a perpetual ascetic, who neither hateth nor desireth ; free from the pairs of opposites, O mighty-armed, he is easily set free from bondage. (3)

ज्ञेयः should be known ; सः he ; नित्य-संन्यासी constant-renouncer; यः who ; न not ; द्वेष्टि hates ; न not ; कांक्षति desires ; निर्द्वंद्वः without the pairs (of opposites) ; हि indeed ; महाबाहो O mighty-armed ; सुखं easily ; बंधात् from bondage ; प्रमुच्यते is freed.

सांख्ययोगौ पृथग्बालाः प्रवदंति न पंडिताः ।
एकमप्यास्थितः सम्यगुभयोर्विंदते फलम् ॥ ४ ॥

Children, not Sages, speak of the Sâṅkhya and Yoga as different ; he who is duly established in one obtaineth the fruits of both. (4)

सांख्ययोगौ = सांख्यः च योगः च Sâṅkhya, and, Yoga, and ; पृथक् separate ; बालाः children ; प्रवदंति say ; न not ; पंडिताः the wise ; एकं one ; अपि even ; आस्थितः established (in) ; सम्यक् together with ; उभयोः of both ; विंदते obtains ; फलं the fruit,

यत्सांख्यैः प्राप्यते स्थानं तद्योगैरपि गम्यते ।

एकं साख्यं च याग चं यः पश्यति स पश्यति ॥५॥

That place which is gained by the Sâṅkhyas is reached by the Yogas also. He seeth who seeth that the Sâṅkhya and the Yoga are one. (5)

यत् that; सांख्यैः by the Sâṅkhyas; प्राप्यते is obtained; स्थानं place; तत् that; योगैः by the Yogas; अपि also; गम्यते is gone to; एकं one; सांख्यं the Sâṅkhya; च and; योगं the yoga; च and; यः who; पश्यति sees; सः he; पश्यति sees.

संन्यासस्तु महाबाहो दुःखमाप्तुमयोगतः ।
योगयुक्तो मुनिर्ब्रह्म न चिरेणाधिगच्छति ॥ ६ ॥

But without yoga, O mighty-armed, renunciation is hard to attain to; the yoga-harmonised Muni swiftly goeth to the ETERNAL. (6)

संन्यासः renunciation; तु indeed; महाबाहो O mighty-armed; दुःखम् hard; आप्तुम् to obtain; अयोगतः from non-yoga; (without yoga); योगयुक्तः = योगेन युक्तः with yoga, joined; मुनिः muni; ब्रह्म to Brahman; न not; चिरेण by a long time; अधिगच्छति goes.

योगयुक्तो विशुद्धात्मा विजितात्मा जितेन्द्रियः ।
सर्वभूतात्मभूतात्मा कुर्वन्नपि न लिप्यते ॥ ७ ॥

He who is harmonised by yoga, the self purified, SELF-ruled, the senses subdued, whose SELF is the SELF of all beings, although acting he is not affected. (7)

योगयुक्तः yoga-united ; विशुद्धात्मा = विशुद्धः आत्मा यस्य सः pure, self, whom, he ; जितेन्द्रियः = जितानि इंद्रियाणि येन सः conquered, senses, by whom, he ; सर्वभूतात्मभूतात्मा = सर्वेषाम् भूतानाम् आत्मा भूतः आत्मा यस्य सः of all, (of) beings, the Self, become, the Self, whose, he ; कुर्वन् acting ; अपि even ; न not ; लिप्यते is affected.

नैव किंचित्करोमीति युक्तो मन्येत तत्त्ववित् ।
पश्यन्श्रृण्वन्स्पृशन्जिघ्रन्नश्नन्गच्छन्स्वपन्श्वसन् ॥८॥

"I do not anything," should think the harmonised one, who knoweth the Essence of things ; seeing, hearing, touching, smelling, eating, moving, sleeping, breathing, (8)

न not ; एव even ; किंचित् anything ; करोमि (I) do ; इति thus ; युक्तः the joined (one) ; मन्यते thinks ; तत्त्ववित् the essence-knower ; पश्यन् seeing ; शृण्वन् hearing ; स्पृशन् touching ; जिघ्रन् smelling ; अश्नन् eating ; गच्छन् going ; स्वपन् sleeping ; श्वसन् breathing.

प्रलपन्विसृजन्गृह्णन्नुन्मिषन्निमिषन्नपि ।
इन्द्रियाणीन्द्रियार्थेषु वर्तंत इति धारयन् ॥ ९ ॥

Speaking, giving, grasping, opening and closing the eyes, he holdeth : "The senses move among the objects of the senses." (9)

प्रलपन् speaking ; विसृजन् giving ; गृह्णन् grasping ; उन्मिषन् opening (the eyes) ; निमिषन् closing (the eyes) ; अपि also ;

इन्द्रियाणि the senses; इन्द्रियार्थेषु = इन्द्रियाणाम् अर्थेषु of the senses, in the objects; वर्तंते exist (move); इति thus; धारयन् maintaining.

ब्रह्मण्याधाय कर्माणि संगं त्यक्त्वा करोति यः ।
लिप्यते न स पापेन पद्मपत्रमिवांभसा ॥ १० ॥

He who acteth, placing all actions in the ETERNAL, abandoning attachment, is unaffected by sin as a lotus leaf by the waters. (10)

ब्रह्मणि in Brahman; आधाय having placed; कर्माणि actions; संगं attachment; त्यक्त्वा having abandoned; करोति acts; यः who; लिप्यते is affected; न not; सः he; पापेन by sin; पद्मपत्रम् = पद्मस्य पत्रम् of the lotus, the leaf; इव like; अंभसा by water.

कायेन मनसा बुद्ध्या केवलैरिन्द्रियैरपि ।
योगिनः कर्म कुर्वंति संगं त्यक्त्वाऽऽत्मशुद्धये ॥ ११ ॥

Yogîs, having abandoned attachment, perform action only by the body, by the mind, by the Reason, and even by the senses, for the purification of the self. (11)

कायेन by the body; मनसा by the mind: बुद्ध्या by the reason; केवलैः (by) only; इंन्द्रियैः by the senses: अपि also; योगिनः yogîs; कर्म action; कुर्वन्ति perform; संगं attachment; त्यक्त्वा having abandoned; आत्मशुद्धये = आत्मनः शुद्धये of the self, for the purification.

युक्तः कर्मफलं त्यक्त्वा शांतिमाप्नोति नैष्ठिकीम् ।
अयुक्तः कामकारेण फले सक्तो निबध्यते ॥१२॥

The harmonised man, having abandoned the fruit of action, attaineth to the eternal Peace; the non-harmonised, impelled by desire, attached to fruit, are bound. (12)

युक्तः the united one ; कर्मफलं = कर्मणः फलं of action, the fruit; त्यक्त्वा having abandoned ; शान्तिम् peace ; आप्नोति odtains; नैष्ठिकीम् final ; अयुक्तः the non-united one ; कामकारेण = कामस्य कारेण of desire, by the impulsion ; फले in (to) fruit ; सक्तः attached ; निबध्यते is bound.

सर्वकर्माणि मनसा संन्यस्यास्ते सुखं वशी ।
नवद्वारे पुरे देही नैव कुर्वन्न कारयन् ॥ १३ ॥

Mentally renouncing all actions, the sovereign dweller in the body resteth serenely in the nine-gated city, [1] neither acting nor causing to act. (13)

सर्वकर्माणि all actions (as before); मनसा by the mind; संन्यस्य having abandoned; आस्ते sits; सुखं happy; वशी the ruler (of himself); नवद्वारे (in) the nine-gated; पुरे in the city; देही the embodied; न not; एव even; कुर्वन् acting; न not; कारयन् causing action.

न कर्तृत्वं न कर्माणि लोकस्य सृजति प्रभुः ।

1 The body, often called the city of Brahman.

न कर्मफलसंयोगं स्वभावस्तु प्रवर्तते ॥ १४ ॥

The Lord of the world produceth not the idea of agency, nor actions, nor the union together of action and its fruit; nature, however, manifesteth. (14)

न not; कर्तृत्वं agency; न not; कर्माणि actions; लोकस्य of the world; सृजति emanates; प्रभुः the Lord; न not; कर्मफलसंयोगं = कर्मणः च फलस्य च संयोगं of action, and, of fruit, and, the union; स्वभावः own-nature; तु indeed; प्रवर्तते exists forth (manifests).

नादत्ते कस्यचित्पापं न चैव सुकृतं विभुः ।
अज्ञानेनावृतं ज्ञानं तेन मुह्यंति जंतवः ॥ १५ ॥

The Lord accepteth neither the evil-doing nor yet the well-doing of any. Wisdom is enveloped by unwisdom; therewith mortals are deluded. (15)

न not; आदत्ते takes; कस्यचित् of anyone; पापं sin; न not; च and; एव even; सुकृतं virtue; विभुः the Lord; अज्ञानेन by ignorance; आवृतं enveloped; ज्ञानं wisdom; तेन by this; मुह्यंति are deceived; जंतवः beings.

ज्ञानेन तु तदज्ञानं येषां नाशितमात्मनः ।
तेषामादित्यवज्ज्ञानं प्रकाशयति तत्परम् ॥ १६ ॥

Verily, in whom unwisdom is destroyed by the wisdom of the SELF, in them wisdom, shining as the sun, reveals the Supreme. (16)

ज्ञानेन by wisdom; तु indeed; तत् that; अज्ञानं ignorance; येषाम् of whom; नाशितम् (is) destroyed; आत्मनः of the Self; तेषाम् of them; आदित्यवत् sunlike; ज्ञानं wisdom; प्रकाशयति shines forth; तत्परं that highest.

तद्बुद्धयस्तदात्मानस्तन्निष्ठास्तत्परायणाः ।
गच्छंत्यपुनरावृत्तिं ज्ञाननिर्धूतकल्मषाः ॥ १७ ॥

Thinking on THAT, merged in THAT, stablished in THAT, solely devoted to THAT, they go whence there is no return, their sins dispelled by wisdom. (17)

तद्बुद्धयः = तस्मिन् बुद्धिः येषां ते in That, mind, whose, they; तदात्मानः = तत् एव आत्मा येषां ते That, only, Self, whose, they; तन्निष्ठाः = तस्मिन् निष्ठा येषां ते in That, establishment, whose, they; तत्परायणाः = तत् परं अयनं येषां ते That, supreme, goal, whose, they; गच्छंति go; अपुनरावृत्तिम् (to) not-again-returning; ज्ञाननिर्धूतकल्मषाः = ज्ञानेन निर्धूताः कल्मषाः येषाम् ते by wisdom, dispelled, sin, whose, they.

विद्याविनयसम्पन्ने ब्राह्मणे गवि हस्तिनि ।
शुनि चैव श्वपाके च पंडिताः समदर्शिनः ॥ १८ ॥

Sages look equally on a Brâhmaṇa adorned with learning and humility, a cow, an elephant, and even a dog, and an outcaste. (18)

विद्याविनयसंपन्ने = विद्यया च विनयेन च संपन्ने with learning, and, with modesty, and, (in) endowed; ब्राह्मणे in (on a) Brâhmaṇa; गवि in (on a) cow; हस्तिनि in (on an) elephant;

शुनि in (on a) dog; च and; एव even; श्वपाके in (on an) outcaste;[1] च and; पंडिताः paṇḍits; समदर्शिनः equal-seeing.

इहैव तैर्जितः सर्गो येषा साम्ये स्थितं मनः ।
निर्दोषं हि समं ब्रह्म तस्माद्ब्रह्मणि ते स्थिताः ॥ १९॥

Even here on earth everything is overcome by those whose mind remains balanced; the ETERNAL is incorruptible and balanced; therefore they are established in the ETERNAL. (19)

इह here, एव even; तैः by those; जितः conquered; सर्गः rebirth or creation; येषाम् of whom; साम्ये in equality; स्थितं established; मनः mind; निर्दोषं spotless; हि indeed; समं equal; ब्रह्म Brahman; तस्मात् therefore; ब्रह्मणि in Brahman; ते they; स्थिताः established.

न प्रहृष्येत्प्रियं प्राप्य नोद्विजेत्प्राप्य चाऽप्रियम् ।
स्थिरबुद्धिरसंमूढो ब्रह्मविद्ब्रह्मणि स्थितः ॥ २० ॥

With Reason firm, unperplexed, the knower of the ETERNAL, established in the ETERNAL, neither rejoiceth on obtaining what is pleasant, nor sorroweth on obtaining what is unpleasant. (20)

न not; प्रहृष्येत् let (him) rejoice; प्रियम् the pleasant; प्राप्य having obtained; न not; उद्विजेत् let (him) be agitated; प्राप्य having obtained; च and; अप्रियम् the unpleasant; स्थिरबुद्धिः = स्थिरा बुद्धिः यस्य सः firm, reason, whose, he; असंमूढः unbewild-

[1] श्वानं पचति, he who cooks, *i. e.,* eats a dog.

ered ; ब्रह्मवित् Brahman-knower ; ब्रह्मणि in Brahman ; स्थितः established.

बाह्यस्पर्शेष्वसक्तात्मा विंदत्यात्मनि यत्सुखम् ।
स ब्रह्मयोगयुक्तात्मा सुखमक्षय्यमश्नुते ॥ २१ ॥

He whose self is unattached to external contacts, and findeth joy in the SELF, having the self harmonised with the ETERNAL by yoga, enjoys happiness exempt from decay. (21)

बाह्यस्पर्शेषु = बाह्येषु स्पर्शेषु in external, (in) contacts ; असक्तात्मा = असक्तः आत्मा यस्य सः unattached, self, whose, he ; विंदति finds ; आत्मनि in the self ; यत् (that) which ; सुखं pleasure ; सः he ; ब्रह्मयोगयुक्तात्मा = ब्रह्मणि योगेन युक्तः आत्मा यस्य सः in Brahman, by yoga, joined, self, whose, he ; सुखं pleasure ; अक्षय्यं imperishable ; अश्नुते enjoys.

ये हि संस्पर्शजा भोगा दुःखयोनय एव ते ।
आद्यंतवंतः कौंतेय न तेषु रमते बुधः ॥ २२ ॥

The delights that are contact-born, they are verily wombs of pain, for they have beginning and ending, O Kaunteya ; not in them may rejoice the wise. (22)

ये (those) which ; हि indeed ; संस्पर्शजाः contact-born ; भोगाः enjoyments ; दुःखयोनयः = दुःखस्य योनयः of sorrow, wombs ; एव only ; ते those ; आद्यंतवंतः having beginning and end ; कौंतेय O Kaunteya ; न not ; तेषु in those ; रमते rejoices ; बुधः the wise.

शक्नोतीहैव यः सोढुं प्राक् शरीरविमोक्षणात् ।
कामक्रोधोद्भवं वेगं स युक्तः स सुखी नरः ॥ २३ ॥

He who is able to endure here on earth, ere he be liberated from the body, the force born from desire and passion, he is harmonised, he is a happy man. (23)

शक्नोति is able to; इह here; एव even; यः who; सोढुं to bear; प्राक् before; शरीरविमोक्षणात् = शरीरात् विमोक्षणात् from the body, (from) liberation; कामक्रोधोद्भवं = कामात् च क्रोधात् च उद्भवः यस्य तं from desire, and, from anger, and, birth, whose, it; वेगं force; सः he; युक्तः united; सः he; सुखी happy; नरः man.

योऽन्तःसुखोऽन्तरारामस्तथान्तर्ज्योतिरेव यः ।
स योगी ब्रह्मनिर्वाणं ब्रह्मभूतोऽधिगच्छति ॥ २४ ॥

He who is happy within, who rejoiceth within, who is illuminated within, that Yogî, becoming the ETERNAL, goeth to the Peace of the ETERNAL. (24)

यः who; अंतःसुखः = अंतः (आत्मनि) सुखं यस्य सः inward, (in the self), pleasure, whose, he; अंतरारामः = अंतः (आत्मनि) आरामः यस्य सः inward, (in the self), enjoyment, whose, he; तथा so (too); अंतर्ज्योतिः = अंतः (आत्मनि) ज्योतिः यस्य सः inward, (in the self), light, whose, he; एव even; यः who; सः that; योगी yogî; ब्रह्मनिर्वाणं = ब्रह्मणः निर्वाणं of Brahman, to the nirvâṇa; ब्रह्मभूतः Brahman-become; अधिगच्छति goes over.

लभंते ब्रह्मनिर्वाणमृषयः क्षीणकल्मषाः ।

छिन्नद्वैधा यतात्मानः सर्वभूतहिते रताः ॥ २५ ॥

Rişhis, their sins destroyed, their duality removed, their selves controlled, intent upon the welfare of all beings, obtain the Peace of the ETERNAL. (25)

लभंते obtain; ब्रह्मनिर्वाणं the Brahma-Nirvâṇa; ऋषयः the Rişhis; क्षीणकल्मषाः = क्षीणाः कल्मषाः येषाम् ते worn away, sins, whose, they; छिन्नद्वैधाः = छिन्नं द्वैधं येषाम ते cut off, dualities, whose, they; यतात्मानः = यतः आत्मा येषाम् ते controlled, self, whose, they; सर्वभूतहिते = सर्वेषाम् भूतानाम् हिते of all, (of) beings, in the welfare; रताः pleased.

कामक्रोधवियुक्तानां यतीनां यतचेतसाम् ।
अभितो ब्रह्मनिर्वाणं वर्तते विदितात्मनाम् ॥ २६ ॥

The Peace of the ETERNAL lies near to those who know themselves, who are disjoined from desire and passion, subdued in nature, of subdued thoughts. (26)

कामक्रोधवियुक्तानां = कामात् च क्रोधात् च वियुक्तानाम् from desire. and, from anger and, (of) the disjoined; यतीनाम् of the controlled ascetics; यतचेतसाम = यतं चेतः येषाम् तेषाम् controlled, mind, whose, of these; अभितः near; ब्रह्मनिर्वाणं Brahma-nirvâṇa; वर्तते exists; विदितात्मनाम् = विदितः आत्मा येषाम् तेषाम् known, of selves, whose, of those.

स्पर्शान्कृत्वा बहिर्बाह्यांश्चक्षुश्चैवांतरे भ्रुवोः ।
प्राणापानौ समौ कृत्वा नासाभ्यंतरचारिणौ ॥ २७ ॥

Having external contacts excluded, and with gaze fixed between the eye-brows; having made equal the outgoing and incoming breaths moving within the nostrils, (27)

स्पर्शान् contacts; कृत्वा having made; बहिः outside; बाह्यान् external; चक्षुः eye (gaze); च and; एव even, अन्तरे in the middle; भ्रुवोः of the (two) eyebrows; प्राणापानौ = प्राणः च अपानः च incoming breath, and, outgoing breath, and; समौ (two) equal; कृत्वा having made; नासाभ्यन्तरचारिणौ = नासायाः अभ्यंतरे चारिणौ of the nostrils, within, moving.

यतेंद्रियमनोबुद्धिर्मुनिर्मोक्षपरायणः ।
विगतेच्छाभयक्रोधो यः सदा मुक्त एव सः ॥ २८ ॥

With senses, mind and Reason ever controlled, solely pursuing liberation, the Sage, having for ever cast away desire, fear and passion, verily is liberated. (28)

यतेंद्रियमनोबुद्धिः = यतानि इन्द्रियाणि च मनः च बुद्धिः च यस्य सः controlled, senses, and, mind, and, reason, and, whose, he; मुनिः the muni; मोक्षपरायणः = मोक्षः परायणं यस्य सः liberation, goal, whose, he; विगतेच्छाभयक्रोधः = विगता इच्छा च भयं च क्रोधः च यस्य सः gone, desire, and, fear, and, anger, and, whose, he; यः who; सदा always; मुक्तः freed; एव even; सः he.

भोक्तारं यज्ञतपसां सर्वलोकमहेश्वरम् ।
सुहृदं सर्वभूतानां ज्ञात्वा मां शांतिमृच्छति ॥ २९ ॥

Having known Me, as the Enjoyer of sacrifice and of

austerity, the mighty Ruler of all the worlds, and the Lover of all beings, he goeth to Peace. (29)

भोक्तारं the enjoyer; यज्ञतपसां = यज्ञानां च तपसां च of sacrifices and, of austerities, and; सर्वलोकमहेश्वरम् = सर्वेषाम् लोकानाम् महेश्वरम् of all, (of) worlds, the great lord; सुहृदं the lover; सर्वभूतानाम् of all creatures; ज्ञात्वा having known; मां me; शांतिम् to peace; ऋच्छति obtains.

इति श्रीमद्भगवद्गीतासूप० संन्यासयोगो नाम पंचमोऽध्यायः ।

Thus in the glorious *Bhagavad-Gîtâ*...the fifth discourse, entitled :

THE YOGA OF THE RENUNCIATION OF ACTION.

SIXTH DISCOURSE.

श्रीभगवानुवाच ।

अनाश्रितः कर्मफलं कार्यं कर्म करोति यः ।
स संन्यासी च योगी च न निरग्निर्न चाऽक्रियः ॥१॥

The Blessed Lord said:

He that performeth such action as is duty, independently of the fruit of action, he is an ascetic, he is a Yogî, not he that is without fire and without rites.[1] (1)

अनाश्रितः not-relying (on); कर्मफलं=कर्मणः फलं of action, the fruit; कार्यं that ought to be done; कर्म action; करोति does; यः who; सः he; संन्यासी Sannyâsî; च and; योगी Yogî; च and; न not; निरग्निः without fire; न not; च and; अक्रियः without action.

यं संन्यासमिति प्राहुर्योगं तं विद्धि पाण्डव ।
न ह्यसंन्यस्तसंकल्पो योगी भवति कश्चन ॥२॥

That which is called renunciation know thou that as yoga, O Pâṇḍava; nor doth any one become a Yogî with the formative will[2] unrenounced. (2)

---

1 The Sannyâsî lights no sacrificial fire, and performs no sacrifices nor ceremonies; but merely to omit these, without true renunciation, is not to be a real Sannyâsî.

2 The imaginative faculty, that makes plans for the future.

यम् which; संन्यासम् renunciation; इति thus; प्राहुः (they) call; योगं yoga; तं that; विद्धि know; पांडव O' Pâṇḍava; न not; हि indeed; असंन्यस्तसंकल्पः = न सन्यस्तः संकल्पः येन सः not, renounced, wishing, by whom, he; योगी yogi; भवति becomes; कश्चन anyone.

आरुरुक्षोर्मुनेर्योगं कर्म कारणमुच्यते ।
योगारूढस्य तस्यैव शमः कारणमुच्यते ॥ ३ ॥

For a Sage who is seeking yoga, action is called the means, for the same Sage, when he is enthroned in yoga, serenity is called the means.

आरुरुक्षोः (of the) wishing to ascend; मुनेः of (a) muni; योगं yoga; कर्म action; कारणम् the cause; उच्यते is called; योगारुढस्य = योगं आरुढस्य (to) yoga, of the ascended; तस्य of him; एव even; शमः peacefulness, कारणम् the cause; उच्यते is called.

यदा हि नेन्द्रियार्थेषु न कर्मस्वनुषज्जते ।
सर्वसंकल्पसंन्यासी योगारूढस्तदोच्यते ॥ ४ ॥

When a man feeleth no attachment either for the objects of sense or for actions, renouncing the formative will, then he is said to be enthroned in yoga. (4)

यदा when; हि indeed; न not; इंद्रियार्थेषु of the sense-objects; न not; कर्मसु in actions; अनुषज्जते is attached; सर्वसंकल्पसंन्यासी = सर्वेषां संकल्पानां संन्यासी of all, of wishings, renouncer; योगारूढः = योगं आरूढः to yoga, attained; तदा then; उच्यते is called.

उद्धरेदात्मनाऽऽत्मानं नात्मानमवसादयेत् ।
आत्मैव ह्यात्मनो बंधुरात्मैव रिपुरात्मनः ॥ ५ ॥

Let him raise the self by the SELF, and not let the self become depressed; for verily is the SELF the friend of the self, and also the SELF the self's enemy; (5)

उद्धरेत् let (him) raise; आत्मना by the self; आत्मानं the self; न not; आत्मानं the self; अवसादयेत् let (him) cause to sink down; आत्मा the self; एव only; हि indeed; आत्मनः of the self; बंधुः the relative; आत्मा the self; एव only; रिपुः the enemy; आत्मनः of the self.

बंधुरात्माऽऽत्मनस्तस्य येनाऽत्मैवाऽत्मना जितः ।
अनात्मनस्तु शत्रुत्वे वर्तेतात्मैव शत्रुवत् ॥ ६ ॥

The SELF is the friend of the self of him in whom the self by the SELF is vanquished; but to the unsubdued self, the SELF verily becometh hostile as an enemy. (6)

बंधुः the relative; आत्मा the self; आत्मनः of the self; तस्य of him; येन by whom; आत्मा the self; एव even; आत्मना by the self; जितः conquered; अनात्मनः = न (जितः) आत्मा यस्य तस्य not (conquered), self, whose, his; तु indeed; शत्रुत्वे in (for) hostility; वर्तेत may (would) become; आत्मा the self; एव even; शत्रुवत् like an enemy.

जितात्मनः प्रशांतस्य परमात्मा समाहितः ।
शीतोष्णसुखदुःखेषु तथा मानापमानयोः ॥ ७ ॥

The higher Self of him who is SELF-controlled and peaceful is uniform in cold and heat, pleasure and pain, as well as in honour and dishonour. (7)

जितात्मनः = जितः आत्मा यस्य तस्य conquered, self, whose, of him; प्रशांतस्य of the peaceful; परमात्मा highest self; समाहितः balanced; शीतोष्णसुखदुःखेषु = शीते च उष्णे च सुखे च दुःखे च in heat, and, in cold, and, in pleasure, and, in pain, and; तथा so; मानापमानयोः = माने च अपमाने च in respect, and, in disrespect, and.

ज्ञानविज्ञानतृप्तात्मा कूटस्थो विजितेंद्रियः ।
युक्त इत्युच्यते योगी समलोष्टाश्मकांचनः ॥ ८ ॥

The Yogî who is satisfied with wisdom and knowledge, unwavering, whose senses are subdued, to whom a lump of earth, a stone and gold are the same, is said to be harmonised. (8)

ज्ञानविज्ञानतृप्तात्मा = ज्ञानेन च विज्ञानेन च तृप्तः आत्मा यस्य सः with wisdom, and, with knowledge, and, satisfied, self, whose, he; कूटस्थः rock-seated; विजितेंद्रियः = विजितानि इंद्रियाणि यस्य सः conquered, senses, whose, he; युक्तः balanced; इति thus; उच्यते is called; योगी yogî; समलोष्टाश्मकांचनः = समानि लोष्टं च अश्मा च कांचनं च यस्मै सः equal, clod, and, rock, and, gold, and, for whom, he.

सुहृन्मित्रार्युदासीनमध्यस्थद्वेष्यबंधुषु ।
साधुष्वपि च पापेषु समबुद्धिर्विशिष्यते ॥ ९ ॥

He who regards impartially lovers, friends, and foes, strangers, neutrals, foreigners and relatives, also the righteous and unrighteous, he excelleth. (9)

सुहृन्मित्रार्युदासीनमध्यस्थद्वेष्यबंधुषु = सुहृत्सु च मित्रेषु च अरिषु च उदासीनेषु च मध्यस्थेषु च द्वेष्येषु च बंधुषु, च in lovers, and, in friends, and, in enemies, and, in apathetics, and, in neutrals, and, in haters, and, in relatives, and; साधुषु in the good; अपि also; पापेषु in the bad; समबुद्धिः = समा बुद्धिः यस्य सः equal, mind, whose, he; विशिष्यते excels.

योगी युंजीत सततमात्मानं रहसि स्थितः ।
एकाकी यतचित्तात्मा निराशीरपरिग्रहः ॥ १० ॥

Let the Yogî constantly engage himself in yoga, remaining in a secret place by himself, with thought and self subdued, free from hope and greed. (10)

योगी the yogî; युंजीत let (him) balance; सततं always; आत्मानं (him) self (his mind); रहसि in secret; स्थितः seated; एकाकी alone; यतचित्तात्मा = यतं चित्तं च आत्मा च यस्य सः controlled, mind, and, self, and, whose, he: निराशीः without-wish; अपरिग्रहः without-taking.

शुचौ देशे प्रतिष्ठाप्य स्थिरमासनमात्मनः ।
नात्युच्छ्रितं नातिनीचं चैलाजिनकुशोत्तरम् ॥ ११ ॥

In a pure place, established on a fixed seat of his own, neither very much raised nor very low, made of a cloth, a black antelope skin, and kusha grass, one over the other, (11)

शुचौ (in a) pure; देशे in a place; प्रतिष्ठाप्य having established; स्थिरं firm; आसनं seat; आत्मनः of self (his own); न not; अत्युच्छ्रितं very-high; न not; अतिनीचं very-low; चैलाजिनकुशोत्तरम् = चैलं च अजिनं च कुशाः च उत्तरं यस्मिन् तत् cloth, and, skin, and, grass, and, in succession, in which, that.

तत्रैकाग्रं मनः कृत्वा यतचित्तेंद्रियक्रियः ।
उपविश्यासने युंज्याद्योगमात्मविशुद्धये ॥ १२ ॥

There, having made the mind one-pointed, with thought and the functions of the senses subdued, steady on his seat, he should practise yoga for the purification of the self. (12)

तत्र there; एकाग्रं one-pointed (concentrated); मनः mind; कृत्वा having made; यतचित्तेंद्रियक्रियः = यताः चित्तस्य च इंद्रियाणाम् च क्रियाः यस्य सः controlled, of mind, and, of senses, the actions, whose, he; उपविश्य being seated; आसने on a seat; युंज्यात् let him practise; योगं yoga; आत्मविशुद्धये = आत्मनः विशुद्धये of the self, for the purification.

समं कायशिरोग्रीवं धारयन्नचलं स्थिरः ।
संप्रेक्ष्य नासिकाग्रं स्वं दिशश्चानवलोकयन् ॥ १३ ॥

Holding the body, head and neck erect, immovably steady, looking fixedly at the point of the nose, with unseeing gaze, (13)

समं straight; कायशिरोग्रीवं = कायः च शिरः च ग्रीवा च body, and, head, and, neck, and; धारयन् holding; अचलं immovable ; स्थिरः steady ; संप्रेक्ष्य looking at ; नासिकाग्रं = नासिकायाः अग्रं of the nose, forepart ; स्वं (his) own ; दिशः the quarters ; च and ; अनवलोकयन् not seeing.

प्रशांतात्मा विगतभीर्ब्रह्मचारिव्रते स्थितः ।
मनः संयम्य मच्चित्तो युक्त आसीत मत्परः ॥ १४ ॥

The self serene, fearless, firm in the vow of the Brahmachârî, the mind controlled, thinking on Me, harmonised, let him sit aspiring after Me. (14)

प्रशांतात्मा = प्रशान्तः आत्मा यस्य सः calmed, self, whose, he ; विगतभीः = विगता भीः यस्य सः gone, fear, whose, he ; ब्रह्मचारिव्रते = ब्रह्मचारिणः व्रते of the Brahmachârî, in the vow ; स्थितः fixed ; मनः the mind ; संयम्य having controlled ; मच्चित्तः = मयि चित्तं यस्य सः in me, mind, whose, he ; युक्तः balanced ; आसीत let him sit ; मत्परः = अहं परः यस्य सः I, supreme, whose, he.

युंजन्नेवं सदाऽऽत्मानं योगी नियतमानसः ।
शांतिं निर्वाणपरमां मत्संस्थामधिगच्छति ॥ १५ ॥

The Yogî, ever united thus with the SELF, with the mind controlled, goeth to Peace, to the supreme Bliss that abideth in Me. (15)

युंजन् balancing ; एवं thus ; सदा always ; आत्मानं the self ; योगी the Yogî ; नियतमानसः = नियतं मानसं यस्य सः controlled, mind, whose, he ; शांतिं to peace ; निर्वाणपरमां = निर्वाणं परमं यस्याः तां nirvâṇa, the end. of which, to that ; मत्संस्थाम् = मयि संस्था

यस्याः तां in me, foundation, of which, to that; अधिगच्छति attains.

नात्यश्नतस्तु योगोऽस्ति न चैकान्तमनश्नतः ।
न चातिस्वप्नशीलस्य जाग्रतो नैव चार्जुन ॥ १६॥

Verily yoga is not for him who eateth too much, nor who abstaineth to excess, nor who is too much addicted to sleep, nor even to wakefulness, O Arjuna. (16)

न not; अत्यश्नतः of the much-eating; तु indeed; योगः yoga; अस्ति is; न not; च and; एकान्तं solely (entirely); अनश्नतः of the un-eating; न not; च and; अतिस्वप्नशीलस्य= अति स्वप्नुं शीलं यस्य तस्य too much, to sleep, tendency, whose, his; जाग्रतः of the waking; न not; एव even; च and; अर्जुन O Arjuna.

युक्ताऽहारविहारस्य युक्तचेष्टस्य कर्मसु ।
युक्तस्वप्नावबोधस्य योगो भवति दुःखहा ॥१७॥

Yoga killeth out all pain for him who is regulated in eating and amusement, regulated in performing actions, regulated in sleeping and waking. (17)

युक्ताहारविहारस्य=युक्तः आहारः च विहारः च यस्य तस्य controlled, food, and, amusement, and, whose, of him; युक्तचेष्टस्य=युक्ता चेष्टा यस्य तस्य controlled, behaviour, whose, of him; कर्मसु in actions; युक्तस्वप्नावबोधस्य=युक्तः स्वप्नः च अवबोधः च यस्य तस्य controlled, sleeping, and, waking, and, whose, of him; योगः yoga; भवति becomes; दुःखहा the pain-killer.

यदा विनियतं चित्तमात्मन्येवावतिष्ठते ।
निःस्पृहः सर्वकामेभ्यो युक्त इत्युच्यते तदा ॥१८॥

When his subdued thought is fixed on the SELF, free from longing after all desirable things, then it is said: "he is harmonised." (18)

यदा when; विनियतं subdued; चित्तं mind; आत्मनि in the self; एव only; अवतिष्ठते sits down; निस्पृहः not-desiring; सर्वकामेभ्यः = सर्वेभ्यः कामेभ्यः (for) all, for (objects of) desires; युक्तः balanced; इति thus; उच्यते is said; तदा then.

यथा दीपो निवातस्थो नेंगते सोपमा स्मृता ।
योगिनो यतचित्तस्य युंजतो योगमात्मनः ॥१९॥

As a lamp in a windless place flickereth not, to such is likened the Yogî of subdued thought, absorbed in the yoga of the SELF. (19)

यथा as; दीपः a lamp; निवातस्थः in (a) windless (-place)-standing; न not; इंगते flickers; सा that; उपमा simile; स्मृता is remembered; योगिनः of the Yogi; यतचित्तस्य = यतं चित्तं यस्य तस्य controlled, mind, whose, of him; युंजतः (of the) practising; योगम् the yoga; आत्मनः of the self.

यत्रोपरमते चित्तं निरुद्धं योगसेवया ।
यत्र चैवात्मनाऽऽत्मानं पश्यन्नात्मनि तुष्यति ॥२०॥

That in which the mind finds rest, quieted by the

practice of yoga; that in which he, seeing the SELF by the SELF, in the SELF is satisfied; (20)

यत्र where; उपरमते comes to rest; चित्तं the mind; निरुद्धं curbed; योगसेवया = योगस्य सेवया of yoga, by the service; यत्र where; च and; एव even; आत्मना by the self; आत्मानं the self; पश्यन् seeing; आत्मनि in the self; तुष्यति is content.

सुखमात्यंतिकं यत्तद्बुद्धिग्राह्यमतींद्रियम् ।
वेत्ति यत्र न चैवाऽयं स्थितश्चलति तत्त्वतः ॥२१॥

That in which he findeth the supreme delight which the Reason can grasp beyond the senses, wherein establised, he moveth not from the Reality; (21)

सुखं pleasure; आत्यंतिकं most final; यत् which; तत् that; बुद्धिग्राह्यम् = बुद्ध्या ग्राह्यं by the reason, graspable; अतीन्द्रियम् = इंन्द्रियाणि अति the senses, more than (beyond); वेत्ति knows; यत्र where; न not; च and; एव even; अयं this; स्थितः fixed; चलति moves; तत्त्वतः from the Reality.

यं लब्ध्वा चाऽपरं लाभं मन्यते नाऽधिकं ततः ।
यस्मिन्स्थितो न दुःखेन गुरुणाऽपि विचाल्यते ॥२२॥

Which, having obtained, he thinketh there is no greater gain beyond it; wherein established, he is not shaken even by heavy sorrow; (22)

यं which; लब्ध्वा having obtained; च and; अपरं another; लाभं gain; मन्यते thinks; न not; अधिकं greater; ततः than that; यस्मिन् in which; स्थितः established; न not; दुःखेन by sorrow;

गुरुणा (by) heavy ; अपि even ; विचाल्यते is moved.

तं विद्याद् दुःखसंयोगवियोगं योगसंज्ञितम् ।
स निश्चयेन योक्तव्यो योगोऽनिर्विण्णचेतसा ॥२३॥

That should be known by the name of yoga, this disconnection from the union with pain. This yoga must be clung to with a firm conviction and with undesponding mind. (23)

तं that; विद्यात् let (him) know; दुःखसंयोगवियोगं = दुःखैः संयोगेन वियोगं with pains, with (from) conjunction, (the) disjunction; योगसंज्ञितम् yoga-named; निश्चयेन surely; योक्तव्यः should be practised; योगः yoga; अनिर्विण्णचेतसा = न निर्विण्णं चेतः यस्य तेन not despondent, mind, whose, by him;

संकल्पप्रभवान्कामांस्त्यक्त्वा सर्वानशेषतः ।
मनसैवेंद्रियग्रामं विनियम्य समंततः ॥ २४ ॥

Abandoning without reserve all desires born of the imagination, by the mind curbing in the aggregate of the senses on every side, (24)

संकल्पप्रभवान् imagination-produced; कामान् desires; त्यक्त्वा having abandoned; सर्वान् all; अशेषतः without remainder; मनसा by the mind; एव even; इंद्रियग्रामं = इंद्रियाणाम् ग्रामं of the senses, collection; विनियम्य having curbed; समंततः on every side.

शनैःशनैरुपरमेद् बुद्ध्या धृतिगृहीतया ।

आत्मसंस्थं मनः कृत्वा न किंचिदपि चिंतयेत् ॥२५॥

Little by little let him gain tranquillity by means of Reason controlled by steadiness : having made the mind abide in the SELF, let him not think of anything. (25)

शनैः gradually ; शनैः gradually ; उपरमेत् let him cease (from activity); बुद्ध्या by the reason : धृतिगृहीतया = धृत्या गृहीतया by firmness, (by) seized ; आत्मसंस्थं self-seated ; मनः the mind ; कृत्वा having made ; न not ; किंचित् anything ; अपि also ; चिंतयेत् let him think.

यतो यतो निश्चरति मनश्चंचलमस्थिरम् ।
ततस्ततो नियम्यैतदात्मन्येव वशं नयेत् ॥ २६ ॥

As often as the wavering and unsteady mind goeth forth, so often reining it in, let him bring it under the control of the SELF. (26)

यतः whence ; यतः whence ; निश्चरति runs out ; मनः mind ; चंचलम् unstable ; अस्थिरम् unsteady ; ततः thence ; नियम्य having restrained ; एतत् this ; आत्मनि in the self ; एव even ; वशं (in) to control ; नयेत् let (him) lead.

प्रशांतमनसं ह्येनं योगिनं सुखमुत्तमम् ।
उपैति शांतरजसं ब्रह्मभूतमकल्मषम् ॥ २७ ॥

Supreme joy is for this Yogî whose mind is peaceful, whose passion-nature is calmed, who is sinless and of the nature of the ETERNAL. (27)

प्रशांतमनसं = प्रशांतं मनः यस्य तं peaceful, mind, whose, him; हि indeed; एनं this; योगिनम् yogî; सुखं pleasure; उत्तमम् highest; उपैति comes; शांतरजसम् = शांतं रजः यस्य तं; subsided, passion-nature, whose, to him; ब्रह्मभूतम् = Brahman-become; अकल्मषम् (to) sinless.

युंजन्नेवं सदाऽऽत्मानं योगी विगतकल्मषः ।
सुखेन ब्रह्मसंस्पर्शमत्यंतं सुखमश्नुते ॥ २८ ॥

The Yogî who thus, ever harmonising the self, hath put away sin, he easily enjoyeth the infinite bliss of contact with the ETERNAL. (28)

युंजन् practising yoga; एवं thus; सदा always; आत्मानं the self; योगी yogî; विगतकल्मषः = विगतः कल्मषः यस्य सः gone, sin, whose, he; सुखेन with ease; ब्रह्मसंस्पर्शम् = ब्रह्मणा संस्पर्शः यस्य तत् with Brahman, touch, whose, that; अत्यंतं ultimate; सुखं pleasure; अश्नुते enjoys.

सर्वभूतस्थमात्मानं सर्वभूतानि चात्मनि ।
ईक्षते योगयुक्तात्मा सर्वत्र समदर्शनः ॥ २९ ॥

The self, harmonised by yoga, seeth the SELF abiding in all beings, all beings in the SELF; everywhere he seeth the same. (29)

सर्वभूतस्थम् = सर्वेषु भूतेषु तिष्ठति तं in all, (in) beings, abides, him; आत्मानं the self; सर्वभूतानि = सर्वाणि भूतानि all, creatures; च and; आत्मनि in the self; ईक्षते sees; योगयुक्तात्मा = योगेन

युक्तः आत्मा यस्य सः by yoga, balanced, self, whose, he; सर्वत्र everywhere; समदर्शनः equal-seeing.

यो मां पश्यति सर्वत्र सर्वं च मयि पश्यति ।
तस्याहं न प्रणश्यामि स च मे न प्रणश्यति ॥ ३० ॥

He who seeth Me everywhere, and seeth everything in Me, of him will I never lose hold, and he shall never lose hold of Me.

यः who; मां me; पश्यति sees; सर्वत्र everywhere; सर्वं all; च and; मयि in me; पश्यति sees; तस्य of him; अहं I; न not; प्रणश्यामि perish (get lost); सः he; च and; मे of (to) me; न not; प्रणश्यति perishes (gets lost).

सर्वभूतस्थितं यो मां भजत्येकत्वमास्थितः ।
सर्वथा वर्त्तमानोऽपि स योगी मयि वर्तते ॥ ३१ ॥

He who, established in unity, worshippeth Me, abiding in all beings, that Yogî liveth in Me, whatever his mode of living. (31)

सर्वभूतस्थितं = सर्वेषु भूतेषु स्थितं in all, (in) beings, sitting; यः who; मां me; भजति worships; एकत्वम् to (in) unity; आस्थितः established; सर्वथा every way; वर्त्तमानः existing; अपि also; सः that; योगी yogî; मयि in me; वर्तते is.

आत्मौपम्येन सर्वत्र समं पश्यति योऽर्जुन ।
सुखं वा यदि वा दुःखं स योगी परमो मतः ॥ ३२ ॥

He who, through the likeness of the SELF, O Arjuna, seeth equality in everything, whether pleasant or painful, he is considered a perfect Yogî. (32)

आत्मौपम्येन = आत्मनः औपम्येन of the self, by the likeness; सर्वत्र everywhere; समं equality; पश्यति sees; यः who; अर्जुन O Arjuna; सुखं pleasure; वा or; यदि if; वा or; दुःखं sorrow; सः he; योगी yogi; परमः highest; मतः is thought.

अर्जुन उवाच ।

योऽयं योगस्त्वया प्रोक्तः साम्येन मधुसूदन ।
एतस्याहं न पश्यामि चंचलत्वात्स्थितिं स्थिराम् ॥३३॥

Arjuna said :

This yoga which Thou hast declared to be by equanimity, O Madhusûdana, I see not a stable foundation for it, owing to restlessness ; (33)

यः which; अयं this; योगः yoga; त्वया by thee; प्रोक्तः declared; साम्येन by equality; मधुसूदन O slayer of Madhu; एतस्य of this; अहं I; न not; पश्यामि see; चंचलत्वात् from restlessness; स्थितिं stability; स्थिराम् firm.

चंचलं हि मनः कृष्ण प्रमाथि बलवद् दृढम् ।
तस्याऽहं निग्रहं मन्ये वायोरिव सुदुष्करम् ॥३४॥

For the mind is verily restless, O Kriṣhṇa ; it is impetuous, strong and difficult to bend ; I deem it as hard to curb as the wind. (34)

चंचलं restless; हि indeed; मनः the mind; कृष्ण O Krishna; प्रमाथि impetuous; बलवत् strong; दृढम् hard; तस्य of it; अहं I; निग्रहं gripping; मन्ये think; वायोः of the wind; इव as; सुदुष्करम् hard to be done.

श्रीभगवानुवाच ।

असंशयं महाबाहो मनो दुर्निग्रहं चलम् ।
अभ्यासेन तु कौंतेय वैराग्येण च गृह्यते ॥३५॥

The Blessed Lord said:

Without doubt, O mighty-armed, the mind is hard to curb and restless; but it may be curbed by constant practice and by dispassion. (35)

असंशयं doubtless; महाबाहो O great-armed; मनः the mind; दुर्निग्रहं hard to grip; चलम् moving; अभ्यासेन by practice; तु indeed; कौंतेय O Kaunteya; वैराग्येण by dispassion; च and; गृह्यते is held.

असंयतात्मना योगो दुष्प्राप इति मे मतिः ।
वश्यात्मना तु यतता शक्योऽवाप्तुमुपायतः ॥३६॥

Yoga is hard to attain, methinks, by a self that is uncontrolled; but by the SELF-controlled it is attainable by properly directed energy. (36)

असंयतात्मना = असंयतः आत्मा यस्य तेन uncontrolled, self, whose, by him; योगः yoga; दुष्प्रापः hard-gained; इति thus; मे my; मतिः opinion; वश्यात्मना = वश्यः आत्मा यस्य तेन controlled, self, whose, by him; तु indeed; यतता (by the) endeavouring; शक्यः possible; अवाप्तुम् to obtain; उपायतः through means.

अर्जुन उवाच ।

अयतिः श्रद्धयोपेतो योगाच्चलितमानसः ।
अप्राप्य योगसंसिद्धिं कां गतिं कृष्ण गच्छति ॥३७॥

Arjuna said :

He who is unsubdued but who possesseth faith, with the mind wandering away from yoga, failing to attain perfection in yoga, what path doth he tread, O Kṛiṣhṇa? (37)

अ-यतिः un-subdued; श्रद्धया by (with) faith; उपेतः endowed; योगात् from yoga; चलितमानसः = चलितं मानसं यस्य सः strayed, mind, whose, he; अ-प्राप्य not having attained; योगसंसिद्धिं = योगस्य संसिद्धिं of yoga, perfection; कां to what; गतिं path; कृष्ण O Kriṣhṇa; गच्छति goes (he).

कच्चिन्नोभयविभ्रष्टश्छिन्नाभ्रमिव नश्यति ।
अप्रतिष्ठो महाबाहो विमूढो ब्रह्मणः पथि ॥३८॥

Fallen from both, is he destroyed like a rent cloud, unsteadfast, O mighty-armed, deluded in the path of the ETERNAL? (38)

कच्चित् is it that; न not; उभयविभ्रष्टः = उभयतः विभ्रष्टः from both, fallen; छिन्नाभ्रं = छिन्नं अभ्रं torn, cloud; इव like; नश्यति is destroyed; अप्रतिष्ठः unstable; महाबाहो O mighty-armed;

विमूढः deluded ; ब्रह्मणः of Brahman ; पथि in the path.

एतन्मे संशयं कृष्ण छेत्तुमर्हस्यशेषतः ।
त्वदन्यः संशयस्यास्य छेत्ता नह्युपपद्यते ॥३९॥

Deign, O Kṛishṇa, to completely dispel this doubt of mine; for there is none to be found save Thyself able to destroy this doubt. (39)

एतत् this ; मे my ; संशयं doubt ; कृष्ण O Kṛishṇa ; छेत्तुम् to resolve ; अर्हसि oughtest ; अशेषतः without remainder ; त्वत् than thou ; अन्यः another ; संशयस्य of doubt ; अस्य (of) this ; छेत्ता the solver ; न not ; हि indeed ; उपपद्यते is to be found.

श्रीभगवानुवाच ।

पार्थ नैवेह नामुत्र विनाशस्तस्य विद्यते ।
नहि कल्याणकृत्कश्चिद्दुर्गतिं तात गच्छति ॥४०॥

The Blessed Lord said :

O son of Pṛithâ, neither in this world nor in the life to come is there destruction for him ; never doth any who worketh righteousness, O beloved, tread the path of woe. (40)

पार्थ O Pârtha ; न not ; एव even ; इह here ; न not ; अमुत्र in the next world ; विनाशः destruction ; तस्य of him ; विद्यते is ; नहि surely ; कल्याणकृत् righteous-doer ; कश्चित् any one ; दुर्गतिं to an evil path (fate) ; तात O beloved ; गच्छति goes.

प्राप्य पुण्यकृतांल्लोकानुषित्वा शाश्वतीः समाः ।
शुचीना श्रीमता गेहे योगभ्रष्टोऽभिजायते ॥४१॥

Having attained to the worlds of the pure-doing, and having dwelt there for immemorial years, he who fell from yoga is reborn in a pure and blessed house. (41)

प्राप्य having obtained; पुण्यकृताम् of the right-doers; लोकान् worlds; उषित्वा having dwelt; शाश्वतीः everlasting; समाः years; शुचीनां of the pure; श्रीमतां of the prosperous; गेहे in the house; योगभ्रष्टः = योगात् भ्रष्टः from yoga, fallen; अभिजायते is born.

अथवा योगिनामेव कुले भवति धीमताम् ।
एतद्धि दुर्लभतरं लोके जन्म यदीदृशम् ॥४२॥

Or he may even be born into a family of wise Yogîs; but such a birth as that is most difficult to obtain in this world. (42)

अथवा or; योगिनाम् of yogis; एव even; कुले in the family; भवति becomes; धीमताम् of wise; एतत् this; हि indeed; दुर्लभतरं very difficult to obtain; लोके in the world; जन्म birth; यत् which; ईदृशं like this.

तत्र तं बुद्धिसंयोगं लभते पौर्वदेहिकम् ।
यतते च ततो भूयः संसिद्धौ कुरुनंदन ॥४३॥

There he recovereth the characteristics belonging

to his former body, and with these he again laboureth for perfection, O joy of the Kurus. (43)

तत्र there; तं that; बुद्धिसंयोगं = बुद्धेः संयोगं of Buddhi, the conjunction; लभते obtains; पौर्वदेहिकम् belonging to the previous body; यतते strives; च and; ततः thence; भूयः again; संसिद्धौ in perfection; कुरुनंदन = कुरूणामं नन्दन of the Kurus, O rejoicer.

पूर्वाभ्यासेन तेनैव ह्रियते ह्यवशोऽपि सः ।

जिज्ञासुरपि योगस्य शब्दब्रह्मातिवर्तते ॥ ४४ ॥

By that former practice he is irresistibly swept away. Only wishing to know yoga, even the seeker after yoga goeth beyond the Brâhmic word. (44)

पूर्वाभ्यासेन = पूर्वेण अभ्यासेन by former, (by) practice; तेन (by) that; एव even; ह्रियते is swept away; हि indeed; अवशः helpless; अपि also; सः he; जिज्ञासुः wishing to know; अपि also; योगस्य of yoga; शब्दब्रह्म sound-Brahman; अतिवर्तते goes beyond.

प्रयत्नाद्यतमानस्तु योगी संशुद्धकिल्बिषः ।

अनेकजन्मसंसिद्धस्ततो याति परां गतिम् ॥ ४५ ॥

But the Yogî, labouring with assiduity, purified from sin, fully perfected through manifold births, he reacheth the supreme goal. (45)

प्रयत्नात् from (with) perseverance; यतमानः striving; तु indeed; योगी the yogi; संशुद्धकिल्बिषः = संशुद्धं किल्बिषं यस्य सः completely purified, sin, whose, he; अनेकजन्मसंसिद्धः = अनेकैः

जन्मभिः संसिद्धः by many, (by) births, perfected; ततः thence; याति goes; पराम् to the highest; गतिम् path.

तपस्विभ्योऽधिको योगी ज्ञानिभ्योऽपि मतोऽधिकः।
कर्मिभ्यश्चाधिको योगी तस्माद्योगी भवाऽर्जुन॥४६॥

The Yogî is greater than the ascetics; he is thought to be greater than even the wise; the Yogî is greater than the men of action; therefore become thou a Yogî, O Arjuna. (46)

तपस्विभ्यः than the ascetics; अधिकः higher; योगी the yogî; ज्ञानिभ्यः than the wise; अपि also; मतः thought; अधिकः greater; कर्मिभ्यः than the actors; अधिकः greater; योगी the yogî; तस्मात् therefore; योगी a yogî; भव be; अर्जुन O Arjuna.

योगिनामपि सर्वेषां मद्गतेनांतरात्मना।
श्रद्धावान्भजते यो मां स मे युक्ततमो मतः॥४७॥

And among all Yogîs, he who, full of faith, with the inner SELF abiding in Me, adoreth Me, he is considered by Me to be the most completely harmonised. (47)

योगिनाम् of yogis; सर्वेषां of all; मद्गतेन = मां गतेन in me, gone; अंतरात्मना with inner self; श्रद्धावान् faith-filled; भजते worships; यः who; मां me; सः he; मे by me; युक्ततमः most-harmonised; मतः is thought.

इति श्रीमद्भगवद्गीता अध्यात्मयोगो नाम षष्ठोऽध्यायः।

Thus in the glorious BHAGAVAD-GÎTÂ...the sixth discourse, entitled:

THE YOGA OF SELF-SUBDUAL.

SEVENTH DISCOURSE.

श्रीभगवानुवाच ।

मय्यासक्तमनाः पार्थ योगं युंजन्मदाश्रयः ।
असंशयं समग्रं मां यथा ज्ञास्यसि तच्छृणु ॥ १ ॥

The Blessed Lord said:

With the mind clinging to Me, O Pârtha, performing yoga, refuged in Me, how thou shalt without doubt know Me to the uttermost, that hear thou. (1)

मयि in me; आसक्तमनाः=आसक्तं मनः यस्य सः attached, mind, whose, he: पार्थ O Pârtha; योगं yoga; युंजन् practising; मदाश्रयः=अहं आश्रयः यस्य सः I, refuge, whose, he; असंशयं doubtless; समग्रं whole; मां me; यथा as; ज्ञास्यसि (thou) shalt know; तत् that; शृणु listen.

ज्ञानं तेऽहं सविज्ञानमिदं वक्ष्याम्यशेषतः ।
यज्ज्ञात्वा नेह भूयोऽन्यज्ज्ञातव्यमवशिष्यते ॥ २ ॥

I will declare to thee this knowledge and wisdom in its completeness, which, having known, there is nothing more here needeth to be known. (2)

ज्ञानं knowledge; ते of (to) thee; अहं I; सविज्ञानम्=विज्ञानेन सह with knowledge, together; इदं this; वक्ष्यामि will declare; अशेषतः without remainder; यत् which; ज्ञात्वा having known; न not; इह here; भूयः more; अन्यत् other; ज्ञातव्यम् (what ought) to be known; अवशिष्यते remains.

मनुष्याणां सहस्रेषु कश्चिद्यतति सिद्धये ।
यततामपि सिद्धानां कश्चिन्मां वेत्ति तत्त्वतः ॥३॥

Among thousands of men scarce one striveth for perfection; of the successful strivers scarce one knoweth Me in essence. (3)

मनुष्याणाम् of men; सहस्रेषु among thousands; कश्चित् some one; यतति strives; सिद्धये for perfection; यतताम् of the striving; अपि also; सिद्धानाम (of) successful; कश्चित् some one; मां me; वेत्ति knows; तत्त्वतः essentially.

भूमिरापोऽनलो वायुः खं मनो बुद्धिरेव च ।
अहंकार इतीयं मे भिन्ना प्रकृतिरष्टधा ॥ ४ ॥

Earth, water, fire, air, ether, Mind and Reason also and Egoism—these are the eightfold division of My nature. (4)

भूमिः earth; आपः water; अनलः fire; वायुः air; खं ether; मनः mind; बुद्धिः reason; एव even; च and; अहंकारः egoism; इति thus; इयं this; मे of me; भिन्ना divided; प्रकृतिः nature; अष्टधा eightfold.

अपरेयमितस्त्वन्यां प्रकृतिं विद्धि मे पराम् ॥
जीवभूतां महाबाहो ययेदं धार्यते जगत् ॥ ५ ॥

This the inferior. Know My other nature, the higher, the life-element, O mighty-armed, by which the universe is upheld. (5)

अपरा lower ; इयं this ; इतः from (than) this ; तु indeed ; अन्यां other ; प्रकृतिम् nature ; विद्धि know ; मे my ; परम् higher जीवभूताम् life-element ; महाबाहो O great-armed ; यया by which ; इदं this ; धार्यते is supported ; जगत् world.

एतद्योनीनि भूतानि सर्वाणीत्युपधारय ।
अहं कृत्स्नस्य जगतः प्रभवः प्रलयस्तथा ॥ ६ ॥

Know this to be the womb of all beings. I am the source of the forthgoing of the whole universe and likewise the place of its dissolving. (6)

एतद्योनीनि = एषा योनिः येषां तानि this, womb, whose, they ; भूतानि beings ; सर्वाणि all ; इति thus ; उपधारय understand ; अहं I ; कृत्स्नस्य (of) whole ; जगतः of world ; प्रभवः (source of) becoming ; प्रलयः (place of) dissolution ; तथा also.

मत्तः परतरं नान्यत्किंचिदस्ति धनंजय ।
मयि सर्वमिदं प्रोतं सूत्रे मणिगणा इव ॥ ७ ॥

There is naught whatsoever higher than I, O Dhanañjaya. All this is threaded on Me, as rows of pearls on a string. (7)

मत्तः than I ; परतरं higher ; न not ; अन्यत् other ; किंचित् any one ; अस्ति is ; धनंजय O Dhanañjaya ; मयि in me ; सर्वं all ; इदम् this ; प्रोतं (is) threaded ; सूत्रे in a string ; मणिगणाः = मणीनाम् गणाः of pearls, rows ; इव like.

रसोऽहमप्सु कौंतेय प्रभाऽस्मि शशिसूर्ययोः ।

प्रणवः सर्ववेदेषु शब्दः खे पौरुषं नृषु ॥ ८ ॥

I the sapidity in waters, O son of Kuntî, I the radiance in moon and sun; the Word of Power in all the Vedas, sound in ether, and virility in men; (8)

रसः the taste; अहं I; अप्सु in waters; कौंतेय O Kaunteya; प्रभा the radiance; अस्मि am (I); शशिसूर्ययोः = शशिनः च सूर्यस्य च of the moon, and, of the sun, and; प्रणवः the praṇava; सर्ववेदेषु = सर्वेषु वेदेषु (in) all, in the Vedas; शब्दः sound; खे in ether; पौरुषं virility; नृषु in men.

पुण्यो गंधः पृथिव्यां च तेजश्चास्मि विभावसौ ।
जीवनं सर्वभूतेषु तपश्चास्मि तपस्विषु ॥ ९ ॥

The pure fragrance of earth and the brilliance in fire am I: the life in all beings am I, and the austerity in ascetics. (9)

पुण्यः pure; गंधः smell; पृथिव्याम् in earth; च and; तेजः light; च and; अस्मि am (I); विभावसौ in fire; जीवनम् life; सर्वभूतेषु = सर्वेषु भूतेषु (in) all, in beings; तपः austerity; च and; अस्मि am (I); तपस्विषु in ascetics.

बीजं मां सर्वभूतानां विद्धि पार्थ सनातनम् ।
बुद्धिर्बुद्धिमतामस्मि तेजस्तेजस्विनामहम् ॥ १० ॥

Know Me, O Pârtha, as the eternal seed of all beings. I am the Reason of the Reason-endowed, the splendour of splendid things am I. (10)

बीजं seed; मां me; सर्वभूतानाम्=सर्वेषाम् भूतानाम् (of) all, of beings; विद्धि know; पार्थ O Pârtha; सनातनम् eternal; बुद्धिः reason; बुद्धिमताम् of the reasonable; अस्मि am (I); तेजः splendour; तेजस्विनाम् of the splendid; अहं I.

बलं बलवतामस्मि कामरागविवर्जितम् ।
धर्माविरुद्धो भूतेषु कामोऽस्मि भरतर्षभ ॥ ११ ॥

And I the strength of the strong, devoid of desire and passion. In beings, I am desire not contrary to duty, O Lord of the Bharatas. (11)

बलं strength; बलवताम् of the strong; अस्मि am (I); कामरागविवर्जितम्=कामेन च रागेण च विवर्जितम् by desire, and, by passion, and, abandoned; धर्माविरुद्धः=धर्मेण अविरुद्धः with (to) duty, not opposed; भूतेषु in beings; कामः desire; अस्मि am (I); भरतर्षभ O Lord of the Bharatas.

ये चैव सात्विका भावा राजसास्तामसाश्च ये ।
मत्त एवेति तान्विद्धि न त्वहं तेषु ते मयि ॥१२॥

The natures that are harmonious, active, slothful, these know as from Me; not I in them, but they in Me. (12)

ये which; च and; एव even; सात्विकाः pure; भावाः natures; राजसाः active; तामसाः inert; च and; ये which; मत्तः from me; एव even; इति thus; तान् these; विद्धि know; न not; तु indeed; अहं I; तेषु in them; ते they; मयि in me.

त्रिभिर्गुणमयैर्भावैरेभिः सर्वमिदं जगत् ।

मोहित नाभिजानाति मामेभ्यः परमव्ययम् ॥१३॥

All this world, deluded by these natures made by the three qualities, knoweth not Me, above these, imperishable. (13)

त्रिभिः (by) three; गुणमयैः (by) the guna-made; भावैः by natures; एभिः (by) these; सर्वम् all; इदं this; जगत् world; मोहितं deceived; न not; अभिजानाति knows well; माम् me; एभ्यः than these; परम् higher; अव्ययम् inexhaustible.

दैवी ह्येषा गुणमयी मम माया दुरत्यया ।

मामेव ये प्रपद्यंते मायामेतां तरंति ते ॥ १४ ॥

This divine illusion of Mine, caused by the qualities, is hard to pierce; they who come to Me, they cross over this illusion. (14)

दैवी divine; हि indeed; एषा this; गुणमयी guṇa-made; मम my; माया illusion; दुरत्यया hard to go beyond; माम् to me; ये who; प्रपद्यंते approach; मायाम् illusion; एताम् this; तरंति cross; ते they

न मां दुष्कृतिनो मूढाः प्रपद्यंते नराधमाः ।

माययाऽपहृतज्ञाना आसुरं भावमाश्रिताः ॥ १५ ॥

The evil-doing, the deluded, the vilest men, they come not to Me, they whose wisdom is destroyed by illusion, who have embraced the nature of demons. (15)

न not; माम् to me; दुष्कृतिनः evil-doers; मूढाः deluded; प्रपद्यंते approach; नराधमाः = नरेषु अधमाः among men, lowest;

मायया by mâyâ; अपहृतज्ञाना: = अपहृतं ज्ञानं येषां ते torn away, wisdom, whose, they; आसुरं âsuric; भावम् nature; आश्रिता: refuged (in).

चतुर्विधा भजंते मां जनाः सुकृतिनोऽर्जुन ।
आर्तो जिज्ञासुरर्थार्थी ज्ञानी च भरतर्षभ ॥ १६ ॥

Fourfold in division are the righteous ones who worship Me, O Arjuna: the suffering, the seeker for knowledge, the self-interested, and the wise, O Lord of the Bharatas. (16)

चतुर्विधा: fourfold; भजंते worship; मां me; जना: people; सुकृतिन: well-doing; अर्जुन O Arjuna; आर्त: the unhappy; जिज्ञासु: wisdom-desiring; अर्थार्थी = अर्थं अर्थयते इति wealth, seeks, thus; ज्ञानी the wise; च and; भरतर्षभ O Lord of the Bharatas.

तेषां ज्ञानी नित्ययुक्त एकभक्तिर्विशिष्यते ।
प्रियो हि ज्ञानिनोऽत्यर्थमहं स च मम प्रियः ॥१७॥

Of these, the wise, constantly harmonised, worshipping the One, is the best; I am supremely dear to the wise, and he is dear to Me. (17)

तेषाम् of these; ज्ञानी the wise; नित्ययुक्त: = नित्यं युक्त: always balanced; एकभक्ति = एकस्मिन् भक्ति: यस्य स: in one, devotion, whose he; विशिष्यते excels; प्रिय: dear; हि indeed; ज्ञानिन: of the wise; अत्यर्थम् excessively: अहं I; स: he; च and; मम of me; प्रिय: dear.

उदाराः सर्व एवैते ज्ञानी त्वात्मैव मे मतम् ।
आस्थितः स हि युक्तात्मा मामेवानुत्तमां गतिम् ॥१८॥

Noble are all these, but I hold the wise as verily Myself; he, SELF-united, is fixed on Me, the highest path. (18)

उदाराः noble; सर्वे all; एव even; एते these; ज्ञानी the wise; तु indeed; आत्मा self; एव even; मे my; मतम् opinion; आस्थितः fixed; सः he; हि indeed; युक्तात्मा = युक्तः आत्मा यस्य सः balanced, self, whose, he; मां me; एव even; अनुत्तमां = न अस्ति उत्तमा यस्याः तां not, is, better, than which, that; गतिम् path.

बहूनां जन्मनामंते ज्ञानवान्मा प्रपद्यते ।
वासुदेवः सर्वमिति स महात्मा सुदुर्लभः ॥ १९ ॥

At the close of many births the man full of wisdom cometh unto Me: "Vâsudeva[1] is all," saith he, the Mahâtmâ, very difficult to find. (19)

बहूनां (of) many; जन्मनाम् of births; अन्ते in (at) the end; ज्ञानवान् the knowledge-possessor; मां to me; प्रपद्यते approaches; वासुदेवः Vâsudeva; सर्वम् all; इति thus; सः he; महात्मा = महान् आत्मा यस्य सः great, self, whose, he; सुदुर्लभः very-hardly-obtained.

कामैस्तैस्तैर्हृतज्ञानाः प्रपद्यंतेऽन्यदेवताः ।

---

1 A name for Shrî Krishṇa, as the son of Vasudeva.

तं तं नियममास्थाय प्रकृत्या नियताः स्वया ॥२०॥

They whose wisdom hath been rent away by desires go forth to other Shining Ones, resorting to various external observances, according to their own natures. (20)

कामैः by desires; तैः (by) them; तैः (by) them; हृतज्ञानाः = हृतं ज्ञानं येषां ते torn away, wisdom, whose, they; प्रपद्यंते approach; अन्यदेवताः = अन्याः देवताः other gods; तं that; तं that; नियमं rule (vow); आस्थाय having taken up; प्रकृत्या by nature; नियताः led; स्वया (by) own.

यो यो यां यां तनुं भक्तः श्रद्धयाऽर्चितुमिच्छति ।
तस्य तस्याचला श्रद्धां तामेव विदधाम्यहम् ॥२१॥

Any devotee who seeketh to worship with faith any such aspect, I verily bestow the unswerving faith of that man. (21)

यः who; यः who; यां which; यां which; तनुं shape; भक्तः devotee; श्रद्धया with faith; अर्चितुम् to worship; इच्छति wishes; तस्य of him; अचलां steady; तस्य of him; श्रद्धां faith; ताम् that; एव even; विदधामि make; अहं I.

स तया श्रद्धया युक्तस्तस्याराधनमीहते ।
लभते च ततः कामान्मयैव विहितान्हितान् ॥२२॥

He, endowed with that faith, seeketh the worship of such a one, and from him he obtaineth his desires, I verily decreeing the benefits; (22)

सः he; तया (with) that; श्रद्धया with faith; युक्तः united, तस्य of it; आराधनम् worship; ईहते wishes; लभते (he) obtains; च and; ततः thence; कामान् desires; मया by me; एव indeed; विहितान् decreed; हितान् benefits.

अंतवत्तु फलं तेषां तद्भवत्यल्पमेधसाम् ।
देवान्देवयजो यांति मद्भक्ता याति मामपि ॥२३॥

Finite indeed the fruit; that belongeth to those who are of small intelligence. To the Shining Ones go the worshippers of the Shining Ones, but My devotees come unto Me. (23)

अंतवत् with an end; तु indeed; फलं the fruit; तेषां of them; तत् that; भवति is; अल्पमेधसाम् = अल्पा मेधा येषां तेषां small, intelligence, whose, of (to) them; देवान् to the gods; देवयजः = देवान् यजन्ते इति gods, worship, thus; यांति go; मद्भक्ताः = मम भक्ताः my, devotees; यांति go; माम् to me; अपि also.

अव्यक्तं व्यक्तिमापन्नं मन्यंते मामबुद्धयः ।
परं भावमजानंतो ममाव्ययमनुत्तमम् ॥ २४ ॥

Those devoid of Reason think of Me, the Unmanifest, as having manifestation, knowing not My supreme nature, imperishable, most excellent. (24)

अव्यक्तं unmanifest; व्यक्तिम to manifestation; आपन्नं arrived; मन्यंते think; माम् me; अबुद्धयः irrational; परं highest; भावम् nature; अजानंतः unknowing; मम my; अव्ययम् imperishable; अनुत्तमम् best.

नाहं प्रकाशः सर्वस्य योगमायासमावृतः ।
मूढोऽयं नाभिजानाति लोको मामजमव्ययम् ॥२५॥

Nor am I of all discovered, enveloped in My creative illusion.[1] This deluded world knoweth Me not, the unborn, the imperishable. (25)

न not; अहं I; प्रकाशः known; सर्वस्य of all; योगमायासमावृतः = योगमायया समावृतः by yoga-mâyâ, covered; मूढः deluded; अयं this; न not; अभिजानाति knows; लोकः world; माम् me; अजम् unborn; अव्ययम् imperishable.

वेदाहं समतीतानि वर्तमानानि चार्जुन ।
भविष्याणि च भूतानि मां तु वेद न कश्चन ॥२६॥

I know the beings that are past, that are present, that are to come, O Arjuna, but no one knoweth Me. (26)

वेद know; अहं I; समतीतानि past; वर्तमानानि present; च and; अर्जुन O Arjuna; भविष्याणि future; च and; भूतानि beings; मां me; तु indeed; वेद knows; न not; कश्चन any one.

इच्छाद्वेषसमुत्थेन द्वंद्वमोहेन भारत ।
सर्वभूतानि संमोहं सर्गे यांति परंतप ॥ २७ ॥

By the delusion of the pairs of opposites, sprung from

1 Yoga-mâyâ is the creative power of yoga, all things being but thought-forms.

attraction and repulsion, O Bhârata, all beings walk this universe wholly deluded, O Parantapa. (27)

इच्छाद्वेषसमुत्थेन = इच्छायाः चः द्वेषात् च समुत्तिष्ठति इति तेन from desire, and, from hate, and, arises, this, by it; द्वंद्वमोहेन = द्वंद्वस्य मोहेन of the pair, by the delusion; भारत O Bhârata; सर्वभूतानि = सर्वाणि भूतानि all beings; संमोहं to delusion; सर्गे in creation; यांति go; परंतप O Parantapa.

येषां त्वंतगतं पापं जनानां पुण्यकर्मणाम् ।
ते द्वंद्वमोहनिर्मुक्ता भजंते मां दृढव्रताः ॥ २८ ॥

But those men of pure deeds, in whom sin is come to an end, they, freed from the delusive pairs of opposites, worship Me, steadfast in vows. (28)

येषाम् of whom; तु indeed; अन्तगतं = अंतं गतं gone, to end; पापं sin; जनानाम् of men; पुण्यकर्मणाम् = पुण्यं कर्म येषाम् तेषाम् pure, action, whose, of them; ते they; द्वंद्वमोहनिर्मुक्ताः = द्वंद्वस्य मोहात् निर्मुक्ताः of pairs, from delusion, freed; भजंते worship; मां me; दृढव्रताः = दृढं व्रतं येषां ते firm, vow, whose, they.

जरामरणमोक्षाय मामाश्रित्य यतंति ये ।
ते ब्रह्म तद्विदुः कृत्स्नमध्यात्मं कर्म चाखिलम् ॥ २९ ॥

They who refuged in Me strive for liberation from birth and death, they know the ETERNAL, the whole SELF-knowledge and all Action. (29)

जरामरणमोक्षाय = जरायाः च मरणात् च मोक्षाय from old age, and, from death, and, for liberation; मां me; आश्रित्य having taken refuge in; यतंति strive; ये who; ते they; ब्रह्म Brahman; तत् that; विदु: know; कृत्स्नम् the whole; अध्यात्मं = आत्मानं अधिकृत्य कृतं to the Âtmâ, having referred, made, (concerning the Self); कर्म action; च and; अखिलं whole.

साधिभूताधिदैवं मां साधियज्ञं च ये विदुः ।
प्रयाणकालेऽपि च मां ते विदुर्युक्तचेतसः ॥३०॥

They who know Me as the knowledge of the Elements, as that of the Shining Ones, and as that of the Sacrifice, they, harmonised in mind, know Me verily even in the time of forthgoing.[1] (30)

साधिभूताधिदैवं = अधिभूतेन च अधिदैवेन च सह with the adhibhuta (concerning the elements), and, with the adhidaiva (concerning the gods), together; साधियज्ञं = अधियज्ञेन सह with the adhiyajña (concerning the sacrifice), together; मां me; च and; ये who; विदुः know; प्रयाणकाले = प्रयाणस्य काले of going-forth, in the time; अपि also; च and; मां me; ते they; विदुः know; युक्तचेतसः = युक्तं चेतः येषाम् ते balanced, mind, whose, they.

इति श्रीमद्भगवद्गीता० ज्ञानयोगो नाम सप्तमोऽध्यायः ।

Thus in the glorious BHAGAVAD-GÎTÂ...the seventh discourse, entitled:

THE YOGA OF DISCRIMINATIVE KNOWLEDGE.

---

1 Death—going forth from the body.

EIGHTH DISCOURSE.

अर्जुन उवाच ।

किं तद्ब्रह्म किमध्यात्मं किं कर्म पुरुषोत्तम ।
अधिभूतं च किं प्रोक्तमधिदैवं किमुच्यते ॥ १ ॥

Arjuna said:

What is that ETERNAL, what SELF-knowledge, what Action, O Purushottama? And what is declared to be the knowledge of the Elements, what is called the knowledge of the Shining Ones? (1)

किं what; तत् that; ब्रह्म Brahman; किं what; अध्यात्मं Adhyâtma; किं what; कर्म karma; पुरुषोत्तम = पुरुषेषु उत्तम among men, O best; अधिभूतं adhibhûta; च and; किम् what; प्रोक्तम declared; अधिदैवम adhidaiva; किम् what; उच्यते is called.

अधियज्ञः कथं कोऽत्र देहेऽस्मिन्मधुसूदन ।
प्रयाणकाले च कथं ज्ञेयोऽसि नियतात्मभिः ॥२॥

What is knowledge of Sacrifice in this body, and how, O Madhusûdana? And how at the time of forthgoing art Thou known by the SELF-controlled? (2)

अधियज्ञः adhiyajña: कथं how; कः who; अत्र here; देहे in body; अस्मिन् this; मधुसूदन O Madhusûdana; प्रयाणकाले in (at) the time of departure; च and; कथं how; ज्ञेयः to be known; असि art (thou); नियतात्मभिः = नियतः आत्मा येषाम् तैः controlled, self, whose, by them.

अक्षरं ब्रह्म परमं स्वभावोऽध्यात्ममुच्यते ।
भूतभावोद्भवकरो विसर्गः कर्मसंज्ञितः ॥ ३ ॥

The Blessed Lord said :

The indestructible, the supreme, is the ETERNAL; His essential nature is called SELF-knowledge; the emanation that causes the birth of beings is named Action; (3)

अक्षरं undecaying; ब्रह्म Brahman; परमं supreme; स्वभावः own being (His nature); अध्यात्मं Adhyâtma; उच्यते is called; भूतभावोद्भवकरः = भूतानाम् भावस्य उद्भवं करोति इति सः of beings, of the nature the birth, makes, thus, that; विसर्गः emanation; कर्मसंज्ञितः = कर्म संज्ञा यस्य सः action, name, whose, that.

अधिभूतं क्षरो भावः पुरुषश्चाधिदैवतम् ।
अधियज्ञोऽहमेवात्र देहे देहभृतां वर ॥ ४ ॥

Knowledge of the Elements concerns My perishable nature, and knowledge of the Shining Ones concerns the life-giving energy;[1] the knowledge of sacrifice tells of Me, as wearing the body, O best of living beings. (4)

अधिभूतं Adhibhuta; क्षरः perishable; भावः nature; पुरुषः man; च and; अधिदैवतम Adhidaiva; अधियज्ञः Adhiyajña;

1 The male creative energy. The supreme Puruṣha is the Divine man, the manifested God.

अहं I; एव only; अत्र here; देहे in the body; देहभृतां=देहं बिभ्रति इति तेषां body, wear, thus, of them; वर O best.

अंतकाले च मामेव स्मरन्मुक्त्वा कलेवरम् ।
यः प्रयाति स मद्भाव याति नास्त्यत्र संशयः ॥५॥

And he who, casting off the body, goeth forth thinking upon Me only at the time of the end, he entereth into My being: there is no doubt of that. (5)

अंतकाले=अंतस्य काले of the end, in the time; च and; माम् me; एव only; स्मरन् remembering; मुक्त्वा having cast off; कलेवरम् body; यः who; प्रयाति goes forth; सः he; मद्भावं=मम भावं my, to nature; याति goes; न not; अस्ति is; अत्र here; संशयः doubt.

यं यं वापि स्मरन्भावं त्यजत्यंते कलेवरम् ।
तं तमेवैति कौंतेय सदा तद्भावभावितः ॥ ६ ॥

Whosoever at the end abandoneth the body, thinking upon any being, to that being only he goeth, O Kaunteya, ever to that conformed in nature. (6)

यं which; यं which; वा or; अपि also; स्मरन् remembering; भावं nature; त्यजति abandons; अंते in the end; कलेवरम् the body; तं to that; तं to that; एव only; एति goes; कौंतेय O Kaunteya; सदा always; तद्भावभावितः=तेन भावेन भावितः (by) that, (by) nature, natured (inspired).

तस्मात्सर्वेषु कालेषु मामनुस्मर युध्य च ।

मय्यर्पितमनोबुद्धिर्मामेवैष्यस्यसंशयम् ॥ ७ ॥

Therefore at all times think upon Me only, and fight. With mind and Reason set on Me, without doubt thou shalt come to Me. (7)

तस्मात् therefore; सर्वेषु in all; कालेषु (in) times; मां me; अनुस्मर remember; युध्य fight; च and; मय्यर्पितमनोबुद्धिः = मयि अर्पिते मनः च बुद्धिः च यस्य सः in Me, placed, mind, and, reason, and, whose, he; माम् to me; एव only; एष्यसि (thou) shalt go; असंशयम् doubtless.

अभ्यासयोगयुक्तेन चेतसा नान्यगामिना ।

परमं पुरुषं दिव्यं याति पार्थानुचिंतयन् ॥ ८ ॥

With the mind not wandering after aught else, harmonised by continual practice, constantly meditating, O Pârtha, one goeth to the Spirit, supreme, divine. (8)

अभ्यासयोगयुक्तेन = अभ्यासेन च योगेन च युक्तेन with practice, and, with yoga, and, (with) united; चेतसा with the mind; न not; अन्यगामिना = अन्यं गच्छति इति तेन to another, goes, thus, by it; परमं the highest; पुरुषं man; दिव्यं divine; याति goes; पार्थ O Pârtha; अनुचिंतयन् thinking on.

कविं पुराणमनुशासितार-

मणोरणीयासमनुस्मरेद्यः ।

सर्वस्य धातारमचिंत्यरूप-

मादित्यवर्णं तमसः परस्तात् ॥ ९ ॥

He who thinketh upon the Ancient, the Omniscient, the All-Ruler, minuter than the minute, the Supporter of all, of form unimaginable, refulgent as the sun beyond the darkness, (9)

कविं the poet; पुराणम् ancient; अनुशासितारम् the ruler of the world; अणोः than the small; अणीयांसं smaller; अनुस्मरेत् may think; यः who; सर्वस्य of all; धातारम् supporter; अचिन्त्य-रूपम् = अचिन्त्यम् रूपम् यस्य तम् inconceivable, form, whose, him; आदित्यवर्णं = आदित्यस्य वर्ण इव वर्णो यस्य तं of the sun, colour, like, color, whose, him; तमसः from darkness; परस्तात् beyond.

प्रयाणकाले मनसाऽचलेन

भक्त्या युक्तो योगबलेन चैव ।

भ्रुवोर्मध्ये प्राणमावेश्य सम्यक्

स तं परं पुरुषमुपैति दिव्यम् ॥ १० ॥

In the time of forthgoing, with unshaken mind, fixed in devotion, by the power of yoga drawing together his life-breath in the centre of the two eye-brows, he goeth to this Spirit, supreme, divine. (10)

प्रया काले in the time of forthgoing; मनसा with mind; अचलेन (with) unshaken; भक्त्या with devotion; युक्तः joined; योगबलेन = योगस्य बलेन of yoga, by strength; च and; एव only; भ्रुवोः of the (two) eyebrows; मध्ये in the middle; प्राणम्

breath; आवेश्य having placed; सम्यक् together; सः he; तं that; परं highest; पुरुषम् man; उपैति goes; दिव्यम् divine.

यदक्षरं वेदविदो वदंति
विशंति यद्यतयो वीतरागाः।
यदिच्छंतो ब्रह्मचर्यं चरंति
तत्ते पदं संग्रहेण प्रवक्ष्ये ॥ ११ ॥

That which is declared indestructible by the Veda-knowers, that which the controlled and passion-free enter, that desiring which Brahmachârya is performed, that path I will declare to thee with brevity. (11)

यत् whom; अक्षरं indestructible; वेदविदः the Veda-knowers; वदंति declare: विशंति enter; यत् (into) whom; यतयः the controlled; वीतरागाः = वीतः रागः येषाम् ते gone, passion, whose, they; यत् whom, इच्छंतः desiring; ब्रह्मचर्यं Brahmacharya; चरंति (they) perform; तत् that; ते of (to) thee; पदं path; संग्रहेण with (as) summary; प्रवक्ष्ये (I) will declare.

सर्वद्वाराणि संयम्य मनो हृदि निरुध्य च।
मूर्ध्न्याधायात्मनः प्राणमास्थितो योगधारणाम् ॥ १२ ॥

All the gates[1] closed, the mind confined in the heart, the life-breath fixed in his own head, concentrated by yoga, (12)

सर्वद्वाराणि = सर्वाणि द्वाराणि all gates; संयम्य having con-

[1] The gates of the body, *i. e.*, the sense organs.

trolled; मन: mind; हृदि in the heart; निरुध्य having confined; च and; मूर्ध्नि in the head; आधाय having placed; आत्मन: of the self; प्राणं breath; आस्थित: established (in); योगधारणाम् = योगस्य धारणाम् of yoga, concentration.

ओमित्येकाक्षरं ब्रह्म व्याहरन्मामनुस्मरन् ।
यः प्रयाति त्यजन्देहं स याति परमां गतिम् ॥१३॥

"Aum!" the one-syllabled Brahman, reciting, thinking upon Me, he who goeth forth, abandoning the body, he goeth on the highest path. (13)

ओम Aum; इति thus; एकाक्षरं one syllabled; ब्रह्म Brahman; व्याहरन् reciting; माम me; अनुस्मरन् remembering; य: who; प्रयाति goes forth; त्यजन् abandoning; देहं the body; स: he; याति goes; परमां (to the) highest; गतिं to the path (goal).

अनन्यचेताः सततं यो मां स्मरति नित्यशः ।
तस्याहं सुलभः पार्थ नित्ययुक्तस्य योगिनः ॥१४॥

He who constantly thinketh upon Me, not thinking ever of another, of him I am easily reached, O Pârtha, of this ever harmonised Yogi. (14)

अनन्यचेता: = न अन्यस्मिन् चेत: यस्य स: not, in another, thoughts, whose, he; सततं always; य: who; माम् me; स्मरति remember; नित्यश: ever; तस्य of him; अहं I; सुलभ: easily obtained; पार्थ O Pârtha; नित्ययुक्तस्य (of) ever-balanced; योगिन: of yogî.

मामुपेत्य पुनर्जन्म दुःखालयमशाश्वतम् ।
नाप्नुवंति महात्मानः संसिद्धिं परमां गताः ॥१५॥

Having come to Me, these Mahâtmâs come not again to birth, the place of pain, non-eternal; they have gone to the highest bliss. (15)

माम् to me; उपेत्य having come; पुनः again; जन्म birth; दुःखालयम् = दुःखानाम् आलयं of sorrows, the place; अशाश्वतम् non-eternal; न not; आप्नुवंति gain; महात्मानः Mahâtmâs; संसिद्धिं to perfection; परमां (to) highest; गताः gone.

आब्रह्मभुवनाल्लोकाः पुनरावर्तिनोऽर्जुन ।
मामुपेत्य तु कौंतेय पुनर्जन्म न विद्यते ॥ १६ ॥

The worlds, beginning with the world of Brahmâ, they come and go, O Arjuna; but he who cometh unto Me, O Kaunteya, he knoweth birth no more. (16)

आ up to; ब्रह्मभुवनात् = ब्रह्मणः भुवनात् of Brahmâ, from the world; लोकाः worlds; पुनरावर्तिनः again-returning; अर्जुन O Arjuna; माम् to me; उपेत्य having gone; तु indeed, कौंतेय O Kaunteya; पुनर्जन्म again-birth; न not; विद्यते is.

सहस्रयुगपर्यंतमहर्यद्ब्रह्मणो विदुः ।
रात्रिं युगसहस्रांता तेऽहोरात्रविदो जनाः ॥१७॥

The people who know the day of Brahmâ, a thousand ages in duration, and the night, a thousand ages in ending, they know day and night. (17)

सहस्रयुगपर्यंतम्=सहस्रं युगानि पर्यं तः यस्य तत् thousand, yugas, boundary, of which, that; अहः day; यत् which; ब्रह्मणः of Brahmâ; विदुः know; रात्रिं the night; युगसहस्रांतां=युगानाम् सहस्रेण अन्तः यस्याः ताम् of yugas, by (a) thousand, end, of which, that; ते they; अहोरात्रविदः=अहः च रात्रिं च विदंति इतिः day, and, night, and, know, thus; जनाः people.

अव्यक्ताद्व्यक्तयः सर्वाः प्रभवंत्यहरागमे ।

रात्र्यागमे प्रलीयंते तत्रैवाव्यक्तसंज्ञके ॥ १८ ॥

From the unmanifested all the manifested stream forth at the coming of day; at the coming of night they dissolve, even in That called the unmanifested. (18)

अव्यक्तात् from the unmanifested; व्यक्तयः the manifested; सर्वाः all; प्रभवंति flow forth; अहरागमे=अह्नः आगमे of day, in the coming; रात्र्यागमे=रात्र्या आगमे of night, in the coming; प्रलीयंते dissolve; तत्र there; एव even; अव्यक्तसंज्ञके=अव्यक्तम् संज्ञा यस्य तस्मिन् unmanifested, name, whose, Its, in that.

भूतग्रामः स एवायं भूत्वा भूत्वा प्रलीयते ।

रात्र्यागमेऽवशः पार्थ प्रभवत्यहरागमे ॥ १९ ॥

This multitude of beings, going forth repeatedly, is dissolved at the coming of night; by ordination, O Pârtha, it streams forth at the coming of day. (19)

भूतग्रामः=भूतानाम् ग्रामः of beings, the aggregate; सः that; even; अयं this; भूत्वा having been; भूत्वा having been;

प्रलीयंते dissolves; रात्र्यागमे in the coming of night; अवशः helpless; पार्थ O Pârtha; प्रभवति flows forth; अहरागमे in the coming of day.

परस्तस्मात्तु भावोऽन्योऽव्यक्तो ऽव्यक्तात्सनातनः ।
यः स सर्वेषु भूतेषु नश्यत्सु न विनश्यति ॥२०॥

Therefore verily there existeth, higher than that unmanifested, another unmanifested, eternal, which, in the destroying of all beings, is not destroyed. (20)

परः higher; तस्मात् than that; तु indeed; भावः nature; अन्यः another; अव्यक्तः unmanifested; अव्यक्तात् (than) the unmanifested; सनातनः ancient; यः who; सः that; सर्वेषु in all; भूतेषु (in) beings; नश्यत्सु (in) the being destroyed; न not; विनश्यति is destroyed.

अव्यक्तोऽक्षर इत्युक्तस्तमाहुः परमां गतिम् ।
यं प्राप्य न निवर्तंते तद्धाम परमं मम ॥ २१ ॥

That unmanifested, "the Indestructible," It is called; It is named the highest Path. They who reach It return not. That is My supreme abode. (21)

अव्यक्तः unmanifested; अक्षरः Indestructible; इति thus; उक्तः called; तम् that; आहुः (they) call; परमां the highest; गतिं path (goal); यं which; प्राप्य having obtained, न not; निवर्तंते return; तत् that; धाम abode; परमं highest; मम my.

पुरुषः स परः पार्थ भक्त्या लभ्यस्त्वनन्यया ।

यस्यांतः स्थानि भूतानि येन सर्वमिदं ततम् ॥२२॥

He, the highest Spirit, O Pârtha, may be reached by unswerving devotion to Him alone, in whom all beings abide, by whom all This[1] is pervaded. (22)

पुरुषः spirit; सः He; परः highest; पार्थ O Pârtha; भक्त्या by devotion; लभ्यः obtainable; तु indeed; अनन्यया without another (object); यस्य of whom; अंतःस्थानि = अंतः तिष्ठंति इति तानि inside. stand, thus, they; भूतानि beings; येन by whom; सर्वम् all; इदम् this; ततम् spread out.

यत्र काले त्वनावृत्तिमावृत्तिं चैव योगिनः ।

प्रयाता याति तं कालं वक्ष्यामि भरतर्षभ ॥ २३ ॥

That time wherein going forth, Yogis return not, and also that wherein going forth they return, that time shall I declare to thee, O prince of the Bharatas. (23)

यत्र where; काले in time; तु indeed; अनावृत्तिम् non-return; आवृत्तिम् return; च and; एव even; योगिनः yogîs; प्रयाताः gone forth; यांति go; तं that; वक्ष्यामि (I) will declare; भरतर्षभ O prince of the Bharatas.

अग्निर्ज्योतिरहः शुक्लः षण्मासा उत्तरायणम् ।

तत्र प्रयाता गच्छंति ब्रह्म ब्रह्मविदो जनाः ॥ २४ ॥

Fire, light, day-time, the bright fortnight, the six

---

1 This, the universe, in opposition to THAT, the source of all.

months of the northern path—then, going forth, the men who know the ETERNAL go to the ETERNAL. (24)

अग्निः fire; ज्योतिः light; अहः day; शुक्लः bright, (fortnight); षण्मासा six months; उत्तरायणम् the northern-going (of the sun); तत्र there; प्रयाता gone forth; गच्छन्ति go; ब्रह्म to Brahman; ब्रह्मविदः Brahma-knowing; जनाः people.

धूमो रात्रिस्तथा कृष्णः षण्मासा दक्षिणायनम्।
तत्र चान्द्रमसं ज्योतिर्योगी प्राप्य निवर्तते ॥ २५ ॥

Smoke, night-time, the dark fortnight also, the six months of the southern path—then the Yogî, obtaining the moonlight,[1] returneth. (25)

धूमः smoke; रात्रिः night; तथा so; कृष्णः dark (fortnight); षण्मासा six months; दक्षिणायनम् the southern going (of the sun); तत्र there; चान्द्रमसं = चन्द्रमसः इदं of the moon, this; ज्योतिः light; योगी the yogî; प्राप्य having obtained; निवर्तते returns.

शुक्लकृष्णे गती ह्येते जगतः शाश्वते मते।
एकया यात्यनावृत्तिमन्ययाऽऽवर्तते पुनः ॥ २६ ॥

Light and darkness, these are thought to be the world's everlasting paths; by the one he goeth who returneth not, by the other he who returneth again. (26)

शुक्लकृष्णे = शुक्ला च कृष्णा च light, and, dark, and; गती (two) paths; हि indeed; एते these; जगतः of the world; शाश्वते

---

1 The lunar, or astral, body. Until this is slain the soul returns to birth.

eternal (two); मते are thought (two); एकया by one; याति (he) goes; अनावृत्तिम् to non-return; अन्यया by another; आवर्तते (he) returns; पुनः again.

नैते सृती पार्थ जानन्योगी मुह्यति कश्चन ।
तस्मात्सर्वेषु कालेषु योगयुक्तो भवार्जुन ॥ २७ ॥

Knowing these paths, O Pârtha, the Yogî is nowise perplexed. Therefore in all times be firm in yoga, O Arjuna. (27)

न not एते these; सृती (two) paths; पार्थ O Pârtha; जानन् knowing; योगी the yogî; मुह्यति is perplexed; कश्चन any one; तस्मात् therefore; सर्वेषु in all; कालेषु (in) times; योगयुक्तः = योगेन युक्तः with yoga, balanced; भव be; अर्जुन O Arjuna.

वेदेषु यज्ञेषु तपःसु चैव
दानेषु यत्पुण्यफलं प्रदिष्टम् ।
अत्येति तत्सर्वमिदं विदित्वा
योगी परं स्थानमुपैति चाद्यम् ॥ २८ ॥

The fruit of meritorious deeds, attached in the Vedas to sacrifices, to austerities, and also to almsgiving, the Yogî passeth all these by having known this, and goeth to the supreme and ancient Seat. (28)

वेदेषु in the Vedas; यज्ञेषु in sacrifices; तपःसु in austerities ; च and ; एव even ; दानेषु in gifts ; यत् what ; पुण्यफलं= पुण्यस्य फलं of merit, the fruit ; प्रदिष्टम् assigned ; अत्येति goes beyond ; तत् that ; सर्वं all ; इदं this ; विदित्वा having known ; योगी the yogî ; परं highest ; स्थानं place ; उपैति goes ; च and ; आद्यम् first.

इति श्रीमद्भगवद्गीता० योगशास्त्रेऽक्षरब्रह्मयोगो नामाष्टमोऽध्यायः ।

Thus in the glorious BHAGAVAD-GÎTÂ...the eighth discourse entitled,

THE YOGA OF THE INDESTRUCTIBLE SUPREME ETERNAL.

NINTH DISCOURSE.

श्रीभगवानुवाच ।

इदं तु ते गुह्यतमं प्रवक्ष्याम्यनसूयवे ।
ज्ञानं विज्ञानसहितं यज्ज्ञात्वा मोक्ष्यसेऽशुभात् ॥ १ ॥

The Blessed Lord said:

To thee, the uncarping, verily shall I declare this profoundest Secret, wisdom with knowledge combined, which, having known, thou shalt be freed from evil. (1)

इदं this ; तु indeed ; ते of (to) thee ; गुह्यतमं most secret ; प्रवक्ष्यामि (I) will declare ; अनसूयवे (to) the uncarping ; ज्ञानं wisdom ; विज्ञानसहितं = विज्ञानेन सहितं with knowledge, together ; यत् which ; ज्ञात्वा having known ; मोक्ष्यसे (thou) shalt be freed ; अशुभात् from sin.

राजविद्या राजगुह्यं पवित्रमिदमुत्तमम् ।
प्रत्यक्षावगमं धर्म्यं सुसुखं कर्तुमव्ययम् ॥ २ ॥

Kingly Science, kingly Secret, supreme Purifier, this, intuitional, according to righteousness, very easy to perform, imperishable. (2)

राजविद्या = विद्यानाम् राजा of sciences, the king ; (or = राज्ञां विद्या of kings, the wisdon) राजगुह्यं = गुह्यानां राजा of secrets, the king ; पवित्रम् purifier ; इदं this ; उत्तमम् highest ; प्रत्यक्षावगमं = प्रत्यक्षेण अवगमः यस्य तत् by direct (intuition), knowledge, whose, that ;

धर्म्यं righteous; सुसुखं very happy; कर्तुम् to do; अव्ययम् imperishable.

अश्रद्दधानाः पुरुषा धर्मस्यास्य परंतप ।
अप्राप्य मां निवर्तन्ते मृत्युसंसारवर्त्मनि ॥ ३ ॥

Men without faith in this knowledge, O Parantapa, not reaching Me, return to the paths of this world of death. (3)

अश्रद्दधानाः unbelieving; पुरुषाः men; धर्मस्य of duty; अस्य (of) this; परंतप O Parantapa; अप्राप्य not having obtained; मां me; निवर्तन्ते return; मृत्युसंसारवर्त्मनि = मृत्योः संसारस्य च वर्त्मनि of death, (of) world, and, in the path.

मया ततमिदं सर्वं जगदव्यक्तमूर्तिना ।
मत्स्थानि सर्वभूतानि न चाहं तेष्ववस्थितः ॥ ४ ॥

By Me all this world is pervaded in My unmanifested aspect; all beings have root in Me, I am not rooted in them. (4)

मया by me; ततम् pervaded; इदं this; सर्वम् all; जगत् world; अव्यक्तमूर्तिना = अव्यक्ता मूर्तिः यस्य तेन unmainifested, aspect, whose, by him; मत्स्थानि = मयि तिष्ठंति इति तानि in me, stand, thus, they; सर्वभूतानि = सर्वाणि भूतानि all being; न not; च and; अहं I; तेषु in them; अवस्थितः placed.

न च मत्स्थानि भूतानि पश्य मे योगमैश्वरम् ।
भूतभृन्न च भूतस्थो ममात्मा भूतभावनः ॥ ५ ॥

Nor have beings root in Me; behold My sovereign yoga! The support of beings, yet not rooted in beings, My SELF their efficient cause. (5)

न not; च and; मत्स्थानि = मयि तिष्ठंति इति in me, stand, thus; भूतानि beings; पश्य see; मे my; योगम् yoga; ऐश्वरम् sovereign; भूतभृत् = भूतानि बिभर्ति इति beings, upholds, thus; न not; च and; भूतस्थः = भूतेषु तिष्ठति इति in beings, sits, thus; मम my; आत्मा self; भूतभावनः = भूतानि भावयति इति, beings, nourishes, thus.

यथाऽकाशस्थितो नित्यं वायुः सर्वत्रगो महान्।
तथा सर्वाणि भूतानि मत्स्थानीत्युपधारय ॥ ६ ॥

As the mighty air everywhere moving is rooted in the Âkâsha, so all beings rest rooted in Me—thus know thou. (6)

यथा as; आकाशस्थितः = आकाशे स्थितः in the ether, placed; नित्यं ever; वायुः the air; सर्वत्रगः = सर्वत्र गच्छति इति every where, goes, thus; महान् great; तथा so; सर्वाणि all; भूतानि beings; मत्स्थानि existing in me; इति thus; उपधारय know.

सर्वभूतानि कौंतेय प्रकृतिं याति मामिकाम्।
कल्पक्षये पुनस्तानि कल्पादौ विसृजाम्यहम् ॥ ७ ॥

All beings, O Kaunteya, enter My lower nature at the end of a world-age; at the beginning of a world-age again I emanate them. (7)

सर्वभूतानि all beings; कौंतेय O Kaunteya; प्रकृतिं to nature;

यांति go; मामिकाम् my; कल्पक्षये = कल्पस्य चये of a kalpa, in the decay; पुनः again; कल्पादौ = कल्पस्य आदौ of a kalpa, in the beginning; विसृजामि emanate; अहं I.

प्रकृतिं स्वामवष्टभ्य विसृजामि पुनः पुनः ।
भूतग्राममिमं कृत्स्नमवशं प्रकृतेर्वशात् ॥ ८ ॥

Hidden in Nature, which is Mine own, I emanate forth again and again all this multitude of beings, helpless, by the force of Nature. (8)

प्रकृतिं nature; स्वाम् own; अवष्टभ्य having embraced; विसृजामि emanate; पुनः again; पुनः again; भूतग्रामम् = भूतानाम् ग्रामं of beings, assemblage; इमं this; कृत्स्नम् all; अवशं helpless; प्रकृतेः of nature; वशात् by force.

न च मां तानि कर्माणि निबध्नंति धनंजय ।
उदासीनवदासीनमसक्तं तेषु कर्मसु ॥ ९ ॥

Nor do these works bind me, O Dhanañjaya, enthroned on high, unattached to actions. (9)

न not; च and; माम् me: तानि these; कर्माणि works; निबध्नंति bind; धनंजय O Dhanañjaya; उदासीनवत् like indifferent; आसीनं seated; असक्तं unattached; तेषु in those; कर्मसु action.

मयाऽध्यक्षेण प्रकृतिः सूयते सचराचरम् ।
हेतुनाऽनेन कौंतेय जगद्विपरिवर्तते ॥ १० ॥

Under Me, as supervisor, Nature sends forth the moving and unmoving; because of this, O Kaunteya, the universe revolves. (10)

मया by me; अध्यक्षेण (by, as) supervisor (lord); प्रकृतिः nature; सूयते sends out; सचराचरम्=चरेण च अचरेण च सह with the moving, and, with the unmoving, and, together; हेतुना by cause; अनेन (by) this; कौंतेय O Kaunteya; जगत् the world; विपरिवर्तते revolves.

अवजानंति मां मूढा मानुषीं तनुमाश्रितम् ।
परं भावमजानंतो मम भूतमहेश्वरम् ॥ ११ ॥

The foolish disregard Me, when clad in human semblance, ignorant of My supreme nature, the great Lord of beings; (11)

अवजानंति despise; मां me; मूढाः the foolish; मानुषीं human; तनुम् form; आश्रितम् refuged (in); परं highest; भावम् nature; अजानंतः unknowing; मम my; भूतमहेश्वरम्=भूतानाम् महेश्वरं of beings, the great Lord.

मोघाशा मोघकर्माणो मोघज्ञाना विचेतसः ।
राक्षसीमासुरीं चैव प्रकृतिं मोहिनीं श्रिताः ॥ १२ ॥

Empty of hope, empty of deeds, empty of wisdom, senseless, partaking of the deceitful, brutal, and demoniacal nature. (12)

मोघाशाः=मोघाः आशाः येषाम् ते vain, hopes, whose, they;

मोघकर्माणः = मोघानि कर्माणि येषाम् ते vain, deeds, whose, they; मोघज्ञानाः = मोघं ज्ञानं येषाम ते vain, knowledge, whose, they; विचेतसः mindless; राक्षसीम râkshasic; आसुरीम âsuric; च and; एव even; प्रकृतिं nature; मोहिनीं deceitful; श्रिताः refuged (in).

महात्मानस्तु मा पार्थ दैवीं प्रकृतिमाश्रिताः ।
भजंत्यनन्यमनसो ज्ञात्वा भूतादिमव्ययम् ॥ १३ ॥

Verily the Mahâtmas, O Pârtha, partaking of My divine nature, worship with unwavering mind, having known Me, the imperishable source of beings. (13)

महात्मानः mahâtmas; तु indeed; मां me; पार्थ O Pârtha; दैवीम् divine; प्रकृतिं nature; आश्रिताः refuged (in;) भजंति worship; अनन्यमनसः = न अन्यस्मिन् मनः येषां ते not, in another, mind, whose, they; ज्ञात्वा having known; भूतादिम = भूतानां आदि of beings, the beginning; अव्ययम imperishable.

सततं कीर्तयंतो मा यतंतश्च दृढव्रताः ।
नमस्यंतश्च मा भक्त्या नित्ययुक्ता उपासते ॥ १४ ॥

Always magnifying Me, strenuous, firm in vows, prostrating themselves before Me, they worship Me with devotion, ever harmonised. (14)

सततं always; कीर्तयंतः praising; मां me; यतंतः striving च and; दृढव्रताः = दृढं व्रतं येषाम् ते firm, vow, whose, they; नमस्यंतः saluting; च and; माम् me; भक्त्या with devotion; नित्ययुक्ताः ever-balanced; उपासते worship.

ज्ञानयज्ञेन चाऽप्यन्ये यजंतो मामुपासते ।
एकत्वेन पृथक्त्वेन बहुधा विश्वतोमुखम् ॥ १५ ॥

Others also sacrificing with the sacrifice of wisdom, worship Me as the One and the Manifold everywhere present. (15)

ज्ञानयज्ञेन = ज्ञानस्य यज्ञेन of wisdom, with the sacrifice; च and; अपि also; अन्ये others; यजंतः sacrificing; मां me; उपासते worship; एकत्वेन by the oneness; पृथक्त्वेन by the manifoldness; बहुधा by the many; विश्वतोमुखम् = विश्वतः मुखं यस्य तम् on all sides, face, whose, him.

अहं क्रतुरहं यज्ञः स्वधाऽहमहमौषधम् ।
मंत्रोऽहमहमेवाज्यमहमग्निरहं हुतम् ॥ १६ ॥

I the oblation; I the sacrifice; I the ancestral offering; I the fire-giving herb; the mantra I; I also the butter; I the fire; the burnt-offering I; (16)

अहं I; क्रतुः the oblation; अहं I; यज्ञः the sacrifice; स्वधा the offering to pitṛis; अहं I; औषधम् the herb; मंत्रः the mantra; अहं I; अहं I; एव even; आज्यं butter; अहं I; अग्निः the fire; अहं I; हुतम् the burnt-offering;

पिताऽहमस्य जगतो माता धाता पितामहः ।
वेद्यं पवित्रमोंकार ऋक् साम यजुरेव च ॥ १७ ॥

I the Father of this universe, the Mother, the Supporter, the Grandsire, the Holy One to be known, the Word of Power, and also the Ṛik, Sâma, and Yajur, (17)

पिता father; अहं I; अस्य of this; जगतः (of) world; माता mother; धाता supporter; पितामहः grandfather; वेद्यं to be known; पवित्रं purifier; ओंकारः the omkâra; ऋक् Ṛik; साम Sâma; यजुः Yajuḥ; एव even; च and;

गतिर्भर्ता प्रभुः साक्षी निवासः शरणं सुहृत् ।
प्रभवः प्रलयः स्थानं निधानं बीजमव्ययम् ॥ १८ ॥

The Path, Husband, Lord, Witness, Abode, Shelter, Lover, Origin, Dissolution, Foundation, Treasure-house, Seed imperishable. (18)

गतिः the path; भर्ता the husband; प्रभुः the lord; साक्षी the witness; निवासः the abode; शरणं the shelter; सुहृत् the lover; प्रभवः the origin; प्रलयः the dissolution; स्थानं the foundation; निधानं the treasure-house; बीजं the seed; अव्ययम् inexhaustible.

तपाम्यहमहं वर्षं निगृह्णाम्युत्सृजामि च ।
अमृतं चैव मृत्युश्च सदसच्चाहमर्जुन ॥ १९ ॥

I give heat; I hold back and send forth the rain; immortality and also death, being and non-being am I, Arjuna. (19)

तपामि burn; अहं I; अहं I; वर्षं rain; निगृह्णामि hold; उत्सृजामि let go; च and; अमृतं immortality; च and; एव even;

मृत्युः death; च and; सत् being; असत् non-being; च and; अहं I; अर्जुन O Arjuna.

त्रैविद्या मा सोमपाः पूतपापा
यज्ञैरिष्ट्वा स्वर्गतिं प्रार्थयंते ।
ते पुण्यमासाद्य सुरेंद्रलोक-
मश्नंति दिव्यान्दिवि देवभोगान् ॥ २० ॥

The knowers of the three, the Soma-drinkers, the purified from sin, worshipping Me with sacrifice, pray of Me the way to heaven; they, ascending to the holy world of the Ruler of the Shining Ones, eat in heaven the divine feasts of the Shining Ones. (20)

त्रैविद्याः = तिस्त्रः विद्याः येषां ते three, sciences (Vedas), whose, they; मां me; सोमपाः = सोमं पिबंति इति the soma, drink, thus; पूतपापाः = पूतं पापं येषाम् ते purified, sin, whose, they; यज्ञैः with; sacrifices; इष्ट्वा having sacrificed; स्वर्गतिं heaven-way; प्रार्थयंते ask; ते they; पुण्यं pure; आसाद्य having reached; सुरेंद्रलोकम् = सुराणां इंद्रस्य लोकं of the Gods, (of) Indra, the world; अश्नंति eat; दिव्यान् divine; दिवि in heaven; देवभोगान् = देवानाम् भोगान् of the Gods, the enjoyments,

ते तं भुक्त्वा स्वर्गलोकं विशालं
क्षीणे पुण्ये मर्त्यलोकं विशंति ।
एवं त्रयीधर्ममनुप्रपन्ना

गतागतं कामकामा लभंते ॥ २१ ॥

They, having enjoyed the spacious heaven-world, their holiness withered, come back to this world of death. Following the virtues enjoined by the three,[1] desiring desires, they obtain the transitory. (21)

ते they; तं that; भुक्त्वा having enjoyed; स्वर्गलोकं svarga-world; विशालं vast; क्षीणे (in the state of being) withered; पुण्ये (in)merit; मर्त्यलोकं = मर्त्यानां लोकं of mortals, the world; विशंति enter; एवं thus; त्रयीधर्म = त्रय्याः धर्मं, of the three (Vedas), the duty; अनुप्रपन्नाः devoted (to); गतागतम् = गतं च आगतम् च going, and, coming, and; कामकामाः = कामानाम् कामः येषाम् ते of (objects of) desire, desire, whose, they; लभंते obtain.

अनन्याश्चिंतयंतो मा ये जनाः पर्युपासते ।

तेषां नित्याभियुक्तानां योगक्षेमं वहाम्यहम् ॥२२॥

To those men who worship Me alone, thinking of no other, to those, ever harmonious, I bring full security. (22)

अनन्याः without-others; चिंतयंतः thinking; मां me; ये who; जनाः men; पर्युपासते worship; तेषाम् of them; नित्याभियुक्तानाम् of the ever-balanced; योगक्षेमं security; वहामि bring; अहं I.

येऽप्यन्यदेवताभक्ता यजंते श्रद्धयाऽन्विताः ।

तेऽपि मामेव कौंतेय यजंत्यविधिपूर्वकम् ॥ २३ ॥

---

1 The three Vedas.

Even the devotees of other Shining Ones who worship full of faith, they also worship Me, O son of Kuntî, though contrary to the ancient rule. (23)

ये who; अपि also; अन्यदेवताभक्ताः = अन्यासां देवतानां भक्ताः (of) other, of gods, devotee; यजंते worship; श्रद्धया with faith; अन्विताः endowed; ते they; अपि also: मां me: एव even; कौंतेय O Kaunteya; यजंति worship; अविधिपूर्वकम् = अविधिः पूर्वं यथा स्यात् तथा non-rule, preceding (guide), as, may be, so.

अहं हि सर्वयज्ञानां भोक्ता च प्रभुरेव च।
न तु मामभिजानंति तत्त्वेनातश्च्यवंति ते ॥२४॥

I am indeed the enjoyer of all sacrifices, and also the Lord, but they know Me not in Essence, and hence they fall. (24)

अहं I; हि indeed; सर्वयज्ञानाम् = सर्वेषाम् यज्ञानाम् of all, (of) sacrifices; भोक्ता the enjoyer; च and; प्रभुः lord; एव even; च and; न not; तु indeed; मां me; अभिजानंति know; तत्त्वेन by essence; अतः hence; च्यवंति fall; ते they.

याति देवव्रता देवान् पितॄन्यांति पितृव्रताः।
भूतानि याति भूतेज्या याति मद्याजिनोऽपि माम् ॥२५॥

They who worship the Shining Ones go to the Shining Ones; to the ancestors go the ancestor-worshippers; to the Elementals go those who sacrifice to Elementals; but My worshippers come unto Me. (25)

यांति go; देवव्रताः=देवेषु व्रतं येषाम् ते in the gods, vow, whose, they; देवान् to the gods; पितॄन् to the pitṛis: यांति go; पितृव्रताः=पितृषु व्रतं येषाम् ते in the pitṛis, vow, whose they; भूतानि to the Bhûtas; यांति go; भूतेज्याः=भूतेभ्यः इज्या येषां ते, for the Bhûtas, sacrifice, whose, they; यांति go; मद्याजिनः=मां यजंते इति me, sacrifice, thus; अपि also; मां to me.

पत्रं पुष्पं फलं तोयं यो मे भक्त्या प्रयच्छति ।
तदहं भक्त्युपहृतमश्नामि प्रयतात्मनः ॥ २६ ॥

He who offereth to Me with devotion a leaf, a flower, a fruit, water, that I accept from the striving self, offered as it is with devotion. (26)

पत्रं a leaf; पुष्पं a flower; फलं a fruit; तोयं water; यः who; मे of (to) me; भक्त्या with devotion; प्रयच्छति offers; तत् that; अहं I; भक्त्युपहृतम्=भक्त्या उपहृतं with devotion, offered; अश्नामि eat; प्रयतात्मनः=प्रयतः आत्मा यस्य तस्य striving, self, whose, of him.

यत्करोषि यदश्नासि यज्जुहोषि ददासि यत् ।
यत्तपस्यासि कौंतेय तत्कुरुष्व मदर्पणम् ॥ २७ ॥

Whatsoever thou doest, whatsoever thou eatest, whatsoever thou offerest, whatsoever thou givest, whatsoever thou doest of austerity, O Kaunteya, do thou that as an offering unto Me. (27)

यत् what; करोषि (thou) doest; यत् what; अश्नासि (thou) eatest; यत् what; जुहोषि (thou) offerest; ददासि (thou) givest;

यत् what ; यत् what ; तपस्यसि (thou) doest of austerity ; कौंतेय O Kaunteya ; तत् that ; कुरुष्व do (thou) ; मदर्पणम्=मयि अर्पणम् in (to) me, offering.

शुभाशुभफलैरेवं मोक्ष्यसे कर्मबंधनैः ।
संन्यासयोगयुक्तात्मा विमुक्तो मामुपैष्यसि ॥२८॥

Thus shalt thou be liberated from the bonds of action, yielding good and evil fruits ; thyself harmonised by the yoga of renunciation, thou shalt come unto Me when set free. (28)

शुभाशुभफलैः=शुभं च अशुभं च फलं येषाम् तैः good, and, evil, and, fruit, of which, by these ; एवं thus : मोक्ष्यसे shall be freed ; कर्मबंधनैः=कर्मणां बंधनैः of karma, by the bonds ; संन्यासयोगयुक्तात्मा=संन्यासस्य योगेन युक्तः आत्मा यस्य सः of renunciation, by yoga, balanced, self, whose, he ; विमुक्तः liberated ; मां to me ; उपैष्यसि shalt come.

समोऽहं सर्वभूतेषु न मे द्वेष्योऽस्ति न प्रियः ।
ये भजंति तु मां भक्त्या मयि ते तेषु चाप्यहम् ॥२९॥

The same am I to all beings; there is none hateful to Me nor dear. They verily who worship Me with devotion, they are in Me, and I also in them. (29)

समः equal ; अहं I ; सर्वभूतेषु=सर्वेषु भूतेषु in all, beings ; न not ; मे of me ; द्वेष्यः hateful ; अस्ति is ; न not ; प्रियः dear ; ये who ; भजंति worship ; तु indeed ; मां me ; भक्त्या with faith ; मयि in me ; ते they ; तेषु in them ; च and ; अपि also ; अहं I.

अपि चेत्सुदुराचारो भजते मामनन्यभाक्।
साधुरेव स मंतव्यः सम्यग्व्यवसितो हि सः॥ ३०॥

Even if the most sinful worship Me, with undivided heart, he too must be accounted righteous, for he hath rightly resolved; (30)

अपि also; चेत् if; सुदुराचार: very-evil-acting; भजते worships; मां me; अनन्यभाक् = न अन्यं भजाति इति not another worships, thus; साधु: righteous; एव even; स: he; मंतव्य: to be thought; सम्यक् well; व्यवसित: resolved; हि indeed; स: he.

क्षिप्रं भवति धर्मात्मा शश्वच्छांतिं निगच्छति।
कौंतेय प्रतिजानीहि न मे भक्तः प्रणश्यति॥ ३१॥

Speedily he becometh dutiful and goeth to eternal peace. O Kaunteya, know thou for certain that My devotee perisheth never. (31)

क्षिप्रं quickly; भवति becomes; धर्मात्मा = धर्मे आत्मा यस्य स: in righteousness, self, whose, he; शश्वत् eternal: शांतिं peace; निगच्छति goes; कौंतेय O Kaunteya; प्रतिजानीहि know; न not; मे my; भक्त: devotee; प्रणश्यति is destroyed.

मां हि पार्थ व्यपाश्रित्य येऽपि स्युः पापयोनयः।
स्त्रियो वैश्यास्तथा शूद्रास्तेऽपि यांति परां गतिम्॥३२॥

They who take refuge with Me, O Pârtha, though of

the womb of sin, women, Vaishyas, even Shûdras, they also tread the highest Path. (32)

मां me; हि indeed; पार्थ O Pârtha; व्यपाश्रित्य having taken refuge (in); ये who; अपि even; स्युः may be; पापयोनयः= पापा योनिः येषाम् ते sinful, womb, whose, they; स्त्रियः women; वैश्याः vaishyas; तथा also; शूद्राः shûdras; ते they; अपि also; यांति go; परां highest; गतिं goal.

किं पुनर्ब्राह्मणाः पुण्या भक्ता राजर्षयस्तथा ।
अनित्यमसुखं लोकमिमं प्राप्य भजस्व माम् ॥३३॥

How much rather then holy Brâhmaṇas and devoted royal saints; having obtained this transient joyless world, worship thou Me. (33)

किं how; पुनः again; ब्राह्मणाः Brâhmaṇas; पुण्याः pure; भक्ताः devoted; राजर्षयः râjarshis; तथा also; अ-नित्यं not lasting; अ-सुखं pleasureless; लोकम् world; इमं this; प्राप्य having obtained; भजस्व worship; मां me.

मन्मना भव मद्भक्तो मद्याजी मां नमस्कुरु ।
मामेवैष्यसि युक्त्वैवमात्मानं मत्परायणः ॥ ३४ ॥

On Me fix thy mind; be devoted to Me; sacrifice to Me; prostrate thyself before Me; harmonised thus in the SELF, thou shalt come unto Me, having Me as thy supreme goal. (34)

मन्मनाः=मयि मनः यस्य सः in me, mind, whose, he; भव be; मद्भक्तः=मम भक्तः my devotee; मद्याजी=मां यजते इति to me, sacrifices, thus; मां me; नमस्कुरु salute; मां to me; एव even; एष्यसि shalt come; युक्त्वा having balanced; एवं thus; आत्मानं the self; मत्परायण := अहं परायणं यस्य स: I, supreme goal, whose, he.

इति श्रीमद्भगवद्गीता० राजविद्याराजगुह्ययोगो नाम नवमोऽध्याय: ।

Thus in the glorious BHAGAVAD-GÎTÂ the......ninth discourse, entitled:

THE YOGA OF THE KINGLY SCIENCE AND THE KINGLY SECRET.

TENTH DISCOURSE.

श्रीभगवानुवाच ।

भूय एव महाबाहो शृणु मे परमं वचः ।
यत्तेऽहं प्रीयमाणाय वक्ष्यामि हितकाम्यया ॥१॥

The Blessed Lord said:

Again, O mighty-armed, hear thou My supreme word, that, desiring thy welfare, I will declare to thee who art beloved. (1)

भूयः again; एव even; महाबाहो O great-armed; शृणु hear; मे my; परमं highest; वचः word; यत् which; ते of (to) thee; प्रीयमाणाय to the being loved; वक्ष्यामि (I) will declare; हितकाम्यया = हितस्य काम्यया of wellbeing, by the desire.

न मे विदुः सुरगणाः प्रभवं न महर्षयः ।
अहमादिर्हि देवानां महर्षीणां च सर्वशः ॥ २ ॥

The multitude of the Shining Ones, or the great Ṛiṣhis, know not My forthcoming, for I am the beginning of all the Shining Ones and the great Ṛiṣhis. (2)

न not; मे my; विदुः know; सुरगणाः = सुराणाम् गणाः of the gods, the hosts; प्रभवं origin; न not; महर्षयः = महान्तः ऋषयः great ṛiṣhis; अहं I; आदिः the beginning; हि indeed; देवानाम् of the gods; महर्षीणाम् of the great ṛiṣhis; च and; सर्वशः everywhere.

यो मामजमनादिं च वेत्ति लोकमहेश्वरम् ।
असंमूढः स मर्त्येषु सर्वपापैः प्रमुच्यते ॥ ३ ॥

He who knoweth Me, unborn, beginningless, the great Lord of the world, he, among mortals without delusion, is liberated from all sin.

यः who; माम् me; अजम् unborn; अनादिं beginningless; च and; वेत्ति knows; लोकमहेश्वरम् = लोकस्य महेश्वरम of the world, the great Lord; असंमूढः undeluded; सः he; मर्त्येषु among mortals; सर्वपापैः = सर्वैः पापैः (by) all, by sins; प्रमुच्यते is quitted.

बुद्धिर्ज्ञानमसंमोहः क्षमा सत्यं दमः शमः ।
सुखं दुःखं भवोऽभावो भयं चाभयमेव च ॥ ४ ॥

Reason, wisdom, non-illusion, forgiveness, truth, self-restraint, calmness, pleasure, pain, existence, non-existence, fear, and also courage, (4)

बुद्धिः reason; ज्ञानम् wisdom; असंमोहः non-illusion; क्षमा forgiveness; सत्यं truth: दमः self-restraint; शमः calmness; सुखं pleasure; दुःखं pain; भवः existence; अ-भावः non-existence; भयं fear; च and; अभयं fearlessness; एव even; च and;

अहिंसा समता तुष्टिस्तपो दानं यशोऽयशः ।
भवंति भावा भूतानां मत्त एव पृथग्विधाः ॥ ५ ॥

Harmlessness, equanimity, content, austerity, almsgiving, fame and obloquy, are the various characteristics of beings issuing from Me. (5)

अहिंसा harmlessness; समता equanimity; तुष्टि: content; तप: austerity; दानं gift; यशः fame; अयशः obloquy; भवंति are; भावा: natures: भूतानाम् of beings; मत्त: from me; एव even; पृथग्विधाः = पृथक् विधाः येषां ते separate, kinds, whose, they.

महर्षयः सप्त पूर्वे चत्वारो मनवस्तथा।

मद्भावा मानसा जाता येषां लोक इमाः प्रजाः॥६॥

The seven great Ṛiṣhis, the ancient Four,[1] and also the Manus, were born of My nature and mind; of them this race was generated. (6)

महर्षयः the great ṛiṣhis; सप्त seven; पूर्वे ancient; चत्वारः four; मनवः manus; तथा also; मद्भावाः = मयिभावो येषां ते in me, being, whose, they; मानसाः mental; जाताः born; येषाम् of whom; लोके in world; इमाः these; प्रजाः races.

एतां विभूतिं योगं च मम यो वेत्ति तत्त्वतः।

सोऽविकंपेन योगेन युज्यते नात्र संशयः॥७॥

He who knows in essence that sovereignty and yoga of Mine, he is harmonised by unfaltering yoga; there is no doubt thereof. (7)

एतां this; विभूतिं sovereignty; योगं yoga; च and; मम of me; यः who; वेत्ति knows; तत्त्वतः by essence; सः he; अविकं-

1 The four Kumâras, or Virgin Youths, the highest in the occult Hierarchy of this earth.

येन = न विकम्पते इति तेन not, shakes, thus, by it; योगेन yoga; युज्यते is balanced; न not; अत्र here; संशयः doubt.

अहं सर्वस्य प्रभवो मत्तः सर्वं प्रवर्तते ।
इति मत्वा भजंते मां बुधा भावसमन्विताः ॥ ८ ॥

I am the Generator of all; all evolves from Me; understanding thus, the wise adore Me in rapt emotion. (8)

अहं I; सर्वस्य of all; प्रभवः the generator; मत्तः from me; सर्वं all; प्रवर्तते evolves; इति thus; मत्वा having thought; भजंते worship; मां me; बुधाः the wise; भावसमन्विताः = भावेन समन्विताः with emotion, endowed.

मच्चित्ता मद्गतप्राणा बोधयंतः परस्परम् ।
कथयंतश्च मां नित्यं तुष्यंति च रमंति च ॥ ९ ॥

Mindful of Me, their life hidden in Me, illumining each other, ever conversing about Me, they are content and joyful. (9)

मच्चित्ताः = मयि चित्तं येषाम् ते in me, mind, whose, they; मद्गतप्राणाः = मां गताः प्राणाः येषाम् ते to me, gone, breaths, whose, they; बोधयंतः illumining (making wise); परस्परम् mutually; कथयंतः talking (of); च and; मां me; नित्यं always; तुष्यंति are content; च and; रमंति rejoice; च and.

तेषां सततयुक्तानां भजतां प्रीतिपूर्वकम् ।
ददामि बुद्धियोगं तं येन मामुपयांति ते ॥ १० ॥

12

To these, ever harmonious, worshipping in love, I give the yoga of discrimination by which they come unto Me. (10)

तेषाम् of these; सततयुक्तानाम्=सततं युक्तानां always, (of the) balanced; भजतां (of the) worshipping; प्रीतिपूर्वकम्=प्रीतिः पूर्वं यथा स्यात् तथा love, before, as, may be, so; ददामि (I) give; बुद्धियोगं=बुद्धेः योगं of reason, the yoga; तं that; येन by which; मां to me; उपयांति come; ते they.

तेषामेवानुकंपार्थमहमज्ञानजं तमः ।
नाशयाम्यात्मभावस्थो ज्ञानदीपेन भास्वता ॥ ११ ॥

Out of pure compassion for them, dwelling within their SELF, I destroy the ignorance-born darkness by the shining lamp of wisdom. (11)

तेषाम् of them; एव even; अनुकंपार्थं=अनुकम्पायाः अर्थं of compassion, for the sake; अहं I; अज्ञानजं=अज्ञानात् जातं from unwisdom, born; तमः darkness; नाशयामि (I) destroy; आत्मभावस्थः=आत्मनः भावे स्थितः of the self, in the nature, seated; ज्ञानदीपेन=ज्ञानस्य दीपेन of wisdom, with the light; भास्वता (with the) shining.

अर्जुन उवाच ।
परं ब्रह्म परं धाम पवित्रं परमं भवान् ।
पुरुषं शाश्वतं दिव्यमादिदेवमजं विभुम् ॥ १२ ॥

Arjuna said:

Thou art the supreme ETERNAL, the supreme

Abode, the supreme Purity, eternal, divine Man, primeval Deity, unborn, the Lord! (12)

परं highest; ब्रह्म Brahman; परं highest; धाम abode; पवित्रं pure (or purifie); परमं highest; भवान् Thou; पुरुषं man; शाश्वतं eternal; दिव्यं divine; आदिदेवं first God; अजं unborn; विभुम् Lord.

आहुस्त्वामृषयः सर्वे देवर्षिर्नारदस्तथा ।
असितो देवलो व्यासः स्वयं चैव ब्रवीषि मे ॥१३॥

All the Rishis have thus acclaimed Thee, as also the divine Rishi, Nârada; so Asita, Devala, and Vyâsa; and now Thou Thyself tellest it me. (13)

आहुः declare; त्वाम् thee; ऋषयः the Rishis; सर्वे all; देवर्षिः divine Rishi; नारदः Nârada; तथा also; असितः Asita; देवलः Devala; व्यासः Vyâsa; स्वयं (thy) self; च and; एव even; ब्रवीषि tellest; मे me.

सर्वमेतदृतं मन्ये यन्मां वदसि केशव ।
नहि ते भगवन्व्यक्तिं विदुर्देवा न दानवाः ॥१४॥

All this I believe true that Thou sayest to me, O Keshava. Thy manifestation, O Blessed Lord, neither Shining Ones nor Dânavas comprehend. (14)

सर्वम् all; एतत् this; ऋतं true; मन्ये (I) think; यत् which मां to me; वदसि thou sayest; केशव O Keshava; न not; हि indeed; ते thy; भगवन् O blessed Lord; व्यक्तिं manifestation; विदुः know; देवाः Gods; न not; दानवाः Dânavas.

स्वयमेवात्मनाऽऽत्मानं वेत्थ त्वं पुरुषोत्तम ।
भूतभावन भूतेश देवदेव जगत्पते ॥ १५ ॥

Thyself indeed knowest Thyself by Thyself, O Purușhottama! Source of beings, Lord of beings, Shining One of Shining Ones, Ruler of the world! (15)

स्वयं (thy) self ; एव only ; आत्मना by (thy) self ; आत्मानं (thy) self ; वेत्थ knowest; त्वम् thou ; पुरुषोत्तम O Purușhottama ; भूतभावन = भूतानि भावयसि इति beings, O thou (that) causest to become, thus ; भूतेश = भूतानाम् ईश of beings, O Lord ; देवदेव = देवानाम् देव of gods, O God ; जगत्पते = जगतः पते of the world, O Ruler.

वक्तुमर्हस्यशेषेण दिव्या ह्यात्मविभूतयः ।
याभिर्विभूतिभिर्लोकानिमांस्त्वं व्याप्य तिष्ठसि ॥ १६ ॥

Deign to tell without reserve of Thine own divine glories, by which glories Thou remainest, pervading these worlds. (16)

वक्तुम् to tell ; अर्हसि shouldst ; अशेषेण by without-remainder ; दिव्याः divine ; हि indeed ; आत्मविभूतयः = आत्मनः विभूतयः of self, glories ; याभिः (by) which ; विभूतिभिः by glories ; लोकान् worlds ; इमान् these ; त्वम् thou ; व्याप्य having pervaded ; तिष्ठसि sittest.

कथं विद्यामहं योगिंस्त्वां सदा परिचिंतयन् ।
केषु केषु च भावेषु चिंत्योऽसि भगवन्मया ॥ १७ ॥

How may I know Thee, O Yogî, by constant meditation? In what, in what aspects art Thou to be thought of by me, O blessed Lord? (17)

कथं how; विद्यामहं may know; अहं I; योगिन् O yogî; त्वाम् thee; सदा always; परिचिंतयन् meditating; केषु (in) what; केषुं (in) what; च and; भावेषु in moods, चिंत्यः to be thought; असि art; भगवन् O blessed Lord; मया by me.

विस्तरेणात्मनो योगं विभूतिं च जनार्दन ।
भूयः कथय तृप्तिर्हि श्रृण्वतो नास्ति मेऽमृतम् ॥ १८ ॥

In detail tell me again of Thy yoga and glory, O Janârdana; for me there is never satiety in hearing Thy life-giving words. (18)

विस्तरेण by (in) detail; आत्मनः of (thy) own; योगं yoga; विभूतिं glory; जनार्दन O Janârdana; भूयः again; कथय tell; तृप्तिः contentment; हि indeed; श्रृण्वतः (of) hearing; न not; अस्ति is; मे of me; अमृतम् nectar.

श्रीभगवानुवाच ।

हंत ते कथयिष्यामि दिव्या ह्यात्मविभूतयः ।
प्राधान्यतः कुरुश्रेष्ठ नास्त्यंतो विस्तरस्य मे ॥ १९ ॥

The Blessed Lord said:

Blessed be thou! I will declare to thee My divine glory by its chief characteristics, O best of the Kurus; there is no end to details of Me. (19)

इत well; ते (to) thee; कथयिष्यामि (I) will declare; दिव्याः divine; हि indeed; आत्मविभूतयः my glories; प्राधान्यतः in the main; कुरुश्रेष्ठ O best of the Kurus; न not; अस्ति is; अन्तः end; विस्तरस्य of detail; मे of me.

अहमात्मा गुडाकेश सर्वभूताशयस्थितः ।
अहमादिश्च मध्यं च भूतानामंत एव च ॥ २० ॥

I, O Guḍâkesha, am the SELF, seated in the heart of all beings; I am the beginning, the midule, and also the end of all beings. (20)

अहं I; आत्मा the self; गुडाकेश O Guḍâkesha; सर्वभूताशयस्थितः = सर्वेषाम् भूतानाम् आशये स्थितः (of) all, of beings, in the heart, seated; अहं I; आदिः the beginning; मध्यं the middle; च and; भूतानाम् of beings; अन्तः the end; एव even; च and.

आदित्यानामहं विष्णुर्ज्योतिषां रविरंशुमान् ।
मरीचिर्मरुतामस्मि नक्षत्राणामहं शशी ॥ २१ ॥

Of the Âdityas I am Vishṇu; of radiances the glorious Sun; I am Marîchi of the Maruts, of the asterisms the Moon am I. (21)

आदित्यानाम् of the Âdityas; अहं I; विष्णुः Vishṇu; ज्योतिषाम् of lights; रविः the Sun; अंशुमान् radiant; मरीचिः Marîchi; मरुताम् of the Maruts; अस्मि (I) am; नक्षत्राणाम् of asterisms; अहं I; शशी the moon.

वेदानां सामवेदोऽस्मि देवानामस्मि वासवः ।

इन्द्रियाणां मनश्चास्मि भूतानामस्मि चेतना ॥ २२ ॥

Of the Vedas I am the Sâma-Veda; I am Vâsava of the Shining Ones; and of the senses I am the mind; I am of living beings the intelligence. (22)

वेदानाम् of the Vedas; सामवेदः the Sâmaveda; अस्मि (I) am; देवानाम् of the gods; अस्मि (I) am; वासवः Vâsava; इंद्रियाणाम् of the senses; मनः mind; च and; अस्मि (I) am; भूतानाम् of beings; अस्मि (I) am; चेतना intelligence.

रुद्राणां शंकरश्चास्मि वित्तेशो यक्षरक्षसाम् ।

वसूनां पावकश्चास्मि मेरुः शिखरिणामहम् ॥ २३ ॥

And of the Rudras Shankara am I; Vittesha of the Yakṣhas and Râkṣhasas; and of the Vasus I am Pâvaka; Meru of high mountains am I. (23)

रुद्राणाम् of the Rudras; शंकरः Shankara; च and; अस्मि (I) am; वित्तेशः Vittesha, or Kubera; यक्षरक्षसाम् = यक्षाणां च रक्षसां च of Yakshas, and of Râkshasas, and; वसूनाम् of Vasus; पावकः Pâvaka; च and; अस्मि (I) am; मेरुः Meru; शिखरिणाम् = शिखराणि एषां संति इति तेषां peaks of which, (there) are, thus, of them; अहं I.

पुरोधसां च मुख्यं मां विद्धि पार्थ बृहस्पतिम् ।

सेनानीनामहं स्कंदः सरसामस्मि सागरः ॥ २४ ॥

And know Me, O Pârtha, of household priests the chief, Brihaspati; of generals I am Skanda; of lakes I am the ocean. (24)

पुरोधसां of house-priests; च and; मुख्यं the chief; मां me; विद्धि know; पार्थ O Pârtha; बृहस्पतिम् Brihaspati; सेनानीनाम् = सेनां नयंति इति तेषां the army, leads, thus, of them; अहं I; स्कंदः Skanda; सरसाम् of lakes; अस्मि (I) am; सागरः the ocean.

महर्षीणां भृगुरहं गिरामस्म्येकमक्षरम् ।
यज्ञानां जपयज्ञोऽस्मि स्थावराणां हिमालयः ॥२५॥

Of the great Ṛishis, Bhrigu; of speech I am the one syllable; of sacrifices I am the sacrifice of silent repetitions; of immovable things the Himâlaya. (25)

महर्षीणां of the great Ṛishis; भृगुः Bhṛigu; अहं I; गिरां of speech; अस्मि (I) am; एकं the one; अक्षरम् syllable; यज्ञानां of sacrifices; जपयज्ञः = जपस्य यज्ञः of repetition, the sacrifice; अस्मि (I) am; स्थावराणाम् of immovable (Things); हिमालयः Himâlaya.

अश्वत्थः सर्ववृक्षाणां देवर्षीणां च नारदः ।
गंधर्वाणां चित्ररथः सिद्धानां कपिलो मुनिः ॥ २६ ॥

Ashvattha of all trees; and of divine Ṛishis Nârada; of Gandharvas Chitraratha; of the perfected the Muni Kapila. (26)

अश्वत्थः Ashvattha; सर्ववृक्षाणाम् = सर्वेषाम् वृक्षाणाम् (of) all, of trees; देवर्षीणाम् of divine Ṛshis; च and; नारदः Nârada; गंधर्वाणाम् of Gandharvas; चित्ररथः Chitraratha; सिद्धानां of the perfect; कपिलः Kapila; मुनिः muni.

उच्चैःश्रवसमश्वानां विद्धि माममृतोद्भवम् ।

ऐरावतं गजेंद्राणां नराणां च नराधिपम् ॥ २७ ॥

Uchchaishravâ of horses know Me, nectar-born; Airâvata of lordly elephants; and of men the monarch. (27)

उच्चैःश्रवसम् Uchchhaishravâ; अश्वानां of horses; विद्धि know; मां me; अमृतोद्भवम् = अमृतात् उद्भवः यस्य सः from amrita, birth, whose, he; ऐरावतं Airâvata; गजेंद्राणां of the lords of elephants; नराणाम् of men; च and; नराधिपम् = नराणां अधिपं of men, the monarch.

आयुधानामहं वज्रं धेनूनामास्मि कामधुक् ।
प्रजनश्चास्मि कंदर्पः सर्पाणामास्मि वासुकिः ॥ २८ ॥

Of weapons I am the thunderbolt; of cows I am Kâmadhuk; I am Kandarpa of the progenitors;' of serpents Vâsuki am I. (28)-

आयुधानाम् of weapons; अहं I; वज्रं the thunderbolt; धेनूनाम् of cows; अस्मि (I) am; कामधुक् = कामान् दोग्धि इति desires, milks, thus (Kâmadhuk); प्रजनः the progenitor; च and; अस्मि (I) am; कंदर्पः Kandarpa; सर्पाणाम् of serpents; अस्मि (I) am; वासुकिः Vâsuki.

अनन्तश्चास्मि नागानां वरुणो यादसामहम् ।
पितॄणामर्यमा चास्मि यमः संयमतामहम् ॥ २९ ॥

And I am Ananta of Nâgas; Varuṇa of sea-dwellers I; and of ancestors Aryamâ; Yama of governors am I. (29)

अनन्तः Ananta; च and; अस्मि (I) am; नागानां of Nâgas; वरुणः Varuṇa; यादसां of sea-beings; अहं I; पितॄणां of ancestors; अर्यमा Aryamâ; च and; अस्मि (I) am; यमः Yama; संयमतां of governors; अहं I.

प्रह्लादश्चास्मि दैत्यानां कालः कलयतामहम् ।
मृगाणां च मृगेन्द्रोऽहं वैनतेयश्च पक्षिणाम् ॥ ३० ॥

And I am Prahlâda of Daityas; of calculators Time am I; and of wild beasts I the imperial beast; and Vainateya of birds. (30)

प्रह्लादः Prahlâda; च and; अस्मि (I) am; दैत्यानां of Daityas; कालः Time; कलयतां of calculators; अहं I; मृगाणां of wild things; च and; मृगेन्द्रः = मृगाणां इन्द्रः of wild things, ruler; अहं I; वैनतेयः = विनतायाः अपत्यं पुमान् of Vinatâ, child, male (Vainateya); च and; पक्षिणाम् of birds.

पवनः पवतामस्मि रामः शस्त्रभृतामहम् ।
झषाणां मकरश्चास्मि स्रोतसामस्मि जाह्नवी ॥ ३१ ॥

Of purifiers I am the wind; Râma of warriors I; and I am Makara of fishes; of streams the Gangâ am I. (31)

पवनः the wind; पवतां of purifiers; अस्मि (I) am; रामः Râma; शस्त्रभृतां = शस्त्राणि बिभ्रति इति तेषां weapons, bears, thus, of them; झषाणां of fishes; मकरः makara; च and; अस्मि (I);

am ; स्रोतसां of streams ; अस्मि (I) am ; जाह्नवी = जह्नोः अपत्यं स्त्री of Jahnu, child, female (Gangâ).

सर्गाणामादिरंतश्च मध्यं चैवाहमर्जुन ।

अध्यात्मविद्या विद्यानां वादः प्रवदतामहम् ॥ ३२ ॥

Of creations the beginning and the ending and also the middle am I, O Arjuna. Of sciences the science concerning the SELF ; the speech of orators I. (32)

सर्गाणां of creations ; आदिः the beginning ; अन्तः the end ; च and ; मध्यं the middle ; च and ; एव even ; अहं I ; अर्जुन O Arjuna ; अध्यात्मविद्या = अध्यात्मनः विद्या of concerning the self, the science ; विद्यानां of sciences ; वादः the speech ; प्रवदतां of orators ; अहं I.

अक्षराणामकारोऽस्मि द्वंद्वः सामासिकस्य च ।

अहमेवाक्षयः कालो धाताऽहं विश्वतोमुखः ॥ ३३ ॥

Of letters the letter A I am, and the dual of all the compounds ;[1] I also everlasting Time ; I the Supporter, whose face turns everywhere. (33)

अक्षराणां of letters ; अकारः the letter A ; अस्मि (I) am ; द्वंद्वः the dvandva ; सामासिकस्य = समासानां समूहः तस्य. of compounds, the group, of that ; च and ; अहं I ; एव even ; अक्षयः everlasting ; कालः time ; धाता the supporter ; अहं I ; विश्वतोमुखः having faces in every direction.

---

1 Among the various kinds of compounds used in Saṃskrit, that called the dvandva, the copulative.

मृत्युः सर्वहरश्चाहमुद्भवश्च भविष्यताम् ।
कीर्तिः श्रीर्वाक्च नारीणां स्मृतिर्मेधा धृतिः क्षमा ॥३४॥

And all-devouring Death am I, and the origin of all to come; and of feminine qualities, fame, prosperity, speech, memory, intelligence, firmness, forgiveness. (34)

मृत्युः death ; सर्वहरः = सर्वं हरति इति all, seizes, thus; च and ; अहं I; उद्भवः the birth; च and; भविष्यतां of future things; कीर्तिः fame; श्रीः prosperity ; वाक् speech; च and; नारीणाम् of feminine things ; स्मृतिः memory ; मेधा intelligence; धृतिः firmness ; क्षमा forgiveness.

बृहत्साम तथा साम्नां गायत्री छंदसामहम् ।
मासानां मार्गशीर्षोऽहमृतूनां कुसुमाकरः ॥ ३५ ॥

Of hymns also Brihatsâman ; Gâyatrî of metres am I; of months I am Margashîrsha ; of seasons the flowery. (35)

बृहत्साम Brihatsâman ; तथा also ; साम्नां of Sâma hymns ; गायत्री Gâyatrî; छंदसाम् metres; अहं I; मासानां of months; मार्गशीर्षः mârgashîrsha ; अहं I; ऋतूनां of seasons ; कुसुमाकरः = कुसुमानां आकरः of flowers, the mine.

द्यूतं छलयतामस्मि तेजस्तेजस्विनामहम् ।
जयोऽस्मि व्यवसायोऽस्मि सत्त्वं सत्त्ववतामहम् ॥ ३६॥

I am the gambling of the cheat, and the splendour

of splendid things I; I am victory, I am determination, and the truth of the truthful I. (36)

द्यूतं the gambling; छलयतां of the cheating; अस्मि (I) am; तेज: the splendour; तेजस्विनां of splendours; अहं I; जय: victory; अस्मि (I) am; व्यवसाय: determination; अस्मि (I) am; सत्वं the truth; सत्ववतां of the truthful; अहं I.

वृष्णीनां वासुदेवोऽस्मि पांडवानां धनंजयः ।
मुनीनामप्यहं व्यासः कवीनामुशना कविः ॥३७॥

Of the Vṛiṣhṇis Vâsudeva am I; of the Pâṇḍavas Dhanañjaya; of the Sages also I am Vyâsa; of poets Ushanâ the Bard. (37)

वृष्णीनां of Vṛiṣhṇis; वासुदेव: Vâsudeva; अस्मि (I) am; पांडवानां Pâṇḍavas; धनंजय: Dhanañjaya; मुनीनां of munis; अपि also; अहं I; व्यास: Vyâsa; कवीनाम् of poets; उशना: Ushanâ; कवि: the poet.

दंडो दमयतामस्मि नीतिरस्मि जिगीषताम् ।
मौनं चैवास्मि गुह्यानां ज्ञानं ज्ञानवतामहम् ॥३८॥

Of rulers I am the sceptre; of those that seek victory I am statesmanship; and of secrets I am also silence; the knowledge of knowers am I. (38)

दंड: the sceptre; दमयतां of rulers; अस्मि (I) am; नीति: policy; अस्मि (I) am; जिगीषतां of the victory-seekers; मौनं silence; च and; एव even; अस्मि (I) am; गुह्यानां of secrets; ज्ञानं the knowledge; ज्ञानवतां of knowers; अहं I.

यच्चापि सर्वभूताना बीजं तदहमर्जुन ।
न तदस्ति विना यत्स्यान्मया भूतं चराचरम् ॥३९॥

And whatsoever is the seed of all beings, that am I, O Arjuna; nor is there aught, moving or unmoving, that may exist bereft of Me. (39)

यत् which; च and; अपि also; सर्वभूतानां of all beings; बीजं seed; तत् that; अहं I; अर्जुन O Arjuna, न not; तत् that; अस्ति is; विना without; यत् which; स्यात् may be; मया by me; भूतं being; चराचरम् = चरं च अचरं च moving, and, unmoving, and.

नांतोऽस्ति मम दिव्यानां विभूतीनां परंतप ।
एष तूद्देशतः प्रोक्तो विभूतेर्विस्तरो मया ॥ ४० ॥

There is no end of My divine powers, O Parantapa. What has been declared is only illustrative of My infinite glory. (40)

न not; अंतः end; अस्ति is; मम my; दिव्यानां (of) divine; विभूतीनां glories; परंतप O Parantapa; एष this; तु indeed; उद्देशतः by (way of) illustration; प्रोक्तः said; विभूतेः of glory; विस्तरः extent; मया by me.

यद्यद्विभूतिमत्सत्वं श्रीमदूर्जितमेव वा ।
तत्तदेवावगच्छ त्वं मम तेजोऽशसंभवम् ॥ ४१ ॥

Whatsoever is glorious, good, beautiful, and mighty,

understand thou that to go forth from a fragment of My splendour. (41)

यत् what; यत् what; विभूतिमत् glorious; सत्त्वं being; श्रीमत् prosperous; ऊर्जितम् mighty; एव even; च and; तत् that; तत् that; एव even; अवगच्छ recognise; त्वम् thou; मम my; तेजोंऽशसंभवम् = तेजसः अंशात् संभवः यस्य तत् of splendour, from portion, origin, of which, that.

अथवा बहुनैतेन किं ज्ञातेन तवार्जुन ।
विष्टभ्याहमिदं कृत्स्नमेकांशेन स्थितो जगत् ॥ ४२ ॥

But what is the knowledge of all these details to thee, O Arjuna? Having pervaded this whole universe with one fragment of Myself, I remain. (42)

अथ now; वा or; बहुना (by) many; एतेन (by) this; किं what; ज्ञातेन by (with being) known; तव of (by) thee; अर्जुन O Arjuna; विष्टभ्य having established; अहं I; इदं this; कृत्स्नं all; एकांशेन by one portion; स्थितः (am) seated; जगत् the world.

इति श्रीमद्भगवद्गीता० विभूतियोगो नाम दशमोऽध्यायः ।

Thus in the glorious BHAGAVAD-GĪTĀ ... the tenth discourse, entitled :

THE YOGA OF SOVEREIGNTY.

ELEVENTH DISCOURSE.

अर्जुन उवाच ।

मदनुग्रहाय परमं गुह्यमध्यात्मसंज्ञितम् ।
यत्त्वयोक्तं वचस्तेन मोहोऽयं विगतो मम ॥ १ ॥

Arjuna said:

This word of the Supreme Secret concerning the SELF, Thou hast spoken out of compassion; by this my delusion is taken away. (1)

मदनुग्रहाय = मम अनुग्रहाय of me, for favour; परमं the highest; गुह्यं secret; अध्यात्मसंज्ञितम् Adhyâtma-named; यत् which; त्वया by Thee; उक्तं spoken; वचः word; तेन by that; मोहः delusion; अयं this; विगतः gone; मम my.

भवाप्ययौ हि भूतानां श्रुतौ विस्तरशो मया ।
त्वत्तः कमलपत्राक्ष माहात्म्यमपि चाव्ययम् ॥ २ ॥

The production and destruction of beings have been heard by me in detail from Thee, O Lotus-eyed, and also Thy imperishable greatness. (2)

भवाप्ययौ = भवः च अप्ययः च the becoming, and, dissolution, and; हि indeed; भूतानां of beings; श्रुतौ (the two) heard; विस्तरशः in detail; मया by me; त्वत्तः from Thee; कमलपत्राक्ष = कमलस्य पत्रं इव अक्षिणी यस्य सः of lotus, leaf, like, eyes, whose, O he; माहात्म्यम् greatness; अपि also; च and; अव्ययं inperishable.

एवमेतद्यथात्थ त्वमात्मानं परमेश्वर ।
द्रष्टुमिच्छामि ते रूपमैश्वरं पुरुषोत्तम ॥ ३ ॥

O supreme Lord, even as Thou describest Thyself, O best of beings, I desire to see Thy Form omnipotent. (3)

एवं thus; एतत् this; यथा as; आत्थ sayest; त्वम् thou; आत्मानं (thy) self; परमेश्वर O highest Lord; द्रष्टुम् to see; इच्छामि (I) desire; ते thy; रूपं form; ऐश्वरं sovereign; पुरुषोत्तम O best of beings.

मन्यसे यदि तच्छक्यं मया द्रष्टुमिति प्रभो ।
योगेश्वर ततो मे त्वं दर्शयात्मानमव्ययम् ॥ ४ ॥

If thou thinkest that by me It can be seen, O Lord, Lord of Yoga, then show me Thine imperishable SELF. (4)

मन्यसे thinkest; यदि if; तत् that; शक्यं possible; मया by me; द्रष्टुम् to see; इति thus; प्रभो O Lord; योगेश्वर = योगस्य ईश्वर of yoga, O Lord; ततः then; मे of (to) me; त्वम् thou; दर्शय show; आत्मानं (thy) self; अव्ययं imperishable.

श्रीभगवानुवाच ।

पश्य मे पार्थ रूपाणि शतशोऽथ सहस्रशः ।
नानाविधानि दिव्यानि नानावर्णाकृतीनि च ॥५॥

Behold, O Pârtha, forms of Me, a hundredfold, a

thousandfold, various in kind, divine, various in colours and shapes. (5)

पश्य behold; मे my; पार्थ O Pârtha: रूपाणि forms; शतशः hundredfold; अथ and; सहस्रशः thousandfold; नानाविधानि of many modes; दिव्यानि divine; नानावर्णाकृतीनि = नाना वर्णाः आकृतयः च येषां तानि many, colors, forms, and, whose, them.

पश्यादित्यान्वसून्रुद्रानश्विनौ मरुतस्तथा ।
बहून्यदृष्टपूर्वाणि पश्याश्चर्याणि भारत ॥ ६ ॥

Behold the Âdityas, the Vasus, the Rudras, the two Ashvins and also the Maruts; behold many marvels never seen ere this, O Bhârata. (6)

पश्य behold; आदित्यान् the Âdityas; वसून् the Vasus; रुद्रान् the Rudras; अश्विनौ the (two) Ashvins; मरुतः the Maruts; तथा also; बहूनि many; अदृष्ट पूर्वाणि = पूर्वं न दृष्टानि before, not, seen; पश्य behold; आश्चर्याणि marvels; भारत O Bhârata.

इहैकस्थं जगत्कृत्स्नं पश्याद्य सचराचरम् ।
मम देहे गुडाकेश यच्चान्यद्द्रष्टुमिच्छसि ॥ ७ ॥

Here, to-day, behold the whole universe, movable and immovable, standing in one in My body, O Gudâkesha, with aught else thou desirest to see. (7)

इह here; एकस्थं = एके स्थितं, in one, standing; जगत् the world: कृत्स्नं all; पश्य behold; अद्य to-day; सचराचरं = चरेण अचरेण च सह (with) moving, (with) unmoving, and, together;

मम my; देहे in body; गुडाकेश O Guḍâkesha; यत् what; च and; अन्यत् other; द्रष्टुम to see; इच्छसि desirest.

न तु मा शक्यसे द्रष्टुमनेनैव स्वचक्षुषा ।
दिव्यं ददामि ते चक्षुः पश्य मे योगमैश्वरम् ॥ ८ ॥

But verily thou art not able to behold Me with these thine eyes; the divine eye I give unto thee. Behold My sovereign Yoga.

न not; तु indeed; मां me; शक्यसे canst (thou); द्रष्टुम to see; अनेन with this; एव even; स्वचक्षुषा with own-eyes; दिव्यं divine; ददामि give (I); ते of (to) thee; चक्षुः the eye; पश्य behold; मे my; योगं yoga; ऐश्वरं sovereign.

संजय उवाच ।

एवमुक्त्वा ततो राजन् महायोगेश्वरो हरिः ।
दर्शयामास पार्थाय परमं रूपमैश्वरम् ॥ ९ ॥

Sañjaya said:

Having thus spoken, O King, the great Lord of Yoga, Hari, showed to Pârtha His supreme form as Lord. (9)

एवं thus; उक्त्वा having spoken; ततः then; राजन् O King; महायोगेश्वरः = महान् योगेश्वरः the great Yoga-Lord; हरिः Hari; दर्शयामास showed; पार्थाय to Pârtha; परमं highest; रूपं form; ऐश्वरम् sovereign.

अनेकवक्त्रनयनमनेकाद्भुतदर्शनम् ।
अनेकदिव्याभरणं दिव्यानेकोद्यतायुधम् ॥ १० ॥

With many mouths and eyes, with many visions of marvel, with many divine ornaments, with many upraised divine weapons ;

अनेकवक्त्रनयनम् = अनेकानि वक्त्राणि च नयनानि च यस्मिन् तत् various, mouths, and, eyes, and, in which, that; अनेकाद्भुतदर्शनं = अनेकानि अद्भुतानि दर्शनानि यस्मिन् तत् various, marvellous, sights, in which, that; अनेकदिव्याभरणं = अनेकानि दिव्यानि आभरणानि यस्मिन् तत् various, divine, ornaments, in which, that; दिव्यानेकोद्यतायुधम् = दिव्यानि अनेकानि उद्यतानि आयुधानि यस्मिन् तत् divine, various, uplifted, weapons, in which, that.

दिव्यमाल्याम्बरधरं दिव्यगंधानुलेपनम् ।
सर्वाश्चर्यमयं देवमनंतं विश्वतोमुखम् ॥ ११ ॥

Wearing divine necklaces and vestures, anointed with divine unguents, the God all-marvellous, boundless, with face turned everywhere. (11)

दिव्यमाल्यांबरधरं = दिव्यानि माल्यानि च अम्बराणि च धरति इति तत् divine, necklaces, and, garments, and, wears, which, that; दिव्यगंधानुलेपनम् = दिव्यः गंधः च अनुलेपनम् च यस्य तत् divine, scent, and, unguents, of which, that; सर्वाश्चर्यमयं full of all marvels; देवम God; अनन्तं endless; विश्वतोमुखं with faces all round.

दिवि सूर्यसहस्रस्य भवेद्युगपदुत्थिता ।

यदि भाः सदृशी सा स्याद्भासस्तस्य महात्मनः ॥ १२॥

If the splendour of a thousand suns were to blaze out together in the sky, that might resemble the glory of that Mahâtmâ. (12)

दिवि in the sky; सूर्यसहस्रस्य = सूर्याणां सहस्रस्य of suns, of a thousand; भवेत् were; युगपत् = simultaneously; उत्थिता arisen; यदि if; भाः splendour; सदृशी like; सा that; स्यात् may be; भासः of a glory; तस्य (of) that; महात्मनः of mahâtmâ.

तत्रैकस्थं जगत्कृत्स्नं प्रविभक्तमनेकधा ।

अपश्यद्देवदेवस्य शरीरे पांडवस्तदा ॥ १३ ॥

There Pâṇḍava beheld the whole universe, divided into manifold parts, standing in one in the body of the God of Gods. (13)

तत्र there; एकस्थं standing-in-one; जगत् the world; कृत्स्नं the whole; प्रविभक्तम् divided; अनेकधा in various ways; अपश्यत् saw; देवदेवस्य = देवानाम देवस्य of the Gods, of the God; शरीरे in the body; पांडवः the Pâṇḍava; तदा then.

ततः स विस्मयाविष्टो हृष्टरोमा धनंजयः ।

प्रणम्य शिरसा देवं कृतांजलिरभाषत ॥ १४ ॥

Then he, Dhanañjaya, overwhelmed with astonishment, his hair upstanding, bowed down his head to the God, and with joined palms spake. (14)

ततः then; सः he; विस्मयाविष्टः = विस्मयेन आविष्टः with astonishment, penetrated; हृष्टरोमा = हृष्टानि रोमाणि यस्य सः excited hairs, whose, he; धनंजयः Dhanañjaya; प्रणम्य having prostrated; शिरसा with head; देवं the God; कृतांजलिः = कृत अंजलिः येन सः made, hand-folding, by whom, he, (saluting); अभाषत said.

अर्जुन उवाच ।

पश्यामि देवास्तव देव देहे
सर्वांस्तथा भूतविशेषसंघान् ।
ब्रह्माणमीशं कमलासनस्थ-
मृषींश्च सर्वानुरगांश्च दिव्यान् ॥ १५ ॥

Arjuna said :

Within Thy form, O God, the Gods I see,
All grades of beings with distinctive marks;
Brahmâ, the Lord, upon His lotus throne,
The Ṛiṣhis all and Serpents, the Divine. (15)

पश्यामि (I) see; देवान् the Gods; तव Thy; देव O God; देहे in the body; सर्वान् all; तथा also; भूतविशेषसंघान् = भूतानाम् विशेषाणाम् संघान् of beings, of (various) species, groups; ब्रह्माणं Brahmâ; ईशं the lord; कमलासनस्थं = कमलस्य आसने स्थितं of lotus, in seat, seated; ऋषीन् Riṣhis; सर्वान् all; उरगान् serpents; च and; दिव्यान् divine.

अनेकबाहूदरवक्त्रनेत्रं
पश्यामि त्वा सर्वतोऽनंतरूपम् ।

नांतं न मध्यं न पुनस्तवादिं
पश्यामि विश्वेश्वर विश्वरूपम् ॥ १६ ॥

With mouths, eyes, arms, breasts, multitudinous,
I see Thee everywhere, unbounded Form.
Beginning, middle, end, nor source of Thee,
Infinite Lord, infinite Form, I find; (16)

अनेकबाहूदरवक्रनेत्रं = अनेके बाहवः उदराणि च वक्राणि च नेत्राणि च यस्य तं many, arms, and stomachs, and, mouths, and, eyes, and, whose, him; पश्यामि (I) see; त्वां thee; सर्वतः everywhere; अनन्तरूपम् = अनन्तानि रूपाणि यस्य तं endless, forms, whose, him; न not अन्तं end; न not; मध्यं middle; न not; पुनः again; तव thy; आदिं origin; पश्यामि (I) see; विश्वेश्वर = विश्वस्य ईश्वर of universe, O Lord; विश्वरूपं = विश्वः रूपं यस्य तं, universe, form, whose, him.

किरीटिनं गादिनं चाक्रिणं च
तेजोराशिं सर्वतो दीप्तिमंतम् ।
पश्यामि त्वां दुर्निरीक्ष्यं समंताद्
दीप्तानलार्कद्युतिमप्रमेयम् ॥ १७ ॥

Shining, a mass of splendour everywhere,
With discus, mace, tiara, I behold:
Blazing as fire, as sun, dazzling the gaze
From all sides in the sky, immeasurable. (17)

किरीटिनं = किरीटं अस्य अस्ति तं diadem, of him, is, him; गदिनं with mace; चाक्रिणं with discus; च and; तेजोराशिं = तेजसः राशिं

of splendour, mass; सर्वतः everywhere ; दीप्तिमन्तं shining ; पश्यामि (I) see; त्वां thee ; दुर्निरीक्ष्यं = दुःखेन निरीक्ष्यं with difficulty, to be seen ; समंतात् from everywhere; दिप्तानलार्कद्युति = दीप्तस्य अनलस्य च अर्कस्य च इव द्युतिः यस्य तं of (the) shining, of fire, and, of sun, and, like, glory, whose, him ; अप्रमेयं immeasurable.

त्वमक्षरं परमं वेदितव्यं
त्वमस्य विश्वस्य परं निधानम् ।
त्वमव्ययः शाश्वतधर्मगोप्ता
सनातनस्त्वं पुरुषो मतो मे ॥ १८ ॥

Lofty beyond all thought, unperishing,
Thou treasure-house supreme ; all-immanent,
Eternal Dharma's changeless Guardian, Thou ;
As immemorial Man I think of Thee. (18)

त्वं Thou ; अक्षरं imperishable ; परम् highest ; वेदितव्यं to be known ; त्वं Thou ; अस्य (of) this ; विश्वस्य of universe; परं highest ; निधानं treasure-house ; त्वं Thou ; अव्ययः inexhaustible; शाश्वतधर्मगोप्ता = शाश्वतस्य धर्मस्य गोप्ता (of the) eternal, of dharma, the Protector ; सनातनः ancient ; त्वं thou ; पुरुषः man ; मतः thought ; मे of me.

अनादिमध्यातमनंतवीर्य-
मनंतबाहुं शशिसूर्यनेत्रम् ।
पश्यामि त्वां दीप्तहुताशवक्त्रं

स्वतेजसा विश्वमिदं तपंतम् ॥ १९ ॥

Nor source, nor midst, nor end ; infinite force,
Unnumbered arms, the sun and moon Thine eyes !
I see Thy face, as sacrificial fire
Blazing, its splendour burneth up the worlds. (19)

अनादिमध्यांतम् = न आदिः मध्यः अंतः यस्य तं not origin, middle, end, whose, him; अनन्तवीर्यं = अनंतं वीर्यं यस्य तं endless, force, whose, him ; अनंतबाहुं = अनन्ताः बाहवः यस्य तं endless, arms, whose, him ; शशिसूर्यनेत्रं = शशी च सूर्यः च नेत्रे यस्य तं moon, and, sun, and, (two) eyes, whose, him ; पश्यामि (I) see ; त्वां Thee ; दीप्तहुताशवक्त्रं = दीप्तः हुताशः इव वक्त्रं यस्य तं light, and, sacrificial, fire, and, face, and, whose, he ; स्वतेजसा by own brightness ; विश्वं the universe ; इदं this ; तपंतम warming.

द्यावापृथिव्योरिदमंतरं हि
व्याप्तं त्वयैकेन दिशश्च सर्वाः ।
दृष्ट्वाऽद्भुतं रूपमुग्रं तवेदं
लोकत्रयं प्रव्यथितं महात्मन् ॥ २० ॥

By Thee alone are filled the earth, the heavens,
And all the regions that are stretched between ;
The triple worlds sink down, O mighty One,
Before Thine awful manifested Form. (20)

द्यावापृथिव्योः = द्यावः च पृथिव्याः च of heaven, and, of earth, and; इदं this; अन्तरं interspace ; हि indeed ; व्याप्तं pervaded; त्वया by Thee; एकेन by (the) One ; दिशः quarters ; च and ; सर्वाः all; दृष्ट्वा

having seen ; अद्भुतं marvellous ; रूपं form ; उग्रं terrible ; तव thy ; इदं this ; लोकत्रयं=लोकानां त्रयं of worlds triplet ; प्रव्यथितं (is) oppressed ; महात्मन् O mahâtmâ.

अमी हि त्वां सुरसंघा विशंति
केचिद्भीताः प्राजलयो गृणंति ।
स्वस्तीत्युक्त्वा महर्षिसिद्धसंघाः
स्तुवंति त्वा स्तुतिभिः पुष्कलाभिः ॥ २१ ॥

To Thee the troops of Suras enter in,
Some with joined palms in awe invoking Thee :
Banded Maharṣhis, Siddhas," Svasti !" cry,
Chanting Thy praises with resounding songs. (21)

अमी these ; हि indeed ; त्वां Thee ; सुरसंघाः=सुराणाम् संघाः of Gods, the hosts ; विशंति enter ; केचित् some ; भीताः frightened ; प्रांजलयः with-joined-palms ; गृणंति utter ; स्वस्ति=सु+अस्ति well is (be it) ; इति thus ; उक्त्वा having said ; महर्षिसिद्धसंघाः=महर्षीणाम् च सिद्धानाम् च संघाः of Maharṣhis, and, of Siddhas, and, hosts ; स्तुवन्ति hymn ; त्वां Thee ; स्तुतिभिः with songs ; पुष्कलाभिः resounding.

रुद्रादित्या वसवो ये च साध्या
विश्वेऽश्विनौ मरुतश्चोष्मपाश्च ।
गंधर्वयक्षासुरसिद्धसंघा
वीक्षंते त्वां विस्मिताश्चैव सर्वे ॥ २२ ॥

Rudras, Vasus, Sâdhyas and Âdityas,
Vishvas, the Ashvins, Maruts, Ushmapas,
Gandharvas, Yakshas, Siddhas, Asuras,
In wondering multitudes beholding Thee. (22)

रुद्रादित्याः = रुद्राः च आदित्याः च Rudras and Adityas, and; वसवः Vasus; ये these; च and; साध्याः Sâdhyas; विश्वे Vishvedevas; अश्विनौ (the two) Ashvins; मरुतः Maruts; च and; ऊष्मपाः Ushmapas; च and; गंधर्वयक्षासुरसिद्धसंघाः = गंधर्वाणां च यक्षाणां च असुराणां च सिद्धानां च संघाः of Gandharvas, and, of Yakshas, and, of Asuras, and of Siddhas, and, hosts; वीक्षंते behold; त्वां Thee; विस्मिताः astonished; च and; एव even; सर्वे all.

रूपं महत्ते बहुवक्त्रनेत्रं
महाबाहो बहुबाहूरुपादम् ।
बहूदरं बहुदंष्ट्राकरालं
दृष्ट्वा लोकाः प्रव्यथितास्तथाऽहम् ॥ २३ ॥

Thy mighty Form, with many mouths and eyes,
Long-armed, with thighs and feet innumerate,
Vast-bosomed, set with many fearful teeth,
The worlds see terror-struck, as also I. (23)

रूपं form; महत् great; ते Thy; बहुवक्त्रनेत्रं = बहूनि वक्त्राणि च नेत्राणि च यस्मिन् तत् many, mouths, and, eyes, and, in which, that; महाबाहो O mighty-armed; बहुबाहूरुपादम् = बहवः बाहवः च ऊरवः च पादाः च यस्मिन् तत् many, arms, and, thighs, and, feet, and, in which, that; बहूदरं = बहूनि उदराणि यस्मिन् तत् many stomachs, in which, that; बहुदंष्ट्राकरालं = बह्वीभिः दंष्ट्राभिः करालं (with) many, with teeth, terrible; दृष्ट्वा having seen; लोकाः the worlds प्रव्यथिताः (are) distressed; तथा also; अहं I.

नभःस्पृशं दीप्तमनेकवर्णं
व्यात्ताननं दीप्तविशालनेत्रम् ।
दृष्ट्वा हि त्वा प्रव्यथितान्तरात्मा
धृतिं न विंदामि शमं च विष्णो ॥ २४ ॥

Radiant Thou touchest heaven; rainbow-hued,
With opened mouths and shining vast-orbed eyes.
My inmost self is quaking, having seen,
My strength is withered, Viṣhṇu, and my peace. (24)

नभःस्पृशं = नभः स्पृशति इति तं heaven, touches, thus; दीप्तं shining; अनेकवर्णं = अनेके वर्णाः यस्य तम् various, colours, whose, him; व्यात्ताननं = व्यात्तानि आननानि यस्य तम् opened, mouths, whose, him; दीप्तविशालनेत्रम् = दीप्तानि विशालानि नेत्राणि यस्य तम् shining, large, eyes, him; दृष्ट्वा having seen; हि indeed; त्वां Thee; प्रव्यथितान्तरात्मा = प्रव्यथितः अन्तरात्मा यस्य सः trembling, mind, whose, he; धृतिं strength; न not; विंदामि (I) find; शमं control; च and; विष्णो O Viṣhṇu.

दंष्ट्राकरालानि च ते मुखानि
दृष्ट्वैव कालानलसंनिभानि ।

दिशो न जाने न लभे च शर्म
प्रसीद देवेश जगन्निवास ॥ २५ ॥

Like Time's destroying flames I see Thy teeth,
Upstanding, spread within expanded jaws;
Nought know I anywhere, no shelter find,
Mercy, O God! refuge of all the worlds! (25)

दंष्ट्राकरालानि = दंष्ट्राभिः करालानि with teeth, terrible; च and; ते thy; मुखानि mouths; दृष्ट्वा having seen; एव even; कालानलसंनिभानि = कालस्य अनलस्य च संनिभानि of time, of the fire, and, resembling; दिशः quarters; न not; जाने know; न not; लभे obtain; च and; शर्म protection; प्रसीद be pleased; देवेश = देवानां ईश of the Gods, O Lord, जगन्निवास = जगतः निवास of the world, O dwelling.

अमी च त्वां धृतराष्ट्रस्य पुत्राः
सर्वे सहैवावनिपालसंघैः ।
भीष्मो द्रोणः सूतपुत्रस्तथासौ
सहास्मदीयैरपि योधमुख्यैः ॥ २६ ॥

The sons of Dhṛitarâshtra, and with them
The multitude of all these kings of earth,
Bhîṣhma, and Droṇa, Sûta's royal son,
And all the noblest warriors of our hosts, (26)

अमी these; च and; त्वां Thee; धृतराष्ट्रस्य of Dhṛitarâṣhtra; पुत्राः sons; सर्वे all; सह with; एव even; अवनिपालसंघैः = अवनि

पालयंति इति तेषां संघैः the earth, (who) protect, thus, of them, with the hosts ; भीष्मः Bhîshma ; द्रोणः Drona ; सूतपुत्रः = सूतस्य पुत्रः of Sûta, the son ; तथा also ; असौ this ; सह with ; अस्मदीयैः with (those) of ours ; योधमुख्यैः = योधानां मुख्यैः of warriors, with the chiefs.

वक्त्राणि ते त्वरमाणा विशंति
दंष्ट्राकरालानि भयानकानि ।
केचिद्विलग्ना दशनान्तरेषु
संदृश्यंते चूर्णितैरुत्तमांगैः ॥ २७ ॥

Into Thy gaping mouths they hurrying rush,
Tremendous-toothed and terrible to see ;
Some caught within the gaps between Thy teeth
Are seen, their heads to powder crushed and ground. (27)

वक्त्राणि mouths ; ते they ; त्वरमाणाः hurrying ; विशंति enter ; दंष्ट्राकरालानि terrible-toothed ; भयानकानि fear-bringing ; केचित् some ; विलग्नाः sticking; दशनान्तरेषु = दशनानाम् अन्तरेषु of teeth, in the gaps ; संदृश्यंते are seen ; चूर्णितैः (with) pulverised ; उत्तमाङ्गैः with highest limbs (heads).

यथा नदीनां बहवोऽम्बुवेगाः
समुद्रमेवाभिमुखा द्रवंति ।
तथा तवामी नरलोकवीरा

विशंति वक्त्राण्यभिविज्वलंति ॥ २८ ॥

As river-floods impetuously rush,
Hurling their waters into ocean's lap,
So fling themselves into Thy flaming mouths,
In haste, these mighty men, these lords of earth. (28)

यथा as; नदीनाम् of rivers; बहवः many; अम्बुवेगाः = अम्बूनां वेगाः of waters, the currents; समुद्रं to the ocean; एव even; अभिमुखाः facing towards; द्रवन्ति run; तथा so; तव of Thee; अमी these; नरलोकवीराः = नराणाम् लोके वीराः of men, in the world, heroes; विशन्ति enter; वक्त्राणि mouths; अभिविज्वलन्ति blazing.

यथा प्रदीप्तं ज्वलनं पतंगा
विशंति नाशाय समृद्धवेगाः ।
तथैव नाशाय विशंति लोका-
स्तवापि वक्त्राणि समृद्धवेगाः ॥ २९ ॥

As moths with quickened speed will headlong fly
Into a flaming light, to fall destroyed,
So also these, in haste precipitate,
Enter within Thy mouths destroyed to fall. (29)

यथा as; प्रदीप्तं blazing; ज्वलनं flame; पतंगाः moths; विशन्ति enter; नाशाय to destruction; समृद्धवेगाः = समृद्धः वेगः येषाम् ते increased, velocity, whose, they; तथा so; एव even; नाशाय

to destruction ; विशंति enter ; लोकाः the people ; तव of Thee अपि also ; वक्त्राणि mouths ; समृद्धवेगाः (with) increased velocity.

लेलिह्यसे ग्रसमानः समंता-
ल्लोकान्समग्रान्वदनैर्ज्वलद्भिः ।
तेजोभिरापूर्य जगत्समग्रं
भासस्तवोग्राः प्रतपंति विष्णो ॥ ३० ॥

On every side, all-swallowing, fiery-tongued,
Thou lickest up mankind, devouring all ;
Thy glory filleth space : the universe
Is burning, Vişhṇu, with Thy blazing rays. (30)

लेलिह्यसे (thou) lickest ; ग्रसमान. grasping ; समंतात् from every side ; लोकान् the worlds ; समग्रान् the whole ; वदनैः with faces ; ज्वलद्भिः (with) fiery ; तेजोभिः with splendours ; आपूर्य having filled ; जगत् the world ; समग्रम् whole ; भासः glory ; तव thy ; उग्राः fierce ; प्रतपंति burning ; विष्णो O Vişhṇu.

आख्याहि मे को भवानुग्ररूपो
नमोऽस्तु ते देववर प्रसीद ।
विज्ञातुमिच्छामि भवंतमाद्यं
न हि प्रजानामि तव प्रवृत्तिम् ॥ ३१ ॥

Reveal Thy SELF ; What awful Form art Thou ?
I worship Thee ! Have mercy, God supreme !

Thine inner being I am fain to know;
This Thy forthstreaming Life bewilders me (31)

आख्याहि declare; मे to me; कः who; भवान् Thou; उग्ररूपः = उग्रं रूपं यस्य सः terrible, form, whose, he; नमः salutation; अस्तु let there be; ते to Thee; देववर = देवानां वर of Gods, O best; विज्ञातुम to know; इच्छामि (I) wish; भवंतम Thee; आद्यं first; न not; हि indeed; प्रजानामि (I) know; तव Thy; प्रवृत्ति desire.

श्रीभगवानुवाच ।

कालोऽस्मि लोकक्षयकृत्प्रवृद्धो
लोकान्समाहर्तुमिह प्रवृत्तः ।
ऋतेऽपि त्वां न भविष्यंति सर्वे
येऽवस्थिताः प्रत्यनीकेषु योधाः ॥ ३२ ॥

The Blessed Lord said:

Time am I, laying desolate the world,
Made manifest on earth to slay mankind!
Not one of all these warriors ranged for strife
Escapeth death; thou shalt alone survive. (32)

कालः time; अस्मि (I) am; लोकक्षयकृत् = लोकानाम् क्षयं करोति इति of the worlds, destruction, makes, thus; प्रवृद्धः vast; लोकान् the worlds; समाहर्तुम् to annihilate; इह here; प्रवृत्तः come forth; ऋते without; अपि also; त्वां thee; न not; भविष्यंति shall be; सर्वे all; ये these; अवस्थिताः arranged; प्रत्यनीकेषु in the rival-armies; योधाः warriors.

तस्मात्त्वमुत्तिष्ठ यशो लभस्व
जित्वा शत्रून्भुङ्क्ष्व राज्यं समृद्धम् ।
मयैवैते निहताः पूर्वमेव
निमित्तमात्रं भव सव्यसाचिन् ॥ ३३ ॥

Therefore stand up! win for thyself renown,
Conquer thy foes, enjoy the spacious realm.
By Me they are already overcome,
Be thou the outward cause, left-handed one. (33)

तस्मात् therefore; त्वं thou; उत्तिष्ठ stand up; यशः fame; लभस्व obtain; जित्वा having conquered; शत्रून् enemies; भुंक्ष्व enjoy; राज्यं the kingdom; समृद्धं wealthy; मया by me; एव even; एते these; निहताः slain; पूर्वं before; एव even; निमित्तमात्रं a mere instrument; भव be; सव्यसाचिन्=सव्येन साचितुं शीलं यस्य सः with the left hand, to aim, habit, whose, he.

द्रोणं च भीष्मं च जयद्रथं च
कर्णं तथाऽन्यानपि योधवीरान् ।
मया हतांस्त्वं जहि मा व्यथिष्ठा
युध्यस्व जेतासि रणे सपत्नान् ॥ ३४ ॥

Droṇa and Bhīshma and Jayadratha,
Karṇa, and all the other warriors here
Are slain by me. Destroy then fearlessly

Fight! thou shalt crush thy rivals in the field. (34)

द्रोणं Droṇa; च and; भीष्मं Bhīshma; च and; जयद्रथं Jayadratha; च and; कर्णं Karṇa; तथा also; अन्यान् others; अपि also: योधवीरान् = योधानां वीरान् of warriors, heroes; मया by me; हतान् slain; त्वं thou; जहि slay; मा not; व्यथिष्ठाः be distressed; युध्यस्व fight; जेतासि shalt conquer; रणे in the battle; सपत्नान् rivals.

संजय उवाच ।

एतच्छ्रुत्वा वचनं केशवस्य
कृतांजलिर्वेपमानः किरीटी ।
नमस्कृत्वा भूय एवाऽह कृष्णं
सगद्गदं भीतभीतः प्रणम्य ॥ ३५ ॥

Sañjaya said:

Having heard these words of Keshava, he who weareth a diadem, with joined palms, quaking, and prostrating himself, spake again to Krishṇa, stammering with fear, casting down his face. (35)

एतत् this; श्रुत्वा having heard; वचनं word; केशवस्य of Keshava; कृतांजलिः = कृतः अञ्जलिः येन सः made, folded-hands by whom, he; वेपमानः trembling; किरीटि the diademed one; नमस्कृत्वा having prostrated; भूयः again; एव even; आह said; कृष्णं to Krishṇa; सगद्गदं = गद्गदेन सह with stammoring, together भीतभीतः frightene, frightened; प्रणम्य having prostrated.

अर्जुन उवाच ।

स्थाने हृषीकेश तव प्रकीर्त्या
जगत्प्रहृष्यत्यनुरज्यते च ।
रक्षांसि भीतानि दिशो द्रवंति
सर्वे नमस्यंति च सिद्धसंघाः ॥ ३६ ॥

Arjuna said :

Hṛishîkesha ! in Thy magnificence
Rightly the world rejoiceth, hymning Thee ;
The Râkṣhasas to every quarter fly
In fear ; the hosts of Siddhas prostrate fall. (36)

स्थाने in (the right) place (rightly) ; हृषीकेश O Hṛishîkesha ; तव Thy ; प्रकीर्त्या by (singing) thy fame ; जगत् the world ; प्रहृष्यति rejoices ; अनुरज्यते is pleased ; च and ; रक्षांसि the Râkṣhasas ; भीतानि terrified ; दिशः to the quarters ; द्रवंति fly ; सर्वे all ; नमस्यंति prostrate ; च and ; सिद्धसंघाः = सिद्धानाम् संघाः of Siddhas, the hosts.

कस्माच्च ते न नमेरन्महात्मन्
गरीयसे ब्रह्मणोऽप्यादिकर्त्रे ।
अनंत देवेश जगन्निवास
त्वमक्षरं सदसत्तत्परं यत् ॥ ३७ ॥

How should they otherwise, O loftiest SELF!
First Cause! Brahmâ Himself less great than Thou.
Infinite, God of Gods, home of all worlds,
Unperishing, Sat Asat, THAT supreme! (37)

कस्मात् wherefore; च and; ते they; न not; नमेरन् may prostrate; महात्मन् O Mahâtmâ; गरीयसे to the greater teacher; ब्रह्मणः of Brahmâ; अपि also; आदिकर्त्रे to the first maker; अनंत O endless one; देवेश O Lord of Gods; जगन्निवास O dwelling of the worlds; त्वं thou; अक्षरं imperishable; सत् Being; असत् non-being; तत् that; परं highest; यत् which.

त्वमादिदेवः पुरुषः पुराण-
स्त्वमस्य विश्वस्य परं निधानम् ।
वेत्ताऽसि वेद्यं च परं च धाम
त्वया ततं विश्वमनंतरूप ॥ ३८ ॥

First of the Gods, most ancient Man Thou art,
Supreme receptacle of all that lives;
Knower and known, the dwelling-place on high;
In Thy vast Form the universe is spread. (38)

त्वं Thou; आदिदेवः first God; पुरुषः Man; पुराणः ancient; त्वं thou; अस्य (of) this; विश्वस्य of world; परं highest; निधानम् treasure-house; वेत्ता knower; असि (thou) art; वेद्यं to be known; च and; परं highest; च and; धाम dwelling; त्वया by Thee; ततं spread; विश्वम् the universe; अनन्तरूप O endless-Formed.

वायुर्यमोऽग्निर्वरुणः शशांकः
प्रजापतिस्त्वं प्रपितामहश्च ।
नमो नमस्तेऽस्तु सहस्रकृत्वः
पुनश्च भूयोऽपि नमो नमस्ते ॥ ३९ ॥

Thou art Vâyu and Yama, Agni, moon,
Varuṇa, Father, Grandsire of all:
Hail, hail to Thee! a thousand times all hail!
Hail unto Thee! again, again, all hail! (39)

वायुः Vâyu; यमः Yama; अग्निः Agni; वरुणः Varuṇa; शशांकः moon; प्रजापतिः Prajâpati; त्वं Thou; प्रपितामहः great-grand-father; च and; नमः hail; नमः hail; ते to thee; अस्तु be; सहस्रकृत्वः thousand times; पुनः again; च and; भूयः again; अपि also; नमः hail; नमः hail; ते to thee.

नमः पुरस्तादथ पृष्ठतस्ते
नमोऽस्तु ते सर्वत एव सर्व, ।
अनंतवीर्याऽमितविक्रमस्त्वं
सर्वं समाप्नोषि ततोऽसि सर्वः ॥ ४० ॥

Prostrate in front of Thee, prostrate behind,
Prostrate on every side to Thee, O All.
In power boundless, measureless in strength,
Thou holdest all: then Thou Thyself art All.
(40)

नमः hail; पुरस्तात् from before; अथ also; पृष्ठतः from behind; ते to Thee; नमः hail; अस्तु be; ते to Thee; सर्वतः on every side; एव even: सर्व O all; अनंतवीर्य=अनंतं वीर्यं यस्य सः endless, strength, whose, he; अमितविक्रमः=अमितः विक्रमः यस्य सः boundless, strength, whose, he; त्वं thou; सर्वं all; समाप्नोषि concludest; ततः thence; असि (thou) art; सर्वः all.

सखेति मत्वा प्रसभं यदुक्तं
हे कृष्ण हे यादव हे सखेति ।
अजानता महिमानं तवेदं
मया प्रमादात्प्रणयेन वापि ॥ ४१ ॥

If, thinking Thee but friend, importunate,
O Kṛishṇa! or O Yâdava! O friend!
I cried, unknowing of Thy majesty,
And careless in the fondness of my love; (41)

सखा friend; इति thus; मत्वा having thought; प्रसभं importunately; यत् which; उक्तं said; हे कृष्ण O Krishṇa; हे यादव O Yâdava: हे सखे O friend; इति thus; अजानता (by) unknowing; महिमानं greatness; तव thy; इदं this; मया by me; प्रमादात् from carelessness; प्रणयेन with affection; वा or; इति thus.

यच्चाऽवहासार्थमसत्कृतोऽसि
विहारशय्यासनभोजनेषु ।
एकोऽथवाऽप्यच्युत तत्समक्षं

तत्क्षामये त्वामहमप्रमेयम् ॥ ४२ ॥

If jesting, I irreverence showed to Thee,
At play, reposing, sitting or at meals,
Alone, O sinless One, or with my friends,
Forgive my error, O Thou boundless One. (42)

यत् which ; च and ; अवहासार्थं = अवहासस्य अर्थे of jesting, for the sake ; असत्कृतः unhonoured ; असि art ; विहारशय्यासनभोजनेषु = विहारे च शय्यां च आसने च भोजने च in play, and, in bed, and in seat, and in feast, and ; एकः alone ; अथवा or ; अपि also ; अच्युत O unfallen one ; तत् so ; समक्षं in company ; तत् that ; क्षामये (I) pray to pardon ; त्वां thee ; अहं I ; अप्रमेयम boundless.

पिताऽसि लोकस्य चराचरस्य
त्वमस्य पूज्यश्च गुरुर्गरीयान् ।
न त्वत्समोऽस्त्यभ्यधिकः कुतोऽन्यो
लोकत्रयेऽप्यप्रतिमप्रभावः ॥ ४३ ॥

Father of worlds, of all that moves and stands,
Worthier of reverence than the Guru's self,
There is none like to Thee. Who passeth Thee?
Pre-eminent Thy power in all the worlds. (43)

पिता father ; असि (thou) art ; लोकस्य of the world ; चराचरस्य of moving and unmoving ; त्वं thou ; अस्य of this ; पूज्य to be reverenced ; च and ; गुरुः the guru ; गरीयान् weightier ; न not ; त्वत्समः = तव समः of the, equal ; अस्ति is ;

अभ्यधिकः surpassing ; कुतः whence ; अन्यः other ; लोकत्रये in the world triplet ; अपि also ; अप्रतिमप्रभावः = अप्रतिमः प्रभावः यस्य सः unrivalled, might, whose, he,

तस्मात्प्रणम्य प्रणिधाय कायं
प्रसादये त्वामहमीशमीड्यम् ।
पितेव पुत्रस्य सखेव सख्युः
प्रियः प्रियायार्हसि देव सोढुम् ॥ ४४ ॥

Therefore I fall before Thee ; with my body
I worship as is fitting ; bless Thou me.
As father with the son, as friend with friend,
With the beloved as lover, bear with me. (44)

तस्मात् therefore ; प्रणम्य having prostrated ; प्रणिधाय having bent ; कायं body ; प्रसादये propitiate ; त्वां Thee ; अहं I ; ईशं the Lord ; ईड्यम् praiseworthy ; पिता father ; इव like ; पुत्रस्य of the son ; सखा friend ; इव like ; सख्युः of the friend ; प्रियः beloved ; प्रियाय to the loved ; अर्हसि shouldst ; देव O God ; सोढुम् to bear.

अदृष्टपूर्वं हृषितोऽस्मि दृष्ट्वा
भयेन च प्रव्यथितं मनो मे ।
तदेव मे दर्शय देव रूपं
प्रसीद देवेश जगन्निवास ॥ ४५ ॥

I have seen That which none hath seen before,
My heart is glad, yet faileth me for fear;
Show me, O God, Thine other Form again,
Mercy, O God of Gods, home of all worlds. (45)

अदृष्टपूर्वं = पूर्वं न दृष्टं before, not, seen; हृषितः glad; अस्मि (I) am; दृष्ट्वा having seen; भयेन with fear; च and; प्रव्यथितं distressed; मनः mind; मे my; तत् that; एव even; मे to me; दर्शय show; देव O God; रूपम् form; प्रसीद be pleased; देवेश O Lord of Gods; जगन्निवास O world-dwelling.

किरीटिनं गदिनं चक्रहस्त-
मिच्छामि त्वां द्रष्टुमहं तथैव ।
तेनैव रूपेण चतुर्भुजेन
सहस्रबाहो भव विश्वमूर्ते ॥ ४६ ॥

Diademed, mace and discus in Thy hand,
Again I fain would see Thee as before:
Put on again Thy four-armed shape, O Lord,
O thousand-armed, of forms innumerate. (46)

किरीटिनं crowned; गदिनं mace-bearing; चक्रहस्तं = चक्रं हस्ते यस्य तं discus, in hand, whose, him; इच्छामि wish; त्वां Thee; द्रष्टुम् to see; अहं I; तथा as (before); एव even; तेन (by) that; एव even; रूपेण by form; चतुर्भुजेन (by) four-armed; सहस्रबाहो = सहस्रं बाहवः यस्य सः thousand, arms, whose, he; भव be; विश्वमूर्ते = विश्वं मूर्तिः यस्य सः the universe, form, whose, he.

श्रीभगवानुवाच ।

मया प्रसन्नेन तवार्जुनेदं

रूपं परं दर्शितमात्मयोगात् ।

तेजोमयं विश्वमनंतमाद्यं

यन्मे त्वदन्येन न दृष्टपूर्वम् ॥ ४७ ॥

The Blessed Lord said:

Arjuna, by My favour thou hast seen
This loftiest form by Yoga's self revealed!
Radiant, all-penetrating, endless, first,
That none except thyself hath ever seen. (47)

मया by me; प्रसन्नेन (by) pleased; तव of (to) thee; अर्जुन O Arjuna; इदं this; रूपं form; परं highest; दर्शितम् (been) shown; आत्मयोगात्=आत्मनः योगात् of Self, from the yoga; तेजोमयं made of light; विश्वं the universe; अनंत endless; आद्यं first; यत् which; मे of me; त्वत् from (thou) thee; अन्येन by another; न not; दृष्टपूर्वम् seen before.

न वेदयज्ञाध्ययनैर्न दानै-

र्न च क्रियाभिर्न तपोभिरुग्रैः ।

एवंरूपः शक्य अहं नृलोके

द्रष्टुं त्वदन्येन कुरुप्रवीर ॥ ४८ ॥

Nor sacrifice nor Vedas, alms nor works,

Nor sharp austerity, nor study deep,
Can win the vision of this Form for man.
Foremost of Kurus, thou alone hast seen. (48)

न not ; वेदयज्ञाध्ययनैः = वेदैः च यज्ञैः च अध्ययनैः च by Vedas, and, by sacrifices, and, by studies, and ; न not ; दानैः by gifts ; न not ; च and ; क्रियाभिः by deeds ; न not : तपोभिः by austerities ; उग्रैः (by) dire ; एवंरूपः thus-formed ; शक्यः (am) possible ; अहं I ; नृलोके = नृणाम् लोके of men, in the world ; द्रष्टुं to see ; त्वत् from (than) thee ; अन्येन by another ; कुरुप्रवीर = कुरूणाम् प्रवीर of (or among) the Kurus, foremost.

मा ते व्यथा मा च विमूढभावो
दृष्ट्वा रूपं घोरमीदृङ्ममेदम् ।
व्यपेतभीः प्रीतमनाः पुनस्त्वं
तदेव मे रूपमिदं प्रपश्य ॥ ४९ ॥

Be not bewildered, be thou not afraid,
Because thou hast beheld this awful Form ;
Cast fear away, and let thy heart rejoice ;
Behold again Mine own familiar shape. (49)

मा not ; ते thee ; व्यथा pain ; मा not ; च and ; विमूढभावः = विमूढस्य भावः of the confused, the condition ; दृष्ट्वा having seen ; रूप form ; घोर terrible ; ईदृक् such ; मम my ; इदम् this ; व्यपेतभीः = व्यपेता भीः यस्य सः departed, fear, whose, he ; प्रीतमनाः = प्रीतं मनः यस्य सः satisfied, mind, whose, he ; पुनः again ; त्वं thou ; तत् that ; एव even ; मे my ; रूपं form ; इदं this ; प्रपश्य behold.

संजय उवाच ।

इत्यर्जुनं वासुदेवस्तथोक्त्वा
स्वकं रूपं दर्शयामास भूयः
आश्वासयामास च भीतमेनं
भूत्वा पुनः सौम्यवपुर्महात्मा ॥ ५० ॥

Sanjaya said :

Vâsudeva, having thus spoken to Arjuna, again manifested His own Form, and consoled the terrified one, the Mahâtmâ again assuming a gentle form. (50)

इति thus; अर्जुनं to Arjuna; वासुदेवः Vâsudeva; तथा thus; उक्त्वा having spoken; स्वकं own; रूपं form; दर्शयामास showed; भूयः again; आश्वासयामास consoled; च and; भीतं the terrified; एनं this (one); भूत्वा having become; पुनः again; सौम्यवपुः=सौम्यं वपुः यस्य सः gentle, form, whose, he; महात्मा mahâtmâ.

अर्जुन उवाच ।

दृष्ट्वेदं मानुषं रूपं तव सौम्यं जनार्दन ।
इदानीमस्मि संवृत्तः सचेताः प्रकृतिं गतः ॥५१॥

Arjuna said :

Beholding again Thy gentle human Form, O Janârdana, I am now collected, and am restored to my own nature. (51)

दृष्ट्वा having seen ; इदं this ; मानुषं human ; रूपं form ; तव thy ; सौम्यं gentle ; जनार्दन O Janârdana ; इदानीम् now ; अस्मि (I) am ; संवृत्तः become ; सचेताः with mind ; प्रकृतिं to nature ; गतः gone.

श्रीभगवानुवाच ।

सुदुर्दर्शमिदं रूपं दृष्टवानसि यन्मम ।
देवा अप्यस्य रूपस्य नित्यं दर्शनकांक्षिणः ॥५२॥

The Blessed Lord said :

This Form of Mine beholden by thee is very hard to see. Verily the Gods ever long to behold this Form. (52)

सुदुर्दर्शम् very hard to see ; इदं this ; रूपं form ; दृष्टवान् (one who) has seen ; असि (thou) art ; यत् which : मम my ; देवाः Gods : अपि also ; अस्य (of) this ; रूपस्य of form : नित्यं always ; दर्शनकांक्षिणः=दर्शनं कांक्षन्ते इति, vision, (they) desire, thus.

नाहं वेदैर्न तपसा न दानेन न चेज्यया ।
शक्य एवंविधो द्रष्टुं दृष्टवानसि मां यथा ॥५३॥

Nor can I be seen as thou hast seen Me by the Vedas, nor by austerities, nor by alms, nor by offerings : (53)

न not ; अहं I ; वेदैः by the Vedas ; न not ; तपसा by austerity; न not; दानेन by gift; न not; च and; इज्यया by offering; शक्यः (am) possible; एवंविधः (of) this—kind: द्रष्टुम् to see; दृष्टवान् (one who) has seen; असि (thou) art; मां me; यथा as.

भक्त्या त्वनन्यया शक्य अहमेवंविधोऽर्जुन।
ज्ञातुं द्रष्टुं च तत्त्वेन प्रवेष्टुं च परंतप॥ ५४॥

But by devotion to Me alone I may thus be perceived, Arjuna, and known and seen in essence, and entered, O Parantapa. (54)

भक्त्या by devotion; तु indeed; अनन्यया (by) without another; शक्यः (am) possible; अहं I; एवंविधः of this kind अर्जुन O Arjuna; ज्ञातुं to know; द्रष्टुं to see; च and; तत्त्वेन by essence; प्रवेष्टुं to enter; च and; परंतप O Parantapa.

मत्कर्मकृन्मत्परमो मद्भक्तः संगवर्जितः।
निर्वैरः सर्वभूतेषु यः स मामेति पांडव॥ ५५॥

He who doeth actions for Me, whose supreme good I am, My devotee, freed from attachment, without hatred of any being, he cometh unto Me, O Pāṇḍava. (55)

मत्कर्मकृत् = मम कर्म करोति इति my, work, does, this; मत्परमः = अहं परमः यस्य सः I, the supreme, whose, he; मद्भक्तः = मम भक्तः my devotee; संगवर्जितः = संगेन वर्जितः by attachment, abandoned; निर्वैरः without enmity; सर्वभूतेषु among all creatures;

यः who ; सः he ; मां to me ; एति goes ; पांडव O Pâṇḍava.

इति श्रीमद्भगवद्गीता० विश्वरूपदर्शनयोगो नामैकादशोऽध्यायः ।

Thus in the glorious BHAGAVAD-GÎTÂ....the eleventh discourse. entitled,

THE YOGA OF THE VISION OF THE UNIVERSAL FORM.

TWELFTH DISCOURSE.

अर्जुन उवाच ।

एवं सततयुक्ता ये भक्तास्त्वां पर्युपासते ।
ये चाप्यक्षरमव्यक्तं तेषां के योगवित्तमाः ॥ १ ॥

Arjuna said :

Those devotees who ever harmonised worship Thee, and those also who worship the Indestructible, the Unmanifested, whether of these is the more learned in yoga? (1)

एवं thus; सततयुक्ताः ever-balanced; ये who; भक्ताः devotees; त्वां Thee; पर्युपासते worship; ये who; च and; अपि also; अक्षरं the undecaying; अव्यक्तं the unmanifested; तेषाम् of these; के who; योगवित्तमाः yoga-learned-most.

श्रीभगवानुवाच ।

मय्यावेश्य मनो ये मां नित्ययुक्ता उपासते ।
श्रद्धया परयोपेतास्ते मे युक्ततमा मताः ॥ २ ॥

The Blessed Lord said :

They who with mind fixed on Me, ever harmonised worship Me, with faith supreme endowed, these in My opinion, are best in yoga. (2)

मयि in me; आविश्य having fixed; मनः the mind; ये who; मां me; नित्ययुक्ताः ever-balanced; उपासते worship; श्रद्धया with faith ; परया (with) supreme ; उपेताः endowed ; ते these ; मे of me ; युक्ततमाः harmonised-best ; मताः thought.

ये त्वक्षरमनिर्देश्यमव्यक्तं पर्युपासते ।
सर्वत्रगमचिंत्यं च कूटस्थमचलं ध्रुवम् ॥३॥

They who worship the Indestructible, the Ineffable, the Unmanifested, Omnipresent and Unthinkable, the Unchanging, Immutable, Eternal, (3)

ये who ; तु indeed ; अक्षरं the undecaying ; अनिर्देश्यं the undefinable ; अव्यक्तं the unmanifested ; पर्युपासते worship ; सर्वत्रगं every-where-going ; अचिंत्यं unthinkable ; च and ; कूटस्थं rock-seated ; अचलं immovable ; ध्रुवं firm.

संनियम्येंद्रियग्रामं सर्वत्र समबुद्धयः ।
ते प्राप्नुवंति मामेव सर्वभूतहिते रताः ॥ ४ ॥

Restraining and subduing the senses, regarding everything equally, in the welfare of all rejoicing, these also come unto Me. (4)

संनियम्य having restrained ; इंद्रियग्रामं = इंद्रियाणाम् ग्रामं of the senses, the aggregate ; सर्वत्र everywhere ; समबुद्धयः = समा बुद्धि येषां ते equal, understanding, whose, they ; ते they ; प्राप्नुवंति obtain ; मां me ; एव even ; सर्वभूतहिते = सर्वेषाम् भूतानाम् हिते (o) all, of beings, in welfare ; रताः rejoicers.

क्लेशोऽधिकतरस्तेषामव्यक्तासक्तचेतसाम् ।
अव्यक्ता हि गतिर्दुःखं देहवद्भिरवाप्यते ॥ ५ ॥

The difficulty of those whose minds are set on the Unmanifested is greater; for the path of the Unmanifested is hard for the embodied to reach. (5)

क्लेश: the trouble; अधिकतर: greater; तेषाम् of those; अव्यक्तासक्तचेतसाम्=अव्यक्ते आसक्तं चेतः येषाम् ते in the unmanifested, attached, mind, whose, they; अव्यक्ता the unmanifested; हि indeed; गतिः path; दुःखं (with) pain; देहवद्भिः by the embodied; अवाप्यते is reached.

ये तु सर्वाणि कर्माणि मयि संन्यस्य मत्पराः ।

अनन्येनैव योगेन मां ध्यायंत उपासते ॥ ६ ॥

Those verily who, renouncing all actions in Me and intent on Me, worship meditating on Me, with whole-hearted yoga, (6)

ये who; तु indeed; सर्वाणि all; कर्माणि actions; मयि in me; संन्यस्य having renounced; मत्पराः intent on me; अनन्येन (by) without another (object); एव even; योगेन by yoga; मां me; ध्यायंतः meditating; उपासते worship.

तेषामहं समुद्धर्ता मृत्युसंसारसागरात् ।

भवामि न चिरात्पार्थ मय्यावेशितचेतसाम् ॥ ७ ॥

These I speedily lift up from the ocean of death and existence, O Pârtha, their minds being fixed on Me. (7)

तेषाम् of those; अहं I; समुद्धर्ता lifter up; मृत्युसंसारसागरात् मृत्योः च संसारस्य च सागरात् of death, and, of procession, and, from the ocean ; भवामि become ; न not ; चिरात् from long ; पार्थ O Pártha ; मयि in me ; आवेशितचेतसाम् = आवेशितं चेतः येषाम् ते षाम् fixed, mind, whose, of them.

मय्येव मन आधत्स्व मयि बुद्धिं निवेशय ।
निवसिष्यासि मय्येव अत ऊर्ध्वं न संशयः ॥ ८ ॥

Place thy mind in Me, into Me let thy Reason enter; then without doubt thou shalt abide in Me hereafter. (8)

मयि in me ; एव even ; मनः the mind ; आधत्स्व place ; मयि in me ; बुद्धिं the reason ; निवेशय cause to enter ; निवसिष्यसि (thou) shalt dwell ; मयि in me ; एव even ; अतः hence ; ऊर्ध्वं above (afterwards) ; न not ; संशयः doubt.

अथ चित्तं समाधातुं न शक्नोषि मयि स्थिरम् ।
अभ्यासयोगेन ततो मामिच्छाप्तुं धनंजय ॥ ९ ॥

But if thou art not able firmly to fix thy mind on Me, then by the yoga of practice seek to reach Me, O Dhananjaya. (9)

अथ now ; चित्तं the mind ; समाधातुं to fix ; न not ; शक्नोषि canst ; मयि in me ; स्थिरम् firmly ; अभ्यासयोगेन = अभ्यासस्य योगेन of practice, by the yoga ; ततः then ; मां me ; इच्छ wish ; आप्तुं to obtain ; धनंजय O Dhananjaya.

अभ्यासेऽप्यसमर्थोऽसि मत्कर्मपरमो भव ।
मदर्थमपि कर्माणि कुर्वन्सिद्धिमवाप्स्यसि ॥ १० ॥

If also thou art not equal to constant practice, be intent on My service; performing actions for My sake, thou shalt attain perfection. (10)

अभ्यासे in practice; अपि also; असमर्थः not-capable; असि (thou) art; मत्कर्मपरमः = मम कर्म परमं यस्य सः my, work, supreme, whose, he; भव be; मदर्थं for my sake; अपि also; कर्माणि actions; कुर्वन् doing; सिद्धिं perfection; अवाप्स्यसि (thou) shalt obtain.

अथैतदप्यशक्तोऽसि कर्तुं मद्योगमाश्रितः।
सर्वकर्मफलत्यागं ततः कुरु यतात्मवान् ॥११॥

If even to do this thou hast not strength, then taking refuge in union with Me, renounce all fruit of action, with the self controlled. (11)

अथ now; एतत् this; अपि also; अशक्तः not able; असि (thou) art; कर्तुं to do; मद्योगं = मम योगं my yoga; आश्रितः refuged (in); सर्वकर्मफलत्यागं = सर्वेषाम् कर्मणां फलस्य त्यागं (of) all, of actions, of fruit, renunciation; ततः then; कुरु act; यतात्मवान् = यतः आत्मा यस्य सः controlled, self, whose, he.

श्रेयो हि ज्ञानमभ्यासाज्ज्ञानाद्ध्यानं विशिष्यते।
ध्यानात्कर्मफलत्यागस्त्यागाच्छांतिरनंतरम् ॥१२॥

Better indeed is wisdom than constant practice; than wisdom meditation is better: than meditation renunciation of the fruit of action; on renunciation follows peace. (12)

श्रेय: better; हि indeed; ज्ञानं wisdom; अभ्यासात् than practice; ज्ञानात् than wisdom; ध्यानं meditation; विशिष्यते excels; ध्यानात् than meditation; कर्मफलत्यागः = कर्मणां फलस्य त्यागः of action, of fruit, renunciation; त्यागात् from renunciation; शांति: peace; अनंतरम् immediately.

अद्वेष्टा सर्वभूतानां मैत्रः करुण एव च ।
निर्ममो निरहंकारः समदुःखसुखः क्षमी ॥ १३ ॥

He who beareth no ill-will to any being, friendly and compassionate, without attachment and egoism, balanced in pleasure and pain, and forgiving, (13)

अद्वेष्टा not hating; सर्वभूतानाम of all creatures; मैत्रः friendly; करुणः merciful; एव even; च and; निर्ममः without-mine (ness); निरहंकारः without egoism; समदुःखसुखः = समे दुःखं च सुखं च यस्य सः equal, sorrow, and, joy, and, whose, he; क्षमी forgiveness-full,

संतुष्टः सततं योगी यतात्मा दृढनिश्चयः ।
मय्यर्पितमनोबुद्धिर्यो मे भक्तः स मे प्रियः ॥१४॥

Ever content, harmonious, with the self controlled, resolute, with mind and Reason dedicated to Me, he, My devotee, is dear to Me. (14)

संतुष्टः contented; सततं always; योगी yogi; यतात्मा self-controlled; दृढनिश्चयः = दृढः निश्चयः यस्य सः firm, resolve, whose, he; मय्यर्पितमनोबुद्धिः = मयि अर्पिते मनः च बुद्धिः च यस्य सः in me, offered up, mind, and, reason, and, whose, he; यः who; मे my; भक्तः devotee; सः he; मे of (to) me; प्रियः dear.

यस्मान्नोद्विजते लोको लोकान्नोद्विजते च यः ।
हर्षामर्षभयोद्वेगैर्मुक्तो यः स च मे प्रियः ॥१५॥

He from whom the world doth not shrink away, who doth not shrink away from the world, freed from the anxieties of joy, anger and fear, he is dear to Me. (15)

यस्मात् from whom ; न not ; उद्विजते is agitated ; लोकः the world ; लोकात् from the world ; न not ; उद्विजते is agitated ; च and ; यः who ; हर्षामर्षभयोद्वेगैः = हर्षस्य च अमर्षस्य च भयस्य च उद्वेगैः of joy, and, of impatience, and, of fear, and, by (from) the agitations ; मुक्तः freed ; यः who ; सः he ; च and ; मे to me ; प्रियः dear.

अनपेक्षः शुचिर्दक्ष उदासीनो गतव्यथः ।
सर्वारंभपरित्यागी यो मद्भक्तः स मे प्रियः ॥१६॥

He who wants nothing, is pure, expert, passionless, untroubled, renouncing every undertaking, he, My devotee, is dear to Me. (16)

अनपेक्षः not looking to (anything) शुचिः pure ; दक्षः skilful ; उदासीनः unconcerned ; गतव्यथः = गता व्यथा यस्य सः gave, pain, whose, he ; सर्वारंभपरित्यागी = सर्वेषाम् आरम्भाणाम् परित्यागी all, (of) undertakings, renouncer ; सः who ; मम my ; भक्तः devotee ; सः he ; मे to me ; प्रियः dear.

यो न हृष्यति न द्वेष्टि न शोचति न काङ्क्षति ।

शुभाशुभपरित्यागी भक्तिमान्यः स मे प्रियः ॥१७॥

He who neither loveth nor hateth, nor grieveth, nor desireth, renouncing good and evil, full of devotion, he is dear to Me. (17)

यः who ; न not ; हृष्यति rejoiceth ; न not : द्वेष्टि hates ; न not ; शोचति grieves ; न not ; कांक्षति desires ; शुभाशुभपरित्यागी = शुभस्य च अशुभस्य च परित्यागी of good, and, of evil, and, the renouncer ; भक्तिमान् devout ; यः who ; सः he ; मे to me ; प्रिय dear.

समः शत्रौ च मित्रे च तथा मानापमानयोः ।

शीतोष्णसुखदुःखेषु समः संगविवर्जितः ॥ १८ ॥

Alike to foe and friend, and also in fame and ignominy, alike in cold and heat, pleasures and pains, destitute of attachment, (18)

समः equal ; शत्रौ (to) in the enemy ; च and ; मित्रे (to) in the friend ; च and ; तथा also ; मानापमानयोः = माने च अपमाने च in fame, and, in ignominy, and ; शीतोष्णसुखदुःखेषु = शीते च उष्णे च सुखे च दुःखे च in cold, and, in heat, and, in pleasure, and, in pain, and ; समः equal ; संगविवर्जितः = संगात् विवर्जितः from attachment, freed.

तुल्यनिंदास्तुतिर्मौनी संतुष्टो येनकेनचित् ।

अनिकेतः स्थिरमतिर्भक्तिमान्मेप्रियो नरः ॥ १९ ॥

Taking equally praise and reproach, silent, wholly

content with what cometh, homeless, firm in mind, full of devotion, that man is dear to Me. (19)

तुल्यनिंदास्तुतिः = तुल्ये निन्दा च स्तुतिः च यस्य सः equal, blame, and, praise, and, whose, he; मौनी silent; संतुष्टः contented; येन केनचित् with anything; अनिकेतः homeless; स्थिरमतिः = स्थिरा मतिः यस्य सः firm, mind, whose, he; भक्तिमान् devout; मे of (to) me; प्रियः dear; नरः the man.

ये तु धर्म्यामृतमिदं यथोक्तं पर्युपासते ।
श्रद्दधाना मत्परमा भक्तास्तेऽतीव मे प्रियाः॥२०॥

They verily who partake of this life-giving wisdom as taught herein, endued with faith, I their Supreme Object, devotees, they are surpassingly dear to Me. (20)

ये who; तु indeed; धर्म्यामृतम् = धर्म्यं च तत् अमृतं च righteous, and, that (same), nectar, and; यथा as; उक्तं said; पर्युपासते worship; श्रद्दधानाः faith-endowed; मत्परमाः (believing in) me (as) the Supreme; भक्ताः devotees; ते they; अति very; इव as if; मे of (to) me; प्रियाः dear.

इति श्रीमद्भगवद्गीता० भक्तियोगो नाम द्वादशोऽध्यायः ।

Thus in the glorious BHAGAVAD-GÎTÂ,...the twelfth discourse entitled:

THE YOGA OF DEVOTION.

THIRTEENTH DISCOURSE.

अर्जुन उवाच ।

प्रकृतिं पुरुषं चैव क्षेत्रं क्षेत्रज्ञमेव च ।
एतद्वेदितुमिच्छामि ज्ञानं ज्ञेयं च केशव ॥[1]

Arjuna said :

Matter and Spirit, also the Field and the Knower of the Field, Wisdom and that which ought to be known, these I fain would learn, O Keshava.

प्रकृतिं matter ; पुरुषं spirit ; च and ; एव even ; क्षेत्रं the field ; क्षेत्रज्ञं the knower of the field ; एव even ; च and ; एतत् this ; वेदितुम् to know ; इच्छामि (I) wish ; ज्ञानं knowledge ; ज्ञेयं what should be known ; च and ; केशव O Keshava.

श्रीभगवानुवाच ।

इदं शरीरं कौंतेय क्षेत्रमित्यभिधीयते ।
एतद्यो वेत्ति तं प्राहुः क्षेत्रज्ञ इति तद्विदः ॥ १ ॥

The Blessed Lord said :

This body, son of Kuntî, is called the Field ; that which knoweth it is called the Knower of the Field by the Sages. (1)

इदं this ; शरीरं body ; कौंतेय O Kaunteya ; क्षेत्रं the field ; इति thus ; अभिधीयते is called ; एतत् this ; यः who ; वेत्ति knows ; तत् that ; प्राहुः (they) call ; क्षेत्रज्ञः the knower of the field ; इति thus ; तद्विदः the knowers of that.

---

1 This verse is omitted in many editions.

क्षेत्रज्ञं चापि मां विद्धि सर्वक्षेत्रेषु भारत ।
क्षेत्रक्षेत्रज्ञयोर्ज्ञानं यत्तज्ज्ञानं मतं मम ॥ २ ॥

Understand Me as the Knower of the Field in all Fields, O Bhârata. Wisdom as to the Field and the Knower of the Field, that in My opinion is the Wisdom. (2)

क्षेत्रज्ञं the knower of the field; च and; अपि also; मां Me; विद्धि know; सर्वक्षेत्रेषु = सर्वेषु क्षेत्रेषु (in) all, in fields; भारत O Bhârata; क्षेत्रक्षेत्रज्ञयोः = क्षेत्रस्य च क्षेत्रज्ञस्य च of the field, and, of the knower of the field, and; ज्ञानं knowledge; यत् which; तत् that; ज्ञानं knowledge; मतं (thought); मम My.

तत्क्षेत्रं यच्च यादृक् च यद्विकारि यतश्च यत् ।
स च यो यत्प्रभावश्च तत्समासेन मे शृणु ॥ ३ ॥

What that Field is and of what nature, how modified, and whence it is, and what He is and what His powers, hear that now briefly from Me. (3)

तत् that; क्षेत्रं field; यत् which; च and; यादृक् what like; च and; यद्विकारि = यः विकारः यस्य तत्, which, modification, whose, that; यतः whence; च and; यत् which; सः He; च and; यः what; यत्प्रभावः = यः प्रभावः यस्य सः which, power, whose, he; च and; तत् that; समासेन by aggregations (compression, brevity); मे of (from) me; शृणु listen.

ऋषिभिर्बहुधा गीतं छंदोभिर्विविधैः पृथक् ।

ब्रह्मसूत्रपदैश्चैव हेतुमद्भिर्विनिश्चितैः ॥ ४ ॥

Rishis have sung in manifold ways, in many various chants, and in decisive Brahma-sûtra words, full of reasonings. (4)

ऋषिभिः by Rishis; बहुधा in many ways; गीतं sung; छंदोभिः by metres; विविधैः (by) various: पृथक् severally; ब्रह्मसूत्रपदैः by Brahma-sûtra-words; च and; एव even; हेतुमद्भिः (by) full of reason; विनिश्चितैः (by) ascertained.

महाभूतान्यहंकारो बुद्धिरव्यक्तमेव च ।
इन्द्रियाणि दशैकं च पंच चेंद्रियगोचराः ॥ ५ ॥

The great Elements, Individuality, Reason and also the Unmanifested, the ten senses, and the one, and the five pastures of the senses; (5)

महाभूतानि = महान्ति भूतानि the great elements; अहंकारः individuality; बुद्धिः reason; अव्यक्तं the Unmanifested; एव even; च and; इंद्रियाणि the senses; दश ten; एकं one; च and; पंच five; च and; इंद्रियगोचराः = इंद्रियाणाम् गोचराः of the senses, the pastures;

इच्छा द्वेषः सुखं दुःखं संघातश्चेतना धृतिः ।
एतत्क्षेत्रं समासेन सविकारमुदाहृतम् ॥ ६ ॥

Desire, aversion, pleasure, pain, combination,[1] intelligence, firmness, these, briefly described, constitute the Field and its modifications. (6)

1 The body.

इच्छा desire; द्वेषः hate; सुखं pleasure; दुःखं pain; संघातः aggregation; चेतना intelligence; धृतिः firmness; एतत् this; क्षेत्रं field; समासेन with brevity; सविकारम् with modification; उदाहृतम् is said.

अमानित्वमदंभित्वमाहिंसा क्षांतिरार्जवम् ।
आचार्योपासनं शौचं स्थैर्यमात्मविनिग्रहः ॥ ७ ॥

Humility, unpretentiousness, harmlessness, rectitude, service of the teacher, purity, steadfastness, self-control, (7)

अमानित्वं unhaughtiness; अदंभित्वं unpretentiousness; अहिंसा harmlessness; क्षांतिः forgiveness; आर्जवं rectitude; आचार्योपासनं = आचार्यस्य उपासनं of the teacher, service; शौचं purity; स्थैर्यं steadfastness; आत्मविनिग्रहः self-control;

इंद्रियार्थेषु वैराग्यमनहंकार एव च ।
जन्ममृत्युजराव्याधिदुःखदोषानुदर्शनम् ॥ ८ ॥

Indifference to the objects of the senses, and also absence of egoism, insight into the pain and evil of birth, death, old age and sickness, (8)

इंद्रियार्थेषु = इंद्रियाणाम् अर्थेषु of the senses, in the objects; वैराग्यं dispassion; अनहंकारः non-egoism; एव even; च and; जन्ममृत्युजराव्याधिदुःखदोषानुदर्शनम् = जन्म च मृत्युः च जरा च व्याधयः च तेषां दुःखस्य च दोषस्य च अनुदर्शनं birth, and, death, and, old age, and, sicknesses, and, of them, of the pain, of the evil, the seeing.

असक्तिरनभिष्वंगः पुत्रदारगृहादिषु ।
नित्यं च समचित्तत्वमिष्टानिष्टोपपत्तिषु ॥९॥

Unattachment, absence of self-identification with son, wife or home, and constant balance of mind in wished-for and unwished-for events, (9)

असक्तिः unattachment; अनभिष्वंगः non-self-identification; पुत्रदारगृहादिषु = पुत्रेषु च दारेषु च गृहेषु च among sons, and among wives, and, among houses, and; नित्यं constant; च and; समचित्तत्वं equal-mindedness; इष्टानिष्टोपपत्तिषु = इष्टानां च अनिष्टानां च उपपत्तिषु of desired, and, of undesired, in the befallings.

मयि चानन्ययोगेन भक्तिरव्यभिचारिणी ।
विविक्तदेशसेवित्वमरतिर्जनसंसदि ॥ १० ॥

Unflinching devotion to Me by yoga, without other object, resort to sequestered places, absence of enjoyment in the company of men. (10)

मयि in Me; च and; अनन्य योगेन = by yoga, without another (object); भक्तिः devotion; अव्यभिचारिणी = unstraying; विविक्तदेशसेवित्वं = विविक्तस्य देशस्य सेवित्वं (if) lovely, of places, resort; अरतिः absence of pleasure; अरतिः non-pleasure; जनसंसदि = जनानां संसदि of men, in the crowd,

अध्यात्मज्ञाननित्यत्वं तत्त्वज्ञानार्थदर्शनम् ।
एतज्ज्ञानमिति प्रोक्तमज्ञानं यदतोऽन्यथा ॥ ११ ॥

Constancy in the Wisdom of the Self, understanding of the object of essential wisdom; that is declared to be the Wisdom; all against it is ignorance. (11)

अध्यात्मज्ञाननित्यत्वं = अध्यात्मनः ज्ञाने नित्यत्वं of the concerning the Self (see vii. 29), in the knowledge, constancy; तत्त्वज्ञानार्थदर्शनम् = तत्त्वस्य ज्ञानस्य अर्थस्य दर्शनम् of the essence, of the knowledge, of the object, the realisation; एतत् this; ज्ञानं knowledge; इति thus; प्रोक्तं said; अज्ञानं ignorance; यत् which; अतः then; अन्यथा otherwise.

ज्ञेयं यत्तत्प्रवक्ष्यामि यज्ज्ञात्वाऽमृतमश्नुते ।
अनादिमत्परं ब्रह्म न सत्तन्नासदुच्यते ॥ १२ ॥

I will declare that which ought to be known, that which being known immortality is enjoyed—the beginningless supreme ETERNAL, called neither being nor non-being. (12)

ज्ञेयं to be known; यत् which; तत् that; प्रवक्ष्यामि (I) will declare; यत् which; ज्ञात्वा being known; अमृतम् nectar; immortality) अश्नुते (the Jiva) enjoyed; अनादिमत् beginningless; परं highest; ब्रह्म Brahman; न not; सत् being; न not; तत् that; असत् non-being; उच्यते is called.

सर्वतः पाणिपादं तत्सर्वतोऽक्षिशिरोमुखम् ।
सर्वतः श्रुतिमल्लोके सर्वमावृत्य तिष्ठति ॥ १३ ॥

Everywhere THAT hath hands and feet, everywhere eyes, heads, and mouths; all-hearing, He dwelleth in the world, enveloping all; (13)

सर्वतः पाणिपादं = सर्वतः पाणयः च पादाः च यस्य तत् everywhere hands, and, feet, and, whose, that; तत् that; सर्वतोऽक्षिशिरोमुखम् = सर्वतः अक्षीणि च शिरांसि च मुखानि च यस्य तत् everywhere, eyes, and, heads, and, mouths, and, whose, that; सर्वतः everywhere; श्रुतिमत् possessing ears; लोके in the world; सर्वं all; आवृत्य having enveloped; तिष्ठति sits.

सर्वेंद्रियगुणाभासं सर्वेंद्रियविवर्जितम् ।
असक्तं सर्वभृच्चैव निर्गुणं गुणभोक्तृ च ॥ १४ ॥

Shining with all sense-faculties without any senses; unattached supporting everything; and free from qualities enjoying qualities.

सर्वेंद्रियगुणाभासं = सर्वेषाम् इंद्रियाणाम् गुणेषु आभासः यस्य तत् (of) all, of senses, in the qualities, the splendour, whose, that; सर्वेन्द्रियविवर्जितम् = सर्वैः इंद्रियैः विवर्जितम् by all, (by) senses, abandoned; असक्तं unattached; सर्वभृत् = सर्वं बिभर्ति इति all, supports, thus; च and; एव even; निर्गुणं without qualities; गुणभोक्तृ = गुणानां भोक्तृ of qualities, the enjoying; च and.

बहिरंतश्च भूतानामचरं चरमेव च ।
सूक्ष्मत्वात्तदविज्ञेयं दूरस्थं चांतिके च तत् ॥ १५ ॥

Without and within all beings, immovable and also movable; by reason of His subtlety imperceptible; at hand and far away is THAT. (15)

बहिः outside; अंतः inside; च and; भूतानां of beings अचरं immovable; चरं movable; एव even; च and; सूक्ष्मत्वात् from subtlety; तत् that; अविज्ञेयं unknowable, दूरस्थं = दूरे तिष्ठति इति in

(all) distance, stands, this ; च and ; अंतिके near ; च and; तत् that.

अविभक्तं च भूतेषु विभक्तमिव च स्थितम् ।

भूतभर्तृ च तज्ज्ञेयं ग्रसिष्णु प्रभविष्णु च ॥ १६ ॥

Not divided amid beings, and yet seated distributively ; THAT is to be known as the supporter of beings ; He devours and He generates. (16)

अविभक्तं undivided ; च and ; भूतेषु in beings ; विभक्तं divided ; इव like ; च and ; स्थितम् seated ; भूतभर्तृ = भूतानां भर्तृ of beings, the supporter ; च and ; तत् that ; ज्ञेयं to be known ; ग्रसिष्णू absorbing ; प्रभविष्णु prevailing ; च and.

ज्योतिषामपि तज्ज्योतिस्तमसः परमुच्यते ।

ज्ञानं ज्ञेयं ज्ञानगम्यं हृदि सर्वस्य धिष्ठितम् ॥ १७ ॥

THAT, the Light of all lights, is said to be beyond darkness ; Wisdom, the object of Wisdom, by Wisdom to be reached, seated in the hearts of all. (17)

ज्योतिषाम् of lights ; अपि also ; तत् That ; ज्योतिः light ; तमसः from darkness ; परं beyond ; उच्यते is called ; ज्ञानं knowledge ; ज्ञेयं that which is to be known ; ज्ञानगम्यं = ज्ञानेन गम्यं by knowledge, to be reached ; हृदि in the heart ; सर्वस्य of all ; धिष्ठितम् seated.

इति क्षेत्रं तथा ज्ञानं ज्ञेयं चोक्तं समासतः ।

मद्भक्त एतद्विज्ञाय मद्भावायोपपद्यते ॥ १८ ॥

Thus the Field, Wisdom and the Object of Wisdom, have been briefly told. My devotee, thus knowing, enters into My Being. (18)

इति thus; क्षेत्रं the Field; तथा also; ज्ञानं wisdom; ज्ञेयं that which is to be known; च and; उक्तं said; समासतः briefly; मद्भक्तः = मम भक्तः my devotee; एतत् this; विज्ञाय having known; मद्भावाय = मम भावाय (to) my, to being; उपपद्यते approaches.

प्रकृतिं पुरुषं चैव विद्ध्यनादी उभावपि ।
विकारांश्च गुणांश्चैव विद्धि प्रकृतिसंभवान् ॥१९॥

Know thou that Matter and Spirit are both without beginning; and know thou also that modifications and qualities are all Matter-born. (19)

प्रकृतिं matter; पुरुषं spirit; च and; एव even; विद्धि know; अनादी beginningless; उभौ both; अपि also; विकारान् modifications; च and; गुणान् qualities; च and; एव even; विद्धि know; प्रकृतिसंभवान् = प्रकृतेः संभवो येषां तान् from matter, origin, whose, them.

कार्यकारणकर्तृत्वे हेतुः प्रकृतिरुच्यते ।
पुरुषः सुखदुःखानां भोक्तृत्वे हेतुरुच्यते ॥ २० ॥

Matter is called the cause of the generation of causes and effects; Spirit is called the cause of the enjoyment of pleasure and pain. (20)

कार्यकारणकर्तृत्वे = कार्याणाम् च कारणानाम् च कर्तृत्वे of acts, and, of causes, and, in the creativeness; हेतुः the cause; प्रकृतिः

matter ; उच्यते is called ; पुरुषः spirit ; सुखदुःखानाम् = सुखानाम् च दुःखानाम् च of pleasures, and, of pains, and ; भोक्तृत्वे in the enjoyingness ; हेतुः the cause ; उच्यते is called.

पुरुषः प्रकृतिस्थो हि भुंक्ते प्रकृतिजान्गुणान् ।
कारणं गुणसंगोऽस्य सदसद्योनिजन्मसु ॥ २१ ॥

Spirit seated in Matter useth the qualities born of Matter; attachment to the qualities is the cause of his births in good and evil wombs. (21)

पुरुषः spirit ; प्रकृतिस्थः = प्रकृतौ तिष्ठति इति, in matter, sits, thus ; हि indeed ; भुंक्ते enjoys ; प्रकृतिजान् = प्रकृतेः जातान् from matter, born ; गुणान् qualities ; कारणं the cause ; गुणसंगः = गुणेषु संगः in the qualities, attachment ; अस्य of his ; सदसद्योनिजन्मसु = सतीषु च असतीषु च योनिषु जन्मानि तेषु (in) good, and, (in) evil, and, in wombs, births, in them.

उपद्रष्टानुमंता च भर्ता भोक्ता महेश्वरः ।
परमात्मेति चाप्युक्तो देहेऽस्मिन्पुरुषः परः ॥ २२ ॥

Supervisor and permitter, supporter, enjoyer, great Lord and also the supreme SELF: thus is styled in this body the supreme Spirit. (22)

उपद्रष्टा supervisor ; अनुमंता permitter ; च and ; भर्ता supporter ; भोक्ता enjoyer ; महेश्वरः the great Lord ; परमात्मा the Supreme Self ; इति thus ; च and ; अपि also ; उक्तः called ; देहे in the body ; अस्मिन् (in) this ; पुरुषः the spirit ; परः highest.

य एवं वेत्ति पुरुषं प्रकृतिं च गुणैः सह ।

सर्वथा वर्तमानोऽपि न स भूयोऽभिजायते ॥ २३ ॥

He who thus knoweth Spirit and Matter with its qualities, in whatsoever condition he may be, he shall not be born again. (23)

यः who; एवं thus; वेत्ति knows; पुरुष spirit; प्रकृति matter; च and; गुणैः with qualities; सह with; सर्वथा in all ways; वर्तमानः existing; अपि also; न not; सः he; भूयः again; अभिजायते is born.

ध्यानेनात्मनि पश्यंति केचिदात्मानमात्मना ।
अन्ये सांख्येन योगेन कर्मयोगेन चापरे ॥ २४ ॥

Some by meditation behold the SELF in the self by the SELF; others by the Sâñkhya Yoga, and others by the Yoga of Action; (24)

ध्यानेन by meditation; आत्मनि in the self; पश्यंति see; केचित् some; आत्मानं the Self; आत्मना by the Self; अन्ये others; सांख्येन (by) the Sâñkhya; योगेन by Yoga; कर्मयोगेन =कर्मणः योगेन of action, by the Yoga; च and; अपरे others.

अन्ये त्वेवमजानंतः श्रुत्वान्येभ्य उपासते ।
तेऽपि चातितरंत्येव मृत्युं श्रुतिपरायणाः ॥ २५ ॥

Others also, ignorant of this, having heard of it from others, worship; and these also cross beyond death, adhering to what they had heard. (25)

अन्ये others; तु indeed; एवं this; अजानंतः not knowing;

श्रुत्वा having heard; अन्येभ्यः from others: उपासते worship; ते they; अपि also; च and; अतितरंति cross over; एव even; मृत्युं death; श्रुतिपरायणाः = श्रुतिः परं अयन येषाम ते scripture, highest, refuge, whose, they.

यावत्संजायते किंचित्सत्वं स्थावरजंगमम् ।
क्षेत्रक्षेत्रज्ञसंयोगात्तद्विद्धि भरतर्षभ ॥ २६ ॥

Whatsoever creature is born, immobile or mobile, know thou, O best of the Bharatas, that it is from the union between the Field and the Knower of the Field. (26)

यावत् whatsoever: संजायते is born; किंचित् any; सत्वं being; स्थावरजंगमम = स्थावरं च जंगमम च unmoving, and, moving, and; क्षेत्रक्षेत्रज्ञसंयोगात् = क्षेत्रस्य च क्षेत्रज्ञस्य च संयोगात् of the field, and, of the field-knower, and, from the union; तत् that; विद्धि know; भरतर्षभ O best of the Bharatas.

समं सर्वेषु भूतेषु तिष्ठंतं परमेश्वरम् ।
विनश्यत्स्वविनश्यंतं यः पश्यति स पश्यति ॥ २७ ॥

Seated equally in all beings, the supreme Lord, unperishing within the perishing—he who thus seeth, he seeth. (27)

समं equal; सर्वेषु (in) all; भूतेषु in beings; तिष्ठंतं seated; परमेश्वरम् the highest Lord; विनश्यत्सु among the perishing; अविनश्यंतं the unperishing; यः who; पश्यति sees; सः he; पश्यति sees.

समं पश्यन्हि सर्वत्र समवस्थितमीश्वरम् ।
न हिनस्त्यात्मनाऽऽत्मानं ततो याति परां गतिम् ॥ २८ ॥

Seeing indeed everywhere the same Lord equally dwelling, he doth not destroy the SELF by the self, and thus treadeth the highest Path. (28)

समं equal; पश्यन् seeing; हि indeed; सर्वत्र everywhere; समवस्थितम् equally dwelling; ईश्वरं lord; न not; हिनस्ति slays; आत्मना by the self; आत्मानं the Self; ततः then; याति goes; परां the highest; गतिं path.

प्रकृत्यैव च कर्माणि क्रियमाणानि सर्वशः ।
यः पश्यति तथात्मानमकर्तारं स पश्यति ॥ २९ ॥

He who seeth that Prakriti verily performeth all actions, and that the SELF is actionless, he seeth. (29)

प्रकृत्या by matter; एव even; च and; कर्माणि actions; क्रियमाणानि (the) being performed; सर्वशः everywhere; यः who; पश्यति sees; तथा so; आत्मानं the Self; अकर्तारं actionless; सः he; पश्यति sees.

यदा भूतपृथग्भावमेकस्थमनुपश्यति ।
तत एव च विस्तारं ब्रह्म संपद्यते तदा ॥ ३० ॥

When he perceiveth the diversified existence of beings as rooted in One, and spreading forth from it, then he reacheth the ETERNAL. (30)

यदा when; भूतपृथग्भावं=भूतानां पृथक् भावम् of beings, several, existence; एकस्थं=एके स्थितं in one, seated; अनुपश्यति discerns; ततः thence; एव even; च and; विस्तारं the spreading; ब्रह्म Brahman; संपद्यते becomes; तदा then.

अनादित्वान्निर्गुणत्वात्परमात्माऽयमव्ययः ।
शरीरस्थोऽपि कौंतेय न करोति न लिप्यते ॥ ३१ ॥

Being beginningless and without qualities, the imperishable supreme SELF, though seated in the body, O Kaunteya, worketh not nor is affected. (31)

अनादित्वात् from beginninglessness; निर्गुणत्वात् from attributelessness; परमात्मा the supreme Self; अयं this; अव्ययः imperishable; शरीरस्थः body-seated; अपि also; कौंतेय O Kaunteya; न not, करोति acts; न not; लिप्यते is affected.

यथा सर्वगतं सौक्ष्म्यादाकाशं नोपलिप्यते ।
सर्वत्रावस्थितो देहे तथात्मा नोपलिप्यते ॥ ३२ ॥

As the omnipresent ether is not affected, by reason of its subtlety, so seated everywhere in the body the SELF is not affected. (32)

यथा as; सर्वगतं the omnipresent; सौक्ष्म्यात् from subtlety; आकाशं ether; न not; उपलिप्यते is affected; सर्वत्र everywhere; अवस्थितः seated; देहे in the body; तथा so; आत्मा the Self; न not; उपलिप्यते is affected.

यथा प्रकाशयत्येकः कृत्स्नं लोकमिमं रविः ।

क्षेत्रं क्षेत्री तथा कृत्स्नं प्रकाशयति भारत ॥ ३३ ॥

As the one sun illumineth the whole earth, so the Lord of the Field illumineth the whole Field, O Bhârata. (33)

यथा as; प्रकाशयति illuminates; एकः one; कृत्स्नं the whole; लोकं world; इमं this; रविः sun; क्षेत्रं the field; क्षेत्री the field-owner; तथा so; कृत्स्नं the whole; प्रकाशयति illuminates; भारत O Bhârata.

क्षेत्रक्षेत्रज्ञयोरेवमंतरं ज्ञानचक्षुषा ।

भूतप्रकृतिमोक्षं च ये विदुर्यांति ते परम् ॥ ३४ ॥

They who by the eye of Wisdom perceive this difference between the Field and the Knower of the Field, and the liberation of beings from Matter, they go to the Supreme. (34)

क्षेत्रक्षेत्रज्ञयोः = क्षेत्रस्य च क्षेत्रज्ञस्य च of the field, and, of the field-knower, and; एवं thus; अंतरं distinction; ज्ञानचक्षुषा = ज्ञानस्य चक्षुषा of knowledge, by the eye; भूतप्रकृतिमोक्षं = भूतानाम् प्रकृतेः मोक्षं of beings, from matter, the liberation; च and; ये who; विदुः know; यांति go; ते they; परं to the highest.

इति श्रीमद्भगवद्गीता॰ क्षेत्रक्षेत्रज्ञविभागयोगो नाम त्रयोदशोऽध्यायः ।

Thus in the glorious BHAGAVAD-GÎTÂ...the thirteenth discourse, entitled:

THE YOGA OF THE DISTINCTION BETWEEN THE FIELD AND THE KNOWER OF THE FIELD.

FOURTEENTH DISCOURSE.

परं भूयः प्रवक्ष्यामि ज्ञानानां ज्ञानमुत्तमम् ।
यज्ज्ञात्वा मुनयः सर्वे परां सिद्धिमितो गताः ॥ १ ॥

The Blessed Lord said:

I will again proclaim that supreme Wisdom, of all wisdom the best, which all the Sages having known have gone hence to the supreme Perfection. (1

परं highest; भूयः again; प्रवक्ष्यामि (I) will declare; ज्ञानानां of wisdoms; ज्ञानं the wisdom; उत्तमम् best; यत् which; ज्ञात्वा having known; मुनयः munis; सर्वे all; परां (to the) highest; सिद्धिं to perfection; इतः hence; गताः gone.

इदं ज्ञानमुपाश्रित्य मम साधर्म्यमागताः ।
सर्गेऽपि नोपजायंते प्रलये न व्यथंति च ॥ २ ॥

Having taken refuge in this Wisdom and being assimilated to My own nature, they are not re-born even in the emanation of a universe, nor are disquieted in the dissolution. (2)

इदं this; ज्ञानं wisdom; उपाश्रित्य having taken refuge in; मम my; साधर्म्यम् (to) similarity of nature; आगताः come; सर्गे in emanation; अपि also; न not; उपजायंते are born; प्रलये in dissolution; न not; व्यथंति suffer; च and.

मम योनिर्महद्ब्रह्म तस्मिन् गर्भं दधाम्यहम् ।

संभवः सर्वभूतानां ततो भवति भारत ॥ ३ ॥

My womb is the great ETERNAL ; in that I place the germ ; thence cometh the birth of all beings, O Bhârata. (3)

मम my ; योनिः womb ; महद्ब्रह्म the great Brahman ; तस्मिन् in this ; गर्भं the germ ; दधामि place ; अहं I ; संभवः the birth ; सर्वभूतानाम् of all beings ; ततः thence ; भवति becomes ; भारत O Bhârata.

सर्वयोनिषु कौंतेय मूर्तयः संभवंति याः ।
तासां ब्रह्म महद्योनिरहं बीजप्रदः पिता ॥ ४ ॥

In whatsoever wombs mortals are produced, O Kaunteya, the ETERNAL is their mighty womb, I their generating father. (4)

सर्वयोनिषु = सर्वासु योनिषु (in) all, in wombs ; कौंतेय O Kaunteya ; मूर्तयः forms ; संभवंति are born ; याः which ; तासां of these ; ब्रह्म Brahman ; महद्योनिः = महती योनिः the great womb ; अहं I ; बीजप्रदः = बीजं प्रददाति इति, the seed, gives, thus ; पिता father.

सत्वं रजस्तम इति गुणाः प्रकृतिसंभवाः ॥
निबध्नंति महाबाहो देहे देहिनमव्ययम् ॥ ५ ॥

Harmony Mobility, Inertia, such are the qualities, Matter-born ; they bind fast in the body, O great-armed one, the indestructible dweller in the body. (5)

सत्वं rhythm (or harmony) ; रजः mobility ; तमः inertia ;

इति thus ; गुणाः the qualities ; प्रकृतिसंभवाः = प्रकृतेः संभवः येषां ते from Prakṛiti, birth, whose, they ; निबध्नंति bind ; महाबाहो O great-armed one ; देहे in the body ; देहिनं the embodied ; अव्ययं indestructible.

तत्र सत्वं निर्मलत्वात्प्रकाशकमनामयम् ।
सुखसंयोगेन बध्नाति ज्ञानसंगेन चानघ ॥ ६ ॥

Of these Harmony, from its stainlessness, luminous and healthy, bindeth by the attachment to bliss and the attachment to wisdom, O sinless one. (6)

तत्र there ; सत्वं harmony ; निर्मलत्वात् from stainlessness ; प्रकाशकं illuminating ; अनामयं healthy ; सुखसंगेन = सुखस्य संगेन pleasure, by the attachment ; बध्नाति binds ; ज्ञानसंगेन = ज्ञानस्य संगेन of wisdom, by the attachment ; च and ; अनघ O sinless one.

रजो रागात्मकं विद्धि तृष्णासंगसमुद्भवम् ।
तन्निबध्नाति कौंतेय कर्मसंगेन देहिनम् ॥ ७ ॥

Mobility, the passion-nature, know thou, isthe source of attachment and thirst for life, O Kaunteya, that bindeth the dweller in the body by the attachment to action. (7)

रजः mobility ; रागात्मकं = रागः आत्मा यस्य तत् desire, self, whose, it ; विद्धि know ; तृष्णासंगसमुद्भवम् = तृष्णा च आसंगः च तयोः समुद्भवः यस्मात् तत् thirst, and attachment, and, from them (two), the source, from which, that ; तत् that ; निबध्नाति binds ;

कौंतेय O Kaunteya; कर्मसंगेन = कर्मण: संगेन of action, by the attachment; देहिनं the embodied.

तमस्त्वज्ञानजं विद्धि मोहनं सर्वदेहिनाम् ।
प्रमादालस्यनिद्राभिस्तन्निबध्नाति भारत ॥ ८ ॥

But Inertia, know thou, born of unwisdom, is the deluder of all dwellers in the body; that bindeth by heedlessness, indolence and sloth, O Bhârata. (8)

तम: inertia; तु indeed; अज्ञानजं = अज्ञानात् जातं from ignorance, born; विद्धि know; मोहनं the causer, of delusion; सर्वदेहिनाम् = सर्वेषां देहिनां (of) all, of embodied; प्रमादालस्यनिद्राभि = प्रमादेन च आलस्येन च निद्रया च by heedlessness and, by indolence, and, by sloth, and; तत् that; निबध्नाति binds; भारत O Bhârata.

सत्वं सुखे संजयति रजः कर्मणि भारत ।
ज्ञानमावृत्य तु तमः प्रमादे संजयत्युत ॥ ९ ॥

Harmony attacheth to bliss, Mobility to action, O Bhârata. Inertia, verily having shrouded wisdom, attacheth on the contrary to heedlessness. (9)

सत्वं harmony; सुखे in pleasure; संजयति attacheth; रजः mobility; कर्मणि in action; भारत O Bhârata; ज्ञानं wisdom; आवृत्य having enveloped; तु indeed; तमः inertia; प्रमादे in heedlessness; संजयति attaches; उत but.

रजस्तमश्चाभिभूय सत्वं भवति भारत ।

रजः सत्वं तमश्चैव तमः सत्वं रजस्तथा ॥ १० ॥

Now Harmony prevaileth, having overpowered Mobility and Inertia, O Bhârata. Now Mobility, having overpowered Harmony and Inertia; and now Inertia, having overpowered Harmony and Mobility. (10)

रजः mobility; तमः inertia; च and; अभिभूय having overpowered; सत्वं harmony; भवति becomes; भारत O Bhârata; रजः mobility; सत्वं harmony; तमः inertia; च and; एव even; तमः inertia; सत्वं harmony; रजः mobility; तथा also.

सर्वद्वारेषु देहेऽस्मिन्प्रकाश उपजायते ।

ज्ञानं यदा तदा विद्याद्विवृद्धं सत्वमित्युत ॥ ११ ॥

When the wisdom-light streameth forth from all the gates of the body, then it may be known that Harmony is increasing. (11)

सर्वद्वारेषु = सर्वेषु द्वारेषु (in) all, in gates; देहे in the body; अस्मिन् in this; प्रकाशः light; उपजायते is born; ज्ञानं wisdom; यदा when; तदा then; विद्यात् let (him) know; विवृद्धं increased; सत्वं harmony; इति thus; उत indeed.

लोभः प्रवृत्तिरारंभः कर्मणामशमः स्पृहा ।

रजस्येतानि जायंते विवृद्धे भरतर्षभ ॥ १२ ॥

Greed, outgoing energy, undertaking of actions, restlessness, desire—these are born of the increase of Mobility, O best of the Bharatas. (12)

लोभः greed ; प्रवृत्तिः forthgoing ; आरंभः beginning ; कर्मणाम् of actions ; अशमः unpeacefulness ; स्पृहा desire ; रजसि in (the state of) mobility ; एतानि these ; जायंते are born ; विवृद्धे (in having become) increased ; भरतर्षभ O best of the Bharatas.

अप्रकाशोऽप्रवृत्तिश्च प्रमादो मोह एव च ।
तमस्येतानि जायंते विवृद्धे कुरुनंदन ॥ १३ ॥

Darkness, stagnation and heedlessness and also delusion—these are born of the increase of Inertia, O joy of the Kurus. (13)

अप्रकाशः darkness ; अप्रवृत्तिः non-forthgoing ; च and ; प्रमादः heedlessness ; मोहः delusion ; एव even ; च and ; तमसि in (the state of) inertia ; एतानि these ; जायंते are born ; विवृद्धे (in having become) increased ; कुरुनंदन O rejoicer of the Kurus.

यदा सत्वे प्रवृद्धे तु प्रलयं याति देहभृत् ।
तदोत्तमविदा लोकानमलान्प्रतिपद्यते ॥ १४ ॥

If Harmony verily prevaileth when the embodied goeth to dissolution, then he goeth forth to the spotless worlds of the great Sages. (14)

यदा when ; सत्वे in (the state of) harmony ; प्रवृद्धे (in having become) increased ; तु indeed ; प्रलयं to dissolution ; याति goes ; देहभृत the supporter of a body ; तदा then ; उत्तमविदाम् = उत्तमं विदंति इति तेषाम् the , (they) know, thus, of them ; लोकान् to the worlds ; अमलान् of the spotless ; प्रतिपद्यते goes .

रजसि प्रलयं गत्वा कर्मसंगिषु जायते ।

तथा प्रलीनस्तमसि मुढयोनिषु जायते ॥ १५ ॥

Having gone to dissolution in Mobility, he is born among those attached to action; if dissolved in Inertia, he is born in the wombs of the senseless. (15)

रजसि in mobility; प्रलयं to dissolution; गत्वा having gone; कर्मसंगिषु = कर्मणि संगः येषां तेषु in action, attachment, whose, amongst them; जायते is born; तथा so; प्रलीनः dissolved; तमसि in inertia; मूढयोनिषु = मूढानाम् योनिषु of the senseless, in the wombs; जायते is born.

कर्मणः सुकृतस्याहुः सात्विकं निर्मलं फलम् ।
रजसस्तु फलं दुःखमज्ञानं तमसः फलम् ॥ १६ ॥

It is said the fruit of a good action is harmonious and spotless; verily the fruit of Mobility is pain, and the fruit of Inertia unwisdom. (16)

कर्मण: of action; सुकृतस्य (of) well-done; आहुः (they) say; सात्विकं harmonious; निर्मलं spotless; फलं the fruit; रजसः of mobility; तु indeed; फलं the fruit; दुःखं pain; अज्ञानं ignorance; तमस. of inertia; फलं the fruit.

सत्वात्संजायते ज्ञानं रजसो लोभ एव च ।
प्रमादमोहौ तमसो भवतोऽज्ञानमेव च ॥ १७ ॥

From Harmony wisdom is born, and also greed from Mobility; heedlessness and delusion are of Inertia, and also unwisdom. (17)

सत्त्वात् from harmony ; संजायते is born ; ज्ञानं wisdom ; रजसः from mobility ; लोभः greed ; एव even ; च and ; प्रमादमोहौ = प्रमादः च मोहः च heedlessness, and, delusion, and ; तमसः from inertia ; भवतः (two) become ; अज्ञानं ignorance ; एव even ; च and.

ऊर्ध्वं गच्छंति सत्वस्था मध्ये तिष्ठंति राजसाः ।
जघन्यगुणवृत्तिस्था अधो गच्छंति तामसाः ॥१८॥

They rise upwards who are settled in Harmony ; the Active dwell in the midmost place ; the Inert go downwards, enveloped in the vilest qualities. (18)

ऊर्ध्वं upwards ; गच्छंति go ; सत्वस्था = सत्त्वे स्थिताः in harmony, seated ; मध्ये in the midst ; तिष्ठंति stand ; राजसाः the active ; जघन्यगुणवृत्तिस्थाः = जघन्यस्य गुणस्य वृत्तौ स्थिताः (of the) lowest, of the guṇa, in the mode, seated ; अधः downwards ; गच्छंति go ; तामसाः the inert.

नान्यं गुणेभ्यः कर्तारं यदा द्रष्टाऽनुपश्यति ।
गुणेभ्यश्च परं वेत्ति मद्भावं सोऽधिगच्छति ॥१९॥

When the Seer perceiveth no agent other than the qualities, and knoweth THAT which is higher than the qualities, he entereth into My nature. (19)

न not ; अन्यं other ; गुणेभ्यः than the qualities ; कर्तारं the doer ; यदा when ; द्रष्टा the Seer ; अनुपश्यति sees ; गुणेभ्यः than the qualities ; च and ; परं the highest ; वेत्ति knows ; मद्भावं = मम भावं my, to being ; सः he ; अधिगच्छति goes.

गुणानेतानतीत्य त्रीन्देही देहसमुद्भवान् ।

जन्ममृत्युजरादुःखैर्विमुक्तोऽमृतमश्नुते ॥ २० ॥

When the dweller in the body hath crossed over these three qualities, whence all bodies have been produced, liberated from birth, death, old age and sorrow, he drinketh the nectar of immortality. (20)

गुणान् the qualities; एतान् these; अतीत्य having crossed beyond; त्रीन् three; देही the embodied; देहसमुद्भवान् = देहात् समुद्भवः येषां तान् from the body, the origin, of whom, them; जन्ममृत्युजरादुःखैः = जन्मनः च मृत्योः च जरायाः च दुःखैः of birth, and, of death, and, of old age, and, by (from) sorrows; विमुक्तः freed; अमृतम् immortality; अश्नुते enjoys.

अर्जुन उवाच ।

कैर्लिंगैस्त्रीन्गुणानेतानतीतो भवति प्रभो ।
किमाचारः कथं चैतांस्त्रीन्गुणानतिवर्तते ॥ २१ ॥

Arjuna said:

What are the marks of him who hath crossed over the three qualities, O Lord? How acteth he, and how doth he go beyond these three qualities? (21)

कैः (by) what; लिंगैः by marks; त्रीन् three; गुणान् qualities; एतान् these; अतीतः crossed; भवति becomes; प्रभो O lord; किमाचारः what-conduct; कथं how; च and; एतान् these; त्रीन् three; गुणान् qualities; अतिवर्त्तते goes beyond.

श्रीभगवानुवाच ।

प्रकाशं च प्रवृत्तिं च मोहमेव च पाण्डव ।
न द्वेष्टि संप्रवृत्तानि न निवृत्तानि काङ्क्षति ॥ २२ ॥

The Blessed Lord said :

He, O Pâṇḍava, who hateth not radiance, nor outgoing energy, nor even delusion, when present, nor longeth after them, absent; (22)

प्रकाशं light; च and; प्रवृत्तिं forthgoing; च and; मोहं delusion; एव even; च and; पांडव O Pâṇḍava; न not; द्वेष्टि hates; संप्रवृत्तानि (when) gone forth; न not; निवृत्तानि (when) returned; कांक्षति desires.

उदासीनवदासीनो गुणैर्यो न विचाल्यते ।
गुणा वर्तंत इत्येव योऽवतिष्ठति नेंगते ॥ २३ ॥

He who, seated as a neutral, is unshaken by the qualities; who saying: "The qualities revolve," standeth apart, immovable, (23)

उदासीनवत् like the neutral; आसीनः seated; गुणैः by the qualities; यः who; न not; विचाल्यते is shaken; गुणाः the qualities; वर्तंते move; इति thus; एव even; यः who; अवतिष्ठति stands away; न not; इंगते moves.

समदुःखसुखः स्वस्थः समलोष्टाश्मकाचनः ।
तुल्यप्रियाप्रियो धीरस्तुल्यनिंदात्मसंस्तुतिः ॥ २४ ॥

Balanced in pleasure and pain, self-reliant, to whom a lump of earth, a rock and gold are alike; the same to loved and unloved, firm, the same in censure and in praise, (24)

समदुःखसुखः = समं दुःखं च सुखं च यस्मै सः the same, sorrow, and, pleasnre, and, for whom, he; स्वस्थः = स्वात्मनि स्थितः in own self, standing; समलोष्टाश्मकांचनः = समः लोष्टः च अश्मा च कांचनं च यस्मै सः equal, clod, and, stone, and, gold, and, for whom, he; तुल्यप्रियाप्रियः = तुल्यः प्रियः च अप्रियः च यस्मै सः equal, loved, and unloved, and, for whom, he; धीरः firm; तुल्यनिंदात्मसंस्तुतिः = तुल्या निंदा च आत्मनः संस्तुतिः च यस्मै सः equal, blame, and, of self, praise, and, for whom, he.

मानापमानयोस्तुल्यस्तुल्यो मित्रारिपक्षयोः ।
सर्वारंभपरित्यागी गुणातीतः स उच्यते ॥ २५ ॥

The same in honour and ignominy, the same to friend and foe, abandoning all undertakings—he is said to have crossed over the qualities. (25)

मानापमानयोः = माने च अपमाने च in honour, and, in dishonour, and; तुल्यः equal; तुल्यः equal; मित्रारिपक्षयोः = मित्रस्य च अरेः च पक्षयोः of the friend, and, of the enemy, in the sides; सर्वारंभपरित्यागी = सर्वेषां आरंभाणां परित्यागी (of) all, of undertakings, the abandoner; गुणातीतः = गुणान् अतीतः the qualities, crossed; सः he; उच्यते is called.

मां च योऽव्यभिचारेण भक्तियोगेन सेवते ।
स गुणान्समतीत्यैतान् ब्रह्मभूयाय कल्पते ॥ २६ ॥

And he who serveth Me exclusively by the yoga of devotion, he, crossing beyond the qualities, he is fit to become the ETERNAL. (26)

मां me; च and; यः who; अव्यभिचारेण without-straying; भक्तियोगेन = भक्त्याः योगेन of devotion, by the yoga; सेवते serves; सः he; गुणान् the qualities; समतीत्य having crossed over; एतान् these; ब्रह्मभूयाय = ब्रह्मणः भूयाय of Brahman, for the becoming; कल्पते is fit.

ब्रह्मणो हि प्रतिष्ठाऽहममृतस्याव्ययस्य च।
शाश्वतस्य च धर्मस्य सुखस्यैकांतिकस्य च॥२७॥

For I am the abode of the ETERNAL, and of the indestructible nectar of immortality, of immemorial righteousness, and of unending bliss. (27)

ब्रह्मणः of Brahman; हि indeed; प्रतिष्ठा abode; अहं I अमृतस्य of nectar; अव्ययस्य (of) inexhaustible; च and; शाश्वतस्य (of) everlasting; च and; धर्मस्य of duty; सुखस्य of pleasure; ऐकांतिकस्य of the uttermost; च and,

इति श्रीमद्भगवद्गीता० गुणत्रयविभागयोगो नाम चतुर्दशोऽध्यायः।

Thus in the glorious BHAGAVAD-GITA...the fourteenth discourse, entitled:

THE YOGA OF SEPARATION FROM THE THREE QUALITIES.

FIFTEENTH DISCOURSE.

श्रीभगवानुवाच ।

ऊर्ध्वमूलमधःशाखमश्वत्थं प्राहुरव्ययम् ।
छंदांसि यस्य पर्णानि यस्तं वेद स वेदवित् ॥ १ ॥

The Blessed Lord said :

With roots above, branches below, the Ashvattha is said to be indestructible ; the leaves of it are hymns ; he who knoweth it is a Veda-knower. (1)

ऊर्ध्वमूलम् = ऊर्ध्वं मूलं यस्य तम् above, the root, whose, it ; अधःशाखं = अधः शाखाः यस्य तम् below, branches, whose, it ; अश्वत्थं the ashvattha ; प्राहुः (they) call ; अव्ययम् indestructible ; छंदांसि hymns ; यस्य of which ; पर्णानि the leaves ; यः who ; तम् that ; वेद knows ; सः he ; वेदवित् Veda-knower.

अधश्चोर्ध्वं प्रसृतास्तस्य शाखाः
गुणप्रवृद्धा विषयप्रवालाः ।
अधश्च मूलान्यनुसंततानि
कर्मानुबंधीनि मनुष्यलोके ॥ २ ॥

Downwards and upwards spread the branches of it, nourished by the qualities ; the objects of the senses its buds ; and its roots grow downwards, the bonds of action in the world of men. (2)

अधः below; च and; ऊर्ध्वं above; प्रसृताः spread; तस्य of that; शाखाः the branches; गुणप्रवृद्धाः = गुणैः प्रवृद्धाः by the qualities, nourished; विषयप्रवालाः = विषयाः प्रवालाः यासां ताः objects of the senses, sprouts, whose, they; अधः below; च and; मूलानि the roots; अनुसंततानि ramified; कर्मानुबंधीनि = कर्म अनुबंधः येषां तानि action, the bond, whose, they; मनुष्यलोके = मनुष्याणाम् लोके of men, in the world.

न रूपमस्येह तथोपलभ्यते
नान्तो न चादिर्न च संप्रतिष्ठा ।
अश्वत्थमेनं सुविरूढमूल-
मसंगशस्त्रेण दृढेन छित्त्वा ॥ ३ ॥

Nor here may be acquired knowledge of its form, nor its end, nor its origin, nor its rooting-place; this strongly-rooted Ashvattha having been cut down by the unswerving weapon of non-attachment, (3)

न not; रूपं form; अस्य of this; इह here; तथा so; उपलभ्यते is obtained; न not; अंतः end; न not; च and; आदिः beginning; न not; च and; संप्रतिष्ठा foundation; अश्वत्थम् ashvattha; एनं this; सुविरूढमूलं = सुविरूढानि मूलानि यस्य तम् well-grown, roots whose, this; असंगशस्त्रेण = असंगस्य शस्त्रेण of non-attachment, by the weapon: दृढेन (by) strong; छित्त्वा having cut;

ततः पदं तत्परिमार्गितव्यं
यस्मिन्गता न निवर्तंति भूयः ।

तमेव चाद्यं पुरुषं प्रपद्ये
यतः प्रवृत्तिः प्रसृता पुराणी ॥ ४ ॥

That path beyond may be sought, treading which there is no return. I go indeed to that Primal Man whence the ancient energy forthstreamed. (4)

ततः then; पदं foot (stepping-place); तत् that; परिमार्गितव्यं should be sought; यस्मिन् in which; गताः gone; न not; निवर्तंति return; भूयः again; तम् to that; एव even; च and; आद्यं original; पुरुषं Man; प्रपद्ये (I) go; यतः whence; प्रवृत्तिः forth-going; प्रसृता issued; पुराणी ancient.

निर्मानमोहा जितसंगदोषा
अध्यात्मनित्या विनिवृत्तकामाः ।
द्वंद्वैर्विमुक्ताः सुखदुःखसंज्ञै-
र्गच्छंत्यमूढाः पदमव्ययं तत ॥ ५ ॥

Without pride and delusion, victorious over the vice of attachment, dwelling constantly in the SELF, desire pacified, liberated from the pairs of opposites known as pleasure and pain, they tread, undeluded, that indestructible path. (5)

निर्मानमोहाः=मानः च मोहः च निर्गतौ येभ्यः ते pride, and, delusion, and, gone, from whom, they; जितसंगदोषाः=जिताः संगस्य दोषाः यैः ते conquered, of attachment, the faults, by whom, they; अध्यात्मनित्याः=अध्यात्मनि नित्याः in the inner self, permanently established; विनिवृत्तकामाः – विनिवृत्ताः कामाः येषां ते departed, desires, whose, they; द्वंद्वैः by (from) the pairs; विमुक्ताः freed; सुखदुःखसंज्ञैः – सुखं च दुःखं च संज्ञा येषां तैः pleasure, and, pain, and, name, whose, by (from) them; गच्छंति go; अमूढाः un-deluded; पदं to the goal, अव्ययं indestructible; तत् that.

न तद्भासयते सूर्यो न शशांको न पावकः ।
यद्गत्वा न निवर्तंते तद्धाम परमं मम ॥ ६ ॥

Nor doth the sun lighten there, nor moon, nor fire; having gone thither they return not; that is My supreme abode. (6)

न not; तत् that; भासयते illuminates; सूर्यः the sun; न not; शशांकः the moon; न not; पावकः fire; यत् to which; गत्वा having gone; न not; निवर्तंते return; तत् that; धाम abode; परमं highest; मम my.

ममैवांशो जीवलोके जीवभूतः सनातनः ।
मनःषष्ठानीन्द्रियाणि प्रकृतिस्थानि कर्षति ॥ ७ ॥

A portion of Mine own Self, transformed in the world of life into an immortal Spirit, draweth round itself the senses of which the mind is the sixth, veiled in Matter. (7)

मम my; एव even; अंशः portion; जीवलोके – जीवानाम् लोके of living things, in the world; जीवभूतः jîva-become; सनातनः ancient; मनःषष्ठानि – मनः षष्ठं येषां तानि mind, sixth, of whom, them; इंद्रियाणि senses; प्रकृतिस्थानि – प्रकृतौ स्थितानि in nature, placed; कर्षति draws.

शरीरं यदवाप्नोति यच्चाप्युत्क्रामतीश्वरः ।
गृहीत्वैतानि संयाति वायुर्गंधानिवाशयात् ॥ ८ ॥

When the Lord acquireth a body and when He abandoneth it, He seizeth these and goeth with them, as the wind takes fragrances from their retreats. (8)

शरीरं a body; यत् which; अवाप्नोति obtains; यत् which; च and; अपि also; उत्क्रामति passes beyond; ईश्वरः the Lord; गृहीत्वा having seized; एतानि these; संयाति goes; वायुः wind; गंधान् fragrances; इव like; आशयात् from retreat.

श्रोत्रं चक्षुः स्पर्शनं च रसनं घ्राणमेव च ।
अधिष्ठाय मनश्चायं विषयानुपसेवते ॥ ९ ॥

Enshrined in the ear, the eye, the touch, the taste and the smell, and in the mind also, He enjoyeth the objects of the senses. (9)

श्रोत्रं the ear; चक्षुः the eye; स्पर्शनं the organ of touch; च and; रसनं the organ of taste; घ्राणं the organ of smell; एव even; च and; अधिष्ठाय presiding over; मनः the mind; च and; अयं this; विषयान् objects of the senses; उपसेवते enjoys.

उत्क्रामंतं स्थितं वापि भुंजानं वा गुणान्वितम् ।
विमूढा नानुपश्यंति पश्यंति ज्ञानचक्षुषः ॥ १० ॥

The deluded do not perceive Him when He

departeth or stayeth, or enjoyeth, swayed by the qualities; the wisdom-eyed perceive. (10)

उत्क्रामंतं departing; स्थितं staying; वा or; अपि also भुंजानं enjoying; वा or; गुणान्वितम् = गुणैः अन्वितं by the qualities, accompanied; विमूढाः the deluded; न not; अनुपश्यंति perceive; पश्यंति see; ज्ञानचक्षुषः = ज्ञानं चक्षुः येषां ते wisdom, eyes, whose, they.

यतंतो योगिनश्चैनं पश्यंत्यात्मन्यवस्थितम् ।
यतंतोऽप्यकृतात्मानो नैनं पश्यंत्यचेतसः ॥ ११ ॥

Yogîs also, struggling, perceive Him, established in the SELF; but, though struggling, the unintelligent perceive Him not, their selves untrained. (11)

यतंतः striving; योगिनः yogîs; च and; एवं thus; पश्यंति see; आत्मनि in the Self; अवस्थितम् established; यतंतः striving; अपि also; अकृतात्मानः = न कृतः आत्मा यैः ते not, made (purified), the Self, by whom, they; न not; एनं this; पश्यंति see; अचेतसः mindless.

यदादित्यगतं तेजो जगद्भासयतेऽखिलम् ।
यच्चंद्रमसि यच्चाग्नौ तत्तेजो विद्धि मामकम् ॥ १२ ॥

That splendour issuing from the sun that enlighteneth the whole world, that which is in the moon and in fire, that splendour know as from Me. (12)

यत् which; आदित्यगतं = आदित्यात् गतं from the sun, gone (forth); तेजः the splendour; जगत् the world; भासयते

lightens; अखिलम् whole; यत् which; चन्द्रमसि in the moon; यत् which; च and; अग्नौ in fire; तत् that; तेजः splendour; विद्धि know; मामकम् mine.

गामाविश्य च भूतानि धारयाम्यहमोजसा ।
पुष्णामि चौषधीः सर्वाः सोमो भूत्वा रसात्मकः ॥ १३ ॥

Permeating the soil, I support beings by My vital energy, and having become the delicious Soma[1] I nourish all plants. (13)

गाम् the earth; आविश्य having entered; च and; भूतानि beings; धारयामि support; अहं I; ओजसा by vitality; पुष्णामि (I) nourish; च and; ओषधीः plants; सर्वाः all; सोमः Soma; भूत्वा having become; रसात्मकः = रसः आत्मा यस्य सः sap, nature, whose, it.

अहं वैश्वानरो भूत्वा प्राणिनां देहमाश्रितः ।
प्राणापानसमायुक्तः पचाम्यन्नं चतुर्विधम् ॥ १४ ॥

I, having become the Fire of Life, take possession of the bodies of breathing things, and united with the life-breaths I digest the four kinds of food. (14)

अहं I; वैश्वानरः Vaishvânara; भूत्वा having become; प्राणिनां of living beings; देहम् the body; आश्रितः sheltered in; प्राणापानसमायुक्तः = प्राणेन च अपानेन च समायुक्तः with the in-breath, and, with the out-breath, and, united; पचामि (I) cook; अन्नं food; चतुर्विधम् fourfold.

---

1 "Having become the watery moon" is the accepted translation.

सर्वस्य चाहं हृदि संनिविष्टो
मत्तः स्मृतिर्ज्ञानमपोहनं च ।
वेदैश्च सर्वैरहमेव वेद्यो
वेदांतकृद्वेदविदेव चाहम् ॥ १५ ॥

And I am seated in the hearts of all, and from Me memory and wisdom and their absence. And that which is to be known in all the Vedas am I; and I indeed the Veda-knower and the author of the Vedânta. (15

सर्वस्य of all ; च and; अहं I; हृदि in the heart; संनिविष्टः seated; मत्तः from me; स्मृतिः memory; ज्ञानं wisdom; अपोहनं absence; च and; वेदैः by the Vedas; च and; सर्वैः (by) all; अहं I; एव even; वेद्यः to be known; वेदांतकृत् Vedânta maker; वेदवित् Veda-knower; एव even; च and; अहं I.

द्वाविमौ पुरुषौ लोके क्षरश्चाक्षर एव च ।
क्षरः सर्वाणि भूतानि कूटस्थोऽक्षर उच्यते ॥ १६ ॥

There are two energies in this world, the destructible and the indestructible; the destructible is all beings, the unchanging is called the indestructible. (16)

द्वौ two; इमौ (in) this; पुरुषौ Purushas (two); लोके in world; क्षरः destructible; च and; अक्षरः indestructible; एव even; च and; क्षरः the destructible; सर्वाणि all; भूतानि beings;

कूटस्थः the rock-seated ; अक्षरः the indestructible ; उच्यते is called.

उत्तमः पुरुषस्त्वन्यः परमात्मेत्युदाहृतः ।
यो लोकत्रयमाविश्य बिभर्त्यव्यय ईश्वरः ॥ १७ ॥

The highest energy is verily Another, declared as the supreme SELF, He, who pervading all, sustaineth the three worlds, the indestructible Lord. (17)

उत्तमः the highest ; पुरुषः spirit ; तु indeed ; अन्यः another ; परमात्मा highest Self ; इति thus ; उदाहृतः called ; यः who ; लोकत्रयम् triple world ; आविश्य having entered ; बिभर्ति sustains ; अव्ययः the imperishable ; ईश्वरः Lord.

यस्मात्क्षरमतीतोऽहमक्षरादपि चोत्तमः ।
अतोऽस्मि लोके वेदे च प्रथितः पुरुषोत्तमः ॥ १८ ॥

Since I excel the destructible, and am more excellent also than the indestructible, in the world and in the Veda I am proclaimed the supreme Spirit. (18)

यस्मात् whereas ; क्षरं destructible ; अतीतः beyond ; अहं I ; अक्षरात् than the indestructible ; अपि also ; च and ; उत्तमः best ; अतः hence ; अस्मि (I) am ; लोके in the world ; वेदे in the Veda ; च and ; प्रथितः declared ; पुरुषोत्तमः the highest spirit.

यो मामेवमसंमूढो जानाति पुरुषोत्तमम् ।
स सर्वविद्भजति मां सर्वभावेन भारत ॥ १९ ॥

He who undeluded knoweth Me thus as the Supreme spirit he, all-knowing, worshippeth Me with his whole being, O Bhârata. (19)

यः who; माम् me; एवं thus; असंमूढः undeluded; जानाति knows; पुरुषोत्तमम् the highest spirit; सः he; सर्ववित् all-knowing; भजति worships; माम् me; सर्वभावेन = सर्वेण भावेन (with) all, with being; भारत O Bhârata.

इति गुह्यतमं शास्त्रमिदमुक्तं मयानघ ।
एतद्बुध्वा बुद्धिमान् स्यात्कृतकृत्यश्च भारत ॥२०॥

Thus by Me this most secret teaching hath been told, O sinless one. This known, he hath become illuminated, and hath finished his work, O Bhârata. (20)

इति thus; गुह्यतमं most secret; शास्त्रम् teaching; इदं this; उक्तं spoken; मया by me; अनघ O sinless one; एतत् this; बुध्वा having known; बुद्धिमान् wise; स्यात् may become; कृतकृत्यः = कृतं कृत्यं येन सः work, done, by whom, he; भारत O Bhârata.

इति श्रीमद्भगवद्गीता० पुरुषोत्तमयोगो नाम पंचदशोऽध्यायः ।

Thus in the glorious BHAGAVAD GITA—the fifteenth discourse, entitled:

THE YOGA OF ATTAINING PURUSHOTTAMA.

SIXTEENTH DISCOURSE.

श्रीभगवानुवाच ।

अभयं सत्वसंशुद्धिर्ज्ञानयोगव्यवस्थितिः ।
दानं दमश्च यज्ञश्च स्वाध्यायस्तप आर्जवम् ॥ १ ॥

Fearlessness, cleanness of life, steadfastness in the Yoga of wisdom, almsgiving, self-restraint and sacrifice and study of the Scripture, austerity and straightforwardness, (1)

अभयं fearlessness ; सत्त्वसंशुद्धिः = सत्त्वस्य संशुद्धिः of being (living), purity ; ज्ञानयोगव्यवस्थितिः = ज्ञाने च योगे च व्यवस्थितिः in wisdom, and, in yoga, and, fixity ; दानं gift ; दमः self-restraint ; च and ; यज्ञः sacrifice ; च and ; स्वाध्यायः study (of Shâstras) ; तपः austerity ; आर्जवं rectitude.

अहिंसा सत्यमक्रोधस्त्यागः शांतिरपैशुनम् ।
दया भूतेष्वलोलुप्त्वं मार्दवं ह्रीरचापलम् ॥ २ ॥

Harmlessness, truth, absence of wrath, renunciation, peacefulness, absence of crookedness, compassion to living beings, uncovetousness, mildness, modesty, absence of fickleness, (2)

अहिंसा harmlessness ; सत्यं truth ; अक्रोधः absence of anger ; त्यागः renunciation ; शांतिः peace ; अपैशुनं absence of guile ; दया compassion ; भूतेषु among beings ; अलोलुप्त्वं uncovetousness ; मार्दवं mildness ; ह्रीः modesty ; अचापलं absence of fickleness.

तेजः क्षमा धृतिः शौचमद्रोहो नातिमानिता ।
भवंति संपदं दैवीमभिजातस्य भारत ॥ ३ ॥

Vigour, forgiveness, fortitude, purity, absence of envy and pride—these are his who is born with the divine properties, O Bhârata. (3)

तेजः splendour; क्षमा forgiveness; धृतिः fortitude: शौचं purity; अद्रोहः absence of malice; न not; अतिमानिता over-pride; भवंति are; संपदं to endowment; दैवीम (to) divine; अभिजातस्य of the born; भारत O Bhârata.

दंभो दर्पोऽभिमानश्च क्रोधः पारुष्यमेव च ।
अज्ञानं चाभिजातस्य पार्थ संपदमासुरीम् ॥ ४ ॥

Hypocrisy, arrogance and conceit, wrath and also harshness and unwisdom, are his who is born, O Pârtha, with demoniacal properties. (4)

दंभः hypocrisy; दर्पः arrogance; अभिमानः pride; च and; क्रोधः wrath; पारुष्यं harshness; एव even; च and; अज्ञानं ignorance; च and; अभिजातस्य of the born, पार्थ O Pârtha; संपदं to the endowment; आसुरीम (to) demoniacal.

दैवी संपद्विमोक्षाय निबंधायासुरी मता ।
मा शुचः संपदं दैवीमभिजातोऽसि पांडव ॥ ५ ॥

The divine properties are deemed to be for liberation, the demoniacal for bondage. Grieve not, thou art born with divine properties, O Pâṇḍava. (5)

दैवी divine; संपद् endowment; विमोक्षाय for liberation; निबंधाय for bondage; आसुरी demoniacal; मता is thought; मा do not; शुचः grieve; संपदं to endowment; दैवीम् (to) divine; अभिजातः born; असि (thou) art; पांडव O Pâṇḍava.

द्वौ भूतसर्गौ लोकेऽस्मिन्दैव आसुर एव च ।
दैवो विस्तरशः प्रोक्त आसुरं पार्थ मे श्रृणु ॥ ६ ॥

Twofold is the animal creation in this world, the divine and the demoniacal; the divine hath been described at length; hear from Me, O Pârtha, the demoniacal. (6)

द्वौ two; भूतसर्गौ = भूतानां सर्गौ of beings, emanations; लोके in world; अस्मिन् (in) this; दैवः divine; आसुरः demoniacal; एव even; च and; दैवः the divine; विस्तरशः in detail; प्रोक्तः said; आसुरं demoniacal; पार्थ O Pârtha; मे of me; श्रृणु hear.

प्रवृत्तिं च निवृत्तिं च जना न विदुरासुराः ।
न शौचं नापि चाचारो न सत्यं तेषु विद्यते ॥ ७ ॥

Demoniacal men know neither right energy nor right abstinence; nor purity, nor even propriety, nor truth is in them. (7)

प्रवृत्तिं forthgoing; च and; निवृत्तिं return; च and; जनाः men; न not; विदुः know; आसुराः demoniacal; न not; शौचं purity; न not; अपि also; च and; आचारः right conduct; न not; सत्यं truth; तेषु in them; विद्यते is.

असत्यमप्रतिष्ठं ते जगदाहुरनीश्वरम् ।
अपरस्परसंभूतं किमन्यत्कामहैतुकम् ॥ ८ ॥

"The universe is without truth, without (moral) basis," they say; "without a God, brought about by mutual union, and caused by lust and nothing else." (8)

असत्यं without-truth; अप्रतिष्ठं without-foundation; ते they; जगत् the world; आहुः say; अनीश्वरम् without-God; अपरस्परसंभूतं = अपरः च परः च ताभ्यां संभूतं another, and, other, and, from them (two), born; किं what; अन्यत् else; कामहैतुकम् = कामः हेतुः यस्य तत् lust, cause, whose, that.

एतां दृष्टिमवष्टभ्य नष्टात्मानोऽल्पबुद्धयः ।
प्रभवंत्युग्रकर्माणः क्षयाय जगतोऽहिताः ॥ ९ ॥

Holding this view, these ruined selves of small understanding, of fierce deeds, come forth as enemies for the destruction of the world. (9)

एतां this; दृष्टिम् view; अवष्टभ्य having held fast; नष्टात्मानः = नष्टाः आत्मानः येषां ते ruined, selves, whose, they; अल्पबुद्धयः = अल्पा बुद्धिः येषाम् ते small, reason, whose, they; प्रभवंति come forth; उग्रकर्माणः = उग्राणि कर्माणि येषाम् ते fierce, actions, whose, they; क्षयाय for destruction; जगतः of the world; अहिताः enemies.

काममाश्रित्य दुष्परं दंभमानमदान्विताः ।
मोहाद्गृहीत्वाऽसद्ग्राहान्प्रवर्ततेऽशुचिव्रताः ॥१०॥

Surrendering themselves to insatiable desires, possessed with vanity, conceit and arrogance, holding evil ideas through delusion, they engage in action with impure resolves. (10)

कामं desire; आश्रित्य having based on; दुष्पूरं hard to fill; दंभमानमदान्विताः = दंभेन च मानेन च मदेन च अन्विताः by vanity, and, by pride, and, by intoxication, and, pursued; मोहात् from delusion; गृहीत्वा having held; असद्ग्राहान् = असतः ग्राहान् evil addictions; प्रवर्तंते engage (in action); अशुचिव्रताः = अशुचीनि व्रतानि येषाम् ते; impure, vows, whose, they.

चिंतामपरिमेयां च प्रलयांतामुपाश्रिताः ।
कामोपभोगपरमा एतावदिति निश्चिताः ॥ ११ ॥

Giving themselves over to unmeasured thought whose end is death, regarding the gratification of desires as the highest, feeling sure that this is all, (11)

चिंतां care; अपरिमेयां unmeasurable; च and; प्रलयांताम् = प्रलयः अन्तः यस्याः तां dissolution, end, whose, it; उपाश्रिताः refuged in; कामोपभोगपरमाः = कामानां उपभोगः परमः येषां ते of (objects of) desires, enjoyment, the supreme (goal), whose, they; एतावत् thus much (is all); इति thus; निश्चिताः assured.

आशापाशशतैर्बद्धाः कामक्रोधपरायणाः ।
ईहंते कामभोगार्थमन्यायेनार्थसंचयान् ॥ १२ ॥

Held in bondage by a hundred ties of expectation, given over to lust and anger, they strive to obtain by unlawful means hoards of wealth for sensual enjoyments. (12)

आशापाशशतैः = आशायाः पाशानां शतैः of hope, of cords, (by) hundreds; बद्धाः bound; कामक्रोधपरायणाः = कामः च क्रोधः च परम् अयनं येषाम् ते desire, and, wrath, and, highest, refuge, whose, they; ईहन्ते (they) strive (to secure); कामभोगार्थे = कामस्य भोगस्य अर्थे of desire, of enjoyment, for the sake of; अन्यायेन = by injustice; अर्थसंचयान् = अर्थस्य संचयान् of wealth, collections.

इदमद्य मया लब्धमिमं प्राप्स्ये मनोरथम् ।
इदमस्तीदमपि मे भविष्यति पुनर्धनम् ॥ १३ ॥

"This to-day by me hath been won, that purpose I shall gain; this wealth is mine already, and also this shall be mine in future. (13)

इदं this; अद्य to-day; मया by me; लब्धं obtained; इमं this; प्राप्स्ये (I) shall obtain; मनोरथम् desire; इदं this; अस्ति is; इदं this; अपि also; मे of me; भविष्यति shall be; पुनः again; धनं wealth.

असौ मया हतः शत्रुर्हनिष्ये चापरानपि ।
ईश्वरोऽहमहं भोगी सिद्धोऽहं बलवान्सुखी ॥१४॥

"I have slain this enemy, and others also I shall slay. I am the Lord, I am the enjoyer, I am perfect, powerful, happy; (14)

असौ this; मया by me; हतः slain; शत्रुः enemy; हनिष्ये (I) shall slay; च and; अपरान् others; अपि also; ईश्वरः ruler; अहं I;

अहं I; भोगी the enjoyer; सिद्धः perfect; अहं I; बलवान् strong; सुखी happy.

आढ्योऽभिजनवानस्मि कोऽन्योस्ति सदृशो मया ।
यक्ष्ये दास्यामि मोदिष्ये इत्यज्ञानविमोहिताः ॥१५॥

"I am wealthy, well-born; what other is there that is like unto me? I will sacrifice, I will give (alms), I will rejoice." Thus deluded by unwisdom, (15)

आढ्यः wealthy; अभिजनवान् well-born; अस्मि (I) am: कः who; अन्यः other; अस्ति is; सदृशः like; मया by me; यक्ष्ये (I) will sacrifice; दास्यामि (I) will give; मोदिष्ये (I) will rejoice; इति thus; अज्ञानविमोहिताः = अज्ञानेन विमोहिताः by unwisdom, deluded.

अनेकचित्तविभ्रांता मोहजालसमावृताः ।
प्रसक्ताः कामभोगेषु पतंति नरकेऽशुचौ ॥ १६ ॥

Bewildered by numerous thoughts, enmeshed in the web of delusion, addicted to the gratification of desire, they fall downwards into a foul hell. (16)

अनेकचित्तविभ्रांताः = अनेकैः चित्तैः विभ्रांताः (by) various, by thoughts, bewildered; मोहजालसमावृताः = मोहस्य जालेन समावृताः of delusion, by the net, covered; प्रसक्ताः attached; कामभोगेषु = कामस्य भोगेषु of desire, in the enjoyments; पतंति fall; नरके into hell; अशुचौ impure.

आत्मसंभाविताः स्तब्धा धनमानमदान्विताः ।

यजंते नामयज्ञैस्ते दंभेनाविधिपूर्वकम् ॥ १७॥

Self-sufficing, obstinate, filled with the pride and intoxication of wealth, they perform lip-sacrifices for ostentation, contrary to scriptural ordinance. (17)

आत्मसंभाविताः = आत्मना संभाविताः by self, glorified; स्तब्धाः stubborn; धनमानमदान्विताः = धनस्य मानेन च मदेन च अन्विताः of wealth, by the pride, and, by the intoxication, and, filled; यजंते worship; नामयज्ञैः by nominal sacrifices; ते they; दंभेन by hypocrisy; अविधिपूर्वकम् contrary to rule.

अहंकारं बलं दर्पं कामं क्रोधं च संश्रिताः ।

मामात्मपरदेहेषु प्रद्विषंतोऽभ्यसूयकाः ॥ १८ ॥

Given over to egoism, power, insolence, lust and wrath, these malicious ones hate Me in the bodies of others and in their own. (18)

अहंकारं (to) egoism; बलं (to) power; दर्पं (to) insolence; कामं (to) desire; क्रोधं (to) wrath; च and; संश्रिताः refuged in; माम् me; आत्मपरदेहेषु = आत्मनः च परेषां च देहेषु of self, and, of others, and, in the bodies,; प्रद्विषंतः hating; अभ्यसूयकाः carping ones.

तानहं द्विषतः क्रूरान्संसारेषु नराधमान् ।

क्षिपाम्यजस्रमशुभानासुरीष्वेव योनिषु ॥ १९ ॥

These haters, evil, pitiless, vilest among men in the world, I ever throw down into demoniacal wombs. (19)

तान् these ; अहं I ; द्विषतः =(the) hating (ones) ; क्रूरान् cruel ; संसारेषु in the worlds ; नराधमान् = नरेषु अधमान् among men, worst ; क्षिपामि (I) throw ; अजस्रम् always ; अशुभान् impure ; आसुरीषु (in) demoniacal ; एव even ; योनिषु in wombs.

आसुरीं योनिमापन्ना मूढा जन्मनि जन्मनि ।
मामप्राप्यैव कौंतेय ततो यात्यधमां गतिम् ॥२०॥

Cast into a demoniacal womb, deluded birth after birth, attaining not to Me, O Kaunteya, they sink into the lowest depths. (20)

आसुरीं demoniacal ; योनिम् womb ; आपन्ना fallen into ; मूढाः deluded ; जन्मनि in birth ; जन्मनि in birth ; मां me ; अप्राप्य not having obtained ; कौंतेय O Kaunteya ; ततः thence ; यांति go ; अधमां to the lowest ; गतिम् path (goal).

त्रिविधं नरकस्येदं द्वारं नाशनमात्मनः ।
कामः क्रोधस्तथा लोभस्तस्मादेतत्त्रयं त्यजेत् ॥२१॥

Triple is the gate of this hell, destructive of the self—lust, wrath and greed ; therefore let man renounce these three. (21)

त्रिविधं triple ; नरकस्य of hell ; इदं this ; द्वारं gate ; नाशनं destructive ; आत्मनः of the self ; कामः desire ; क्रोधः wrath ; तथा also ; लोभः greed ; तस्मात् therefore ; एतत् this ; त्रयं triplet ; त्यजेत् let him throw away.

एतैर्विमुक्तः कौंतेय तमोद्वारैस्त्रिभिर्नरः ।

आचरत्यात्मनः श्रेयस्ततो याति परां गतिम् ॥२२॥

A man liberated from these three gates of darkness, O son of Kuntī, accomplisheth his own welfare and thus reacheth the highest goal. (22)

एतैः by these, विमुक्तः liberated ; कौंतेय O Kaunteya ; तमोद्वारैः=तमसः द्वारैः of darkness ; by gates ; त्रिभिः (by) three ; नरः the man ; आचरति acts ; आत्मनः own ; श्रेयः bliss ; ततः thence ; याति goes ; परां highest ; गतिम् path.

यः शास्त्रविधिमुत्सृज्य वर्तते कामकारतः ।

न स सिद्धिमवाप्नोति न सुखं न परां गतिम् ॥२३॥

He who having cast aside the ordinances of the Scriptures, followeth the promptings of desire, attaineth not to perfection, nor happiness, nor the highest goal. (23)

यः who ; शास्त्रविधिं=शास्त्राणाम् विधिं of the Shâstras, the rule ; उत्सृज्य having cast away ; वर्तते goes ; कामकारतः from the impulsion of desire ; न not ; सः he ; सिद्धिम् perfection ; आप्नोति obtains ; न not ; सुखं pleasure ; न not ; परां highest ; गतिम् path.

तस्माच्छास्त्रं प्रमाणं ते कार्याकार्यव्यवस्थितौ ।

ज्ञात्वा शास्त्रविधानोक्तं कर्म कर्तुमिहार्हसि ॥२४॥

Therefore let the Scriptures be thy authority, in determining what ought to be done, or what ought not to be done. Knowing what hath been declared by the ordinances of the Scriptures, thou oughtest to work in this world. (24)

तस्मात् therefore; शास्त्रं Shâstra; प्रमाणं authority; ते of thee; कार्याकार्यव्यवस्थितौ = कार्यस्य च अकार्यस्य च व्यवस्थितौ of duty, and, of non-duty, and, in the determination; ज्ञात्वा having known; शास्त्रविधानोक्तं = शास्त्रस्य विधानेन उक्तं of Shâstra, by the rule, spoken; कर्म action; कर्तुम to do; इह here; अर्हसि oughtest.

इति श्रीमद्भगवद्गीता० दैवासुरसंपद्विभागयोगो नाम षोडशोऽध्यायः ।

Thus in the glorious BHAGAVAD-GÎTÂ... the sixteenth discourse, entitled:

THE YOGA OF DIVISION BETWEEN THE DIVINE AND THE DEMONIACAL.

SEVENTEENTH DISCOURSE.

अर्जुन उवाच ।

ये शास्त्रविधिमुत्सृज्य यजंते श्रद्धयाऽन्विताः ।
तेषा निष्ठा तु का कृष्ण सत्वमाहो रजस्तमः ॥१॥

Arjuna said :

Those that sacrifice full of faith, but casting aside the ordinances of the Scriptures, what is verily their condition, O Kṛishṇa ? Is it one of Purity, Passion or Darkness? (1)

ये who; शास्त्रविधिम् the rule of the Shâstras; उत्सृज्य having cast away; यजंते sacrifice; श्रद्धया with faith; अन्विताः endowed; तषाम् of them; निष्ठा state; तु indeed; का what; कृष्ण O Kṛishṇa; सत्वं Satva; आहो or; रजः Rajaḥ; तमः Tamaḥ.

श्रीभगवानुवाच ।

त्रिविधा भवति श्रद्धा देहिना सा स्वभावजा ।
सात्विकी राजसी चैव तामसी चेति तां शृणु ॥ २ ॥

The Blessed Lord said :

Threefold is by nature the inborn faith of the embodied—pure, passionate and dark. Hear thou of these. (2)

त्रिविधा threefold; भवति is; श्रद्धा faith; देहिनां of the embodied; सा this; स्वभावजा = स्वभावात् जाता from own nature, born; सात्त्विकी sâtvic; राजसी râjasic; च and; एव even; तामसी tâmasic; च and; इति thus; तां it; शृणु hear.

सत्वानुरूपा सर्वस्य श्रद्धा भवति भारत ।
श्रद्धामयोऽयं पुरुषो यो यच्छ्रद्धः स एव सः ॥ ३ ॥

The faith of each is shaped to his own nature, O Bhârata. The man consists of his faith;[1] that which his faith is, he is even that. (3)

सत्वानुरूपा = सत्त्वस्य अनुरूपा of the being, following the form; (according to) सर्वस्य of all; श्रद्धा faith; भवति is; भारत O Bhârata; श्रद्धामयः faith-formed; अयं this; पुरुषः man; यः who; यच्छ्रद्धः या श्रद्धा यस्य सः whatever, faith, whose, he; सः that; एव even, सः he.

यजंते सात्विका देवान्यक्षरक्षांसि राजसाः ।
प्रेतान्भूतगणांश्चान्ये यजंते तामसाः जनाः ॥ ४ ॥

Pure men worship the Gods; the passionate the gnomes and giants; the others, the dark folk, worship ghosts and troops of nature-spirits. (4)

यजंते worship; सात्विकाः the sâtvic; देवान् the Gods; यक्षरक्षांसि = यक्षांसि च रक्षांसि च Yakshas, and, Râkshasas, and; राजसाः the râjasic; प्रेतान् ghosts; भूतगणान् = भूतानाम् गणान् of elementals, the hosts; च and; अन्ये others; यजंते worship; तामसाः tâmasic; जनाः people.

---

[1] That is, the man's faith shows what is the man's character.

अशास्त्रविहितं घोरं तप्यंते ये तपो जनाः ।
दंभाहंकारसंयुक्ताः कामरागबलान्विताः ॥ ५ ॥

The men who perform severe austerities, unenjoined by the Scripture, wedded to vanity and egoism, impelled by the force of their desires and passions, (5)

अशास्त्रविहितं = न शास्त्रेण विहितं not, by the Shâstras, ordained; घोरं terrible; तप्यंते endure; ये who; तपः austerity; जनाः people; दंभाहंकारसंयुक्ताः = दंभेन च अहंकारेण च संयुक्ताः with vanity, and, with egoism, and, joined; कामरागबलान्विताः = कामस्य च रागस्य च बलेन अन्विताः of desire, and, of passion, and, by force, filled.

कर्षयंतः शरीरस्थं भूतग्राममचेतसः ।
मां चैवांतःशरीरस्थं तान्विद्ध्यासुरनिश्चयान् ॥ ६ ॥

Unintelligent, tormenting the aggregated elements forming the body, and Me also, seated in the inner body, know these demoniacal in their resolves. (6)

कर्षयंतः tormenting; शरीरस्थं = शरीरे स्थितं in the body, seated; भूतग्रामम् = भूतानाम् ग्रामम् of elements, assemblage; अचेतसः unintelligent; मां me; च and; एव even; अन्तःशरीरस्थं = अंतः शरीरे स्थितं within, in the body, seated; तान् them; विद्धि know; आसुरनिश्चयान् = आसुराणां निश्चयः येषाम् ते of asuras, resolve, whose, they.

आहारस्त्वपि सर्वस्य त्रिविधो भवति प्रियः ।
यज्ञस्तपस्तथा दानं तेषां भेदमिमं शृणु ॥ ७ ॥

The food also which is dear to each is threefold, as also sacrifice, austerity and almsgiving. Hear thou the distinction of these. (7)

आहार: food; तु indeed; अपि also; सर्वस्य of all; त्रिविध: threefold; भवति is; प्रिय: dear; यज्ञ: sacrifice; तप: austerity; तथा also; दानं gift; तेषाम of these, भेदं distinction; इमं this; शृणु hear.

आयु:सत्वबलारोग्यसुखप्रीतिविवर्धना: ।

रस्या: स्निग्धा: स्थिरा हृद्या आहारा: सात्विकप्रिया:।८।

The foods that augment vitality, energy, vigour, health, joy and cheerfulness, delicious, bland, substantial and agreeable, are dear to the pure. (8)

आयु:सत्वबलारोग्यसुखप्रीतिविवर्धना: = आयु: च सत्वं च बलं च आरोग्यं च सुखं च प्रीति: च तासाम् विवर्धना: vitality, and, purity, and, strength, and, health, and, pleasure, and, cheerfulness, and, these, the increasers; रस्या: delicious; स्निग्धा: bland; स्थिरा: substantial; हृद्या: agreeable; आहारा: foods; सात्विकप्रिया: = सात्विकानां प्रिया: of the sâtvic, dear.

कट्वम्ललवणात्युष्णतीक्ष्णरूक्षाविदाहिन: ।

आहारा राजसस्येष्टा दु:खशोकामयप्रदा: ॥ ९ ॥

The passionate desire foods that are bitter, sour, saline, over-hot, pungent, dry and burning, and which produce pain, grief and sickness. (9)

कट्वम्ललवणात्युष्णतीक्ष्णरूक्षविदाहिनः = कटुः च अम्लः च लवणः च अत्युष्णः च तीक्ष्णः च रूक्षः च विदाही च bitter, and, sour, and, salt, and, very hot, and, pungent, and, dry, and, burning, and ; आहाराः foods ; राजसस्य of the râjasic ; इष्टाः desired ; दुःखशोकामयप्रदाः = दुःखं च शोकं च आमयं च प्रददति इति sorrow, and, grief, and, disease, give, thus.

यातयामं गतरसं पूति पर्युषितं च यत् ।

उच्छिष्टमपि चामेध्यं भोजनं तामसप्रियम् ॥ १० ॥

That which is stale and flat, putrid and corrupt, leavings also and unclean, is the food dear to the dark. (10)

यातयामं = यातः यामः यस्य तत् gone, a watch (of ours), whose, it ; गतरसं = गतः रसः यस्य तत् gone, taste, whose, it ; पूति putrid ; पर्युषितं stale ; च and ; यत् which ; उच्छिष्टम् left ; अपि also ; च and ; अमेध्यं unclean ; भोजनं food ; तामसप्रियम् = तामसानाम् प्रियम् of the tâmasic, dear.

अफलाकांक्षिभिर्यज्ञो विधिदृष्टो य इज्यते ।

यष्टव्यमेवेति मनः समाधाय स सात्विकः ॥ ११ ॥

The sacrifice which is offered by men without desire for fruit as enjoined by the ordinances, under the firm belief that sacrifice is a duty, that is pure. (11)

अफलाकांक्षिभिः = न फलस्य कांक्षिभिः not, of fruit, by the desirous ; यज्ञः sacrifice ; विधिदृष्टः = विधौ दृष्टः in the rule (of the Shâstra), seen (prescribed) ; यः which ; इज्यते is offered ; यष्टव्यम्

ought to be offered; एव even; इति thus; मनः the mind; समाधाय having fixed; सः that; सात्त्विकः sâttvic.

अभिसंधाय तु फलं दंभार्थमपि चैव यत् ।
इज्यते भरतश्रेष्ठ तं यज्ञं विद्धि राजसम् ॥ १२ ॥

The sacrifice offered with a view verily to fruit, and also indeed for self-glorification, O best of the Bhâratas; know thou that to be of passion. (12)

अभिसंधाय having aimed at; तु indeed; फलं fruit; दंभार्थम् = दंभस्य अर्थे of hypocrisy, for the sake; अपि also; एव even; च and; यत् which; इज्यते is offered; भरतश्रेष्ठ O best of the Bharatas; तं that; यज्ञं sacrifice; विद्धि know; राजसम् râjasic.

विधिहीनमसृष्टान्नं मंत्रहीनमदक्षिणम् ।
श्रद्धाविरहितं यज्ञं तामसं परिचक्षते ॥ १३ ॥

The sacrifice contrary to the ordinances, without distributing food, devoid of words of power and without gifts, empty of faith, is said to be of darkness. (13)

विधिहीनं = विधिना हीनं by rule, wanting; असृष्टान्नं = न सृष्टं अन्नं यस्मिन् तत् not, given, food, in which, that; मंत्रहीनं mantra-without; अदक्षिणम् giftless; श्रद्धाविरहितं = श्रद्धया विरहितं by (of) faith, devoid; यज्ञं sacrifice; तामसं tâmasic; परिचक्षते (they) declare.

देवद्विजगुरुप्राज्ञपूजनं शौचमार्जवम् ।

ब्रह्मचर्यमहिंसा च शारीरं तप उच्यते ॥ १४ ॥

Worship given to the Gods, to the twice-born, to the teachers and to the wise, purity, straightforwardness, continence and harmlessness, are called the austerity of the body. (14)

देवद्विजगुरुप्राज्ञपूजनं = देवानां च द्विजानां च गुरूणां च प्राज्ञानां च पूजनं of the Gods, and, of the twice-born, and, of the gurus, and, of the wise, and, worship; शौचं purity; आर्जवम् rectitude; ब्रह्मचर्यम् continence; अहिंसा harmlessness; च and; शारीरं bodily तपः austerity; उच्यते is called.

अनुद्वेगकरं वाक्यं सत्यं प्रियहितं च यत् ।

स्वाध्यायाभ्यसनं चैव वाङ्मयं तप उच्यते ॥१५॥

Speech causing no annoyance, truthful, and beneficial, the practice of the study of the Scriptures, are called the austerity of speech. (15)

अनुद्वेगकरं = न उद्वेगं करोति इति not, excitement, causes, thus; वाक्यं speech; सत्यं truthful; प्रियहितं = प्रियं च हितं च pleasant, and, beneficial, and; च and; यत् which; स्वाध्यायाभ्यसनं = स्वाध्यायस्य अभ्यसनं of the study, practice; च and; एव even; वाङ्मयं of speech; तपः austerity; उच्यते is called.

मनःप्रसादः सौम्यत्वं मौनमात्मविनिग्रहः ।

भावसंशुद्धिरित्येतत्तपो मानसमुच्यते ॥ १६ ॥

Mental happiness, equilibrium, silence, self-control,

purity of nature—this is called the austerity of the mind. (16)

मनःप्रसादः = मनसः प्रसादः of the mind, happiness; सौम्यत्वं equanimity; मौनम् silence; आत्मविनिग्रहः self-restraint; भावसंशुद्धिः = भावस्य संशुद्धिः of nature, purity; इति thus; एतत् this; तपः austerity; मानसम् mental; उच्यते is called.

श्रद्धया परया तप्तं तपस्तत्त्रिविधं नरैः ।
अफलाकांक्षिभिर्युक्तैः सात्विकं परिचक्षते ॥ १७ ॥

This threefold austerity, performed by men with the utmost faith, without desire for fruit, harmonised, is said to be pure. (17)

श्रद्धया by faith; परया (by) highest; तप्तं suffered; तपः austerity; तत् that; त्रिविधं threefold; नरैः by men; अफलाकांक्षिभिः = (by) not-desirous-of-fruit; युक्तैः by balanced; सात्विकं sâttvic; परिचक्षते (they) declare.

सत्कारमानपूजार्थं तपो दंभेन चैव यत् ।
क्रियते तदिह प्रोक्तं राजसं चलमध्रुवम् ॥ १८ ॥

The austerity which is practised with the object of gaining respect, honour and worship, and for ostentation, is said to be of passion, unstable and fleeting. (18)

सत्कारमानपूजार्थं = सत्कारः च मानः च पूजा च तासां अर्थं respect, and, honour, and, worship, and, of these, for the sake; तपः austerity; दंभेन by hypocrisy; च and; एव even; यत् which;

क्रियते is done; तत् that; इह here; प्रोक्तं is said; राजसं râjasic; चलं movable; अध्रुवम् unsteady.

मूढग्राहेणात्मनो यत्पीडया क्रियते तपः ।
परस्योत्सादनार्थं वा तत्तामसमुदाहृतम् ॥ १९ ॥

That austerity done under a deluded understanding, with self-torture, or with the object of destroying another, that is declared of darkness. (19)

मूढग्राहेण = मूढेन ग्राहेण by foolish, seizing, (stubbornness); आत्मनः of the self; यत् which; पीडया with torture; क्रियते is done; तपः austerity; परस्य of another; उत्सादनार्थं = उत्सादनस्य अर्थे of destruction, for the sake; वा or; तत् that; तामसम् tâmasic; उदाहृतम् is called.

दातव्यमिति यद्दानं दीयतेऽनुपकारिणे ।
देशे काले च पात्रे च तद्दानं सात्त्विकं स्मृतम् ॥२०॥

That alms given to one who does nothing in return, believing that a gift ought to be made, in a fit place and time, to a worthy person, that alms is accounted pure. (20)

दातव्यम् ought to be given; इति thus; यत् that; दानं gift; दीयते is given; अनुपकारिणे to the non-requiting; देशे in place; काले in time; च and; पात्रे in a right person; च and; तत् that; दानं gift; सात्त्विकं sâtvic; स्मृतं is remembered.

यत्तु प्रत्युपकारार्थं फलमुद्दिश्य वा पुनः ।

दीयते च परिक्लिष्टं तद्दानं राजसं स्मृतम् ॥ २१ ॥

That given with a view to receiving in return, or looking for fruit again, or grudgingly, that alms is accounted of passion. (21)

यत् which ; तु indeed ; प्रत्युपकारार्थं = प्रत्युपकारस्य अर्थे of return-benefit, for the sake ; फलं fruit ; उद्दिश्य having looked for ; वा or ; पुनः again ; दीयते is given ; च and ; परिक्लिष्टं painful (grudgingly) ; तत् that ; दानं gift ; राजसं râjasic ; स्मृतम् is remembered.

अदेशकाले यद्दानमपात्रेभ्यश्च दीयते ।

असत्कृतमवज्ञातं तत्तामसमुदाहृतम् ॥ २२ ॥

That alms given at unfit place and time, and to unworthy persons, disrespectfully and contemptuously, that is declared of darkness. (22)

अदेशकाले = न देशे काले च not, in right place, and, in (right) time, and ; यत् that ; दानं gift ; अपात्रेभ्यः to unfit persons ; दीयते is given ; असत्कृतम् unhonored ; अवज्ञातं contemned ; तत् that ; तामसम् tâmasic ; उदाहृतम् is called.

ओं तत्सदिति निर्देशो ब्रह्मणस्त्रिविधः स्मृतः ।

ब्राह्मणास्तेन वेदाश्च यज्ञाश्च विहिताः पुरा ॥२३ ॥

"AUM TAT SAT," this has been considered to be the threefold designation of the ETERNAL. By that were ordained of old Brâhmaṇas, Vedas and sacrifices. (23)

ओं तत् सत् Aum, That, Being ; इति thus ; निर्देशः designation ; ब्रह्मणः of Brahman ; त्रिविधः threefold ; स्मृतः remembered ; ब्राह्मणाः Brâhmaṇas ; तेन by this ; वेदाः Vedas ; च and ; यज्ञाः sacrifices ; च and ; विहिताः ordained ; पुरा formerly.

तस्मादोमित्युदाहृत्य यज्ञदानतपःक्रियाः ।
प्रवर्तंते विधानोक्ताः सततं ब्रह्मवादिनाम् ॥ २४ ॥

Therefore with the pronunciation of "AUM" the acts of sacrifice, gift and austerity, as laid down in the ordinances, are always commenced by the knowers of the ETERNAL. (24)

तस्मात् therefore ; ओं Aum ; इति thus ; उदाहृत्य having said ; यज्ञदानतपःक्रियाः = यज्ञस्य च दानस्य च तपसः च क्रियाः of sacrifice, and, of gift, and, of austerity, and, acts ; प्रवर्तंते go forth ; विधानोक्ताः = विधानेन उक्ताः by the rule, said ; सततं always ; ब्रह्मवादिनाम् of Brahman-declarers.

तदित्यनभिसंधाय फलं यज्ञतपःक्रियाः ।
दानक्रियाश्च विविधाः क्रियंते मोक्षकांक्षिभिः ॥ २५ ॥

With the pronunciation of "TAT" and without aiming at fruit are performed the various acts of sacrifice, austerity and gift, by those desiring liberation. (25)

तत् that ; इति thus ; अनभिसंधाय without having aimed at ; फलं fruit ; यज्ञतपःक्रियाः acts of sacrifice and austerity ; दानक्रियाः acts of gift ; च and ; विविधाः various ; क्रियंते are done ; मोक्षकांक्षिभिः = मोक्षस्य कांक्षिभिः of liberation, by the desirers.

सद्भावे साधुभावे च सदित्येतत्प्रयुज्यते ।
प्रशस्ते कर्मणि तथा सच्छब्दः पार्थ युज्यते ॥२६॥

"SAT" is used in the sense of reality and goodness likewise, O Pârtha, the word "SAT" is used in the sense of a good work. (26).

सद्भावे in (reference to) reality ; साधुभावे in (reference to) goodness ; च and ; सत् being ; इति thus ; एतत् this ; प्रयुज्यते is spoken ; प्रशस्ते in praiseworthy ; कर्मणि actions ; तथा also ; सत् Being ; शब्दः word ; पार्थ O Pârtha ; युज्यते is used.

यज्ञे तपसि दाने च स्थितिः सदिति चोच्यते ।
कर्म चैव तदर्थीयं सदित्येवाभिधीयते ॥ २७ ॥

Steadfastness in sacrifice, austerity and gift is also called "SAT," and an action for the sake of the supreme is also named "SAT." (27)

यज्ञे in sacrifice ; तपसि in austerity ; दाने in gift ; च and ; स्थितिः firmness ; सत् true ; इति thus ; च and ; उच्यते is called ; कर्म action ; च and ; एव even ; तदर्थीयं=सः अर्थः यस्य तत् that, the meaning, whose, it ; सत् Being ; इति thus ; एव even ; अभिधीयते is named.

अश्रद्धया हुतं दत्तं तपस्तप्तं कृतं च यत् ।
असदित्युच्यते पार्थ न च तत्प्रेत्य नो इह ॥२८॥

Whatsoever is wrought without faith, oblation, gift,

austerity, or other deed, "Asat" it is called, O Pârtha; it is nought, here or hereafter. (28)

अश्रद्धया by without-faith; हुतं offered; दत्तं given; तपः austerity; तप्तं suffered; कृतं done; च and; यत् which; असत् untrue; इति thus; उच्यते is called; पार्थ O Pârtha; नो not; च and; तत् that; प्रेत्य having gone (hereafter); नो not; इह here.

इति श्रीमद्भगवद्गीता० श्रद्धात्रयविभागयोगो नाम सप्तदशोऽध्यायः

Thus in the glorious BHAGAVAD-GÎTÂ,—the seventeenth discourse, entitled:

THE YOGA OF THE DIVISION OF THREEFOLD FAITH.

EIGHTEENTH DISCOURSE.

अर्जुन उवाच ।

संन्यासस्य महाबाहो तत्त्वमिच्छामि वेदितुम् ।
त्यागस्य च हृषीकेश पृथक्केशिनिषूदन ॥ १ ॥

Arjuna said:

I desire, O mighty-armed, to know severally the essense of renunciation, O Hrishîkesha, and of relinquishment, O Keshinishûdana. (1)

सन्यासस्य of renunciation; महाबाहो O mighty-armed; तत्त्वम् the essence; इच्छामि (I) wish; वेदितुम् to know; त्यागस्य of abandonment; च and; हृषीकेश O Hrishîkesha; पृथक् severally; केशिनिषूदन = केशिनः निषूदन of Keshi, O slayer.

श्रीभगवानुवाच ।

काम्यानां कर्मणां न्यासं संन्यासं कवयो विदुः ।
सर्वकर्मफलत्यागं प्राहुस्त्यागं विचक्षणाः ॥ २ ॥

The Blessed Lord said:

Sages have known as renunciation the renouncing of works with desire; the relinquishing of the fruit of all actions is called relinquishment by the wise. (2)

काम्यानां (of) desireful; कर्मणां of actions; न्यासं renouncing; संन्यासं renunciation; कवयः poets; विदुः know; सर्वकर्मफलत्यागं = सर्वेषाम् कर्मणाम् फलस्य त्यागं (of) all, of works, of fruits, renunciation ;' प्राहुः declare ; त्यागं abandonment ; विचक्षणाः the wise.

त्याज्यं दोषवदित्येके कर्म प्राहुर्मनीषिणः ।
यज्ञदानतपः कर्म न त्याज्यमिति चापरे ॥ ३ ॥

"Action should be relinquished as an evil," declare some thoughtful men ; "acts of sacrifice, gift and austerity should not be relinquished," say others. (3)

त्याज्यं should be abandoned ; दोषवत् full of evil ; इति thus ; एके ones (some) ; कर्म action ; प्राहुः say ; मनीषिणः the wise ; यज्ञदानतपःकर्म acts of sacrifice, gift, and austerity ; न not ; त्याज्यम् to be abandoned ; इति thus ; च and ; अपरे others.

निश्चयं श्रृणु मे तत्र त्यागे भरतसत्तम ।
त्यागो हि पुरुषव्याघ्र त्रिविधः संप्रकीर्तितः ॥ ४ ॥

Hear my conclusions as to that relinquishment, O best of the Bharatas : since relinquishment, O tiger of men, has been explained as threefold. (4)

निश्चयं conclusion ; श्रृणु hear ; मे my ; तत्र there ; त्यागे in (respect of) abandonment ; भरतसत्तम O best of the Bharatas ; त्यागः abandonment ; हि indeed ; पुरुषव्याघ्र O tiger of men ; त्रिविधः threefold ; संप्रकीर्तितः is declared.

यज्ञदानतपःकर्म न त्याज्यं कार्यमेव तत् ।
यज्ञो दानं तपश्चैव पावनानि मनीषिणाम् ॥ ५ ॥

Acts of sacrifice, gift and austerity should not be relinquished, but should be performed ; sacrifice, gift and also austerity are the purifiers of the intelligent. (5)

यज्ञदानतपःकर्म acts of sacrifice. gift, and austerity ; न not ; त्याज्यं should be abandoned ; कार्यम् to be done ; एव even ; तत् that ; यज्ञं sacrifice ; दानं gift ; तपः austerity ; च and ; एव even ; पावनानि purifiers ; मनीषिणाम् of the wise.

एतान्यपि तु कर्माणि संगं त्यक्त्वा फलानि च ।
कर्तव्यानीति मे पार्थ निश्चितं मतमुत्तमम् ॥ ६ ॥

But even these actions should be done leaving aside attachment and fruit, O Pârtha ; that is my certain and best belief. (6)

एतानि these ; अपि also ; तु indeed ; कर्माणि actions ; संगं attachment ; त्यक्त्वा having abandoned ; फलानि fruits ; च and ; कर्तव्यानि to be done (obligatory) ; इति thus ; मे my ; पार्थ O Pârtha ; निश्चितं certain ; मतं opinion ; उत्तमम् best.

नियतस्य तु संन्यासः कर्मणो नोपपद्यते ।
मोहात्तस्य परित्यागस्तामसः परिकीर्तितः ॥ ७ ॥

Verily renunciation of actions that are prescribed is not proper ; the relinquishment thereof from delusion is said to be of darkness. (7)

नियतस्य of prescribed ; तु indeed ; संन्यासः renunciation ; कर्मणः of action ; न not ; उपपद्यते befits ; मोहात् from delusion ;

तस्य of that; परित्यागः abandonment; तामसः tamasic; परिकीर्तितः is declared.

दुःखमित्येव यत्कर्म कायक्लेशभयात्त्यजेत् ।
स कृत्वा राजसं त्यागं नैव त्यागफलं लभेत् ॥८॥

He who relinquisheth an action from fear of physical suffering, saying, "Painful," thus performing a passionate relinquishment, obtaineth not the fruit of relin-quishment. (8)

दुःखं pain; इति thus; एव even; यत् which; कर्म action; कायक्लेशभयात्—कायस्य क्लेशस्य भयात् of body, of pain, from fear; त्यजेत् may abandon; सः he; कृत्वा having done; राजसं râjasic; त्यागं abandonment; न not; एव even; त्यागफलं—त्यागस्य फलं of abandonment, the fruit; लभेत may obtain.

कार्यमित्येव यत्कर्म नियतं क्रियतेऽर्जुन ।
संगं त्यक्त्वा फलं चैव स त्यागः सात्विको मतः ॥९॥

He who performeth a prescribed action, saying, "It ought to be done," O Arjuna, relinquishing attachment and also fruit, that relinquishment is regarded as pure. (9)

कार्यम् ought to be done; इति thus; एव even; यत् which; कर्म action; नियतं prescribed; क्रियते is done; अर्जुन O Arjuna; संगं attachment; त्यक्त्वा having abandoned; फलं fruit; च and; एव even; सः that; त्यागः abandonment; सात्त्विकः sâttvic; मतः is thought.

न द्वेष्ट्यकुशलं कर्म कुशलं नानुषज्जते ।
त्यागी सत्वसमाविष्टो मेधावी छिन्नसंशयः ॥१०॥

The relinquisher pervaded by purity, intelligent and with doubts cut away, hateth not unpleasurable action nor is attached to pleasurable. (10)

न not; द्वेष्टि hates; अकुशलं unpleasant; कर्म action; कुशले in pleasant; न not; अनुषज्जते is attached; त्यागी the abandoner; सत्वसमाविष्टः satva-pervaded; मेधावी intelligent; छिन्नसंशयः = छिन्नः संशयः यस्य सः cut, doubt, whose, he.

नहि देहभृता शक्यं त्यक्तुं कर्माण्यशेषतः ।
यस्तु कर्मफलत्यागी स त्यागीत्यभिधीयते ॥ ११ ॥

Nor indeed can embodied beings completely relinquish action; verily he who relinquisheth the fruit of action he is said to be a relinquisher. (11)

न not; हि indeed; देहभृता by the embodied; शक्यं possible; त्यक्तुं to abandon; कर्माणि actions; अशेषतः without remainder; यः who; तु indeed; कर्मफलत्यागी = कर्मणः फलस्य त्यागी of action, of fruit, abandoner; सः he; त्यागी abandoner; इति thus; अभिधीयते is called.

अनिष्टमिष्टं मिश्रं च त्रिविधं कर्मणः फलम् ।
भवत्यत्यागिनां प्रेत्य न तु संन्यासिनां क्वचित् ॥ १२ ॥

Good, evil and mixed—threefold is the fruit of action hereafter for the non-relinquisher; but there is none ever for the renouncer. (12)

अनिष्टम् unwished ; इष्टं wished ; मिश्रं mixed ; च and ; त्रिविधं threefold ; कर्मण: the fruit ; भवति is ; अत्यागिनाम् of non-abandoners ; प्रेत्य having departed (hereafter); न not.

पंचैतानि महाबाहो कारणानि निबोध मे ।
सांख्ये कृतांते प्रोक्तानि सिद्धये सर्वकर्मणाम् ॥१३॥

These five causes, O mighty-armed, learn of Me as declared in the Sâñkhya system for the accomplishment of all actions :— (13)

पंच five ; एतानि these ; महाबाहो O mighty-armed ; कारणानि causes ; निबोध learn ; मे of me ; सांख्ये in the Sâñkhya ; कृतांते =कृतस्य अंतः यत्र तस्मिन् of action, the end, where, in that ; प्रोक्तानि (are) declared ; सिद्धये success ; सर्वकर्मणाम् = सर्वेषाम् कर्मणाम् (of) all, of actions.

अधिष्ठानं तथा कर्ता करणं च पृथग्विधम् ।
विविधाश्च पृथक्चेष्टा दैवं चैवात्र पंचमम् ॥१४॥

The body, the actor, the various organs, the divers kinds of energies, and the presiding deities also, the fifth. (14)

अधिष्ठानं the body ; तथा also ; कर्ता the doer ; करणं organ ; च and ; पृथग्विधम् severally ; विविधाः various ; च and ; पृथक् several ; चेष्टाः activities ; दैवं divinity ; च and ; एव even ; अत्र here ; पंचमं fifth.

शरीरवाङ्मनोभिर्यत्कर्म प्रारभते नरः ।

न्याय्यं वा विपरीतं वा पंचैते तस्य हेतवः ॥१५॥

Whatever action a man performeth by his body, speech and mind, whether right or the reverse, these five are the cause thereof. (15)

शरीरवाङ्मनोभिः = शरीरेण च वाचा च मनसा च with body, and, with speech, and, with mind, and; यत् which; कर्म action; प्रारभते undertakes; नरः a man; न्याय्यं just; वा or; विपरीतं evil; वा or; पंच five; एते these; तस्य of that; हेतवः causes.

तत्रैवं सति कर्तारमात्मानं केवलं तु यः ।
पश्यत्यकृतबुद्धित्वान्न स पश्यति दुर्मतिः ॥१६॥

That being so, he verily who—owing to untrained Reason—looketh on his SELF, which is isolated, as the actor, he, of perverted intelli ence, seeth not. (16)

तत्र there; एवं thus; सति in being; कर्तारं actor; आत्मानं the Self; केवलं alone; तु indeed; यः who; पश्यति sees; अकृतबुद्धित्वात् = न कृता बुद्धिः येन, तस्य भावात् not, achieved, intelligence, by whom, of him, from the condition; न not; सः he; पश्यति sees; दुर्मतिः evil-minded.

यस्य नाहंकृतो भावो बुद्धिर्यस्य न लिप्यते ।
हत्वापि स इमाँल्लोकान्न हंति न निबध्यते ॥१७॥

He who is free from the egoistic notion, whose Reason is not affected, though he slay these peoples, he slayeth not, nor is bound. (17)

यस्य of whom ; न not ; अहंकृतः egoistic ; भावः notion ; बुद्धिः reason ; यस्य of whom ; न not ; लिप्यते is affected ; हत्वा having slain ; अपि also ; सः he ; इमां these ; लोकान् peoples ; न not ; हंति slays ; न not ; निबध्यते is bound.

ज्ञानं ज्ञेयं परिज्ञाता त्रिविधा कर्मचोदना ।
करणं कर्म कर्तेति त्रिविधः कर्मसंग्रहः ॥१८॥

Knowledge, the knowable and the knower, the threefold impulse to action; the organ, the action, the actor, the threefold constituents of action. (18)

ज्ञानं knowledge ; ज्ञेयं the knowable ; परिज्ञाता the knower ; त्रिविधा threefold ; कर्मचोदना = कर्मणां चोदना to action, incentive ; करणं the organ ; कर्म the action ; कर्ता the actor ; इति thus ; त्रिविधः threefold ; कर्मसंग्रहः = कर्मणः संग्रहः of action, the assemblage.

ज्ञानं कर्म च कर्त्ता च त्रिधैव गुणभेदतः ।
प्रोच्यते गुणसंख्याने यथावच्छृणु तान्यपि ॥१९॥

Knowledge, action and actor in the category of qualities are also said to be severally threefold, from the difference of qualities; hear thou duly these also. (19)

ज्ञानं knowledge ; कर्म action ; च and ; कर्ता actor ; च and ; त्रिधा threefold ; एव even ; गुणभेदतः = गुणानाम् भेदतः of gunas from the division ; प्रोच्यते is said : गुणसंख्याने = गुणानाम् संख्याने of gunas, in the enumeration ; यथावत् exactly ; शृणु hear ; तानि these ; अपि also.

सर्वभूतेषु येनैकं भावमव्ययमीक्षते ।
अविभक्तं विभक्तेषु तज्ज्ञानं विद्धि सात्विकम्॥२०॥

That by which one indestructible Being is seen in all beings, inseparate in the separated, know thou that knowledge as pure. (20)

सर्वभूतेषु in all beings; येन by which; एकं one; भावं being; अव्ययं indestructible; ईक्षते sees; अविभक्तं inseparate; विभक्तेषु in the separate; तत् that; ज्ञानं wisdom; विद्धि know; सात्विकम् sâtvic.

पृथक्त्वेन तु यज्ज्ञानं नानाभावान्पृथग्विधान् ।
वेत्ति सर्वेषु भूतेषु तज्ज्ञानं विद्धि राजसम् ॥२१॥

But that knowledge which regardeth the several manifold existences in all beings as separate, that knowledge know thou as of passion. (21)

पृथक्त्वेन by separateness; तु indeed; यत् which; ज्ञानं wisdom; नाना various; भावान् natures; पृथग्विधान् of various kinds; वेत्ति knows; सर्वेषु (in) all; भूतेषु in beings; तत् that; ज्ञानं knowledge; विद्धि know; राजसं râjasic.

यत्तु कृत्स्नवदेकस्मिन् कार्ये सक्तमहैतुकम् ।
अतत्त्वार्थवदल्पं च तत्तामसमुदाहृतम् ॥ २२ ॥

While that which clingeth to each one thing as if it were the whole, without reason, without grasping the reality, narrow, that is declared to be dark. (22)

यत् which ; तु indeed ; कृत्स्नवत् like the whole ; एकस्मिन् in one ; कार्ये in action ; सक्तं attached ; अहैतुकं without cause ; अतत्त्वार्थवत् without essential significance ; अल्पं small ; च and ; तत् that ; तामसं tâmasic ; उदाहृतम् is called.

नियतं संगरहितमरागद्वेषतः कृतम् ।
अफलप्रेप्सुना कर्म यत्तत्सात्त्विकमुच्यते ॥ २३ ॥

An action which is ordained, done by one undesirous of fruit, devoid of attachment, without love or hate, that is called pure.

नियतं prescribed ; संगरहितं = संगेन रहितं by (of) attachment, devoid ; अरागद्वेषतः = न रागात् वा द्वेषात् वा इति not, from love, or, from hate, or, thus ; कृतं done ; अफलप्रेप्सुना = न फलस्य प्रेप्सुना not, of fruit, by desirer ; कर्म action ; यत् which ; तत् that ; सात्त्विकम् sâtvic ; उच्यते is called.

यत्तु कामेप्सुना कर्म साहंकारेण वा पुनः ।
क्रियते बहुलायासं तद्राजसमुदाहृतम् ॥ २४ ॥

But that action that is done by one longing for desires, or again with egoism, or with much effort, that is declared to be passionate. (24)

यत् which ; तु indeed ; कामेप्सुना = कामस्य ईप्सुना of desire, by desirer ; कर्म action ; साहंकारेण = अहंकारः यस्य अस्ति तेन egoism, whose, is by him ; वा or ; पुनः again ; क्रियते is, done ; बहुलायासं = बहुलः आयासः यस्मिन् तत् great, labor, in which, that ; तत् that ; राजसं râjasic ; उदाहृतं is called.

अनुबंधं क्षयं हिंसामनपेक्ष्य च पौरुषम् ।
मोहादारभ्यते कर्म यत्तत्तामसमुच्यते ॥ २५ ॥

The action undertaken from delusion, without regard to capacity and to consequences—loss and injury to others—that is declared to be dark. (25)

अनुबंधं consequence ; क्षयं loss ; हिंसाम् injury ; अनपेक्ष्य without regarding ; च and; पौरुषं exertion; मोहात् from delusion ; आरभ्यते is begun ; कर्म action ; यत् which ; तत् that ; तामसं tâmasic ; उच्यते is called.

मुक्तसंगोऽनहंवादी धृत्युत्साहसमन्वितः ।
सिद्ध्यसिद्ध्योर्निर्विकारः कर्त्ता सात्विक उच्यते ॥२६॥

Liberated from attachment, not egoistic, endued with firmness and confidence, unchanged by success or failure, that actor is called pure. (26)

मुक्तसंगः = मुक्तः संगः येन सः abandoned, attachment, by whom, he; अनहंवादी = न अहं वदति इति not, I, says, thus; धृत्युत्साहसमन्वितः = धृत्या च उत्साहेन च समन्वितः with firmness, and, with confidence, and, endowed ; सिद्ध्यसिद्ध्योः = सिद्धौ च असिद्धौ च in success, and, in failure, and ; निर्विकारः unchanged ; कर्ता actor ; सात्विकः sâtvic ; उच्यते is called.

रागी कर्मफलप्रेप्सुर्लुब्धो हिंसात्मकोऽशुचिः ।
हर्षशोकान्वितः कर्ता राजसः परिकीर्तितः ॥२७॥

Impassioned, desiring to obtain the fruit of actions, greedy, harmful, impure, moved by joy and sorrow, such an actor is pronounced passionate. (27)

रागी passionate; कर्मफलप्रेप्सुः = कर्मणः फलस्य प्रेप्सुः of action, of the fruit, desirous; लुब्धः greedy; हिंसात्मकः = हिंसा आत्मनि यस्य सः cruelty, in self, whose, he; अशुचिः impure; हर्षशोकान्वितः = हर्षेण च शोकेन च अन्वितः with joy, and, with sorrow, and, followed, कर्ता actor; राजसः râjasic; परिकीर्तितः is named.

अयुक्तः प्राकृतः स्तब्धः शठो नैष्कृतिकोऽलसः।
विषादी दीर्घसूत्री च कर्ता तामस उच्यते ॥ २८ ॥

Discordant, vulgar, stubborn, cheating, malicious, indolent, despairful, procrastinating, that actor is called dark. (28)

अयुक्तः unbalanced; प्राकृतः vulgar; स्तब्धः stubborn; शठः cheating; नैष्कृतिकः malicious; अलसः lazy; विषादी despairing; दीर्घसूत्री procrastinating; च and; कर्ता actor; तामसः tâmasic.

बुद्धेर्भेदं धृतेश्चैव गुणतस्त्रिविधं शृणु।
प्रोच्यमानमशेषेण पृथक्त्वेन धनंजय ॥ २९ ॥

The division of Reason and of firmness also, threefold according to the qualities, hear thou related, unreservedly and severally, O Dhanañjaya. (29)

बुद्धेः of reason; भेदं division; धृतेः of firmness; च and; एव even; गुणतः from (according to) qualities; त्रिविधं threefold; शृणु hear; प्रोच्यमानम् being declared; अशेषेण without remainder ; पृथक्त्वेन by severalness ; धनंजय O Dhanañjaya.

प्रवृत्तिं च निवृत्तिं च कार्याकार्ये भयाभये ।
बंधं मोक्षं च या वेत्ति बुद्धिः सा पार्थ सात्विकी ॥३०॥

That which knoweth energy and abstinence, what ought to be done and what ought not to be done, fear and fearlessness, bondage and liberation, that Reason is pure, O Pârtha. (30)

प्रवृत्तिं forthgoing ; च and ; निवृत्तिं return ; च and ; कार्याकार्ये = कार्यं च अकार्यं च right-doing, and, wrong-doing, and ; भयाभये = भयं च अभयं च fear, and, fearlessness, and ; बंधं bondage ; मोक्षं liberation ; च and ; वा or ; वेत्ति knows ; बुद्धिः reason ; सा that ; पार्थ O Pârtha ; सात्विकी sâtvic.

यया धर्ममधर्मं च कार्यं चाकार्यमेव च ।
अयथावत्प्रजानाति बुद्धिः सा पार्थ राजसी ॥३१॥

That by which one understandeth awry Right and Wrong, and also what ought to be done and what ought not to be done, that Reason, O Pârtha, is passionate. (31)

यया by which ; धर्मम् right ; अधर्मम् wrong ; च and ; कार्यं what should be done ; च and ; अकार्यं what should not be done ; एव even ; च and ; अयथावत् incorrectly ; प्रजानाति understands ; बुद्धिः reason ; सा that ; पार्थ O Pârtha ; राजसी râjasic.

अधर्मं धर्ममिति या मन्यते तमसा वृता ।

सर्वार्थान् विपरीतांश्च बुद्धिः सा पार्थ तामसी ॥३२॥

That which, enwrapped in darkness, thinketh Wrong to be Right, and seeth all things subverted, that Reason O Pârtha, is of darkness. (32)

अधर्मं wrong; धर्मं right; इति thus; या which; मन्यते thinks; तमसा with darkness; वृता covered; सर्वार्थान्=सर्वान् अर्थान् all, things; विपरीतान् perverted; बुद्धिः reason; सा that; पार्थ O Pârtha; तामसी tâmasic.

धृत्या यया धारयते मनःप्राणेंद्रियक्रियाः ।
योगेनाव्यभिचारिण्या धृतिः सा पार्थ सात्विकी ॥३३॥

The unwavering firmness by which, through yoga, one restraineth the activity of the mind, of the life-breaths and of the sense-organs, that firmness, O Pârtha, is pure. (33)

धृत्या by firmness; यया (by) which; धारयते holds; मनःप्राणेंद्रियक्रियाः=मनसः च प्राणानाम् च इंद्रियाणाम् च क्रियाः of the mind, and, of the life-breaths, and, of the sense-organs, and. actions; योगेन by yoga; अव्यभिचारिण्या (by) unwavering; धृतिः firmness; सा that; पार्थ O Pârtha; सात्विकी sâtvic.

यया तु धर्मकामार्थान् धृत्या धारयतेऽर्जुन ।
प्रसंगेन फलाकांक्षी धृतिः सा पार्थ राजसी ॥ ३४॥

But the firmness, O Arjuna, by which, from attachment desirous of fruit, one holdeth fast duty, desire and wealth, that firmness, O Pârtha, is passionate. (34)

यया (by) which ; तु indeed ; धर्मकामार्थान् = धर्मः च कामः च अर्थः च तान् duty, and, pleasure, and, wealth, and, them ; धृत्या by firmness ; धारयते holds ; अर्जुन O Arjuna ; प्रसंगेन by attachment ; फलाकांक्षी = फलस्य आकांक्षी of fruit, desirous ; धृतिः firmness ; सा that ; पार्थ O Pârtha ; राजसी râjasic.

यया स्वप्नं भयं शोकं विषादं मदमेव च ।
न विमुंचति दुर्मेधा धृतिः सा पार्थ तामसी ॥३५॥

That by which one from stupidity doth not abandon sleep, fear, grief, despair, and also vanity, that firmness, O Pârtha, is dark. (35)

यया by which ; स्वप्नं sleep ; भयं fear ; शोकं grief ; विषादं despair ; मदं intoxication ; एव even ; च and ; न not ; विमुंचति abandons ; दुर्मेधाः evil-witted ; धृतिः firmness ; सा that ; पार्थ O Pârtha ; तामसी tâmasic.

सुखं त्विदानीं त्रिविधं शृणु मे भरतर्षभ ।
अभ्यासाद्रमते यत्र दुःखान्तं च निगच्छति ॥३६॥

And now the threefold kinds of pleasure hear thou from Me, O bull of the Bharatas. That in which one by practice rejoiceth, and which putteth an end to pain ; (36)

सुखं pleasure ; तु indeed ; इदानीं now ; त्रिविधं threefold ; शृणु hear ; मे of me ; भरतर्षभ O bull of the Bharatas ; अभ्यासात् from practice ; रमते rejoices ; यत्र where ; दुःखान्तं = दुःखस्य अन्तं of pain, the end ; च and ; निगच्छति goes.

यत्तदग्रे विषमिव परिणामेऽमृतोपमम् ।
तत्सुखं सात्विकं प्रोक्तमात्मबुद्धिप्रसादजम् ॥३७॥

Which at first is as venom but in the end is as nectar; that pleasure is said to be pure, born of the blissful knowledge of the SELF. (37)

यत् which; तत् that; अग्रे in beginning; विषम् poison; इव like; परिणामे in end; अमृतोपमम्=अमृतं उपमा यस्य तत् nectar, simile, whose, it; तत् that; सुखं pleasure; सात्विकम् sâtvic; प्रोक्तं is called; आत्मबुद्धिप्रसादजम्=आत्मनः बुद्धेः प्रसादात् जातं of the Self, of knowledge, from the placidity, born.

विषयेंद्रियसंयोगाद्यत्तदग्रेऽमृतोपमम् ।
परिणामे विषमिव तत्सुखं राजसं स्मृतम् ॥ ३८ ॥

That which from the union of the senses with their objects at first is as nectar, but in the end is like venom, that pleasure is accounted passionate. (38)

विषयेंद्रियसंयोगात्=विषयेभ्यः इंद्रियाणाम् संयोगात् with the objects, of the senses, from union; यत् which; तत् that; अग्रे in the beginning; अमृतोपमम् like nectar; परिणामे in the end; विषम् poison; इव like; तत् that; सुखं pleasure; राजसं râjasic; स्मृतम् remembered.

यदग्रे चानुबंधे च सुखं मोहनमात्मनः ।
निद्रालस्यप्रमादोत्थं तत्तामसमुदाहृतम् ॥ ३९ ॥

That pleasure which both at first and afterwards is

delusive of the self, arising from sleep, indolence and heedlessness dark, that is declared tâmasic. (39)

यत् which ; अग्रे in the beginning ; च and ; अनुबंधे in the consequence ; च and ; सुखं pleasure ; मोहनं delusive ; आत्मन: of the self ; निद्रालस्यप्रमादोत्थं = निद्रा च आलस्यं च प्रमादः च, तेभ्यः उत्थितं sleep, and, sloth, and, heedlessness, and, from them, risen ; तत् that ; तामसम् tâmasic ; उदाहृतम् is called.

न तदस्ति पृथिव्यां वा दिवि देवेषु वा पुनः ।
सत्त्वं प्रकृतिजैर्मुक्तं यदेभिः स्यात्त्रिभिर्गुणैः ॥ ४० ॥

There is not an entity, either on the earth or again in heaven among the Shining Ones, that is liberated from these three qualities, born of matter. (40)

न not ; तत् that ; अस्ति is ; पृथिव्यां in the earth ; वा or ; दिवि in heaven ; देवेषु among the Gods ; वा or ; पुन: again ; सत्त्वं a being ; प्रकृतिजैः by (from) nature-born ; मुक्तं freed ; यत् which ; एभिः from these ; स्यात् may be ; त्रिभिः from three; गुणैः by (from) qualities.

ब्राह्मणक्षत्रियविशां शूद्राणां च परंतप ।
कर्माणि प्रविभक्तानि स्वभावप्रभवैर्गुणैः ॥ ४१ ॥

Of Brâhmaṇas, Kṣhattriyas, Vaishyas and Shûdras, O Parantapa, the duties have been distributed, according to the qualities born of their own natures. (41)

ब्राह्मणक्षत्रियविशाम् = ब्राह्मणानां च क्षत्रियाणां च विशां च of Brâhmaṇas, and, of Kṣhattriyas, and, of Vaishyas, and ; शूद्रा-

णाम् of Shûdras ; च and ; परंतप O Parantapa ; कर्माणि actions ; प्रविभक्तानि (are) distributed ; स्वभावप्रभवैः by own-nature-produced ; गुणैः by qualities.

शमो दमस्तपः शौचं क्षांतिरार्जवमेव च ।
ज्ञानं विज्ञानमास्तिक्यं ब्रह्मकर्म स्वभावजम् ॥४२॥

Serenity, self-restraint, austerity, purity, forgiveness and also uprightness, wisdom, knowledge, belief in God, are the Brâhmaṇa duty, born of his own nature. (42)

शमः calm ; दमः self-control ; तपः austerity ; शौचं purity ; क्षांतिः forgiveness ; आर्जवम् rectitude ; एव even ; च and ; ज्ञानं wisdom ; विज्ञानं knowledge ; आस्तिक्यं belief ; ब्रह्मकर्म = ब्रह्मणः कर्म of the Brâhmaṇa, the action.

शौर्यं तेजो धृतिर्दाक्ष्यं युद्धे चाप्यपलायनम् ।
दानमीश्वरभावश्च क्षात्रं कर्म स्वभावजम् ॥ ४३ ॥

Prowess, splendour, firmness, dexterity, and also not flying from battle, generosity, the nature of a ruler, are the Kṣhattriya duty, born of his own nature. (43)

शौर्यं prowess ; तेजः splendour ; धृतिः firmness ; दाक्ष्यं dexterity ; युद्धे in battle ; च and ; अपि also ; अपलायनम् not fleeing ; दानं gift ; ईश्वरभावः = ईश्वरस्य भावः of a lord, the nature ; च and ; क्षात्रं belonging to the Kṣhattriya ; कर्म action ; स्वभावजं own-nature-born.

कृषिगोरक्ष्यवाणिज्यं वैश्यकर्म स्वभावजम् ।

परिचर्यात्मकं कर्म शूद्रस्यापि स्वभावजम् ॥ ४४ ॥

Ploughing, protection of kine, and trade are the Vaishya duty, born of his own nature. Action of the nature of service is the Shûdra duty, born of his own nature. (44)

कृषिगोरक्ष्यवाणिज्यं = कृषिः च गोरक्ष्यं च वाणिज्यं च ploughing, and, cow-protection, and, trade, and ; वैश्यकर्म = वैश्यानां कर्म of Vaishyas, the action ; स्वभावजम् own-nature-born ; परिचर्यात्मकं = परिचर्या आत्मा यस्य तत् service, nature, whose, that ; कर्म action ; शूद्रस्य of the Shûdra ; अपि also ; स्वभावजं own-nature-born.

स्वे स्वे कर्मण्यभिरतः संसिद्धिं लभते नरः ।
स्वकर्मनिरतः सिद्धिं यथा विंदति तच्छृणु ॥ ४५ ॥

Man reacheth perfection by each being intent on his own duty. Listen thou how perfection is won by him who is intent on his own duty. (45)

स्वे in own ; स्वे in own ; कर्मणि in action ; अभिरतः engaged ; संसिद्धिं perfection ; लभते obtains ; नरः a man ; स्वकर्मनिरतः = स्वस्य कर्मणि निरतः of own, in action, enjoyed ; सिद्धिं perfection ; यथा also ; विंदति finds ; तत् that ; शृणु hear.

यतः प्रवृत्तिर्भूताना येन सर्वमिदं ततम् ।
स्वकर्मणा तमभ्यर्च्य सिद्धिं विंदति मानवः ॥ ४६ ॥

He from whom is the emanation of beings, by Whom all This is pervaded, by worshipping Him in his own duty a man winneth perfection. (46)

यतः from whom; प्रवृत्तिः forthcoming; भूतानाम् of beings; येन by whom; सर्वं all; इदं this; ततं spread; स्वकर्मणा by own-action; तम् Him; अभ्यर्च्य having worshipped; सिद्धिं perfection; विंदति finds; मानवः man.

श्रेयान् स्वधर्मो विगुणः परधर्मात्स्वनुष्ठितात् ।
स्वभावनियतं कर्म कुर्वन्नाप्नोति किल्बिषम् ॥४७॥

Better is one's own duty, though destitute of merits, than the well-executed duty of another. He who doeth the duty laid down by his own nature incurreth not sin. (47)

श्रेयान् better; स्वधर्मः own-duty; विगुणः without quality; परधर्मात् = परस्य धर्मात् of another, than duty; स्वनुष्ठितात् (than) well-practised; स्वभावनियतं = स्वभावेन नियतं by own-nature ordained; कर्म action; कुर्वन् doing; न not; आप्नोति obtains; किल्बिषम् sin.

सहजं कर्म कौंतेय सदोषमपि न त्यजेत् ।
सर्वारंभा हि दोषेण धूमेनाग्निरिवावृताः ॥ ४८ ॥

Congenital duty, O son of Kuntī, though defective, ought not to be abandoned. All undertakings indeed are clouded by defects as fire by smoke. (48)

सहजं congenital; कर्म action; कौंतेय O Kaunteya; सदोषम् with fault; अपि even; न not; त्यजेत् let (him) abandon;

सर्वारंभाः = सर्वे आरंभाः all, undertakings ; हि indeed; दोषेण by fault ; धूमेन by smoke ; अग्निः fire ; इव like ; आवृताः enwrapped.

असक्तबुद्धिः सर्वत्र जितात्मा विगतस्पृहः ।
नैष्कर्म्यसिद्धिं परमां संन्यासेनाधिगच्छति ॥४९॥

He whose Reason is everywhere unattached, the self subdued, dead to desires, he goeth by renunciation to the supreme perfection of freedom from obligation. (49)

असक्तबुद्धिः = असक्ता बुद्धिः यस्य सः unattached, reason, whose, he ; सर्वत्र everywhere ; जितात्मा = जितः आत्मा यस्य सः conquered, self, whose, he; विगतस्पृहः = विगता स्पृहा यस्मात् सः gone, desires, from whom, he ; नैष्कर्म्यसिद्धिं = निर्गतानि कर्माणि यस्मात् सः निष्कर्मा तस्य भावः नैष्कर्म्यं, तस्य सिद्धिम् gone, actions, from whom, he—his condition—of that, the perfection ; परमां highest ; संन्यासेन by renunciation ; अधिगच्छति obtains.

सिद्धिं प्राप्तो यथा ब्रह्म तथाप्नोति निबोध मे ।
समासेनैव कौंतेय निष्ठा ज्ञानस्य या परा ॥ ५० ॥

How he who hath attained perfection obtaineth the ETERNAL, that highest state of wisdom learn thou from Me only succinctly, O Kaunteya. (50)

सिद्धिं perfection ; प्राप्तः attained ; यथा as ; ब्रह्म Brahman ; तथा so ; आप्नोति obtains ; निबोध learn ; मे of me ; समासेन by summary ; एव even ; कौंतेय O Kaunteya ; निष्ठा state ; ज्ञानस्य of wisdom ; या or ; परा highest.

बुद्ध्या विशुद्धया युक्तो धृत्यात्मानं नियम्य च ।

शब्दादीन्विषयांस्त्यक्त्वा रागद्वेषौ व्युदस्य च ॥५१॥

United to the Reason purified, controlling the self by firmness, having abandoned sound and the other objects of the senses, having laid aside passion and malice, (51)

बुद्ध्या by reason ; विशुद्धया (by) purified ; युक्तः united ; धृत्या by firmness ; आत्मानं the self ; नियम्य having controlled ; च and ; शब्दादीन् = शब्दः आदिः येषाम् तान् hearing, beginning, whose, they ; विषयान् objects (of the senses) ; त्यक्त्वा having abandoned ; रागद्वेषे = रागः च द्वेषः च passion, and, hatred, and ; व्युदस्य having thrown off ; च and.

विविक्तसेवी लघ्वाशी यतवाक्कायमानसः ।
ध्यानयोगपरो नित्यं वैराग्यं समुपाश्रितः ॥५२॥

Dwelling in solitude, abstemious, speech, body and mind subdued, constantly fixed in meditation and yoga, taking refuge in dispassion, (52)

विविक्तसेवी = विविक्तं सेवते इति solitude, serves, thus ; लघ्वाशी = लघु अश्नाति इति little, eats, thus ; यतवाक्कायमानसः = यता वाक् च कायः च मानसं च यस्य सः controlled, speech, and, mind, whose, he ; ध्यानयोगपरः = ध्यानं च योगः च परः यस्य सः meditation, and, yoga, and, supreme, whose, he ; नित्यं always ; वैराग्यं dispassion ; समुपाश्रितः taking refuge in.

अहंकारं बलं दर्पं कामं क्रोधं परिग्रहम् ।
विमुच्य निर्ममः शांतो ब्रह्मभूयाय कल्पते ॥५३॥

Having cast aside egoism, violence, arrogance, desire, wrath, covetousness, selfless and peaceful—he is fit to become the ETERNAL. (53)

अहंकारं egoism; बलं violence; दर्पं arrogance; कामं desire; क्रोधं anger; विमुच्य having abandoned; निर्ममः without-mineness; शांतः peaceful; ब्रह्मभूयाय = ब्रह्मणः भूयाय of Brahman, for the nature; कल्पते is fit.

ब्रह्मभूतः प्रसन्नात्मा न शोचति न कांक्षति ।
समः सर्वेषु भूतेषु मद्भक्तिं लभते पराम् ॥ ५४ ॥

Becoming Brahman, serene in the SELF, he neither grieveth nor desireth; the same to all beings, he obtaineth supreme devotion unto Me. (54)

ब्रह्मभूतः Brahman-become; प्रसन्नात्मा = प्रसन्नः आत्मा यस्य सः tranquil, self, whose, he; न not; शोचति grieves; न not; कांक्षति desires; समः equal; सर्वेषु among all; भूतेषु among beings; मद्भक्तिं = मयि भक्तिं in me, devotion; लभते obtains; पराम् highest.

भक्त्या मामभिजानाति यावान्यश्चास्मि तत्त्वतः ।
ततो मां तत्त्वतो ज्ञात्वा विशते तदनंतरम् ॥ ५५ ॥

By devotion he knoweth Me in essence, who and what I am; having thus known Me in essence he forthwith entereth into the Supreme. (55)

भक्त्या by devotion; मां me; अभिजानाति (he) knows; यावान् how much; यः who; च and; अस्मि (I) am; तत्त्वतः essentially; ततः thence; मां me; तत्त्वतः essentially; ज्ञात्वा

having known; विशते (he) enters; तत् that; अनंतरम् afterwards.

सर्वकर्माण्यपि सदा कुर्वाणो मद्व्यपाश्रयः ।
मत्प्रसादादवाप्नोति शाश्वतं पदमव्ययम् ॥ ५६ ॥

Though ever performing all actions, taking refuge in Me, by My grace he obtaineth the eternal indestructible abode. (56)

सर्वकर्माणि = सर्वाणि कर्माणि all, actions; अपि also; सदा always; कुर्वाणः doing; मद्व्यपाश्रयः = अहं व्यपाश्रयः यस्य सः I, refuge, whose, he; मत्प्रसादात् = मम प्रसादात् my, by favour; अवाप्नोति obtains; शाश्वतं eternal; पदम् goal; अव्ययं indestructible.

चेतसा सर्वकर्माणि मयि संन्यस्य मत्परः ।
बुद्धियोगमुपाश्रित्य मच्चित्तः सततं भव ॥ ५७ ॥

Renouncing mentally all works in Me, intent on Me, resorting to the yoga of discrimination have thy thought ever on Me. (57)

चेतसा with the mind; सर्वकर्माणि all actions; मयि in me; सन्यस्य having renounced; मत्परः intent on me; बुद्धियोगम् the yoga of reason; उपाश्रित्य having taken refuge in; मच्चित्तः = मयि चित्तं यस्य सः in me, mind, whose, he; सततं always; भव be.

मच्चित्तः सर्वदुर्गाणि मत्प्रसादात्तरिष्यसि ।
अथ चेत्त्वमहंकारान्न श्रोष्यसि विनंक्ष्यसि ॥ ५८ ॥

Thinking on Me, thou shalt overcome all obstacles by My grace; but if from egoism thou wilt not listen, thou shalt be destroyed utterly. (58)

मच्चित्तः intent on me; सर्वदुर्गाणि = सर्वाणि दुर्गाणि all obstacles, मत्प्रसादात् by my grace; तरिष्यसि (thou) shalt cross over; अथ now; चेत् if; त्वं thou; अहंकारात् from egoism; न not; श्रोष्यसि wilt listen: विनंक्ष्यसि (thou) shalt be destroyed.

यदहंकारमाश्रित्य न योत्स्य इति मन्यसे ।
मिथ्यैष व्यवसायस्ते प्रकृतिस्त्वां नियोक्ष्यति ॥५९॥

Entrenched in egoism, thou thinkest, "I will not fight;" to no purpose thy determination; nature will constrain thee. (59)

यत् which; अहंकारम् egoism; आश्रित्य having taken refuge in; न not; योत्स्ये (I) will fight; इति thus; मन्यसे (thou) thinkest; मिथ्या vain; एष this; व्यवसायः resolution; ते thy; प्रकृतिः nature; त्वाम् thee; नियोक्ष्यति will compel.

स्वभावजेन कौंतेय निबद्धः स्वेन कर्मणा ।
कर्त्तुं नेच्छसि यन्मोहात्करिष्यस्यवशोऽपि तत् ॥६०॥

O son of Kuntî, bound by thine own duty, born of thine own nature, that which from delusion thou desirest not to do, even that helplessly thou shalt perform. (60)

स्वभावजेन by own-nature-born; कौंतेय O Kaunteya; निबद्धः bound; स्वेन by own; कर्मणा by action; कर्त्तुं to do; न not;

इच्छसि (thou) wishest ; यत् that ; मोहात् from delusion ; करिष्यसि (thou) shalt do ; अवश: helpless ; अपि also ; तत् that.

ईश्वरः सर्वभूतानां हृद्देशेऽर्जुन तिष्ठति ।
भ्रामयन्सर्वभूतानि यंत्रारूढानि मायया ॥ ६१ ॥

The Lord dwelleth in the hearts of all beings, O Arjuna, by His illusive power, causing all beings to revolve, as though mounted on a potter's wheel. (61)

ईश्वर: the Lord ; सर्वभूतानाम् of all beings ; हृद्देशे = हृदःदेशे of heart, in place ; अर्जुन O Arjuna ; तिष्ठति sits ; भ्रामयन् turning ; सर्वभूतानि all beings ; यंत्रारूढानि = यंत्रे आरूढानि in (on) machine, mounted ; मायया by illusion.

तमेव शरणं गच्छ सर्वभावेन भारत ।
तत्प्रसादात्परां शांतिं स्थानं प्राप्स्यासि शाश्वतम् ॥ ६२ ॥

Flee unto Him for shelter with all thy being, O Bhârata ; by His grace thou shalt obtain supreme peace, the everlasting dwelling-place. (62)

तम् to Him ; एव even ; शरणं shelter ; गच्छ go ; सर्वभावेन सर्वेण भावेन (with) all, with nature ; भारत O Bhârata ; तत्प्रसादात् = तस्य प्रसादात् his, by grace ; परां highest ; शांतिं peace ; स्थानं place ; प्राप्स्यसि (thou) shalt obtain ; शाश्वतम everlasting

इति ते ज्ञानमाख्यातं गुह्याद्गुह्यतरं मया ।
विमृश्यैतदशेषेण यथेच्छसि तथा कुरु ॥ ६३ ॥

Thus hath wisdom, more secret than secrecy itself, been declared unto thee by Me; having reflected on it fully, then act thou as thou listest. (63)

इति thus; ते to thee; ज्ञानम् wisdom; आख्यातं declared; गुह्यात् than the secret; गुह्यतरं more secret; मया by me; विमृश्य having considered; एतत् this; अशेषेण without remainder; यथा as; इच्छसि (thou) wishest; तथा so; कुरु do.

सर्वगुह्यतमं भूयः श्रृणु मे परमं वचः ।
इष्टोऽसि मे दृढमिति ततो वक्ष्यामि ते हितम् ॥६४॥

Listen thou again to My supreme word, most secret of all; beloved art thou of Me, and steadfast of heart, therefore will I speak for thy benefit. (64)

सर्वगुह्यतमं = सर्वेभ्यः गुह्यतमं than all, most secret; भूयः again; श्रृणु listen; मे my; परमं highest; वचः word; इष्टः beloved; असि (thou) art; मे of me; दृढम् strongly; इति thus; ततः thence; वक्ष्यामि (I) will speak; ते thy; हितं benefit.

मन्मना भव मद्भक्तो मद्याजी मां नमस्कुरु ।
मामेवैष्यसि सत्यं ते प्रतिजाने प्रियोऽसि मे ॥६५॥

Merge thy mind in Me, be My devotee, sacrifice to Me, prostrate thyself before Me, thou shalt come even to Me. I pledge thee My troth; thou art dear to Me. (65)

मन्मना with mind fixed on me; भव be; मद्भक्तः my devotee; मद्याजी = मां यजते इति to me, sacrifices, thus; माम् me; नमस्कुरु

salute; मां to me; एव even; एष्यसि (thou) shalt come; सत्यं truth; ते to thee; प्रतिजाने (I) promise; प्रियः dear; असि (thou) art; मे of me.

सर्वधर्मान्परित्यज्य मामेकं शरणं व्रज।
अहं त्वा सर्वपापेभ्यो मोक्षयिष्यामि मा शुचः॥६६॥

Abandoning all duties, come unto Me alone for shelter: sorrow not, I will liberate thee from all sins. (66)

सर्वधर्मान्=सर्वान् धर्मान् all duties; परित्यज्य having abandoned; मां to me; शरणं refuge; व्रज come; अहं I; त्वां thee; सर्वपापेभ्यः=सर्वेभ्यः पापेभ्यः (from) all, from sins; मोक्षयिष्यामि will free; मा not; शुचः grieve.

इदं ते नातपस्काय नाभक्ताय कदाचन।
न चाशुश्रूषवे वाच्यं न च मां योऽभ्यसूयति॥६७॥

Never is this to be spoken by thee to anyone who is without asceticism, nor without devotion nor to one who desireth not to listen, nor yet to him who speaketh evil of Me. (67)

इदं this; ते of (by) thee; न not; अतपस्काय to (one) without asceticism; न not; अभक्ताय to (one) without devotion; कदाचन at any time; न not; च and; अशुश्रूषवे to (one) not wishing to listen; वाच्यं to be spoken; न not; च and; मां me; यः who; अभ्यसूयति cavils at.

य इदं परमं गुह्यं मद्भक्तेष्वभिधास्यति।

भक्तिं मयि परां कृत्वा मामेवैष्यत्यसंशयः ॥६८॥

He who shall declare this supreme secret among My devotees, having shown the highest devotion for Me, without doubt he shall come to Me. (68)

यः who ; इदं this ; परमं highest ; गुह्यं secret ; मद्भक्तेषु = मम भक्तेषु my, among devotees ; अभिधास्यति shall declare ; भक्तिं devotion ; मयि in (for) me ; परां highest ; कृत्वा having done ; माम् to me ; एव even ; एष्यति shall come ; असंशयः doubtless.

न च तस्मान्मनुष्येषु कश्चिन्मे प्रियकृत्तमः ।
भविता न च मे तस्मादन्यः प्रियतरो भुवि ॥ ६९ ॥

Nor is there any among men who performeth dearer service to Me than he, nor any other shall be more beloved by Me on earth than he. (69)

न not ; च and ; तस्मात् than he ; मनुष्येषु among men ; कश्चित् any one ; मे of me ; प्रियकृत्तमः most well-doing ; भविता will be ; न not ; च and ; मे of me ; तस्मात् than he ; अन्यः another ; प्रियतरः dearer ; भुवि in the earth.

अध्येष्यते च य इमं धर्म्यं संवादमावयोः ।
ज्ञानयज्ञेन तेनाहमिष्टः स्यामिति मे मतिः ॥७०॥

And he who shall study this sacred dialogue of ours, by him I shall be worshipped with the sacrifice of wisdom. Such is My mind. (70)

अध्येष्यते shall study; च and; य who; इमं this; धर्म्यं sacred; संवादं dialogue; आवयोः of us (two); ज्ञानयज्ञेन = ज्ञानस्य यज्ञेन of wisdom, by the sacrifice; तेन by him; अहं I; इष्टः worshipped; स्याम् may be; इति thus; मे my; मतिः opinion.

श्रद्धावाननसूयश्च शृणुयादपि यो नरः ।
सोऽपिमुक्तःशुभाँल्लोकान्प्राप्नुयात्पुण्यकर्मणाम्॥ ७१॥

The man also who, full of faith, merely heareth it unreviling, even he, freed trom evil, obtaineth the radiant worlds of the righteous. (71)

श्रद्धावान् full of faith; अनसूयः uncarping; च and; शृणुयात् may hear; अपि also; यः who; नरः man; सः he; अपि also; मुक्तः liberated; शुभान् radiant; लोकान् worlds; प्राप्नुयात् may obtain; पुण्यकर्मणाम् = पुण्यं कर्म येषां तेषां meritorious, action, whose, of them.

कच्चिदेतच्छ्रुतं पार्थ त्वयैकाग्रेण चेतसा ।
कच्चिदज्ञानसंमोहः प्रनष्टस्ते धनंजय ॥ ७२ ॥

Has this been heard, O son of Pṛitha, with one-pointed mind? Has thy delusion, caused by unwisdom, been destroyed, O Dhanañjaya? (72)

कच्चित् whether; एतत् this; श्रुतं heard; पार्थ O Pârtha; त्वया by thee; एकाग्रेण (by) one-pointed; चेतसा by mind; कच्चित् whether; अज्ञानसंमोहः = अज्ञानस्य संमोहः of ignorance, delusion; प्रणष्टः destroyed; ते they; धनंजय C Dhanañjaya.

अर्जुन उवाच ।

नष्टो मोहः स्मृतिर्लब्धा त्वत्प्रसादान्मयाच्युत ।
स्थितोऽस्मि गतसंदेहः करिष्ये वचनं तव ॥ ७३ ॥

Arjuna said :

Destroyed is my delusion. I have gained knowledge through Thy grace, O Immutable One. I am firm, my doubts have fled away. I will do according to Thy word (73)

नष्टः destroyed ; मोहः delusion ; स्मृतिः memory ; लब्धा obtained ; त्वत्प्रसादात् = तव प्रसादात् of thee, by grace ; मया by me ; अच्युत O Achyuta ; स्थितः firm ; अस्मि (I) am ; गतसंदेहः गतः संदेहः यस्य सः gone, doubt, whose, he ; करिष्ये (I) will do ; वचनं word ; तव Thy.

संजय उवाच ।

इत्यहं वासुदेवस्य पार्थस्य च महात्मनः ।
संवादमिममश्रौषमद्भुतं रोमहर्षणम् ॥ ७४ ॥

Sañjaya said :

I heard this marvellous dialogue of Vâsudeva and of the great-souled Pârtha, causing my hair to stand on end ; (74)

इति thus ; अहं I ; वासुदेवस्य of Vâsudeva ; पार्थस्य of Pârtha ; च and ; महात्मनः of the great-souled ; संवादं dialogue ;

इमम् this; अश्रौषम् heard; अद्भुतं marvellous; रोमहर्षणम् = रोम्णां हर्षणम् यस्मात् तत् of the hair, excitement, from which, that.

व्यासप्रसादाच्छ्रुतवानेतद्गुह्यमहं परम् ।
योगं योगेश्वरात्कृष्णात्साक्षात्कथयतः स्वयम् ॥७५॥

By the favour of Vyâsa I listened to this secret and supreme yoga from the Lord of Yoga, Kṛishṇa Himself speaking before mine eyes. (75)

व्यासप्रसादात् = व्यासस्य प्रसादात् of Vyâsa, from the favour; श्रुतवान् heard; एतत् this; गुह्यं secret; अहं I; परं highest: योगं yoga; योगेश्वरात् = योगस्य ईश्वरात् of yoga, from the Lord; कृष्णात् from Kṛishṇa; साक्षात् directly; कथयतः (from) the declaring; स्वयम् Himself.

राजन्संस्मृत्य संस्मृत्य संवादमिममद्भुतम् ।
केशवार्जुनयोः पुण्यं हृष्यामि च मुहुर्मुहुः ॥ ७६ ॥

O King, remembering, remembering this marvellous and holy dialogue between Keshava and Arjuna, I rejoice again and again. (76)

राजन् O King; संस्मृत्य having remembered; संस्मृत्य having remembered; संवादम् dialogue; इमं this; अद्भुतं marvellous; केशवार्जुनयोः = केशवस्य च अर्जुनस्य च of Keshava, and, of Arjuna, and; पुण्यं holy; हृष्यामि (I) rejoice; च and; मुहुः again; मुहुः again.

तच्च संस्मृत्य संस्मृत्य रूपमत्यद्भुतं हरेः ।

विस्मयो मे महान् राजन् हृष्यामि च पुनः पुनः॥७७॥

Remembering, remembering, also that most marvellous form of Hari, great is my wonder, O King. I rejoice, again and again. (77)

तत् that; च and; संस्मृत्य having remembered; संस्मृत्य having remembered; रूपं the form; अत्यद्भुतं very marvellous; हरेः of Hari; विस्मयः astonishment; मे my; महान् great; राजन् O King; हृष्यामि (I) rejoice; च and; पुनः again; पुनः again.

यत्र योगेश्वरः कृष्णो यत्र पार्थो धनुर्धरः।
तत्र श्रीर्विजयो भूतिर्ध्रुवा नीतिर्मतिर्मम ॥ ७८ ॥

Wherever is Kṛiṣhṇa, Yoga's Lord, wherever is Pârtha, the archer, assured are there prosperity, victory and happiness. So I think. (78)

यत्र where; योगेश्वरः the Lord of yoga; कृष्णः Kriṣhṇa; यत्र where; पार्थः Pârtha; धनुर्धरः the archer; तत्र there; श्रीः prosperity; विजयः victory; भूतिः happiness; ध्रुवा firm; नीतिः policy; मतिः opinion; मम my.

इति श्रीमद्भगवद्गीतासूपनिषत्सु ब्रह्मविद्यायां योगशास्त्रे श्रीकृष्णार्जुनसंवादे संन्यासयोगो नामाष्टादशोऽध्यायः ॥ १८ ॥

श्रीकृष्णार्पणमस्तु ॥ शुभं भवतु ॥

Thus in the glorious Upanishats of the BHAGAVAD-GÎTÂ, the

science of the ETERNAL. the scripture of Yoga, the dialogue between Shrî Kṛishṇa and Arjuna, the eighteenth discourse, entitled:

THE YOGA OF LIBERATION BY RENUNCIATION.

To the Blessed Kṛishṇa be homage. May there be happiness.

Thus the BHAGAVAD-GÎTÂ hath ending.

PEACE BE TO ALL WORLDS.

APPENDIX.

The following variations of the text and one or two new interpretations are printed as likely to be of use to the student. The different readings have been mostly gathered together by Bâbu Govinda Dâsa of Benares from various MSS. and different commentaries. The new interpretations have been suggested by Paṇḍit Vrindâvana Sârasvata of Benares, who passed away only in this year (1905 A. D.). The interpretations are worthy of attention because of their *prima facie* aptness. This gentleman used to say that he had practically studied only two works in the course of a fairly long life, the *Bhagavad-Gita* and the *Yoga-Vasishtha*; and the kind of study he gave to these may be inferred from the fact that, as he said shortly before his death, he had read the *Yoga-Vasishtha* through one-hundred and sixty-five times—and the work consists of sixty-four thousand lines-while the *Gitâ* was read through too often to be counted. Under these circumstances it is easy to see that his interpretations are at least as notable as many older ones.

For	Read	Remarks.
i. 8. तथैव च	जयद्रथः	Adds the name of one of the principal warriors.
i. 10. बलं भीमाभि-रक्षितं	धृष्टद्युम्नाभि-रक्षितं	Dhṛishṭadyumna was the Commander-in-chief of the Pâṇḍava army.
i. 19. व्यनु-	ऽभ्यनु	The prefix वि has no special significance here, while अभि gives the sense of "on all sides."
i. 36. स्वबान्धवान्	सबांधवान्	The alternative here is scarcely preferable, as it means 'with their relations'; the text, on the other hand, '*our own* relatives', is stronger.
ii. 26. नैनं	नैवं	"Not thus" (shouldst thou grieve, even so).

ii. 53. श्रुतिविप्रतिपन्ना Pt. Vrindâvana interprets this as meaning: श्रुत्या श्रवणेन श्रुतौ श्रुत्यर्थे विशेषेण प्रतिपन्ना ज्ञानवती, "having, by listening (to my teaching) acquired knowledge of the *true* and particular significance of the Veda".

For	Read	Remarks.
ii. 62. क्रोधः	लोभः	This is an emendation suggested by Paṇḍit Vrin-dâvana, on the ground that anger does not arise from desire but from defeat
ii. 63. क्रोधात्	लोभात्	

			of desire, while लोभ, blind craving, is the natural consequence of desire. The emendation has a doubtful value, however, because it is not supported by any manuscripts inspected, and the addition of "defeat of" is no very serious strain on the interpretation of the verse.
iv. 23.	मुक्तस्य	युक्तस्य	The context refers to one who is still striving after deliverance, युक्तस्य, and not to one who has already attained it, मुक्तस्य.
v. 21.	यत्सुखं	यः सुखं	In view of the following सः, यः is distinctly the better reading grammatically; यत् confuses the prose order and the sense, and does not fit in.
vi. 39.	एतन्मे	एतम् मे	The alternative is correct according to modern grammar, and the other incorrect, because संशय, with which the pronoun is in apposition, is masculine and not neuter,

Ref.	Text	Alternative	Remarks
vii. 19.	सुदुर्लभः	स दुर्लभः	"He is difficult to find" instead of "very difficult to find".
viii. 5.	असंशयं	असंशयः	The text means "undoubtedly"; the alternative "free of doubt thyself". The text seems to be the stronger reading.
viii. 8.	मान्यगामिना	ऽनन्यगामिना	The alternative makes no change of meaning, but is more in accordance with modern grammar.
viii. 20.	ऽव्यक्तो व्यक्तात्	व्यक्ताव्यक्तात्	"(More ancient) than both the manifested and the (lower) unmanifested." Cf. xv. 16 & 18, xi. 37.
x. 7.	ऽविकंपेन	ऽविकल्पेन	The alternative means "abstract, without Vikalpa, without alternative, doubt, or lower attraction". It is more in keeping with the technicality of Yoga.
xi. 28.	अभिविज्वलन्ति	अभितो ज्वलंति	"Flaming on all sides." The alternative seems to make better sense. The text has a superfluous and weak prefix वि.
xi. 41.	इदं	इदम्	The alternative is gramma-

tically correct, as the माहिमा which the pronoun qualifies is masculine, not neuter.

xiii. 5. अव्यक्तम् here is interpreted by Pt. Vrindâvana as meaning the Linga Sharîra.

xiv. 1. ज्ञानानां ज्ञानिनां "(The highest knowledge) of the wise" instead of "of all knowledges".

xiv. 3. 4. In these two shlokas, the current commentaries interpret the word महत् as 'great' and regard it as qualifying ब्रह्म, Brahman; and further they construe both the shlokas as meaning that "the great Brahman is the womb and I the depositor of the seed". Pt. Vrindâvana says the construction should be as follows: "mahat-tattva is the womb and I, Brahman, am the seed-giver".

xv. 23. अवतिष्ठति अनुतिष्ठति "And acts in pursuance." This gives additional meaning; the other merely repeats the sense of नेंगते.

xvii. 23. ब्राह्मणास्तेन ब्रह्मणा तेन "By that Brahmâ, or by that Brahman." Cf. iv. 32.

INDEX.

अंश—x. 41, 42—xv. 7.

अकर्त्ता—iv. 13—v. 14—vii. 5. 6. 12. 25. 26—ix. 5. 9. 19—x. 6—xi.37—xiii. 21. 31—xiv. 12. 19—xviii. 14. 16.

अकर्म—ii. 47—iii. 5. 8—iv. 16. 17. 18.

अकार्य—xvi. 24—xviii. 30. 31.

अकाल—ii. 34.

अकृत—iii. 18—xv. 11—xviii. 6. 16.

अकृत्स्न—iii. 29.

अक्रिय—vi. 1.

अक्रोध—xvi. 2.

अक्षय—v. 31—x. 33.

अक्षर—iii. 15—viii. 3. 11. 13. 21—x. 25. 33—xi. 18. 37—xii. 1. 3—xv. 16. 18.

अखिल—iv. 33—vii. 29—xv. 12.

अग्नि—iv. 37—viii. 24—ix. 16—xi. 39—xv. 12—xviii. 48.

अचल—ii. 24. 53. 70—vi. 13—vii. 21—viii. 10—xii. 3.

अचेतः—iii. 32—xv. 11—xvii. 6.

अच्युत—i. 21—xi. 42—xviii. 73.

अज—ii. 21—iv. 6—vii. 25—x. 3. 12.

अजानत्—vii. 24—xi. 41—xiii. 25.

अज्ञान—iv. 42—v. 15. 16—x. 11—xiii. 11—xiv. 8. 16. 17—xvi. 4. 15—xviii. 72.

अणीय—viii. 9.

अधर्म—i. 40. 41—iv. 7—xviii. 31. 32.

अधिगम्—ii. 71—iv. 39—v. 6. 24—vi. 15—xiv. 19—xviii. 49.

अधिदैव—vii. 30—viii. 1. 4., (also अधिभूत, अधियज्ञ)

अधिष्ठान—iii. 40—iv. 6—xiii. 17—xv. 9—xviii. 14.

अध्यात्म—iii. 30—vii. 29—viii. 1. 3—x. 32—xi. 1—xv. 5—xiii. 11—xv. 5.

अनन्तरूप—xi. 16. 38.

अनामय—ii. 51—xiv. 6.

अनुशोचन्ति—ii. 11. 25 *seq.*—iv. 8.

अनुस्मर—viii. 7. 9. 13.

अनेक—vi. 45—xi. 10. 13. 16. 24—xvi. 16.

अन्त—ii. 16. 55. 72—v. 24—vi. 26—vii. 19. 28—viii. 5. 6—x. 19. 32. 40—xi. 16—xv. 3.

अन्तर—v. 24—vi. 47—xi. 20—xiii. 34.

अन्न—iii. 14.—xv. 14.

अन्यदेवता—vii. 20—ix. 53.

अपर—ii. 22—iv. 4. 25. 27-30—vi. 22—vii. 5—xiii. 24—xvi. 8. 14—xviii. 3.

अपहृत—ii. 44—vii. 15.

अपात्र—xvii. 22.

अप्राप्य—vi. 37—ix. 3—xvi. 20.

अफल—xvii. 11. 17—xviii. 23.

अभय—x. 4—xvi. 1—xviii. 30.

अभाव—ii. 16. 66—x. 4.

अभिजानाति—iv. 14—vii. 13. 25—ix. 24—xviii. 55.

अभ्यास—vi. 35. 44—viii. 8—xii. 9. 10. 12—xviii. 36.

अभ्यासयोग—viii. 8—xii. 9.

अमानित्व—xiii. 7.

अमूढ—xv. 5.

अमृत—iv. 31—ix. 19—x. 18—xiii. 12—xiv. 20. 27.

अमृतोपम—xviii. 37. 38.

अयज्ञ—iv. 31.

अयति—vi. 37.

अयुक्त—ii. 66—v. 12—xviii. 28.

अरागद्वेषतः—xviii. 23.

अवध्य—ii 30.

अवश—iii. 5—vi. 44—viii. 19—ix. 8—xviii. 60.

अविकार्य—ii 25.

अविभक्त—xiii. 16—xviii. 20.

अव्यक्त—ii. 25. 28—vii. 24—viii. 18. 20. 21—ix. 4—xii. 1. 3. 5. 6—xiii. 5.

अव्यय—ii. 17. 21. 34—iv 1. 13—vii. 13. 24. 25—ix. 2. 13. 18—xi. 2 4. 18—xiii. 31—xiv. 5. 27—xv. 1. 5. 17—xviii. 20 56.

अव्यवसायी—ii. 41.

अशान्त—ii 66.

असक्त—iii. 7. 19. 25—v. 21—ix. 9—xiii. 9. 14—xviii. 49.

असङ्गशस्त्र—xiii. 5.

असत्—ii 16—ix. 19—xi 37—xiii. 12—xvii. 28.

असन्न्यस्तसङ्कल्प—vi. 2.

असिद्धि—ii 48—iv. 22—xviii. 26.

असुर—xi. 22.

अहंकार—iii. 27—vii. 4—xiii. 5—xvi. 18—xvii. 5—xviii. 17. 58. 59.

आत्मा—ii. 55—iii. 13. 17. 43—iv. 7. 35. 38. 42—v. 7. 16 21—vi 5. 6. 7. 8. 10. 11. 15. 18. 19. 20. 26—vii. 18—viii. 12—ix. 5. 28. 34—x. 15. 18. 20—xi. 3. 4—xiii. 24. 28. 29 32—xv. 11—xvi. 21. 22—xvii. 19—xviii. 16. 39. 51.

आत्मवत्—ii 45—iv. 41.

आवृ—iii. 38. 39. 40—v. 15—xiv. 9—xviii. 32. 48.

आसुर—vii. 15—ix. 19—xvi. 4. 5. 6, 7. 19. 20—xvii. 6.

आहार—xvii. 7. 8. 9.

इन्द्रिय—ii 8. 58. 60. 61. 64. 67—iii. 7. 34. 40. 41. 42—iv. 26. 27—v. 9. 11—x. 22—xii. 14—xiii. 5—xv. 7—xviii. 33. 38—vi. 24.

ईश्वर—iv. 6—xiii. 28—xv. 8. 17—xvi. 14.

उत्तरायण—viii. 24.

उत्स्था—ii. 3. 37—iv. 42—xi. 12. 33.

उदार—vii. 18.

उदास—vi. 9—ix. 9—xii. 16—xiv. 23.

एक—ii. 41—iii. 2—v. 1. 4, 5—vi. 31—viii. 26—ix. 15.—x. 25. 42—xi. 7. 13. 20. 42—xiii. 5..30. 33—xviii. 3. 20. 22. 66.

ओम—xvii. 23. 24.

कर्तृ—iii. 24. 27—iv. 13—v. 14—xiii. 20—xiv. 19—xviii. 14. 16. 18. 19. 26. 27. 28.

कर्मचोदना—xviii. 18.

कर्मज—ii. 51—iv. 12 32.

कर्म—ii. 47. 48. 49. 50—iii. 1. 4. 5. 8. 9. 15. 19. 20. 22. 23. 24. 25. 27. 30. 31—iv. 9. 12. 14. 15. 16. 17. 18. 20. 21. 23. 33. 41—v. 1. 10. 11. 14—vi. 1. 3. 4. 17—vii. 29—viii. 1—ix. 9—xii. 6. 10—xiii. 29—xiv. 9. 12. 16—xvi. 24—xvii 26 27—xviii. 2. 3. 6. 7. 8. 9. 10. 11. 12. 15. 18. 19. 23. 24. 25. 41. 43. 44. 45. 47. 48. 60.

कर्मफल—iv. 14—v. 12—vi. 1—xii. 11. 12—xviii. 11.

कर्मयोग—iii. 3. 7—v. 2—xiii. 24.

काम—ii. 55. 62. 70. 71—iii. 37—vi. 24—vii. 11. 20. 22—xvi. 10. 18. 21—xvii. 5—xviii. 34. 53.

कूटस्थ—vi. 8—xii. 3—xv. 16.

कौशल—ii. 50.

क्रोध—ii. 62. 63—iii. 37—xvi. 4. 18. 21—xviii. 53.

क्षेत्र—xiii. 1. 2, 3. 6. 18. 26. 33. 34.

क्षेत्रज्ञ—xiii. 1. 2. 26. 34.

गतव्यथ—xii 16.

गतसङ्ग—iv. 23.

गुण—iii. 5. 27. 28. 29—iv. 13—xiii. 19. 21. 23—xiv. 5. 19. 20. 21. 23. 26—xviii. 29 40. 41.

गुह्य—x. 38—xi. 1—xviii. 63. 68. 75.

गुह्यतम—ix. 1—xv. 20—xviii. 64.

चञ्चल—vi. 26. 33. 34.

चतुर्विध—vii. 16—xv. 14.

चित्त—vi. 18. 20—xii. 9.

चेतस्—i. 38—ii. 7—viii. 8—xviii. 57. 72.

छिद्—ii. 23—iv. 42—v. 25—vi. 38. 39—xv. 3—xviii. 10.

जगत्—vii. 5. 6 13—viii. 26—ix. 4. 10. 17—x. 42—xi. 7. 13. 30. 36—xv. 12—xvi. 8. 9.

जन्—i. 29. 41—ii 27—iii. 26—x. 6—xiv. 12. 13. 15.

ज्ञा—i. 38—iv 15. 16. 32. 35—v. 3 29.—vii. 1. 2—viii. 2. 27—ix. 13—xi. 25. 54—xiii. 12. 16. 17. 18—xiv. 1—xv. 19—xvi. 24—xviii 18. 55.

ज्ञान—iii. 39. 40. 41—iv. 33. 34. 38. 39—v. 15. 16—vi. 8—vii. 2—ix. 1—x. 4. 38. 42—xii. 12—xiii. 2. 11. 17. 18—xiv. 1. 2. 9. 11. 17—xv. 15—xvi. 1—xviii. 18. 19. 20. 21. 42. 50. 63.

ज्ञानयज्ञ—iv. 33—ix. 15—xviii. 70.

ज्ञानी—iii. 39—iv. 34—vi. 46—vii. 16. 17. 18.

तत्त्व—vi. 21—ix. 24—xi. 54—xviii. 1.

तत्त्वतस्—iv. 9.—vii. 3—x. 7—xviii. 55.

तमस्—x. 11—xiii. 17—xiv. 8. 9. 10. 13. 15. 16. 17—xvi. 52—xvii. 1—xviii. 32.

तुल्य—xii. 19—xiv. 24. 25.

त्रिविध—xvi. 21—xvii. 2. 7. 17. 23—xviii. 4. 12. 18. 29. 36.

दान—viii. 28—x. 5.—xi. 48. 53—xvi. 1—xvii. 7. 20. 21. 22. 24. 25. 27—xviii. 3. 5. 43.

दानव—x. 14.

दुःख—ii. 56—vi. 22. 23. 32—x. 4—xiii. 6. 8—xiv. 16—xvii. 9.

देह—ii. 13. 18. 30—iv. 9—viii. 2. 4. 13—xi. 7. 15—xiii. 22. 32—xiv. 5. 11—xv. 14.

देहभृत्—viii. 4—xiv. 14—xviii. 11.

देही—ii. 13. 22. 30. 59—iii. 40—xiv. 5. 7. 20—xvii. 2.

देव—iv. 25—vii. 14—ix. 13—xvi. 3. 5. 6—xviii. 14.

द्विष—ii. 57—v. 3—vi. 9—iv. 29—xii. 17—xiv. 22—xvi. 19—xviii. 10.

धर्म—i. 40—ii. 7. 40—iv. 7. 8—ix. 3—xiv. 27—xviii. 31. 32. 34.

निराशीः—iii. 30—iv. 21—vi. 10.

निर्मम—ii. 71—iii. 30—xviii. 53.

निर्योगक्षेम—ii. 45.

पञ्च—xiii. 5—xviii. 13. 15.

फल ii. 47. 49 51.—v. 4. 12.—vii. 23—ix. 26—xiv. 16—xvii. 12. 21. 25—xviii. 6. 9. 12.

बन्ध—iv. 14.—xiv. 6.—xvi. 12.

बन्धु—v. 3.—xviii. 30.

बहूनि जन्मानि—iv. 5—vii. 19.

बीज—vii. 10—ix. 18—x. 39.—xiv. 4

बुद्धि—(and derivatives) ii. 39. 41. 44. 49. 50. 51. 52. 53. 65.

66.—iii. 1. 8. 26. 40. 42. 43.—iv. 17. 18. 19—v. 11—vi. 21. 22. 25. 43—vii. 4. 10—x. 4. 8. 9. 10—xii. 8—xiii. 5.—xv. 20—xviii. 17. 29. 30. 32. 51. 57.

ब्रह्मकर्मन्—xviii. 42.

ब्रह्मकर्मसमाधिना—iv. 24.

ब्रह्मचर्यम्—xvii. 14.

ब्रह्मचारिव्रत—vi. 14.

ब्रह्म—iii. 15—iv. 24. 31. 32—v. 6 10. 19—vi. 38—vii. 29—viii. 1. 3. 17. 24—x. 12—xi. 15. 37—xiii. 12. 30—xiv. 3. 4. 27—xvii. 23—xviii. 50.

ब्रह्मनिर्वाण—ii. 72—v. 24. 25. 26.

ब्रह्मभुवन—viii. 16.

ब्रह्मभूत—v. 24—vi. 27—xviii. 54.

ब्रह्मभूय—xiv. 26—xviii. 53.

ब्रह्मयोग—v. 21.

ब्रह्मवादिन्—xvii. 24.

ब्रह्मवित्—viii. 24.

ब्रह्मसंस्पर्श—vi. 28.

ब्रह्मसूत्र—xiii. 4.

ब्रह्माग्नि न—iv. 24. 25.

ब्रह्मोद्भव—iii. 15.

ब्राह्मी—ii. 72.

ब्राह्मणे—ii. 46—v. 18—ix. 33—xvii. 23—xviii. 41.

भक्त्या—viii. 10. 22—ix. 14. 26. 29—xi. 54—xviii. 55.

भक्ति—ix. 26—xii. 17. 19—xiii. 10—xviii. 54. 68

भक्तियोग—xiv. 26.

भक्त—ix. 3—vii. 21—ix. 23. 31. 33. 34—xii. 1. 20

भस्मसात्—iv. 37.

भाव—ii. 16—vii. 12. 13. 15. 24—viii. 4. 5. 6. 20—x. 5. 17—xviii. 17. 20.

भूतानि—ii. 28. 34. 69—iii. 14. 33—iv. 6. 35—vii. 11. 26—viii. 20. 22—ix. 5. 25—x. 5. 20. 22. 39—xi. 2.—xiii. 15. 16. 27. 30—xiv. 3—xv. 13. 16—xvi. 2—xviii. 21. 46. 54.

भूतप्रकृति—xiii. 34.

भोक्तृ—v. 29—ix. 24—xiii. 22.

मत्पर—ii. 61—vi. 14—xii. 6—xviii. 57.

मत्परम—xi. 55—xii. 20.

मत्परायण—ix. 34.

मत्संस्था—vi. 15.

मत्स्थानि—ix. 4. 5. 6.

मद्भक्त—vii. 23—ix. 34—xi. 55—xii. 14. 16—xiii. 18—xviii. 65. 68.

मद्भाव—iv. 10—x. 6—xiii. 18—xiv. 19.

मद्—iii. 28—xi. 41.

मत—iii. 1. 31. 32—vi. 32. 46. 47—vii. 18—viii. 26—xi. 18—xii. 2—xiii. 2—xvi. 5—xviii. 6. 9.

मनःप्रसाद—xvii. 16.

मनःषष्ठ—xv. 7

मनस्—i. 30. 60—ii. 55. 67—iii. 6. 7. 40. 42—v. 11. 13. 19—vi. 12. 14. 24. 25. 26. 34. 35—vii. 4—viii. 10—ix. 34—x. 22—xi. 45—xii. 2. 8—xv. 9—xvii. 11—xviii. 15. 33. 65.

मनुष्य—i. 44—iii. 23—iv. 18—vii. 3—xviii. 69.

मनुष्यलोके—xv. 2.

मन्मनस—ix. 34—xviii. 65.

मन्मय—iv. 10

मर्त्यलोक—ix. 21.

महद्ब्रह्म—xiv. 3.

महद्योनिः—xiv. 4.

महात्मन्—vii. 19—viii. 15—ix. 13—xi. 12. 20. 37. 50—xviii. 74.

महापाप्मा—iii. 37.

महाभूत—xiii. 5.

महेश्वर—v. 29—x. 3—xiii. 22.

मानस्—i. 47—x. 7—xvii. 16.

माया—vii. 14. 15—xviii. 61.

मुक्तसंग—iii. 9.—xviii. 26.

मुच्यन्ते—iii. 13. 31.

मुक्त—v. 28—xii. 15—xviii. 40. 71.

मुक्त्वा—viii. 5.

मुमुक्षु—iv. 15.

मूढयोनि—xiv. 15.

मूर्त्ति—iv. 4.

मूल—xv. 2.

मृत—ii. 26. 27.

मृत्यु—ii. 27—ix. 3 19—x. 34—xii. 7—xiii. 8. 25.—xiv. 20.

मोक्ष्यसे—iv. 16—ix. 28.

मोक्ष—v. 28—vii. 29—xiii. 34—xvii. 25—xviii. 30.

मोघ—iii 16—ix. 12.

मोह—iv 35—xi. 1—xiv. 13. 17. 22—xvi. 10—xviii. 7. 25. 60.73.

मोहकलिल—ii. 52.

मोहजाल—xvi. 16.

मोहन—ix. 12—xiv. 8—xviii. 39.

मौन—x. 38—xii. 19—xvii. 16.

यजन्त—iv. 12—ix. 15. 23—xvi. 15. 17—xvii. 4. 11. 12—xviii. 70.

यज्ञ—iii. 9. 12. 13. 14. 15—iv. 23. 25. 30. 31. 32. 33—v. 29—viii. 28—ix. 16. 20—x. 25—xi. 48—xvi. 1—xvii. 7. 11.

12. 13. 23. 24. 25. 27—xviii. 3. 5.

यतचेतस् – v. 26.

यति—iv. 28—v. 26—viii. 11.

युक्तचेतस्—vi. 17. 47—vii. 18. 30—xii. 2.

युक्त—i. 14—ii. 39. 61—iii. 26—iv. 18. 23—v. 8. 12. 23—vi. 8. 14. 18—vii. 22—viii. 8. 10—xvii. 17—xviii. 51.

युज—ii. 38. 50—vi. 10. 12. 15. 19. 23—vii. 1—ix. 34—x. 7—xvii. 26.

योग—ii. 39. 48. 50. 53—iv. 1. 2. 3. 28. 38. 41. 42—v. 1. 4. 5—vi. 2. 3. 4. 12. 16. 17. 19. 20. 23. 33. 36. 37. 44—vii. 1.—viii. 10. 12—ix. 5. 22.—x. 7. 18—xii. 1. 6. 11—xiii. 24.—xvi. 1—xviii. 33. 75.

योगमाया—vii. 25.

योगयुक्त—v. 6. 7—viii. 27—आत्मन् vi. 29.

योगिन्—iii. 3.—iv. 25—v. 11. 24—vi. 1. 2. 8. 10. 15. 19. 27. 28. 31. 32. 42. 45. 46. 47—viii. 14. 23. 25. 27. 28—x. 17.—xii. 14—xv. 11.

योगेश्वर—xi. 4—xviii. 75. 78.

योनि—xiv. 3. 4—xvi. 19. 20.

रजस्—iii. 37—xiv. 7. 9. 10, 12. 15. 16. 17—xvii. 1.

रस—ii. 59—vii. 8.—आत्मक xv. 13.

रहस्य—iv. 3.

राग—ii. 64—iii. 34—vii. 11—xvii. 5—xviii. 51. आत्मक xiv. 7.

रागिन्—xviii. 27.

राजगुह्य—ix. 2.

राजविद्या—ix. 2.

राजस—vii. 12—xiv. 18—xvii. 2. 4. 9. 12. 18. 21—xviii. 8. 21. 24. 27. 31. 34. 38.

रात्रि—viii. 17. 25.

लोक—iii. 3. 9. 20. 21. 22. 24. 25—iv. 12. 31. 40—v. 14—vi. 41. 42—vii. 25—viii. 16—ix. 33—x. 3. 6. 16—xi. 20. 23. 29. 30. 32. 43—xii. 15—xiii. 33—xiv. 14—xv. 16. 17. 18—xvi. 6—xviii. 17. 71.

विद्या—v. 18—x. 32.

विभूति—x. 7. 16. 18. 40. 41.

विषय—ii. 59. 62. 64—iv. 26—xv. 2. 9—xviii. 38. 51.

विषाद—xviii. 35.

विष्णु—x. 21—xi. 24. 30.

विसर्ग—viii. 3.

विसृज्—i. 47—v. 9—ix. 7. 8.

वेद—ii. 42. 45. 46—viii. 28—x. 22—xi. 48. 53—xv. 15. 18—xvii. 23.

वैराग्य—vi 35.—xiii. 8—xviii. 52.

वैरिन्—iii. 37.

शम—vi. 3—x. 4—xi. 24—xviii. 42.

शय्या—xi. 42.

शरण—ii. 49—ix. 18—xviii. 62. 66.

शरीर—i. 29—ii. 18 22—iii. 8—v. 23—xi. 13—xiii. 1. 31—xv. 8.—xviii. 6. 15.

शास्त्र—xv. 20—xvi. 23. 24—xvii. 1.

शिष्य—i. 3—ii. 7.

शीतोष्ण—ii. 14—vi. 7.

शुचि—vi. 11. 41—xii. 16.

शुभाशुभ—ii. 57—xii 17—ix. 28.

शोक—i. 47—ii. 8—xvii. 9—xviii. 27. 35.

शौच—xiii. 7—xvi. 3. 7—xvii. 14—xviii. 42.

श्रद्धा—iii. 31—iv. 39—xi. 37. 47—vii. 21. 22—ix. 23—xii. 2. 20—xvii. 2. 3. 13. 17—xviii. 71.

श्रुति—ii. 53—xiii. 25.

षण्मासाः—viii. 24. 25.

संयतेन्द्रिय—vi. 39.

संयम्य—ii. 61—iii. 6—vi. 14—viii. 12.

संयोग—vi. 23—xiii. 26—xviii. 38.

संशय—iv. 40. 42—vi. 39—viii. 5—x. 7—xii. 8.

संसार—ix. 3—xii. 7—xvi. 19.

संसिद्धि—iii. 20—vi. 43—xiii. 15—xviii. 45.

संसिद्ध—vi. 45.

संकल्प—vi. 4—प्रभव vi. 24.

संग्रह—viii. 11.

सचराचर—ix. 10—xi. 7.

सक्त—iii. 25—v. 12—xviii. 22.

सज्जते—iii. 28. 29—xiv. 9.

सञ्जनयन्—i. 11.

सत्—ii. 16—ix. 19—xi. 37—xiii. 12—xvii. 23. 26. 27.

सततम्—iii. 19—vi. 10—viii. 14—ix. 14—xii. 14—xvii. 24—xviii. 57.

सततयुक्त—x. 10—xii. 1.

सत्कार—xvii 18.

सत्त्व—x. 36. 41—xiii. 26—xiv. 1. 6. 9. 10. 11. 14. 17. 18—xvii. 1. 3. 8—xviii. 10. 40.

सत्य—x. 4—xvi. 2. 7—xvii 15—xviii. 65.

सदसद्योनि—xiii. 21.

सनातन—i. 30—ii. 24—iv. 31—vii. 10—viii. 20—xi. 18—xv. 7.

सन्नियम्य—xii. 4.

सन्निविष्ट—xv. 15.

सन्न्यस्य—iii. 30—v. 13—xii. 6—xviii. 57.

सन्न्यसन—iii. 4.

सन्न्यास—v. 1. 2. 6—vi. 2—xviii. 1. 2. 7. 49. °योग ix. 28.

सन्न्यासिन्—vi. 1. 4—xviii. 12.

समचित्तत्व—xiii. 9.

समदर्शन—vi. 29.

समदर्शिन्—v. 18.

समदुःखसुख—ii. 15—xii. 13—xiv. 24.

समधिगच्छति—iii. 4.

समबुद्धि—vi. 9—xii. 4.

समलोष्टाश्म—vi. 8—xiv. 24.

समवस्था—xiii. 28.

समाचर—iii. 9. 19. 26.

समाधि—ii. 44. 53. 54.

समायुज्—xv. 14.

समावृत—vii. 25—xvi. 16.

समास—xiii. 3. 6. 18—xviii. 50.

सर्ग—v. 19—vii. 27—x. 32—xiv. 2.

साक्षी—ix. 18.

सांख्य—ii. 39—iii. 3—v. 4. 5—xiii. 24—xviii. 13.

सात्त्विक—vii. 12—xiv. 16—xvii. 2. 4. 11. 17. 20—xviii. 9. 20. 23. 26. 30. 33. 37.

साधर्म्य—xiv. 2.

साधिभूताधिदैव—vii. 30.

साधियज्ञ—vii. 30.

साधु—iv. 8—vi. 9—ix. 30.

सिद्धि—ii. 49—iii. 4—iv. 12. 22—vii. 3—xii. 10—xiv. 1. xvi.

23—xviii. 13. 26. 45. 46. 49. 50.

सिद्ध—vii. 3—x. 26—xvi. 14.

सुकृत्—ii. 50—v. 15—xiv. 16.

सुकृतिन्—vii. 16.

सुख—i. 32. 45. 56—ii. 66—iv. 40—v. 21—vi. 21. 27. 28. 32—x. 4—xiii. 6—xiv. 9. 27—xvi. 23—xvii. 8—xviii. 36. 37. 38. 39.

सुखदुःख—ii. 7—vi. 7—xii. 18—xiii. 20 ° संज्ञैः xv. 5.

सुखदुःखद—ii. 14.

सुखम्—v. 3. 13. ° संगेन xiv. 6.

सुखिन्—i. 37—ii. 32—v. 23—xvi. 14.

हतम्—ii. 19. 37—xi. 34—xvi. 14.

हन्ति—ii. 19. 21—xviii. 17.

हन्यते—ii. 19. 20.

हेतु—i. 35—ix. 10—xiii. 20—xviii. 15.

हेतुमत्—xiii. 4.

———:0:———